Myanmar's Education Reforms

Myanmar's Education Reforms
A pathway to social justice?

Marie Lall

First published in 2020 by
UCL Press
University College London
Gower Street
London WC1E 6BT

Available to download free: www.uclpress.co.uk

Text © Author, 2021
Images © Author and copyright holders named in captions, 2021

Marie Lall has asserted her rights under the Copyright, Designs and Patents Act 1988 to be identified as the author of this work.

A CIP catalogue record for this book is available from The British Library.

This book is published under a Creative Commons 4.0 International licence (CC BY 4.0). This licence allows you to share, copy, distribute and transmit the work; to adapt the work and to make commercial use of the work providing attribution is made to the authors (but not in any way that suggests that they endorse you or your use of the work). Attribution should include the following information:

Lall, M. 2020. *Myanmar's Education Reforms: A pathway to social justice?* London: UCL Press. https://doi.org/10.14324/111.9781787353695

Further details about Creative Commons licences are available at http://creativecommons.org/licenses/

Any third-party material in this book is published under the book's Creative Commons licence unless indicated otherwise in the credit line to the material. If you would like to re-use any third-party material not covered by the book's Creative Commons licence, you will need to obtain permission directly from the copyright holder.

ISBN: 978-1-78735-404-3 (Hbk.)
ISBN: 978-1-78735-387-9 (Pbk.)
ISBN: 978-1-78735-369-5 (PDF)
ISBN: 978-1-78735-410-4 (epub)
ISBN: 978-1-78735-416-6 (mobi)
DOI: https://doi.org/10.14324/111.9781787353695

For those who were part of this 16-year research journey: the Egress sisterhood – Nan Theingi, Khin Moe Samm, Thei Su San, Phyo Thandar and my Myanmar family – Aung Htun, Nwe Nwe San and their daughter Mia.

Figure 0.1 Khin Moe Samm, Phyo Thandar, Nan Theingi and Nwe Nwe San at Thei Su San's wedding, Yangon, 2015. Source: Author.

Contents

List of figures and tables ix
List of abbreviations xi
Acknowledgements xix

	Introduction	1
1	The state of education, pre-reform	30
2	Education reform and effects on basic education	58
3	The alternative: Monastic education	101
4	Higher education: Towards international standards in a neo-liberal world	130
5	Teacher education and training: Is changing practice possible?	159
6	Ethnic education: Language and local curriculum issues	197
7	Ethnic education: Recognising alternative systems run by ethnic armed organisations	238
	Conclusion: Whither social justice in Myanmar?	273

References 286
Index 297

List of figures and tables

Figures

0.1	Khin Moe Samm, Phyo Thandar, Nan Theingi and Nwe Nwe San at Thei Su San's wedding, Yangon, 2015	v
0.2	Map of Myanmar	2
2.1	Rural government school, 2014	63
2.2	Education protests, 2015	72
2.3	Leadership and management seminars for informed decision making for the Ministry of Education, 2019	83
3.1	Monastic school, 2010	109
3.2	Monastic teacher training: Network of CCA trainers, 2010	114
3.3	Phaung Daw Oo Monastic School, 2010 teachers' focus group discussion	115
3.4	Monastic school parents Yangon Region, 2010 parents' focus group discussion	117
3.5	Monastic school in Mandalay, 2010	121
4.1	Transforming Higher Education Programme, senior management from 11 Universities, 2018	136
4.2	First National Higher Education Conference with Minister of Education, 2018	136
4.3	Second National Higher Education Conference, 2018: Building Quality and Equity in Higher Education	149
6.1	Ethnic education representatives meet Comprehensive Education Sector Review (CESR) team, 2013	202
6.2	Conversation with the Akha community, 2018	222
6.3	Members of the Dainet community, 2018	225
6.4	Members of the PNO, PDN, PWEF and PLCO with Daw Aye Aye Tun, 2016	226
6.5	Shan State Pa-O Teacher Education College, 2018	227

7.1	Nationwide Ceasefire Agreement (NCA) ceremony 2015 with General Min Aung Hlaing on the screen as he prepares to sign	245
7.2	Mon National School, 2013	248
7.3	Shan language books developed by the Shan Literature and Culture Associations (LCA)	253
7.4	Kaw Dai, Shan State, 2018	257
7.5	Kachin State non-government teacher workshop, 2015	263
7.6	Joint MNEC and Mon SEO workshop 2018, led by Viren Lall with Mi Kun Chan Non translating	265

Tables

6.1	Adult literacy rates by sex, urban and rural areas, states/regions, 2014 Census	212
6.2	School attendance rates by age, sex, states/regions, 2014 Census	213
6.3	Proportion of population aged 25 and over with no schooling by sex, urban and rural areas, states/regions, 2014 Census	214
6.4	Children aged 7–15 by school attendance, states/regions, 2014 Census	215
6.5	Percentage of population aged 25 and over by highest completed level of education by sex, states/regions, 2014 Census	217
7.1	Typology of ethnic schools	242

List of abbreviations

AANZFTA	ASEAN–Australia/New Zealand Free Trade Area
ABSFU	All Burma Federation of Students' Unions
ACDE	Action Committee for Democratic Education
ADB	Asian Development Bank
ADRA	Adventist Development and Relief Agency
ANP	Arakan National Party
APEF	Asia Peace and Education Foundation
APR	Annual Progress Review(s)
AQRF	ASEAN Qualifications Reference Framework
ASEAN	Association of Southeast Asian Nations
ASL	Athletic, Stationary and Library
ATEO	Assistant Township Education Officers AUN – ASEAN University Network
AUN-QA	ASEAN University Network Quality Assurance Framework
AUN	ASEAN University Network
AUSAID	(now Department of Foreign Affairs and Trade – DFAT)
AY	Academic Year
BC	British Council
BCP	Burmese Communist Party
BGF	Border Guard Force,
BIM	Burnet Institute Myanmar
BUPE	Burma UK Partnership for Education
CBO	Community Based Organisation
CCA	Child-Centred Approaches (in Education)
CCRP	COVID-19 Comprehensive Relief Plan
CDF	Capacity Development Fund
CDT	Curriculum Development Team
CESR	Comprehensive Education Sector Review
CLC	Community Learning Centre
CPD	Continuous Professional Development
CPME	Centre for the Promotion of Monastic Education

CREATE	Curriculum Reform at Primary Level of Basic Education
CRED	Centre for Rural Education and Development
CSO	Civil Society Organisations
CTUM	Confederation of Trade Unions – Myanmar
DANIDA	Danish International Development Agency
DASSK	Daw Aung San Suu Kyi
DANIDA	Danish International Development Agency
DBE	Department of Basic Education
DDGs	Deputy Director Generals
DEO	District Education Office/r(s)
DEPT	Department of Educational Planning and Training
DERPT	Department of Education Research, Planning and Training
DFAT	Department of Foreign Affairs and Trade (Australia)
DFID	Department for International Development (UK)
DG	Director General
DHE	Department of Higher Education
DKBA	Democratic Karen Benevolent/Buddhist Army
DMER	Department of Myanmar Education Research
DPCG	Development Partner Coordination Group
DTEd	Diploma in Teacher Education
DTET	Department of Teacher Education and Training
DWT	Daily Wage Teachers
EAG	Ethnic Armed Groups
EAO	Ethnic Armed Organisations
EBEP	Ethnic Basic Education Providers
ECCD	Early Childhood Care and Development
ECCE	Early Childhood Centres for Education
EDGE	Education Directory and Guide for Everyone
EFA	Education for All
EfECT	English for Education College Trainers
EMIS	Education Management Information System(s)
EPIC	Education Promotion Implementation Committee
ES4E	English Skills for Everyone
ESCC	Education Sector Coordination Committee
ESRC	Education Sector Reform Contract
ETWG	Education Technical Working Group
EYE	Equipping Youth for Employment Project
FESR	Framework for Social and Economic Reforms
FGD	Focus Group Discussion
GDP	Gross Domestic Product
GEI	Gender Inequality Index

GER	Gross Enrolment Ratio(s)
GESI	Gender Equality and Social Inclusion
GIZ	Gesellschaft für Internationale Zusammenarbeit (German Corporation for International Cooperation)
GPE	Global Partnership for Education
HDI	Human Development Index
HE	Higher Education
HEI	Higher Education Institution
HES	Higher Education Subsector
HRD	Human Resource Development
IBE	International Bureau of Education
ICJ	International Court of Justice
ICT	Information and Communication Technology
IDP	Internally Displaced person/ people
IGA	Income Generating Activities
IHLCA	Integrated Household Living Conditions Assessment
IHLCS	Integrated Household Living Conditions Survey
ILAS	Institute of Liberal Arts and Sciences
ILBC	International Language and Business Centre
ILO	International Labour Organisation
IMF	International Monetary Fund
INGOs	International Non-governmental Organisation
INSET	In-service and teacher education
IoE	Institute(s) of Education
IPE	Irrawaddy Policy Exchange
IT	Information Technology
JAT	Junior Assistant Teachers
JESWG	Joint Education Sector Working Group
JICA	Japan International Cooperation Agency
KAS	Konrad Adenauer Stiftung
KDA	Kachin Defense Army
KEC	Kachin Education Consortium
KED	Karen Education Department
KESAG	Karen State Education Assistance Group
KG	Kindergarten
KHRG	Karen Human Rights Group
KIA	Kachin Independence Army
KIO	Kachin Independence Organisation
KIO-ED	Kachin Independence Organisation – Education Department
KnEDN	Karenni Education and Development Network
KNPP	Karenni National Progressive Party

KNU	Karen National Union
KRCEE	Karen Refugee Committee Education Entity
KSEAG	Karen State Education Assistance Group
KTWG	Karen Teacher Working Group
LC	Local Curriculum
LCA	Literature and Culture Associations
LCC	Literature and Culture Committees
LDU	Lahu Democratic Union
LESC	Language, Education and Social Cohesion Initiative
LoI	Language of Instruction
MC	Monthly Curriculum
MDEF	Multi-Donor Education Fund
MDG	Millennium Development Goal(s)
ME	Myanmar Egress
MEC	Myanmar Education Consortium
MEDG	Monastic Education Development Group
MEPP	Myanmar Education Partnership Project
MERB	Myanmar Education Research Bureau
MESC	Monastic Education Supervisory Committees
MFF	Myanmar Fisheries Federation
MIMU	Myanmar Information Management Unit
MINE	Myanmar/Burma Indigenous Network for Education
MLRC	Myanmar Literacy Resource Centre
MMCWA	Myanmar Maternal and Child Welfare Association
MNEC	Mon National Education Committee
MNS	Mon National Schools
MoA	Memoranda of Agreements
MoE	Ministry of Education
MoEA	Ministry of Ethnic Affairs
MoFA	Ministry of Foreign Affairs
MoPF	Ministry of Planning and Finance
MoRA	Ministry for Religious Affairs
MoU	Memoranda of Understanding
MP	Members of Parliament
MPBND	Ministry of the Progress of Border Areas and National Races
MPC	Myanmar Peace Centre
MSLBC	Mon Summer Literacy and Buddhist Culture
MSW	Ministry for Social Welfare
MTB-MLE	Mother Tongue Based Multi-Lingual Education
MTR	Mid Term Review
MUDE	Mandalay University of Distance Education

MUPE	Myanmar-UK Partnership for Education
MWAF	Myanmar Women's Affairs Federation
NAQAC	National Accreditation and Quality Assurance Committee
NCA	Nationwide Ceasefire Agreement
NCC	National Curriculum Committee
NDA-K	New Democratic Army-Kachin
NEL	National Education Law
NER	Net Enrolment Ratio
NEPC	National Education Policy Commission
NESP	National Education Strategic Plan (since 2016) / National Education Sector Plan (pre 2016)
NGO	Non-Government Organisation(s)
NIHED	National Institute of Higher Education Development
NLD	National League for Democracy
NMSP	New Mon State Party
NNER	National Network for Education Reform
NPA	National Plan for Action
NPT	Nay Pyi Taw (Myanmar's capital)
NUS	National University of Singapore
OCA	Organisational Constraints Analysis
OECD	Organisation for Economic Co-operation and Development
OECD/DAC	OECD's Development Assistance Committee
OHCHR	Office of the High Commissioner for Human Rights (UN Human Rights).
OOCS	Out of School Children
OPM	Oxford Policy Management
OSF	Open Society Foundation
OSY	Out-of-School Youth
PACE	People's Alliance for Credible Elections
PAT	Primary Assistant Teacher
PDN	Parami Development Network
PEPC	Parliamentary Education Promotion Committee
PNLA	Pa-O National Liberation Army (PNLA)
PNO	Pa-O National Organisation
PPE	Post-Primary Education
PPTT	Pre-Primary Teacher Training
PTA	Parent Teacher Association
QBEP	Quality Basic Education Programme
RC	Rectors' Committee
RCSS	Restoration Council of Shan State (Political wing of a Shan State Army)

RCSS-ED	Restoration Council of Shan State – Education Department
REO	Regional Education Office
RISE	Rural Indigenous Sustainable Education
RSSDF	Rural Shan State Development Foundation
RWCT	Reading, Writing and Critical Thinking
SAT	Senior Assistant Teacher
SAZ	Self Administered Zone
SDG	Sustainable Development Goals
SES	Secondary Education Sub-sector
SEO	State Education Office(r)
SEZ	Special Economic Zones
SIF	School Improvement Funds
SISP	School Improvement Support Programme
SITE	School-based In-service Teacher Education
SJN	*SaJaNa* – Shan State Kachin Baptist Union
SLCA	Shan Literature and Cultural Association
SLORC	State Law and Order Restoration Council
SNLD	Shan Nationalities League for Democracy
SPDC	State Peace and Development Council
SSA	Shan State Army
SSPP	Shan State Progressive Party
STEM	Strengthening Pre-service Teacher Education in Myanmar
SUOE	Sagaing University of Education
TA	Teaching Assistant(s)
TBC	The Border Consortium
TCA	Teacher Centred Approach
TCSF	Teacher Competency Standards Framework
TET	Teacher Education Team
TEO	Township Education Office(r)
ToR	Terms of Reference
TREE	Towards Results in Education and English
TTCs	Teacher Training Colleges
TTSs	Teacher Training Schools
TVET	Technical and Vocational Education and Training
UDNR	University for Development of National Races
UGC	Union Election Commission
UNDP	United Nations Development Programme
UNGA	United Nations General Assembly
UEC	Union Election Commission
UNESCO	United Nations Educational, Scientific and Cultural Organisation

UNICEF	United Nations International Children's Emergency Fund
UNOCHA	United Nations Office for the Coordination of Humanitarian Affairs
USDA	Union Solidarity and Development Association
USDP	Union Solidarity and Development Party
USIP	United States Institute of Peace
WB	World Bank
YU	Yangon University
YUDE	Yangon University of Distance Education
YUOE	Yangon University of Education
YWCA	Young Women's Christian Association

Acknowledgements

Much of the research on the ground – especially before 2013 – would have been impossible without the research team I was able to build at Myanmar Egress. This book is therefore dedicated to the Egress sisterhood Moe, Phyo, TG and Thei Su as well as Aung Htun and Nwe Nwe San, who accompanied me on multiple trips around the country.

Over the past five years, it has become somewhat easier to do research in Myanmar's education institutions. In this time, I have worked with a large number of people, but my fondest memories go to my time in the field with Aye Aye Tun who has become a very dear friend.

I have many colleagues and friends to thank in Mon, Kachin, Karen and Shan States – in particular, Mi Kun Chan Non, Mi Sardar (especially for that unforgettable trip to Nyisar) in Mon State, Dr Lu Awn in Kachin State and Daw Nang Wah Nu, who made it possible for me to travel across southern Shan State. Many thanks also to Kaw Dai for the warm welcome in their HQs, they do truly amazing work.

In NPT, my thanks go to the many patient MoE officials who have spent numerous days with me discussing many aspects of the education reform process. Their work is super hard and yet they are not tiring of it (and of all the foreigners who regularly come and bug them). Also thank you to Susannah Hla Hla Soe and Ma Shwe Latt, who manage to make time to meet in between the busy parliamentary sessions

In Yangon, my thanks go to my very old friends Tin Maung Thann and U Hla Maung Shwe, who I wish I could see more of as well as Ma Thanegi and of course Dr Nay Win Maung's mother – Mummy to me – who still feeds me on every one of my visits.

This book could not have been written without the help and collaboration of all the teachers, parents, teacher educators, student teachers, TEO officials, SEO officials, monastic heads, academic colleagues, LCA/LCC members, EAO representatives and Civil Society Organisation members who gave their time to answer questions, explain the local situation and relate their views. I hope this book does justice to their voices.

In Tokyo, my thanks go to my colleagues and friends, who have spent many hours talking about the country with me. In particular discussions with Ikuko Okamoto, Kei Nemoto and Yukako Iikuni who have spent years working on Myanmar were invaluable. Special thanks also to the Myanmar JICA teams in Tokyo and Yangon who made time to explain the various Japanese programmes. This book would not have been written had I not been able to access the Tokyo Metropolitan Library over the summer and winter 2019. This serene, quiet space in the midst of the Arisugawa-no-miya Memorial Park, far away from the London (and Yangon rush) was my sanctuary and my inspiration.

Many thanks to ANU who have allowed me to reproduce one of their maps of Myanmar and Gerard McCarthy who helped me to get the right permission.

In London, much thanks are due to my editor Pat Gordon-Smith, who turned this book around in record time.

As always, my thanks and love to my husband who over the last 25 years has put up with my absence, but who did join me on one of my last Myanmar trips as a part of my team.

Marie Lall
London, during the COVID-19 lockdown, June 2020

Introduction

A policy window for change

The landslide election victory of the National League for Democracy (NLD) in 2015 offered a window for change – a so called 'policy window' (Marshall, 2000) – to lead Myanmar's reform process according to the original NLD values that included a left-leaning view of social justice and the empowerment of the poorest and most disadvantaged communities as a part of the political and economic transformation of Myanmar.[1] This book, written from mid-2019 to mid-2020, is a snapshot taken towards the end of the first five years of NLD rule, evaluating the progress made, nevertheless casting an eye on the future of Myanmar beyond the 2020 elections.

The reality on the ground after almost ten years of reforms – five years under President Thein Sein and almost five years under Daw Aung San Suu Kyi – does not point to a social justice agenda. The most marginalised remain at the fringes. A recent report by the Myanmar Information Management Unit (MIMU) on vulnerability bears out how the reforms are failing the wider Myanmar population and exacerbating inequalities (MIMU, 2018). This multi-sectoral review holds that Myanmar's success in meeting the Sustainable Development Goals (SDGs) largely depends on how well the government targets the poorest and most marginalised in society. In its summary findings, the report points to the urban–rural differences as follows (MIMU, 2018: 2):

> Stark disparities were found in living conditions and economic freedoms between the residents of urban and rural areas: 72% of rural villages are not electrified and persons in rural areas have markedly lower access to safe drinking water and sanitation; educational outcomes vary significantly and secondary school attendance in rural areas is half of that in urban areas.

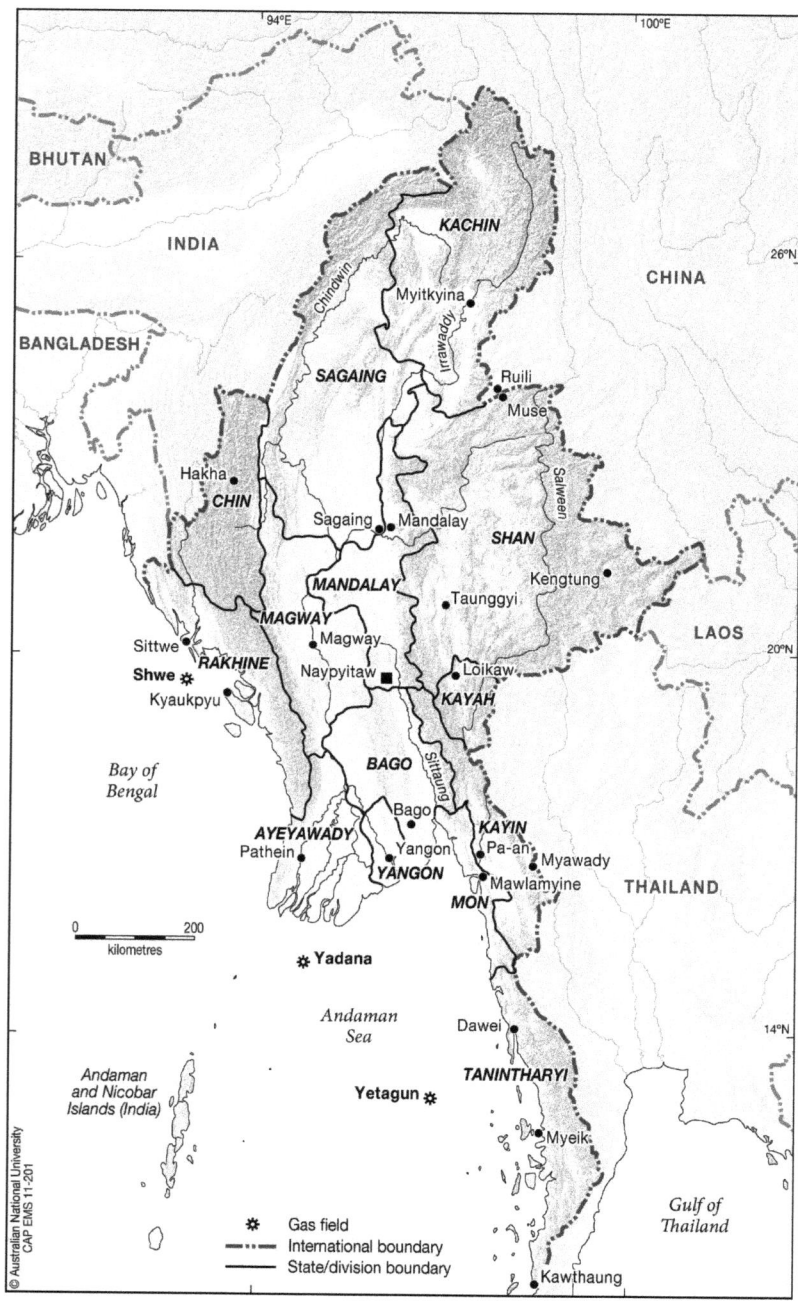

Figure 0.2 Map of Myanmar. Source: CartoGIS Services, College of Asia and the Pacific, The Australian National University.

With regard to health, the report again shows the stark disparities that are not being alleviated by the reforms (MIMU, 2018: 3):

> There are wide geographic, ethnic and socio-economic disparities; infant mortality rates are highest in the districts of Labutta in Ayeyarwady and Mindat in Chin, whereas Magway, Sagaing and Tanintharyi have particularly high early years mortality rates. Children in rural areas are more likely to be chronically undernourished (32% stunting) than those in urban areas (20%).

With regard to education the report finds (MIMU, 2018: 3):

> Literacy is particularly low in Shan State which accounts for 18 of the 19 townships countrywide where more than half of children have never attended school; Mongkhet township is especially prominent with 85% of children never having attended school. Other townships with particularly high numbers of persons with no education are in Kayin, Magway and Rakhine. Children from rural families, poor or otherwise disadvantaged groups are less likely to transition from primary to secondary education, or to complete their secondary education.

Much of this is of course the legacy of decades of junta rule, yet the decade of reforms could have made a significant difference if development priorities had targeted the most vulnerable – the poor and conflict-affected communities.

In part, the types of development being prioritised is due to the international aid and development community, whose philosophy comes from a neo-liberal tradition, and who are driving the reform process. This has resulted in too much being changed at once, with tight targets exceeding the capacities of local departments and organisations. It has also resulted in large development contracts being awarded to Western firms who have little knowledge of Myanmar rather than supporting bottom-up grassroots civil society and local NGOs who understand the local context.[3] The kind of development taking place is nevertheless also due to the gap between NLD policy and priorities, between what was promised and what this first NLD Government is actually delivering. Daw Aung San Suu Kyi has changed the tune of the government, asking local people to look to each other for help and support rather than to the state (McCarthy, 2019).

While the reforms have not yet resulted in Myanmar adopting an overall market approach to public services, including education, the

Myanmar Government ministries are adopting other aspects of neo-liberalism – including the vocabulary of efficiency and effectiveness. The 'market' is being looked at to offer choice to the urban middle classes. Some reforms are being rolled out to improve the lives of the majority rural and poor population by improving the quality of the government services, but Myanmar's first democratic decade has seen a dramatic increase in the inequalities between urban and rural, middle classes and poorer sections of society. This is disappointing to many Myanmar citizens[4] who had put all their hopes into Daw Aung San Suu Kyi and her NLD Government. They had not expected much from the Union Solidarity and Development Party (USDP) Government led by President Thein Sein that ruled from 2011 to 2015 that was largely viewed as no more than a political vehicle for the military. There was a clear expectation that once the NLD obtained power, the country would be governed in a manner that would strive to bring equality and justice to all. People did not use the term 'social justice', but in effect that is what they were referring to when speaking about access to education and health and public services, no matter where they lived and from what ethnic group they originated.

Today, the NLD has been in power for almost five years and people across the country complain about having been let down. Some look for excuses, for example, that Daw Aung San Suu Kyi has not had a free hand in governing the country, but must constantly appease the military. Yet many know that the military contingent in parliament[5] is not preventing Daw Aung San Suu Kyi from delivering on their hopes. In fact, there was more than hope, rather the many promises in the 2015 NLD election manifesto that all reflect the issues that one would group under 'social justice', even if this exact term was not used.[6]

One of the overall promises in the NLD election manifesto (priority 3 of 4) was: 'To change the lives of our people, the NLD will strive for a system of government that will fairly and justly defend the people' (NLD, 2015: 4). With regard to ethnic affairs and peace the NLD promises 'solidarity with all ethnic groups' and 'principles of freedom, equal rights and self-determination' (NLD, 2015: 5). This is also reflected in the section in the Constitution (NLD, 2015: 6) where the NLD promises: 'to guarantee ethnic rights' and 'to defend and protect the equal rights of citizens'. In particular, the NLD mentions agricultural workers (NLD, 2015: 11) and states that 'farmers' rights and economic well-being must be secure'. Workers (NLD, 2015: 14) are being promised the following:

- 'We will establish opportunities for workers to develop their skills and expertise.
- We will implement policies aimed at ensuring that workplaces are safe and fair for all, and that workers receive an appropriate salary.
- No worker should be discriminated against, and every worker should receive equal compensation for equivalent work.
- Every worker shall have the right to freely establish and be part of workers' organisations that protect their rights and benefits.
- We will end all forms of forced labour.'

In order to secure these opportunities for workers and agricultural workers, the NLD promises to: 'strive to establish access to electricity in all areas, both urban and rural' (NLD, 2015: 19) and the urban poor, many of whom are migrants from conflict and disaster areas are promised to be rehoused: 'We will establish, as quickly as possible, a programme for the rehousing of homeless migrants, who have moved to the cities as a result of natural disasters, economic opportunities, and land confiscation' (NLD, 2015: 25). Women are also promised equality (NLD, 2015: 22):

- 'We will strive to ensure that existing laws are implemented effectively so that women in all sectors – whether government, business, or social – have equal rights with men.
- We will take action as necessary to end the persecution, insecurity, violence, and other forms of harassment and bullying suffered by women.
- We will work to ensure that female workers receive the same compensation as their male counterparts for equivalent work, and that there is no gender discrimination with regard to workplace promotions.'

And most importantly for this book, with regard to education (NLD, 2015: 15), the NLD promises the following:

- 'We will prioritise the needs of schools in less-developed areas where schools currently lack necessary facilities and equipment, in order to make middle school and high school education more accessible to all.
- For the improvement of the quality of life of people with limited educational qualifications, we will establish opportunities for

further education through programmes for continuing basic middle and high school study, and in-school and out-of-school vocational training opportunities of equivalent standard.
- We will establish effective education services that do not place a burden on parents and communities.'

As can be seen from the above, the 2015 election manifesto did indeed promise *social justice*, despite the absence of this term.[7] The social justice framework cuts across the various chapters, as education is a key element if one is to build a just and equal society, and it is crucial for other reforms to succeed. The fact that the promises made by the NLD go well beyond the education sector strengthens the case this book is making.

After the manifesto, the election: November 2015 – Myanmar's first free and fair election since 1990[8]

On Sunday 8 November 2015, Myanmar went to the polls with more than 90 parties contesting seats for the two houses of parliament as well as the 14 state and regional assemblies. Despite the large number of parties, all eyes were on the opposition NLD and the regime USDP. The NLD swept the polls. In order to control the government, the NLD needed 67 per cent of the seats (or 329 seats), as 25 per cent were allocated to unelected appointees of the military; but the NLD did far better than this, winning almost 80 per cent of elected seats. Crossing this threshold meant that Myanmar could become a very different country – it offered a policy window to transform Myanmar. The losing military-based USDP was bitterly disappointed with the result, yet despite this, neither the military nor the USDP tried to hinder the transfer of power in any way.

The elections were followed by an almost three-month transition period during which time the old government was still in power. The new parliament convened only after the old parliament dissolved on 30 January 2016. The NLD's first task was to select a new President, as Daw Aung San Suu Kyi, the leader of the NLD, was barred by the constitution from the position due to her having sons with British citizenship. To circumvent this restriction, Daw Aung San Suu Kyi declared that she would be 'above the president' in all the decisions – a promise she has kept. In any event, Daw Aung San Suu Kyi's close childhood friend Htein Kyaw[9] was appointed to the presidency and the post of 'State Councillor' was created for Daw Aung San Suu Kyi.[10]

The challenges faced by the National League for Democracy (NLD)

After winning the election, the NLD's first challenge was to develop cordial relations with the military. Myanmar has mainland Southeast Asia's largest standing army, and the constitution guarantees their place in parliament, and together with their control over key ministries they remain significant stakeholders in the political system. The NLD had to find a way to cooperate with the Chief of Staff as well as the military members of parliament (MPs). The NLD's campaign pledge to alter the Constitution, and in particular change Article 436 which ensured a veto by the military for any constitutional change, was likely to bring the party into conflict with the military leadership, and as such it was quickly shelved.

The second major challenge was to rule and administer the country. The NLD did not do much in this regard between 2012 and 2015 as they had only 43 MPs. With the exception of wanting to change the constitution, the NLD campaign was devoid of clear and detailed policy priorities, keeping things rather general and focusing on promising major changes. As seen above, the NLD manifesto did, however, promise to govern the country on the lines of social justice, promising to represent the poorest and most disadvantaged in society.

The main challenge facing the new Myanmar Government at the time of the transfer of power was addressing the country's ethnic and religious tensions. An ultra-nationalist Buddhist movement led by monks – called *Ma Ba Tha* ('Society for the Protection of Race and Religion') had gained traction since 2012 and had been fuelling anti-Muslim sentiment across the country. Ma Ba Tha's influence not only resulted in four 'race and religion protection laws' being passed in 2014 (which clearly discriminate against Muslims), it also resulted in Muslim electoral candidates not being able to contest seats in the election, and not one of the 1,051 NLD candidates was a Muslim. The result has been a parliament without a single Muslim MP, despite about 4 per cent of Myanmar's population identifying as Muslim. At the time of the elections in November 2015 (and in the subsequent four years), the NLD did not speak up for the disenfranchised Rohingya for fear of being branded a 'foreigner friendly' party.

Another challenge to unity and fairness included the representation of ethnic people, as around 38 per cent of Myanmar's population are ethnic minorities and there are a large number of ethnic political parties.[11] In 2010, the ethnic MPs formed the first legal opposition to the USDP dominated parliament. Despite local ethnic leaders' misgivings (Lall et al., 2015) the NLD fielded candidates in all ethnic majority areas. Consequently, many locals feared the vote would be split, leading to an end of the vibrant ethnic politics that had been an unforeseen result of the 2010 elections. After the ballots had been counted, it was clear that the NLD had displaced most of the ethnic parties.[12] The main reason for this result appears to be that a large number of ethnic parties had been created to contest the 2015 elections, but subsequently, the ethnic electorate seems to have decided that if the country was to change, a united vote for the NLD was going to be more powerful than many small ethnic parties with little mandate. The lack of a clearly defined ethnic voice in parliament was, however, to have grave consequences for equal representation. The NLD has always maintained that democracy is their first priority and ethnic grievances can be addressed later. Given the protracted peace process with the ethnic armed groups, a sizeable ethnic representation would have been essential so as to represent the ethnic civilian voice.

At the time of the electoral win in November 2015, euphoria across Myanmar's electorate was high. The results that they had been denied in 1990 came through 25 years later. People expected the NLD to transform the country. However, in the past five years there have been increasing voices of discontent, and at the time of writing – as the NLD is completing its fifth year in power – the overall mood across Myanmar has changed from hope to resignation. The list of challenges confronting the government seem almost unchanged from when the NLD took power, with the country's progress seemingly stalled, stuck in quagmires for which there are no easy solutions.

The key issue remains the stagnant peace process, and more specifically how to link the wider reforms and the peace process. The lack of decentralisation means that ethnic states still do not have the required mandate to engage with issues specific to their state or their ethnic groups, which is underpinned by the lack of ethnic voices in parliament and in wider politics, as mentioned above. Whilst the NLD does have ethnic MPs in certain areas, they have not been able to speak up specifically for local and ethnic issues as ethnic parties had done in the past.[13]

Other problems include the lack of freedom of expression for the press,[14] the lack of decentralisation of power (even within ministries), and stagnating economic growth that rather than delivering inclusive development is widening the gap between urban and rural, rich and poor.[15] Ministries are working towards change according to strategic plans that they have co-developed with development partners, however, many have reached a point where they cannot take any more capacity building, nor spend the aid money that has been allocated to drive change. While ministries are supposed to drive change in all sectors, the lack of agency they are allowed at different levels means the direction of instructions remains top-down, begging the question of how Myanmar will ever move to a more participatory administration. The lack of agency is also due to the deep mistrust the NLD holds of the civil service: 'due to the military background and loyalties of many bureaucrats' (Stokke et al., 2018: 12). The role of the international community is not blameless in these developments, as the lack of coordination between development partners means that ministries are pushed and pulled in different directions, and those most senior (such as director generals) have to cope with unbearable workloads to try to keep all the funders happy.

A defining feature of Myanmar's reform journey has been the contestations over narratives and understandings of citizenship and national identity. There has been a growing sense that Buddhism as part of the national identity has served to discriminate and divide rather than unite. An increasingly large number of citizens within the Buddhist ethnic groups (i.e. not only the Bamar) equate citizenship with religion, or seem to think that in order to be a Myanmar citizen one must also be Buddhist (Lall et al., 2014). This religious nationalism that reared its head earlier this decade has not been dealt with carefully, and has alienated other groups with different religious identities. Debates in the press and social media have been galvanised by the crisis in Rakhine that has pitted Buddhists and Muslims against each other, however, the issue is central across ethnic states as well. It has of course also deeply affected Myanmar's image abroad as countries that have supported Myanmar's transition have turned to castigating the government for not doing enough for the Muslims in northern Rakhine. At the heart of this issue is Myanmar's decades of unequal treatment of ethnic groups, a clear social justice issue.

At this point in 2020, just before the next elections, it is therefore pertinent to ask about the NLD's vision for the reform process. It is unclear what is driving the choice of priorities.[16] Coming from a left wing political tradition that espouses the state's responsibility towards its citizens through the provision of public services underpinned by social equality, the NLD's key promise was to deliver reforms and social justice if it came to power. Some change is indeed evident, but the country is not united in these changes, and a relatively small urban elite is benefitting far more from the reform process than is the wider population. In fact, Daw Aung

San Suu Kyi has asked citizens to rely on themselves rather than look to the state (McCarthy, 2019).

As seen above, there is a widening gap between rural and urban Myanmar, at social, economic and political levels. Inflation has made the income divide between the urban middle classes and rural poor much starker. Land is now at a premium, so the agricultural poor are losing their livelihoods to development schemes, not least due to the establishment of Special Economic Zones (SEZs) that are being created to bring more foreign investment to Myanmar. Social justice has not been sufficiently part of the reform agenda, despite it being promised as a pillar by President Thein Sein in his inaugural speech in 2011, reiterated in his 2015 New Year message and then taken up as an NLD campaign pledge. The only difference with 'before' is that now those who have been wronged can protest, so there are loud and visible protests about land ownership and other social justice concerns. This widening gap and the trajectory Myanmar is on raises questions about the commitment to social justice that the NLD chose as a basis for its political mandate.

Social justice in a neo-liberal era

Myanmar is of course not alone and the global context shows that inequality has been on the rise. Brown and Lauder pointed out that since the 1970s, the income share of the richest 20 per cent of the world's population as compared to the poorest 20 per cent of the world's population increased from 30:1 to 61:1 (Brown and Lauder, 2003). Alvaredo et al. in 'The World Inequality Report' (Alvaredo et al., 2018) note that inequality has increased everywhere in the world despite substantial geographical differences, with the richest 1 per cent twice as wealthy as the poorest 50 per cent. This widening gap, both within countries and between countries, raises global questions around equality and social justice. There are broadly two opposing policy views regarding social justice – one emanating from social democracy based on social relationships and the needs of people within a community, and another, neo-liberal view that believes that social justice can be achieved through market individualism where people get what they deserve, rejecting any redistributive notions. The two positions represent very different, contrasting views of the world and Rizvi and Lingard in their epic book on globalisation remind us that (Rizvi and Lingard, 2010: 158) '... market individualism and social democracy rest on very different understandings of the nature of the relationship between justice and the market.' Hatcher puts it bluntly (Hatcher, 2001: 58):

> ... the starting point has to be the recognition that there are two distinct logics at work. One is a logic of education, based on social and individual need, and notions of equity and democracy. The other is a logic of business, whose bottom line is profit. Not everything business wants to do is incompatible with education interests. But the logic of business is incompatible with the logic of education.

The path of social democracy and redistribution marked the post-World War II (mostly Western) world.[17] At the core was the state's responsibility to provide equal public services – including education – to all its citizens, although more recently the neo-liberal vision of market-based social justice has dominated. It is argued that the marketisation of society has influenced all spheres of life, including education, and this has led to profound changes in the nature of social relations, in particular, the narrowing of the notion of 'student' into that of consumer, and a concomitant commodification of the learning experience (Giroux, 2004). The emphasis on competition and increased performance means increased surveillance and evaluation, which has led to the development of national curricula, national testing regimes and managerialist systems of performance evaluation which have eroded teacher's professional autonomy (Apple, 2004).[18]

At the heart of a neo-liberal system is the changing nature of the state from a provider to a regulator (Olssen and Peters, 2005; Wrigley, 2007). Consequently, neo-liberalism is not about lessening state control, but rather represents a new form of state involvement. As the market logic is extended to the public sector, the state becomes a regulator rather than a provider of such services, with the state being instrumental in facilitating the market to take on these responsibilities. As such, the state uses the market as a new control mechanism. Whilst there is a general withdrawal of the state, it is not in the arena of control, but rather in its position as the entity responsible for safeguarding all citizens, especially the weaker sections of society, a key socio-democratic function of the state. Globalisation has ensured that these notions have influenced the development and aid agenda, with aid agencies exporting these notions to the Global South (Lall and Rao, 2011).

Reforms pushing public services to adapt to markets have been particularly supported by the growing middle classes in middle income and poorer countries, as they tend to benefit most from policies of choice and have the ability to buy themselves out of the public system to the detriment of the poorer and weaker sections of society (Hill and Rosskam, 2009: xvii). Globally, the middle classes have been seen to access the lion's share of opportunities that have come with the new economy, using education as a key cultural resource.

The new economic realities across the developing world have led to increased disaggregation, deregulation, commodification, emphasis on measurable outputs, managerialism and accountability. Neo-liberal market-orientated reforms have affected education at all levels in developed and developing countries. In many countries, primary and secondary education have opened up to the market allowing new private providers to offer educational services, competing with public education provided by the state. This has brought with it a new education discourse which changes the aim of education and is developing a society which is adapted to the new knowledge economy both at domestic and international levels. As Gamarnikow notes:

> In the social democratic era, education was constructed as a public good and a collective form of welfare provision, a key element of Marshall's social citizenship (Marshall, 1950). In the current neo-liberal era, by contrast, policy discourses construct education as a positional good for individuals, and as the site for human capital formation for the globalised economy. What has not changed is the importance ascribed to education. (Gamarnikow, 2009: 158)

There have been similar effects in the higher education (HE) sector: marketisation across the sector has made performance and accountability cornerstones of HE policies today. The pressure to increase the number of students, account for how time is spent and the general concern with national and international rankings are all effects of the changing understanding of the aims of HE. The role of the university is no longer that of a public interest institution, but that of a site of 'knowledge production' in light of the economic imperatives of the 'knowledge economy'. As academics are ranked according to the number of their publications, their universities compete internationally for those students who will bring in the highest fees.

The central question in all this concerns the role of the state, and what role it has to play in ensuring a socially just society. Those concerned with equality and social justice in education have voiced concern about the changing discourse on social justice with the ascendance of the neo-liberal paradigm in education, pointing to widening disparities between social groups while emphasising emerging and deepening inequalities as a result of new state policies and programmes. There has been a significant volume of research (as well as official statistics) that show that groups that experience discrimination and disadvantage because of identities of race, caste and ethnic identity show lower participation and achievement rates in schools and HE (Lall and Rao, 2011).

Regimes of competition that include standardised testing of high skills (within and across nations) are becoming widespread as nations strive to make their school systems more efficient in order to gain a competitive edge in the global market for education and labour. The growing preoccupation with testing and competition and the resulting narrowing and fragmenting of the larger objectives of education leads to the neglect of inclusive cultures and practices.

The purpose of education reforms

Education reforms in developing countries are often 'pushed through' as part of a wider reform process, one underpinned by an international development agenda spearheaded by international agencies such as the World Bank (WB) and the International Monetary Fund (IMF). The Washington consensus ensured for decades that inefficient public systems that were attempting to serve poor communities across developing countries had to change their funding models to achieve 'fiscal reforms'. The dominant Western economic perspective on education reform (Wolf, 2002) focuses on its role in producing future benefits, largely drawing on human capital theory (Hanushek, 2013; Sweetland, 1996). Whilst research has begun to highlight the limitations of the human capital theory approach (Brown, 2001; Marginson, 2019), many fundamental questions about the role of, and alternatives to, human capital theory remain unanswered (Kapur and Crowley, 2008). What is increasingly clear is that the perspective of human capital theory and its role in driving the comparative advantage in the global economy as part of many a national education policy does not allow for all groups to benefit equally. Often these neo-liberal reforms pay lip-service to social justice, mainly in terms of expanding provision for hitherto excluded groups. However, the increasingly differentiated systems of education, the spread of for-profit schooling and tight controls and accountability structures, along with the standardised assessment practices that schools are being drawn into have grave consequences for the purposes of education and social justice.

Why 'social justice' as a basis to review education reforms in Myanmar?

As noted above, despite important improvements across the globe that include better living standards both in the Western and the developing world, there are enduring problems including a rising gap between the poor and the middle classes; social class and ethnicity still largely determine life chances and political influence is polarised according to wealth and class. Education has been heralded as a panacea to resolve inequalities and deliver more socially just societies across the globe. It is thought that education will empower any individual to rise to his or her full potential and to break free from poverty and inequality. However, in order for education to deliver such outcomes, the education system itself needs to offer not only equality of access and opportunity (quality) but also equality of outcome and condition. Education delivered in public schools by poorly trained teachers in rural or remote areas cannot compete with education delivered by high-end urban private schools because the conditions are vastly different.

Education reforms in developing countries therefore need to go beyond the access agenda propagated by the Millennium Development Goals (MDGs) and beyond the quality agenda propagated subsequently by the Sustainable Development Goals (SDGs) in order to consider how those most disadvantaged can attain equal outcomes to the more privileged with regard to future opportunities and equality of conditions. Policies for distribution and redistribution are necessary but not sufficient. Recognition is also important. Taylor et al. reminds us that any policies for educational justice have to deal with a complex web of issues that go beyond access and equity (Taylor et al., 1997: 151):

> ... but also [include] issues of identity, difference, culture and schooling. That is, the way things are named and represented, the manner in which difference is treated and the way in which the values and norms which govern life in schools are negotiated and established. These are all matters central to the concerns both of social justice and education.

The MDG proposal of a way forward to deliver a more socially just world was based on the distributive paradigm that focuses on resources – essentially on 'who gets what?' It can be argued that this model drew undue attention to the allocation of education. Education was seen as a social good and it was access to that social good and the resources given to it that were important. Social justice was therefore furthered by more equitable access. This paradigm, however, was never sufficient to capture the complexities of injustice. Content and quality were overlooked. Realising that just getting more children into classrooms and 'giving everyone their due' did not actually raise their achievement levels brought about the debate of quality that underpins the SDGs. An argument emerged that: the *how much* cannot be separated from the *what*' (Connell, 1993: 18). The 17 SDGs and in particular goal four, 'quality education', place quality and content at the heart of the agenda, while the SDG agenda also promises to address 'intersecting inequalities' as the goals are interrelated.

For social justice to truly underpin the governance of education and public services, *relational justice* is a better model. This refers to the power structures within society both in terms of how people interact with each other at a micro level, how individuals connect with wider society, as well as the macro socio-economic relations that: 'are mediated by institutions such as the state and the market' (Gewirtz, 1997: 471). Particular policies that target particular groups are known as 'politics of identity' and risk becoming deterministic. On the pathway to social justice we should not and cannot ignore differences within groups. What needs to be developed is a system that stresses: 'balancing the rights and freedoms of individuals to pursue their own interests with an equal interest in the rights and interests of the community' (Olssen et al., 2004: 235). The first step in this direction is to understand how the education reforms promote (or not) social justice through a theoretical model. One such model[19] is Iris Young's 'five faces of oppression' that includes consideration of exploitation, marginalisation, powerlessness, cultural imperialism and violence (Young, 2005).[20] When examining education reforms these factors identified by Young can be used to assess how the education policies support, interrupt or subvert:

- exploitative relationships within and beyond educational institutions
- the processes of marginalisation and inclusion within and beyond the education system
- the promotion of relationships based on recognition, respect, care and mutuality or produce powerlessness for education workers and students
- practices of cultural imperialism – and which cultural differences should be affirmed, which should be universalised and which rejected?

These questions will form the basis for the analysis of the various education reforms that have been undertaken by the Myanmar Government since 2011, but in particular since the NLD took power in 2016. The lens of social justice (Taylor et al., 1997; Gerwitz, 1997; Connell 1993) is used throughout these chapters to engage with a critique of the reforms undertaken over the past decade and the outcomes as they are visible today, just a few months before Myanmar is due to go to the polls again. The basis for the critique is what Marshall terms a 'policy window', a space that opens because of a change in the political stream (a change in administration, a shift in parliament or national mood); or it opens because a new problem captures the attention of policy-makers (Marshall, 2000; 127).

Taking a comprehensive view over 16 years, this book argues that the 2015 elections represented a policy window for the NLD that could have set Myanmar on a social justice trajectory, but that this policy window has been missed. It argues in particular that despite the education reform priorities espoused by the NLD Ministry of Education (MoE) explicitly advocating greater equality and equity,[21] Myanmar has missed an historic opportunity to use the education reform process to engage with deep-seated social justice issues, both in terms of granting more equitable long-term outcomes to poorer sections of society as well as rectifying existing inequalities between the majority Bamars and ethnic nationality communities.[22]

The book's aim is to review the education reform process as an example of policy reform and draw out the lessons learnt for Myanmar's Government and citizens, as well as for the aid and development community who have underpinned the reforms. Although locating itself in the education reform process, this book addresses interests beyond education, as education links in with many of the other reforms such as the peace process and economic and labour reforms. In doing so, the book aims to give voice to those most implicated in and affected by the changing landscape of Myanmar's education and wider reform process. This is important because these voices of students and their parents of all ethnic backgrounds, as well as those of teachers, student teachers and university staff engaged in education are rarely heard. Yet if readers (some of whom might be policy makers) are to understand what has been successful (or not) and why, it is important to look at the effects of the reforms on the ground and how ordinary lives have changed – or not. The book also engages with the voice of key policy makers in Myanmar and their views on the transformation of their country.

Why education?

Education is at the heart of Myanmar's transformation. The education story does not start with the Comprehensive Education Sector Review (CESR) in 2012. It starts in 2005–6 when different civil society groups saw education as the principal way in which to bring about change to the country's military dictatorship from within. Lall charts how Myanmar came to start a domestically-led transition from military dictatorship to a more participatory system between 2005 and 2010, resulting in an NLD Government between 2015 and 2020 (Lall, 2016a). It is clear that education was a catalyst for the movement of new civil society organisations that emerged and pushed for change.

After the 1988 and 1990 student protests, the universities had largely been closed. Undergraduate provision had been moved outside of the cities into remote areas and distance university education was encouraged, officially to enable the poorer students to study at home, but mostly to avoid students from getting together and becoming politically active. A whole generation was not able to access education beyond the metric examination and the quality of government education overall, and the quality of tertiary education particularly, had fallen dramatically over the decades of isolation due to under-investment and a lack of contact with the outside world.[23] The generation that was the last to complete their university education before 1988 realised that they had been the lucky ones, and that those who came after them would not have access to a comprehensive form of HE. Now in their 40s or older, some started to think about how the country could and would be able to change, and how a growing number of uneducated young adults in the population would make change ever more difficult. Some joined together to form civil society organisations (CSOs) to develop education programmes for the middle classes to compensate for the decade long closure of key universities prior to the 2010 elections (Lall, 2016a). In the mid-2000s, these organisations were supported by mostly German political foundations, and together with Myanmar Egress (ME), the most significant civil society organisation to emerge in 2006 to support the change process, have been pivotal in the country's reforms. ME was made up of a group of friends who had managed to complete their studies prior to 1988 and understood the transformative power of education. Their view was that if change was going to come to Myanmar, it was only going to occur by expanding the space from within, and not through either a revolution (as had been attempted in 1988) or through pressure from the outside (as the sanctions had been attempting since the 1990s).

The idea of an institution that would serve as a training institute, a think tank, a liaison office for reform-minded military government officials and as a catalyst for change can be credited to Dr Nay Win Maung, a medical doctor who had left medicine first for business, and then left business for journalism.[24]

The main aim of ME was first and foremost the training and education of young adults – the generation that had not had the chance to go to university, and those who could be catalysts for change. A series of courses was developed by ME ranging from a few days to six months to educate the youth about basic economic and political concepts and prepare them to vote in the 2010 elections.[25] Education was at the core of Myanmar's local move to engender change and it was these types of classes conducted by civil society that brought young people together, not on the streets in protest as in 1988, but binding them together with the aim of jointly transforming their country. ME was also used to create political space and develop a political and social identity amongst the young middle class Myanmar citizens who had missed out on 'proper' education. The idea was to recruit those who were enthusiastic, even if they had limited skills and few qualifications, and develop them into change agents. There were mostly three types of students – those who wanted to continue with their studies, those who wanted a career change, and those who were already working as NGO workers or activists. Recruitment happened through the networks of students who had completed the course, snowballing the number of applications. In the end, the number of students wanting to enrol far exceeded the number of places and all candidates had to be interviewed for the final selection. Some of the graduates of early courses then joined ME as staff for research and training.

Education – as can be seen from the above – is much more than what happens in schools and universities. It is at the heart of the political process in Myanmar. It is what has been at the origins of all the student protests that brought the country to a standstill in 1988 and 1990, and what pulled the country out of its stasis before the 2010 elections. It is therefore right that the country's transformation, especially since 2015, is reviewed in light of the education reforms that happened across the various education sectors – formal and informal – and by using education as a platform to give voice to the Myanmar people across the country who are living the change process. To successfully undertake this, a lot of primary data is required. The section below reviews the primary qualitative and quantitative data sets that have been collected through fieldwork across the whole of Myanmar.

Introducing the data that underpins this book

Based on 16 years of engagement, and over 10 years of (education) data collected in Myanmar across the whole country, this book gives a holistic view of both government and non-government education sectors, the reform process and how the transition has played out across schools, universities and wider society. This book refers to secondary sources, however, at the heart of the narrative are 13 large education studies that were conducted between 2010 and 2019. This book also draws on information gathered across three other very large studies, one on young people's views on citizenship another on the peace process, and a third on ethnic political parties.

Data for Chapter 1 on the background of education before the reforms started was collected as part of a 2012 study entitled 'Teachers' Voice' (Lall et al., 2013) Data was collected in 19 schools (most were government schools, but there were a few monastic and two private schools) in the Yangon Region.[26] Of these, four were primary level, seven were middle, and eight were high schools. Surveys were conducted with 308 teachers (out of 443 working in these schools). Follow-on in-depth focus groups with 84 teachers and interviews with 16 head teachers were conducted so as to get a comprehensive view on issues including the curriculum, the examination system, teacher salaries, teacher training and teaching methods. Schools were deliberately chosen so as to reflect the diversity of education institutions. Schools that agreed to take part were urban and suburban, and based in both middle class and poor areas. The aim of the project was to inform the incoming government of the on-the-ground needs and challenges faced by teachers in light of the expected reforms. The research was the first project of three conducted as part of the research training of research staff whilst supporting the establishment of a research centre at ME. Both the research centre and the research were funded by the Friedrich Naumann Stiftung Foundation from Germany and the EU as part of a large capacity building project.

Data on the education reforms in basic education and other education sectors, including the Comprehensive Education Sector Review (CESR) and the Education Promotion Implementation Committee (EPIC), were collected by the author whilst holding the position of Education Advisor for Fragile States for AUSAID (now Department of Foreign Affairs and Trade – DFAT) between 2012 and 2014, and being part of a team supporting the CESR that was led by the Myanmar MoE. This also included work on education in ethnic and conflict-affected areas that involved the organising and leading of two ground breaking ethnic education workshops in Yangon with representatives of all Ethnic Armed Organisation (EAO) education departments, workshops that have fed into the chapters on ethnic education.

More data on how the reforms were being carried out in the field were collected in 2013 as part of the United Nations International Children's Emergency Fund (UNICEF) funded and American University-led 'Mon State Situation Analysis (SITAN)' (Mehta et al., 2014), that examined decentralisation issues in the service delivery of education. This project included detailed discussion with MoE officers at State and Township levels. There was further engagement with the Union MoE through a series of two-day workshops and seminars between 2018–9 for the director generals and their deputies supporting reforms (funded by the Danish International Development Agency – DANIDA and delivered through the UCL Institute of Education).

The primary data for Chapter 3 on monastic education emanate from two large studies conducted in 2011 and 2016. Both studies were funded by the Pyoe Pin programme, a British Council (BC) supported programme that became an independent entity in 2018. The first was research conducted on child-centred teaching and learning methods in monastic schools across Myanmar. This involved fieldwork in 11 schools in three divisions – Ayeyarwady, Yangon and Mandalay (as regions were then called) in 2010, as well as conducting a workshop for stakeholders. The second focused on non-state education across Myanmar (not only monastic schools) leading to an advocacy policy paper in 2016. This involved fieldwork in Yangon, Northern Shan and Karen States.

Data for Chapter 4 on HE is taken from the BC funded project 'Supporting the Transformation of Higher Education in Myanmar' in 2018. Though not based on research, this allowed engagement with 11 Myanmar universities from across the country in developing leadership capacity through a series of four one-week-long intense training modules, workshops and two conferences. The project also involved supporting the development of a new government institution for HE (National Institute for Higher Education Development) that is to take on the future training of senior university staff in light of the reforms.

Chapter 5 on teacher education draws on three BC funded projects; a review of leadership needs for head teachers across Yangon in 2013–4; the baseline research for the Connecting Classrooms pilot project involving 15 schools across Yangon, Mandalay Region and Mon State; and a project surveying 2,000 teacher trainees over two consecutive years (2014–6) regarding the attributes and motivations of those who become teachers. Data were collected in all Myanmar education colleges (20 at the time) around the country and two batches studying in two different year groups that were compared with each other.

The data for ethnic education were collected during fieldwork undertaken between 2011 and 2019, primarily in Karen, Mon, Kachin, Shan and Rakhine-populated areas. The first round of data collection (together with Ashley South) was in 2011–2, funded by the Open Society Institute, focusing in particular on mapping ethnic minority education systems in Mon and Karen States, where interviews and focus groups were conducted with 93 people across 8 locations, including in jungle and conflict-affected areas. Communities were accessed through local colleagues who have been instrumental in delivering education services in hard-to-reach places. Most meetings were held in schools, but in some cases respondents preferred to meet at sites where they felt less exposed to scrutiny. All interviews were conducted in the local language with a trained translator. Further data collection (funded by USAID as part of their transition support programme, together with Ashley South) happened between 2014 and 2016 across 10 locations in Mon, Karen and Kachin States, and neighbouring China and Thailand, in both government and EAO-controlled areas. This included interviews with 150 people and 30 focus groups conducted with 8–10 participants each, as well as larger meetings with stakeholders from EAOs, ethnic education departments, political parties and local civil society actors who were contacted through the EAO education departments and education Community Based Organisations (CBOs). In addition, teachers, parents and students at ethnic schools were either interviewed or took part in focus groups. All meetings were conducted either in the local language or in Burmese with the help of a trained translator. Subsequently, the findings were validated through a series of five workshops in Mon and Kachin States conducted around four to six months after the original fieldwork had taken place. The workshops included state education officials so as to better understand how the Myanmar Government was developing education policy in ethnic areas. A further set of data comes from 28 interviews we conducted as a part of a Pyoe Pin-funded research project in 2016, which investigated the funding and teacher training challenges faced by non-state education institutions. This last round of data collection focused on ethnic education providers in very hard-to-reach areas, including northern Shan State where conflict is ongoing. In that setting, it was too dangerous to meet parents, so only teachers and other official stakeholders were interviewed.[27]

What the book covers

Chapter 1 reviews the state of education prior to the 2010 elections, including the period under military rule, including issues pertaining to textbooks. The chapter then looks at the limited changes that took place between 2000 and 2012, including the rise of a parallel system of private education as an alternative for the urban middle classes, which began to divide society into those who could afford to buy services and those dependent on what the state provided. Drawing on original interview and Focus Group Discussion (FGD) data in 19 Yangon schools in 2012 just prior to the start of the education reform process, it reflects the voices of teachers who were asked what they felt were the priorities for education reform, revealing the tension between the weighty curriculum and the examination system with improving teaching methods in the classroom – particularly Child-Centred Approaches (CCA) to teaching and learning. The chapter then engages with the challenges faced by the teachers in the public education sector in terms of teacher salaries that are too low for daily living (and the related problem of tuition that is used by teachers to compensate for the difference); teacher-to-student ratios that are overly large (especially in primary schools, and even more so in rural and remote regions); the lack of classroom materials and teaching aids; and societal pressure for teachers not to marry so they can dedicate their life to society. These pressures have made teaching an increasingly unattractive profession. The chapter sets the scene for the social justice issues that the education reforms have promised to address, in order to understand how far the post-2012 changes have actually made a difference in the Myanmar government school classrooms.

Chapter 2 details the effects of the reforms in basic education by introducing the education reforms that started in the second half of 2012 under the Thein Sein Government, including the CESR, and the role played by the aid agencies. The chapter engages with the tensions between the various stakeholders including the MoE (which remained quite detached between 2012 and 2015), the CESR, the Parliamentary Committee lead by Daw Aung San Suu Kyi and the National Network for Education Reform (NNER), a civil society-led consortium campaigning for more radical education reforms. It explains why President Thein Sein brought in EPIC to side-line the influence of the international development agencies, and how all of this resulted in the National Education Sector Plan (NESP)[28] and the New Education Law.[29] The chapter also looks at the student protests of 2015, their demands based on social justice, and their engagement with the government leading to limited changes in the New Education Law.

The second part of the chapter engages with the NLD Government's development of the education reform process, including the continuity of policy by largely accepting the NESP unchanged. Priorities for education remain access, quality, curricular reforms and teacher training reforms, thus addressing a few issues faced by Myanmar's poor, yet not engaging with the issues associated with ethnic and linguistic diversity that have resulted in a largely inequitable education system. As of this point, all chapters will contrast education policy and the education experience on the ground. The chapter draws on original data collected during training sessions and meetings with the MoE between 2012 and 2019.

Chapter 3 considers monastic education. Myanmar's education system has historically been closely linked with Buddhism, and Myanmar traditional values reflect Buddhist values of service to the community. Society supports monks and monasteries through donations as part of their religious duty, and monasteries have been the main vehicle for inclusion in education by offering schooling to poor and disadvantaged children. This chapter engages with the role of monasteries in bringing about change in the classroom, even before the government reforms began. Whilst monastic schools have always catered to the poorest and the most disadvantaged of society, their relative independence and status outside of the purview of the MoE allowed them to pioneer the CCA in their classrooms. Phaung Daw Oo, the largest monastic school in the country, based in Mandalay, is led by Sayadaw U Nayaka who can be credited with bringing large-scale change to teaching methods across all monastic schools by founding a centre for monastic teacher training that was supported by local donors as well as international aid money. Drawing on original interviews and FGD data of monastic teachers collected in 2010 and 2016, the chapter looks at how CCA spread across monastic networks and the role of both local and international teacher training agents across the country. In the end, it was monastic schools that led the way in reforms that affected teaching methods beyond monastic schools, especially CCA in the classroom, with the state sector following suit a few years later. The chapter discusses how children from the most disadvantaged backgrounds were ultimately subject to better teaching practice than those at government schools because of the work pioneered in Phaung Daw Oo. The chapter draws on original FGD data with parents whose children attended these schools, and their views on the role of monasteries in educating Myanmar society. Lastly, the chapter describes the role of monasteries in maintaining ethnic nationality languages and culture, especially in Mon, Karen, Shan and Pa-O societies through summer school language and literature programmes; a theme that will be considered again in Chapter 6 on ethnic languages.

Chapter 4 reviews the state of HE. The quality of HE has deteriorated sharply in Myanmar since independence, prior to which Rangoon University was seen as a leading higher education institution (HEI) in the region. The chapter gives a snapshot of Yangon and Mandalay Universities in 2005 and 2006, when the author was teaching there during the summer months, before moving on to the main HE reform agenda, including the development of the National Institute of Higher Education Development (NIHID)[30] that is due to start training senior academic staff across the HE sector. The chapter engages with the vexed issue of decentralisation including the rotation of staff appointments, the changing role of research and how universities are starting to engage with issues of access and quality, and designing their own curriculum. The chapter contrasts the views of leading academics[31] on the purpose of HE and its reforms, contrasting neo-liberal views that have emerged through the engagement with Western aid and development agencies with more traditional Myanmar views based on Buddhist values.

At the time of writing, access to HE, although almost free and despite the presence of over 150 institutions across Myanmar, is only accessible to a small number of mostly middle class students, with the poorer students enrolling in one of the world's largest (and possibly the worst) distance HE system. The chapter discusses the issues of limited access of ethnic minority young people due to severe language disadvantage[32] that emanates from their lack of access to basic education, and how this is something with which most Myanmar universities, including those based in ethnic states, do not have the capacity to engage.

Chapter 5 reviews the issues faced by student teachers and teacher educators across the 20 education colleges in Myanmar, drawing on original survey data collected in the midst of the reform process. It engages with the views, hopes, challenges and fears faced by those who want to become teachers. It explains the special challenges faced by the very few ethnic nationality teacher trainees who manage to get into the education colleges. The chapter also looks at the reforms of teacher education that started with the BC funded 'English for Education College Trainers' (EfECT) project that focused on upgrading teacher educators' English and teaching methodology. At the time of writing, the curriculum for teacher education is being reformed, yet this is not in sync with the curricular reforms of basic education, as these are supported by different aid agencies with little, if any, communication or coordination.

The chapter discusses the tensions that arise from these uncoordinated efforts to improve education across Myanmar.

Chapter 6 discusses Myanmar's struggle with ethnic and linguistic diversity. Despite the reforms, education has remained highly centralised, with only Burmese being allowed as a means of instruction. Policy under the NLD Government has not changed much. While ethnic minority languages are now allowed as 'classroom language' to help explain concepts when necessary, mother tongue-based multi-lingual education (MTB-MLE) is *not* presently Myanmar education policy, marginalising ethnic hopes and concerns.[35] The only concession from the government has been the introduction of a 'local curriculum' (LC) of one period a day in Kindergarten (KG), Grade 1 and Grade 2 that is locally developed and can be taught in an ethnic language. The development of this LC and its roll-out is haphazard and uneven, privileging larger, more organised ethnic groups. This chapter engages with the often overlooked voices of minorities within minorities regarding their views on language, education and Language of Instruction (LoI), and how this shapes their relationship with both the more dominant ethnic groups as well as the ruling Burman majority. It argues that whilst all minorities within minorities consulted as part of fieldwork research in 2018, work hard to preserve their ethnic language and culture, they all argue that they want Burmese to remain the main LoI. Many emphasised that Burmese was the essential language for their children to be able to get good jobs and bring their families and communities out of poverty. The communities therefore do not support an MTB-MLE system and prefer multilingual local teachers who can explain the Burmese textbooks to their children.

The chapter also engages with a potential solution to the need for more ethnic nationality teachers in government schools. It looks at the alternative teacher education college established by the Pa-O to specifically train those ethnic nationality candidates that failed to get into the education colleges. The lack of ethnic teachers is a serious issue for ethnic nationality children who cannot understand Burmese, so the training of such teachers by an ethnic organisation is an interesting alternative solution to the problem. Based on original data collected at this college in Shan State, the chapter explains how despite its recognition by the government authorities, this college is not able to fulfil its mission as its teachers are sent to work in ethnic areas where they do not speak the local language, defeating the original purpose of its creation.

Chapter 7 discusses the structural challenges in alternative systems run by EAOs and uses the education systems under the authority of four major EAOs to discuss the relationship between ethnic nationality communities and the state. Drawing on data collected (between 2011 and 2018) in schools under the New Mon State Party's (NMSP)[34] Mon National Education Committee, the Kachin Independence Organisation's (KIO) Education Department,[35] the Karen National Union's (KNU) Education Department, and the Revolutionary Council of Shan State's (RCSS)[36] Education Department as well as their administrations, the chapter discusses the issue of recognition of alternative and separate education systems that have in effect been filling the gap for education provision in remote and conflict-affected areas for the Myanmar Government. Whilst addressing the language issue (also discussed in Chapter 6) is a key part to finding a sustainable resolution to armed conflict, the chapter engages with the key problems of recognition of EAO authority in education in areas under their control, and how the issues of the peace process, language policy and federalism are inextricably intertwined with each other.

The book is essentially about the Myanmar education reform process and how this is affecting key stakeholders and the wider population. Therefore, the *conclusion* returns first to the NESP Mid Term Review and its assessment on what has been achieved with regard to equity. It is clear that the MoE and the wider government understand that there are wider issues of social justice at play that are not being resolved through the education and wider reform processes. In light of the 2020 elections and the path Myanmar has chosen through the lenses of education and ethnicity, the conclusion asks – 'What future for Myanmar's youth?'

Areas that are not covered by the book include disability and inclusive education, vocational education and education for out-of-school children, and recent developments in private education. Disabled people are largely invisible in Myanmar society, and disabled students are not often seen in schools. While this is a key issue of social justice and equality, the invisibility of the less able means that there was not enough available data, and writing anything substantial on this problem would be virtually impossible. Vocational education and the education of out-of-school children, although now part of the education reform process through its inclusion in the NESP, was until recently quite separate from the formal education sector. This again has meant a lack of substantial data, making its inclusion in the book impossible.[37] The focus being on the effects of the government reforms, the book also does not cover Chinese schools (some of which exist in Shan State close to the border, for example, in the Wa Autonomous Region) as well as in cities such as Yangon and Mandalay, nor other religious schools and HEIs – such as those run by the Baptist or Adventist churches, nor any religious education institutions catering to the Muslim population, that remain largely unaffected by the government reforms. Lastly, a separate book could be written on the rise of the private parallel system that has increased so dramatically over the past decade. The early development of this sector is covered in Chapter 1. However, the book's focus means that the more recent rise of the private education sector, still a largely urban phenomenon serving the middle classes and the rich, is less relevant. Given that much of the private education sector is not recognised by the government, it is also not included in the reform processes and remains a separate, parallel, largely business orientated development.

Notes

1 Although she is no longer on the website, Daw Aung San Suu Kyi was a honorary President of Socialist International, a worldwide organisation of social democratic, socialist and labour parties. The NLD's first election manifesto of 1989 focuses on democracy, but has strong sections on farmer, student and labour unions as well. The NLD might have reinvented itself, but its roots lie on the left side of the political spectrum.
2 The Norwegian Government's commissioned Political Economy Analysis states: 'Myanmar is a new place for many donors that have entered the country since 2011. Many of them have little experience and poor understanding of how to address the opportunities and challenges that have emerged from Myanmar's democratic opening. Insufficient country knowledge on the part of development actors is a risk that can potentially do harm.' (Stokke et al., 2018: XX).
3 It has to be said that the NLD is not supportive of CSOs and local Non-Government Organisations (NGOs) receiving aid funds to undertake development work, and prefer international funds to be received by the government so that the programmes can be controlled. This is in stark contrast to the government under President Thein Sein (2010–5) who allowed CSOs and local NGOs to receive donor funds and to run programmes as they saw fit (Lall, 2016a).
4 Over the 15 years that the author has been speaking with ordinary Myanmar people across the whole country – most of whom she met (parents and teachers) through her education research, as well as many young people through her work on citizenship and many ethnic respondents/members of armed groups through her work on conflict and the peace process.
5 The 25 per cent military seats in parliament are there to stop the constitution from being changed. They make sure the Tatmadaw leadership has a free hand in dealing with ethnic conflict and border affairs the way it sees fit. To date, they have not stopped any policy that focused on issues of health, education and access to public services.
6 The 2015 NLD Manifesto was also very much in tune both with the anti-colonial cries for economic justice espoused in the pre-independence period that were taken up by the post-independence governments, as well as Daw Aung San Suu Kyi's accusations that the State Peace and Development Council (SPDC) government had made economic inequalities worse during their rule, due to their socio-economic mismanagement.
7 This chapter will not try to engage with the semantics of the terminology in Burmese and how the terms were used, as this will detract from the core aim of the book, which is to engage with the education reforms. The issue at heart is that the NLD as a political party promised a Myanmar version of social justice and the wider electorate understood this promise.
8 It has been argued that the 2015 elections cannot be considered fair and free as 25 per cent of seats in all legislative assemblies were reserved for the military. See Tonkin for more on the 1990 election (Tonkin, 2007).

9   He was replaced by President Win Myint on the 30 March 2018, after President Htein Kyaw resigned 'to take a rest'. https://frontiermyanmar.net/en/president-u-htin-kyaw-resigns-u-win-myint-tipped-as-replacement.
10 Despite their constitutional mandate neither of the two presidents seem to have had much say in any of the government's policy making, and Daw Aung San Suu Kyi has kept control of the government. The post of 'State Councillor' was specially created for her – it does not exist in the Constitution. The creation of this post shows the power of the NLD, whose majority in Parliament meant that they were able to override the 25 per cent military vote who were opposed to the creation of such an official position.
11 It is estimated that non-Burman communities make up around 30–40 per cent of the population including Shan 9 per cent, Karen 7 per cent, Rakhine 4 per cent, Chinese 3 per cent, Indian 2 per cent, Mon 2 per cent, and other 5 per cent. https://www.cia.gov/library/publications/the-world-factbook/geos/bm.html.
12 With the exception of the Shan Nationalities League for Democracy (SNLD) and the Arakan National Party (ANP).
13 Informal discussions with ethnic nationality NLD MPs in NPT in 2017, 2018 and 2019.
14 The most famous cases being the two Reuters journalists, Wa Lone and Kyaw Soe Oo, who were detained in Myanmar on 12 December 2017 for reporting on the killings of Rohingya men. They were freed as part of an amnesty in May 2019.
15 Economic growth – but not inclusive and sustainable development. Myanmar has seen an economic liberalisation and opening that has been followed by increased investment in key sectors, above all in natural resource extraction. The lack of redistributive mechanisms and the continuing cronyism hinder inclusive growth and sustainable development. (Stokke et al., 2018: xviii).
16 An example of this is the peace process versus reforming the constitution. The NLD decided to give constitutional change another push despite the peace process being stuck. It proved to be a fruitless battle with the military MPs, not unlike what occurred at the end of 2015.
17 The social democratic framework as the foundation for governance was also the basis for India's development, as well as a number of other post-colonial developing countries.
18 Quite a lot has been written about how teachers have been affected by neo-liberal education reforms. However, the Mike Apple reference of 2004 shows that this is nothing new.
19 There are of course other models and theoretical frameworks for social justice, but this one focuses on structures rather than individuals, encapsulating much of the social justice issues in Myanmar. In the last two chapters that focus on ethnic education issues, another social justice model – Novelli et al.'s '4 R framework' of redistribution, recognition, representation and reconciliation (Novelli et al., 2015) – is used in addition to Young's 'Five Faces of Oppression' model (1990 and 2005), since Novelli et al.'s model links in with peace and reconciliation issues, that are particularly relevant in light of Myanmar's peace process.
20 Young's 'Five Faces of Oppression' is a model cited in much recent literature pertaining to oppression, and first appeared in Iris Young, 1990, 'Justice and the politics of difference': **Exploitation** (the transfer of the fruits of labour from one group to another, as, for example, in the cases of workers giving up surplus value to capitalists or women in the domestic sphere transferring the fruits of their labour to men); **Marginalisation** (the expulsion of people from useful participation in social life so that they are 'potentially subjected to severe material deprivation and even extermination'); **Powerlessness** (the lack of that 'authority, status and sense of self' which would permit a person to be listened to with respect); **Cultural imperialism** (stereotyping in behaviours as well as in various forms of cultural expression such that the oppressed group's own experience and interpretation of social life finds little expression that touches the dominant culture, while that same culture imposes on the oppressed group its experience and interpretation of social life). **Violence** (the fear and actuality of random, unprovoked attacks which have 'no motive except to damage, humiliate or destroy the person').
21 As the MoE's NESP 2016–2021 notes in its Executive Summary (7): 'Quality, equitable and relevant education is essential if we are to provide our children with new knowledge and competencies, creativity and critical thinking skills and cultural and ethical values that will enable them to excel in their chosen careers and contribute to Myanmar's socio-economic development in the 21st century.'
22 In Myanmar, ethnic minorities prefer to be referred to as 'ethnic nationality communities' or simply 'ethnic'. They reject being labelled as minorities.

23 More on the student protests in Chapter 4.
24 More on Dr Nay Win Maung, his life and work in Lall (2016a).
25 As detailed in Lall (2016a), the military regime had announced elections as part of their 'roadmap to democracy' in 2004. However, no one knew when these elections would be held and it was clear that the process would be tightly controlled.
26 There was not enough funding for the research team to collect data outside of Yangon.
27 In 2018, the author was the Lead Consultant at Covenant Consult for the World Bank and the Myanmar Education Consortium (MEC) working across all ethnic states and leading a team of 12 international and Myanmar specialist consultants. Data from this project (Informing Partnerships between Government and Ethnic Basic Education Providers – MEPP) has not been directly used in this book, however, the views from respondents in that project are reflected in Chapters 6 and 7. In 2019 and 2020, the author was an advisor to the Department for International Development (DFID) funded Myanmar–UK Partnership for Education (MUPE) project that involved data collection across the various departments of Myanmar's MoE. Data from this project has not been directly used for this book, however, the views from policy makers and development partners in that project are reflected across the volume.
28 Renamed 'National Education Strategic Plan' (thus still 'NESP') by the NLD government after 2016.
29 The author was special education advisor to AUSAID in Myanmar at the time, therefore accessing both the MoE and CESR staff as well as the international agencies.
30 Author was part of a small team training the NIHED senior trainers, and supporting NIHED in its first HE training of 11 universities.
31 Who took part in a training programme co-led by the author.
32 This is a double disadvantage as HE is supposed to be in English, and the books are in English, even if the actual teaching is in Burmese. Many ethnic nationality students are unable to matriculate because of their poor levels of Burmese, making it impossible for them to access HE. Those who do make it then find that course materials in English present a double challenge.
33 Using any ethnic language in the classroom effectively would require recruiting local teachers, or teachers who have learnt an ethnic language. According to UNICEF, 70 per cent of teachers working in ethnic areas do not speak local languages (Joliffe and Speers, 2016: 37).
34 Maintained a ceasefire with the government since 1995.
35 Which saw its 17-year ceasefire collapse in 2011.
36 Both EAOs agreed to sign the 2015 'Nationwide Ceasefire Agreement' (NCA), following decades of armed conflict.
37 There is a substantial MoE report on education of out-of-school children, but internal MoE politics in 2018–9 means that there is now not so much focus on the issue, as (allegedly) the MoE does not wish to acknowledge the fact that this problem exists. (From personal interviews with a number of development partners in the summer of 2019.)

1
The state of education, pre-reform

Introduction

This chapter reviews the state of education in the decades preceding the 2010 elections, during which the country was primarily under military rule. It starts with a brief history of education in Myanmar and discusses it in the context of the post-independence military governments' attempts to instil nationalism under the banner of a Bamar identity. The chapter considers the limited changes that took place between 2000 and 2012, including the rise of a parallel system of private education that provided an alternative for the urban middle classes, thus dividing society into those who could afford private offerings, and those dependent on what the state provided. The information here draws from interview and focus group data obtained from 19 Yangon schools in 2012, just prior to the start of the education reform process. It reflects the voices of teachers who were asked what they believed should be the priorities for education reform, and reveals the tension between the weighty curriculum and examination system in relation to the aim of improving teaching methods in the classroom – particularly the use of CCA to teaching and learning. The chapter then identifies some key challenges faced by teachers in the public education sector: very low teacher salaries; the related problem of tuition as a means for teachers to enhance their incomes; overly large teacher-to-student ratios, especially in primary schools, and even more so in rural and remote regions; the lack of classroom materials and teaching aids; and societal pressure on teachers not to marry so they can dedicate their life to their work. These challenges have made teaching an increasingly un-attractive profession. Thus, this chapter sets the scene for the social justice issues that the education reforms have promised to address, in order to understand how far the post-2012 changes have actually made a difference in the Myanmar government school classrooms.

History of education

The best known history of Myanmar's traditional education before and during the colonial era is that of U Kaung's detailed dissertation submitted to the University of London in 1920, and later published in the *Journal of Burma Research* (U Kaung, 1963). In it he describes how traditional Myanmar education functioned under the ancient monarchies, with mainly monastic settings serving boys, and a parallel system of lay schools developed to educate girls.[1] U Kaung identifies the influence of European missionaries who came to Myanmar over the centuries, and whose fortunes rose and waned, depending on which dynasty was in power and where in the country they were based. Missionaries shaped education in a lasting way in certain ethnic areas, more so than in the Bamar heartlands where monastic education held sway.

'Modern' education in Myanmar began with the British colonising Burma from 1824. In 1885, after the third Anglo–Burmese war when Burma was made part of British India, the state became responsible for education and a larger number of students, both girls and boys, were able to access some form of government education. Monastic education, perceived as traditional and backward by the colonisers, declined. According to Thein Lwin, the three types of school in pre-World War II Burma were as follows (Thein Lwin, 2000: 4–5):

- Vernacular schools, administered by local education authorities in which the medium of instruction was Burmese or one of the recognised local languages. These were the schools serving the majority of the country's children.
- Anglo–vernacular schools in which English was taught as a second language and instruction was in both English and Burmese.
- English schools, in which the medium of instruction was English, with Burmese as the second language. These schools served the elites and were geared for students who aspired to government employment.

Because English was the language of the colonial powers, vernacular schools were seen as second class. A domestic reaction to the dominance of the colonial language took shape with the creation of national schools in the 1920s, where the language of instruction was Burmese and Buddhist holidays were observed as opposed to the British ones. These schools did not survive beyond the 1930s, however, nationalism in the form of anti-colonialism continued to grow across educational institutions. In the early twentieth century, colleges and universities became centres of social and political activism, playing their part in the anti-colonial movement. By the 1920s, university students had begun to strike against the University Act Bill that established English as the medium of instruction and which set fees for instruction that placed universities out of reach of most Burmese (Zobrist and McCormick, 2017).

While the Japanese occupation was short lived (1942–5), the end of the colonial control of Burma resulted for the first time in a single schooling system with a unified curriculum and Burmese as the medium of instruction, making it accessible to all Burmese. It did not, however, result in a revival of the monastic education system. According to Salem-Gervais and Metro, 'In spite of some government documents deeming religion essential to a "sound educational tradition", and some policies leaning towards an increased role for the Sangha in schooling, a specific policy of religious teaching in schools was conspicuous by its absence.' (Salem-Gervais and Metro, 2012: 61). Thein Lwin reports that in 1947, the Education Reconstruction Committee, chaired by the Honourable Sir Htoon Aung Gyaw, reviewed Burma's education system and proposed the concept of a homogenous system of schools provided and controlled by the state (Thein Lwin, 2000). On 1 June 1950, a new policy came into force promising free education for all pupils in state schools from primary to university level. Private schools were allowed in their own school buildings under the registration of the 1951 Private Schools Act. Shortly thereafter in 1952, a modern school curriculum was introduced nationwide, followed by textbooks in Burmese in all subjects. The curriculum for the state schools introduced vocational subjects according to local needs rather than a unified qualification system, resulting in an academic–vocational divide, an urban–rural divide, and inequality of opportunity between girls and boys (Thein Lwin, 2000: 9). In 1958, the Ministry of Education (MoE) announced that the medium of instruction was to be Burmese in schools and English was to be taught only from the Fifth Standard onwards (Union of Myanmar, 1992 cited in Thein Lwin, 2000). No consideration was given to the use of ethnic languages for pupils whose mother tongue was not Burmese. However, there were still private, Christian and Buddhist monastic schools functioning legally around the country, and private and Christian schools taught English from the beginning of primary education. In ethnic majority areas, community schools used ethnic languages. At university, Burmese also became the medium of instruction for all undergraduate subjects, with

English becoming the medium of instruction in postgraduate Honours and Masters classes (Thein Lwin, 2000: 8–9).

After the April 1962 coup led by General Ne Win, the Revolutionary Council proclaimed 'The Burmese Way to Socialism' as its political programme. The new government's view of education was inspired by its socialist aims. 'The Revolutionary Council believes the existing educational system un-equated with livelihood will have to be transformed. An educational system equated with livelihood and based on socialist moral values will be brought about; science will be given precedence in education' (Thein Lwin, 2000: 9). The syllabus put more emphasis on vocational education to support the socialist cause. Universities also changed, with the new 1964 University Act decreasing the size of Rangoon and Mandalay Universities by splitting off specialist subject areas such as technology and medicine. Since the arts and humanities were seen as lower ranking courses, children with high matriculation results tended to study medicine regardless of whether they wanted to become doctors or not. In 1965, all schools were nationalised, including mission schools and schools operated for the Chinese and Indian communities (Zobrist and McCormick, 2017). In 1974, the military rule changed to a constitutional dictatorship (Silverstein, 1977) with Article 152 of the new 1974 Constitution stating that, 'every citizen shall have the right to education' and that 'basic education' would be compulsory, while Article 10 stated, 'the State shall cultivate and promote the all-round physical, intellectual and moral development of youth'. However, very little changed across educational institutions. In 1988, as a result of nationwide protests in which students took a leading role, the 1974 Constitution was abolished and replaced by absolute military rule under the State Law and Order Restoration Council (SLORC). General Saw Maung, the Head of State at the time, said that education was not the military regime's responsibility, but would be that of the next elected government. Elections were held in 1990, but the military refused to recognise the NLD win, ultimately entrenching military rule for another two decades.[2] The quality of education across schools and universities continued its slow and steady decline. Control by SLORC – renamed the State Peace and Development Council (SPDC) in 1997 – came to an end through the development of a new constitution in 2008, and subsequent 2010 elections that brought a partly civilian government into power in 2011. The new constitution that was enacted in 2008 made some changes to education. These are discussed in the next chapter.

Education and nationalism: Cementing military rule

The roots of 20th century Burmese nationalism lay in growing Burmese perceptions that they were second-class citizens in their own country, in British 'divide and rule' policies and the loss of traditional authority structures and in the exploitation by the British and other foreigners of Burma's rich natural resources. (Herbert, 1991 cited in Thein Lwin, 2000: 1).

Education had been one means of developing and cementing nationalism from as far back as the colonial period, where the national schools and HEIs promoted anti-colonial patriotism. National schools had worked towards a return to pre-colonial education – as led historically by monasteries – coupled with new demands for civil liberties, prioritising Burmese language, literature and history. The National Education Committee that led this movement aimed for both progress and renewal: 'Patriotism is the new religion of the new generation, and it is best propagated through National Schools' (Cheesman, 2002: 53). According to Cheesman, students at national schools recited the Five Buddhist Precepts in place of 'The Prayer for the King–Emperor', were permitted to wear Burmese traditional clothes, and were free to read any publications (Cheesman, 2002). The national schools also reintroduced six letters of the Burmese alphabet that had been dropped from government schools. Unfortunately, problems with funding and factionalism led to their decline and eventual demise in the late 1930s.

From independence in 1948 onwards, the school curriculum was standardised and centrally determined by the government without regional or other special allowances. However, as seen earlier, private and ethnic alternatives were tolerated until the 1960s, just not as part of the state education narrative. After the 1962 coup, these alternatives were closed down and outlawed. Nationalism in Myanmar's education system, no longer serving an anti-colonial purpose, had two main functions: to cement the Burman culture and language as central to the nation's unity – a process referred to as 'Burmanisation'– and to help justify military rule.

Education and Burmanisation: Post-1962 focus

Burmanisation is the hallmark of post-1962 education. This was based on a belief that the country needed a unifying national identity based on one culture, one language and one religion. Since independence, there had been conflict with separatist ethnic movements on the Thai and Chinese borders, with the Karen National Union (KNU) in particular calling for an independent Karen homeland. Further north, located in ethnic areas, the Burmese Communist Party (BCP) was fighting the Burmese central government.⁵ These conflicts provided the reasons both for the 1962 military coup ('to prevent the disintegration of the nation') as well as for the process of enforcing Burmanisation on all non-Bamar ethnic groups across the country.

It is important to note that Bamar-centred nationalism did not suddenly appear after 1962. Nationalism had been historically linked with the majority Bamar, both under the Bamar kings in pre-colonial and later during the anti-colonial pre-independence periods. Thant Myint-U and Michael Charney have described the formation of a 'myanma' identity centred around Buddhism, Burmese language and Burman ethnicity during the Konbaung Dynasty (1752–1885) (Thant Myint-U, 2001; Charney, 2006). Thant Myint-U argues that the concept of *myanma lu-myò* was consolidated around Burmese language, Buddhism and the political and legal institutions based in the Konbaung dynasty court at Ava during the late eighteenth century (Thant Myint-U, 2001: 88). This identity was spread by itinerant monks in what was later described as a process of 'Burmanisation', in which non-myanma people were given incentives or pressured to adopt myanma customs (Houtman, 1999). Because *lu-myò* was more flexible than twentieth-century conceptions of ethnicity, people could 'become' myanma by changing their political allegiance or behaviour – the category myanma was capable of retaining its purity while incorporating other groups (Charney, 2006: 41). As Thant Myint-U argues, 'the strength and political dominance of a Burmese/Myanma identity based on older Ava-based memories has never allowed the development of a newer identity which would incorporate the diverse peoples inhabiting the modern state' (Thant Myint-U, 2001: 254). The 1930s nationalist *Dòbáma* ('We-báma') organisation took as its slogan a series of phrases that can be translated as '*Báma* country, our country; *báma* literature, our literature; *báma* language, our language' (Khin Yi, 1988: 5). Although this 'Burmanisation', as it was called, was primarily an attempt to combat the dominance of 'foreign' English and Hindi languages (Khin Yi, 1988: 6), it also served to exclude non-Burmese speaking ethnic groups from nationalists' conception of *báma*/myanma (Metro, 2011: 47).

As shall be seen in later chapters, the conflict between ethnic armed groups and the Burmese military ('Tatmadaw') arose largely because of unequal rights as well as the forced assimilation process of 'Burmanisation', best exemplified by the requirement that only the Bamar language was allowed as the language of instruction in schools and for official transactions. This excluded the culture and languages of over 100 ethnic groups that comprise modern Burma. In essence, though this was nothing new – the history of the Mon, Shan and Arakanese kingdoms were not part of the monastic curricula that dominated education for hundreds of years (Salem-Gervais and Metro, 2012), nor do they appear in post-independence textbooks. As noted above, the tension between Bamar and other ethnic groups is undoubtedly ancient, and was deepened during the period immediately pre-independence when the Karen, Kachin and some other ethnic groups fought with the British against the Japanese–Burman alliance. In the post-independence era, the majority Bamar again instituted measures to control other ethnic groups. In fact, the primacy of one ethnicity (Bamar) over the others became a tactic the Tatmadaw used to attempt to legitimise itself through primary school textbooks. Cheesman found that according to the textbooks' normative model, the ideal citizen had distinct ethnic (Bamar), religious (Buddhist) and gender (male) characteristics, and worked to benefit the state (Cheesman, 2002: iii). 'Part of the aim of the textbooks was to instil an understanding of "the Union" that conflates the state, nation, territory and people' (Cheesman, 2002: 1). After 1962, schools had to serve as an aid for the realisation of the revolutionary government's socialist goal. This is when schools were nationalised, Burmese was made the official language of instruction, Buddhism the national religion and minority languages were removed from state schools.[4] The aim seems to have been to force a unitary Bamar-dominated national identity across all ethnicities. The first Basic Education Law (1966), enacted under General Ne Win, tightened the supervision of schools, including monastic schools (Cheesman, 2002: 64).

Promoting the martial kings and forgetting Aung San: Post-1988 focus

Under the SLORC/SPDC regime, the core aims of basic education remained unchanged from the preceding socialist period. Students were still expected to become citizens who served the state, with the aims being as follows (UNESCO–IBE, 2006/7):

- to enable every citizen of the Union of Myanmar to become a physical and mental worker well equipped with basic education, good health and moral character

- to lay foundations for vocational education for the benefit of the Union of Myanmar
- to give precedence to the teaching of science capable of strengthening and developing productive forces
- to give precedence to the teaching of arts capable of preservation and development of culture, fine arts and literature of the state
- to lay a firm and sound educational foundation for the further pursuance of university education.

Buddhism, interestingly, was not included in the syllabus, rather it was part of co-curricular activities and teachers were encouraged by the state to develop their students' spiritual character outside of school hours (Cheesman, 2002: 75). Cheesman recounts how Secretary One of the SPDC (Lieutenant-General Khin Nyunt) personally travelled throughout the country in order to give instructions on how education should support the state and promote nationalism (Cheesman, 2002: 72–3). Addressing students of monastic schools, Khin Nyunt urged the trainee teachers to study:

> … with the aim of being able to organize and lead the youths in safeguarding the nation against the danger of some foreign super powers who are disrupting national consolidation, peace and stability of the State and development, and to study with the aim of keeping national unity ever alive and flourishing of the Union Spirit, which are the true strengths to prevent the infiltration in political, economic and cultural sectors with the use of e-technologies and to counterattack the fabrications of the neo-colonialists and their follower expatriates group. (*New Light of Myanmar*, 2001: 16)

Cheesman notes how such speeches exemplify the contradictions of the regime's simultaneous focus on the 'modern nation' and 'traditional values' (Cheesman, 2002: 90–1). Part of a wider endeavour of promoting nationalism and restoring the glory of the dynastic era, the SPDC changed the official name of the country from Burma to Myanmar in 1989 (Houtman, 1999: 48). Nationalism post-1988 changed focus in that the 'Myanmar identity' was now meant to include the other ethnic groups so that Myanmar means the Bamar plus other ethnic groups (although not ethnic Chinese or Indian). Houtman describes this process as 'myanmafication', the creation of a unitary myanma identity, which parallels the processes of Burmanisation carried out in earlier eras (Houtman, 1999). Callahan points out that myanmafication entails both a simultaneous homogenisation and differentiation of ethnic identity: ethnic people are 'infantilised', mostly represented by traditional costumes and dance styles, with no mention of their cultures or history (Callahan, 2004).[5] When looking at this process in the textbooks, Cheesman finds that Bamar people appear 'natural', whereas those of non-Bamar groups 'are contrived and often comical' (Cheesman, 2002: 157).[6]

In line with Khin Nyunt's sample speech above, the SPDC used school textbooks to reinforce links between the military regime and Myanmar's past, creating the myth that the Bamar kings defeated ethnic minorities and ruled supreme. Metro shows that what she calls a 'trinity of activities – national unification, economic development, and religious patronage' are carried out by the SPDC and by all kings who are 'hero-ised' in the textbooks (Metro, 2011: 56). The result of this was to relegate anti-colonial nationalists to the second rung of heroes, behind the Great Kings. The prioritisation of the Great Kings[7] meant that almost all of the history sections of history and geography textbooks were dedicated to Kings Anawratha, Kyansittha, Bayinnaung, Alaungpaya and Mindon. In textbooks, the actions of these Kings mirrored the actions of the SPDC, lending a spurious legitimacy to the military regime, a point developed by Metro (Metro, 2011). However, the kings and heroes of the other ethnic groups are only mentioned in relation to the Burman kings, so that the Mon, whose history is more closely related to the Burmans than other ethnic groups, received more textbook space than other ethnic historical figures.

In promoting the military as part of Myanmar's history, the SPDC reduced the focus on the period of independence, in which General Aung San, seen by many as the founder of the Union, played a leading role.[8] According to Salem-Gervais and Metro, it is a popular misconception that the SPDC erased Aung San from the textbooks (Salem-Gervais and Metro, 2012). Rather, his role was reduced in light of the longer and wider history of historical kings, so that while in textbooks from the late 1970s he was often referred to as the 'Architect of Independence', and he appeared in numerous lessons, by the 1990s the process of downplaying Aung San's role had occurred. According to the *Democratic Voice of Burma* (Naw Say Phaw, 2008), some extracts of his speeches were removed in 2008.

Though the focus on the kings was paramount, the role of the kings nevertheless changed according to what the regime in power was aiming to achieve. In the first chapter of her PhD dissertation 'Myanma identity and the shifting value of the classical past: A case study of King Kyansittha in Burmese history textbooks, 1829–2010', Metro argues that

Burmese history textbook discourse from the dynastic era to the present illustrates the 'ethnification' of Burmese (*myanma*) identity[9] and shows that the SPDC was using the past to underpin its policies, which was not new, rather it continued a tradition that has been in use for two centuries (Metro, 2011). She argues, however, that the SPDC fails in constructing an all-inclusive Myanmar identity that includes other ethnic groups, rather the term Myanmar most often refers only to the Bamar majority, in effect erasing the other ethnic groups.

This argument is also underlined by Cheesman who explains that the Union of Myanmar – also called *Pyidaunzu Myanmar Naingandaw* – is essentially 'Bamar' (Cheesman, 2002: 226):

> From start to finish, the textbooks link national identity with the dominant ethnic group. State rhetoric speaks to 'Myanmar' identity in terms of 'national races'; in the textbooks this narrative is marginalised and subverted by a stream of text indicating the contrary. [...] Culture, tradition, history, civility and normalcy are all associated with being Bamar. But all of these things are also 'Myanmar'. The lines are blurred: overtly, 'Myanmar' is 'national races', covertly it is Bamar. No better illustration for this exists than the fact that the language in which the readers are written, Burmese – with all its concomitant cultural and historical baggage – is signified as 'Myanmar language, our language'.

Beyond promoting nationalism and the Union, the SPDC still had to ensure literacy and numeracy of the Myanmar citizens. As the quality of education declined, and unfavourable comparisons with Association of Southeast Asian Nations (ASEAN) started to emerge, the government began to develop a plan for the education sector.

Signing up to 'Education for All'

In 2001, the MoE set up a 30-year-long Basic Education Plan that was to be implemented in six five-year phases. In addition, it formulated a special 4-year Education Development Plan from 2000–1 to 2003–4 to develop the education sector, specifically to improve enrolment rates, review the curriculum, revise the assessment system, establish multi-media classrooms and upgrade teacher training institutions (Government of Myanmar, 2004). The 30-year Education Plan contained 10 programmes for basic education with the purpose of promoting greater access to, and quality of, basic education, and 36 programmes for the HE sector (Min Zaw Soe et al., 2017).

The Myanmar Government signed up to the objectives of the World Declaration on Education for All (EFA) and the Millennium Development Goals (MDGs), nevertheless education remained woefully underfunded, receiving only 0.5 per cent of the gross national product compared to an average of 2.7 per cent in other Southeast Asian Countries (Thein Lwin, 2000). In order to meet its EFA responsibilities, the government organised an EFA Forum in May 2002 and established the EFA National Plan for Action (NPA), adopting six national goals for EFA under the EFA NPA 2003–2015.[10] The NPA was linked to the 30-year Long-Term Education Plan, and developed activity plans for access to and quality of basic education, Early Childhood Centres for Education (ECCE), non-formal and continuing education, and Education Management Information Systems (EMIS). The government set the following goals that were to be achieved through the implementation of the NPA with various government and non-government organisations (NGOs) working together:[11]

- ensuring that significant progress is achieved so that basic education of good quality is compulsory and completely free for all school-age children by 2015
- improving all aspects of the quality of basic education: teachers, education personnel and curriculum
- achieving significant improvement in the levels of functional literacy and continuing education by 2015
- ensuring that the learning needs of young people and adults are met through non-formal education, life-skills training and preventive education
- expanding and improving comprehensive early childhood care and education and
- strengthening EMIS.

One of the flagship projects was 'Child-Friendly Schools', supported by the United Nations International Children's Emergency Fund (UNICEF). For the wider community in meeting literacy goals, the focus was on Community Learning Centres (CLCs), and other non-formal education examples such as inclusive education initiatives. At the seventh EFA coordinators meeting in Bangkok in Thailand in October 2005, Myanmar presented slides that showed programmes for disabled children, over-aged students and the building of CLCs, as well as the introduction of human rights to the Myanmar School Curriculum.[12] With regard to targeting disadvantaged groups through non-formal education, unpublished MoE documents detailed how the CLCs that focused on literacy acquisition as of 1994, expanded from 7 centres established with United Nations Educational, Scientific and Cultural Organisation (UNESCO) assistance to over 70 centres in 11 townships. The CLCs rolled out a 3R (reading, writing and arithmetic) programme in rural and disadvantaged urban areas to support adults and help meet EFA literacy targets. The CLCs also served as community information and resource centres, building capacity with short-term courses and skills-based training. In addition, there was a special 3R programme developed for the border areas and implemented by the Ministry of the Progress of Border Areas and National Races (MPBND), Department of Basic Education (DBE) and Department of Educational Planning and Training (DEPT), with technical assistance from Department of Myanmar Education Research (DMER) that increased from 7 townships in Kokant, Wa, Eastern Kyaingtong and Rakhine in 1996 to 68 townships by 2007.[13] Another measure was a special primary-level curriculum and syllabus for over-aged school children developed by DEPT in June 2003. The accelerated programme was intended to help children over 7 or 8 years old to complete primary education in two years.[14]

It is unclear if the signing-up to the EFA goals shaped part of the 30-year policy or if what was prioritised in the 30-year policy was identified before the EFA framework. However, the policy plan of 2004 describes the details of the 30-year plan and they seem to show that the Government of Myanmar was aware of some severe shortcomings of its education system, particularly of issues related to social justice and equality. Long before the formulation of the National Education Strategic Plan (NESP) in 2016, and eight years before the start of the reforms, the policy document engages with access to schools, mentioning in particular the border and conflict affected areas, gender disparity in schools, the lack of post-primary schools and the promotion of access to over-aged children. Information and Communication Technology (ICT) and assessment that does not rely on rote learning and teacher education (both pre- and in-service) are also mentioned as priority areas for reform. In addition, the document provides details on changes that are required in HE, such as improving access, quality and delivering modern ICT. For example, Section 7.2 summarises priorities under the heading of 'Developing Learner Maturity, Creativity, Analytical Skills and Ability to utilise Modern Technology'.[15] The section on HE even suggests that HEIs should cater to the needs of the local communities and help develop the regions in which they are located. Although not as detailed as the NESP, this policy document is a valuable precursor. It seems that the issue the

MoE faced was more with the implementation of change rather than with the realisation that change was needed.

Myanmar's progress was reviewed in 2010. In an unpublished advisory document to the MoE,[16] a Myanmar consultant and education expert for the government states:

> Net enrolment ratio in primary education in Myanmar was 65.7% in 1990. Though it rose sharply to 73.6% in 1995, it rose gradually to 77% in 2000. In 2005, 82.2% (about 1% per year) has been gained. In 2009, it was 84.1%. Hence, in order to accomplish the MDG target (95%) in 2015, it needs to increase, at least, by about 2% growth rate per year. In other words, more concerted efforts and investment are, indeed, required to achieve this target. (…) The proportion of pupils starting grade 1 who reach grade 5, in 1990, was 24.5%. In 1995, it was improved by about 12% to 37.1%. Likewise, it was progressed by about 12% to 48.5% in 2000. While the increase rate of this proportion (12%) was doubled to gain 73.4% in 2005, it was only 74.4% in 2009. In other words, it had only increased by 1% over the period from 2005 to 2009. Therefore, this indicator is too slow to reach its target and Myanmar must invest all possible effort to achieve its target 90% by 2015 (pp. 2–3). […] The dropout rate in primary education is still existing in all the Grades. […] The highest number of dropout rates is in Grade 1, indicating 17.52% in 2001–02, 18.44% in 2000–01, 20.13% in 1999–00 and 23.17% in 1998–99 academic year.

It is clear from the above that the MoE was made aware of the shortcomings of its programmes well before the 2012 Comprehensive Education Sector Review (CESR) and that they were aware of the challenges in catching up with other nations in the region.

Child-Centred Approaches, international donors and the failure of a new method

Part and parcel of the first round of education 'reforms' that followed the Myanmar government's commitment to work towards EFA outcomes, was the introduction of a new teaching and learning method called Child-Centred Approaches (CCA).[17] This was first introduced in cooperation with the Japan International Cooperation Agency (JICA) in 2004–5 to promote the development of children's creativity, analytical skills, critical thinking and problem-solving skills (JICA, 2013: 61). However, as shall be seen below, since the curriculum was developed before the CCA method was introduced, the two did not integrate well. Part of the problem was that the MoE published a syllabus rather than a comprehensive curriculum.

> The Monthly Curriculum (MC) developed by the Regional Education Office (REO) and authorized by DBE is the well-known school syllabus despite being called 'curriculum'. In addition to that, modifications relating to school curricula are made during an annual conference in April – the 'Seminar on National Education Promotion' – without updating the current curriculum documents. DBE merely notifies schools about decisions and modifications through Regional Education Offices (REO), District Education Offices (DEC) and Township Education Offices (TEO). (JICA, 2013: 61)

The problems of practicing CCA go beyond the mismatch between curriculum, syllabus, method and lack of communication noted by JICA. In a study in 2009–10 on teaching methods, most teachers who had received some form of CCA training had no difficulty explaining what they saw as the main elements of CCA or the benefits they experienced when using CCA. The teachers, however, struggled to apply this approach due to logistical problems such as high teacher-to-student ratios, lack of space, lack of teaching aids and lack of time. Teachers all agreed that CCA required a lot more work overall (Lall, 2010: 1–2).

A further issue with this change has been cultural; CCA has been perceived as a 'foreign' or 'Western' way to teach. Teachers were not always used to the self-reflection and collaborative procedures which underlie such teaching and were worried that they might be asked questions they would not be able to answer (Lall, 2010: 27). The issue of respect and how the students view teachers and parents or other elders remains central, as many see the main difficulty in balancing this new approach – seen as the 'modern' and 'Western' way – with traditional Myanmar culture. Parents were especially worried that children would become too disrespectful and reject the traditional hierarchies at home (Lall, 2010: 27).

Lall et al.'s study, conducted prior to the start of the reforms in 2012, focused on what teachers[18] themselves had to say about the current education system in Myanmar and what education reforms they felt were needed. Some quotes from the teachers who took part are listed below (Lall et al., 2013: 18–19):

- 'We don't have time. Let me say. For biology we need 18 periods for teaching, 4 periods for practicals, so it is altogether 22 periods. But in practice I have only 21 periods for this month. [...] We are in haste every month, we feel like changing it.'
- 'To finish the course in time set by the MoE, CCA is used less than Teacher Centred Approach (TCA).'
- 'But in our opinion we don't think the current syllabus is fit for CCA. Not only children but also teachers prefer CCA but in the meanwhile a limit of time, lots of lessons to teach, examinations and the number of children more than we can manage are things hindering CCA to be successful in current Myanmar schools. [...] With CCA we cannot assess each and every child thoroughly. We don't have time. Current exam system does not go well with CCA. If we are to use CCA, we are obliged to reduce the curriculum.'

One of the main reasons that CCA could not be applied was incompatibility with the exam system, also referred to as the 'Pass System', used from Grade 1 to Grade 8. The intention of this system has been to make sure that the whole class passes the final exams with a basic understanding of each and every lesson. However, there were some constraints to exercising this principle. In the primary and high schools, teachers had to finish the given curriculum within a limited timeframe, and exams had to be held on target dates. Because of this time limitation, teachers chose some lessons out of the overall curriculum and taught the students through rote learning so that they would finish teaching the lessons on time and the students could then sit the exams.

The exam system included monthly exams, with questions designed in a manner that students only needed to memorise what had been taught in the classroom and to write down the exact answer. After the exams, the students' pass rate was used as an indicator for both teacher and school evaluations. If students failed the exams, the teachers had to prepare reports to their respective Township Education Office/Officer (TEOs), and they had to teach the students again in the summer so that they could attempt the exam again and move on to the next grade. Most of the schools skipped this process and just allowed all students to pass in the first stage, otherwise the process consumed too much time and money – and some said they felt that students would not learn better anyway.

Other reasons for not applying CCA included insufficient teaching aids, inappropriate class sizes and large teacher-to-student ratios, small class spaces and out-dated curriculum in some subjects, especially science subjects. There were also issues with regard to inequities between teachers' qualifications and teachers' salaries. Since older teachers had not received regular in-service training after entering into service, their understanding of teaching methodology and child psychology was not up to date; they were nevertheless the 'senior' teachers who had to be listened to.

Another issue that teachers complained about was their salary, the salary scheme for public servants pre-2012 being unrealistic. The need to subsidise teaching salaries meant that tuition became a popular business for teachers, especially in urban areas, to meet the costs of living. Unfortunately, the need to make money outside the classroom reduces teaching capacity in schools as well as creating conditions conducive to corruption. Students come to rely on tuition and only students who can afford tuition get high marks and high grades in exams. A deputy director from a TEO interviewed in 2012 added:

> Most of the teachers do not want to change CCA. They think CCA is good, but there are some problems such as parents' economic and education status, student-teacher ratio imbalance, time, curriculum, exam system, and teachers' salaries. They think these factors make problems for CCA. In the current situation, they want to use TCA, not only CCA.

The fact that parents expect students to pass exams means that teachers also feel they have to teach to the test rather than for learning:

> We have to spoon-feed here in our country. They have to learn by heart. We don't have self-study, though children from international schools have self-study.
> [...] We have to teach for exams, not to teach them so that they really learn! (Lall et al, 2013: 20).

> It takes time, for CCA system is related with the intelligence of the children. There will be problems for this system because of our 'all pass' system. [...] We are weak in every sector in comparison with foreign countries. There should be music halls and sports halls for the children to cope with every aspect. The spacious classrooms and teaching aids should also be well installed. (Lall et al, 2013: 20)

In effect, teachers agreed that the whole system needed to be adapted to the teaching method. Just changing the method without changing the exam system and without addressing issues of time and space would not lead to a successful adaptation of CCA. As one head teacher explained: 'It is important to be provided with material resources together with system change. For example, to change into CCA we need enough teachers' (Lall et al., 2013: 20).

The main findings of the research showed deep incompatibility between CCA and the exam system. The pass system meant that teachers were under time pressure to get through the curriculum, and the lack of space and time reduced their ability to use the CCA method. Capacity constraints both infrastructural and curriculum-related were the second issue, with oversized classes leading to inattention and rote learning methods, and a profession in need of greater professional pride and modernisation. Teachers did, however, speak of the pressure from head teachers to change the teaching method to accord with Myanmar's education policy. The lack of parental involvement and the proliferation of tuition in the state sector resulted in profoundly inequitable outcomes for children, as children left school with different foundations depending on which school they attended. This then affected their ability to enter HE. In the end, those studying for the teaching profession were not the top achievers from the school system, in turn affecting teaching quality (Lall et al., 2013: 27).

The findings above, though based on research only across Yangon, are reflected in another, much larger UNICEF and University of York Institute for Effective Education Study (Hardman et al., 2012) that used a stratified sample of 800 schools from 20 townships covering a range of urban/rural, multi-grade/mono-grade settings and schools of different sizes. The schools had many of the traditional impediments noted in the earlier research (Hardman et al., 2012: 9).

> Many of the teachers observed were working in an environment of genuine constraints caused by lack of adequate investment in school buildings: schools lacked electricity, learning resources and other facilities. Nearly 80% of the schools observed were multi-grade without walls or partitions between classes. Classrooms were often overcrowded, hot and noisy, with insufficient desks and chairs available and buildings were in a poor state of repair, particularly in rural areas.

The study used a pre-/post-test, quasi-experimental design to investigate the impact of an in-service and teacher education (INSET) programme on classroom processes and learning outcomes. The findings were basically the same as noted in the Yangon study, in that teachers were unable to use the CCA method (Hardman et al., 2012: 9).

> The majority of lessons observed used a transmission model of teaching in which the teacher often used a chalk board and/or textbook to transmit recipe knowledge for recall. There appeared to be very little difference in the underlying pedagogic approach used by teachers in the teaching of mathematics and Myanmar language at Grades 3 and 5. [...] Teacher feedback on responses did not occur in nearly 80 per cent of the questioning sequences as they were usually answered by a choral response with little opportunity for follow-up.

Private schools: The middle class looks for alternatives

Government schools and public education provision were increasingly seen as poor and inadequate, especially by the middle classes. Yet legally there were no alternatives. As had been mentioned earlier, in the post-independence period from 1948 to 1962 private education was accepted, but during the socialist era of 1962–1988 all private institutions were closed down. The Myanmar government website consulted in 2007 stated:

> ... though the private sector has not yet formally been granted a status of setting up Universities with privileges to confer degrees, it has increasingly played an important role in the education market in consonance with the adoption of market mechanisms in the country's economy. The Private Tuition Law of 1964 permits setting up of private schools to teach single subjects per se. Permission is not granted to set up private schools to teach the full curriculum.

Dorothy Guyot describes how when the government shut down all universities in 1996 in reaction to the student boycott, families started to look for alternatives. This gap led to an opening for the private sector to start providing education services as a business, and even a school directory, the 'Education Directory and Guide for Everyone' (EDGE) which was published by U Myo Kyaw in 2000. Guyot[19] wrote to U Myo Kyaw's assistant Daw Tahnee Wade, who recollected:

> Students would go from course to course at private tuition companies while they waited for universities to open. The problem

was that the education establishments were not allowed to advertise, so the students did not know what was out there for them. Many of the schools were legally illegal. They were not allowed to open by law, but the government of the time ignored them. I still do not know how we managed to get permission for the Education Directory, but I do remember going to the Censor office with a sample and getting permission. We were able to include adverts from the tuition centres and schools, and even had an ad from the British Council.

Many schools did not advertise themselves, and those that did used headings such as 'tutors, foreign language schools/centres, or education services'. Preschools were the only private Myanmar schools that the government officially allowed, since education before kindergarten (KG) was under the authority of the Ministry of Social Welfare, not the MoE. The only schools that announced their presence in EDGE in 2000 were 10 international schools and 75 preschools. Slowly, the sector started to grow and by 2006–7, private schools had sprung up at pre-elementary, elementary, secondary and HE levels to cater for popular demand for English language, computing, accounting and business-related training.[20] Some schools offered a wider curriculum, some focused only on a few subjects. Most operated as supplementary schools, where children came after their day at the government schools, others were full-time schools operating under the radar.[21] Officially in 2006–7, private schools were still not allowed to operate as an alternative to the state system (although there were a few that had special status, such as the Yangon International School and the Diplomatic School in Yangon). The state tried to regulate these new schools by limiting the number of subjects they were allowed to teach, but schools managed to teach mathematics and science subjects under the guise of 'Information Technology' and other arts and language subjects under the title of 'English'.[22] Some private organisations, sometimes calling themselves schools and sometimes education centres, were also engaged in preparing students for examinations held by overseas universities and professional institutes.

Despite the regulations, some larger consortiums managed to set up large private education centres around the country. The International Language and Business Centre (ILBC) was such a venture and catered to a wide age group of learners of English and other subjects.[23] *The Khit Myanmar Weekly* (2006) reports that there were also summer schools that ran as businesses, such as the Summit International Learning Centre in Yangon that focused on English skills as well as maths and sciences.

In the 2002 Education Directory section entitled 'General Education', the sub-headings were: Day Care (61), KG (17), Preschool (89), Primary (18), International Schools (11), GCE 'O' levels (20), Libraries (4), plus Basic Education Schools as well as Universities and Colleges (these last three categories were government institutions). It is clear from the listings that most private institutions catered to the pre-primary age (which includes both preschool and KG), nevertheless offering a variety of subjects such as Myanmar, English, Maths and general knowledge as well as singing, playing and drawing. In certain cases, other languages such as Mandarin Chinese were also on offer. The day-care centres/KGs catered to those aged 3–5, but some offered their services from the age of one. The prices for 2002 ranged from around 500 MMK per month to 30,000 MMK per month. The older the children, the more variety of subjects (including IT, Geography, History, Science, Arts and Physical Education) and the more expensive. The Montessori Children's house seemed at the time to be the most expensive pre-primary option at 45,000 MMK per month. Guyot et al. remember this as well (Guyoy et al., 2016):

> The visible growth area was outside the purview of the Ministry of Education – preschools. The heads of preschools often quietly accommodated parents' pleading to let their English language school grow with their children. An example of the quiet growth is ES4E (English Skills for Everyone), housed in a simple single story building on Kaba Aye Road. When Dorothy first visited the preschool in 2003 looking for a service placement site for Pre-Collegiate students, it had been teaching 3–5 year olds since 1998. When she dropped in a few years later its signboard and façade were unchanged, but in the back there were five new classrooms for five new grades.

Parents were keen to send their children to formal institutions, although the quality of tuition was not verified or regulated. An article from a local Burmese weekly (cited in Lall, 2009: 141), explains:[24]

> Private Schools ending with 'School' are chosen over those that end with 'Centre'.
>
> If the name ends with 'school', private schools are more likely to be chosen than if it ends with 'centre' said a principal of the private international school which opens in Yangon, Myanmar. The parents

choose this as it is related to the international private school field. In this field, more credible names end with 'school' rather than having a name ending with 'centre'. According to the same principal over ninety per cent of parents did not check the credibility of the school. These parents send their children to what was perceived as popular schools.

What is clear from the above is that while the government schools were failing, urban middle class parents were looking for alternatives, and in light of the political changes expected after the 2008 Constitution had been enacted, the scene was set for a major overhaul of the education system.

Tuition

It is good to remember that all parents – not only middle class parents in urban areas – are key stakeholders in any education system. In Myanmar's poorer households, parental involvement in education has been historically low, not because parents were not interested in education, but because traditional hierarchies accorded teachers considerable esteem and respect along with a belief that teachers know best and will do their best for the children. Parents of all classes and across all states and regions[25] place a high value on education, which they connect with character development and socio-emotional skills, such as self-control, discipline, manners and ethics. At the same time, poorer households do not support schooling beyond the minimum amount thought necessary for their children, unless they perceive that the quality of education will allow their children to have a better future. The poorest households always have to appraise the school versus work choice for their children.

Parents at the end of the first decade of the twenty-first century in Myanmar knew that the system was failing them and their families. Education was not a conduit out of poverty for the more disadvantaged, and it rarely offered a brighter future to those in remote and conflict-affected areas. Despite this, and possibly because there were no alternatives, parents and communities subsidised government education to about 70 per cent of total expenditure (Mehta et al., 2014). Historically, there have been two main forms of community-based funding of education: parental contributions and community-based donors.[26] In the government schools, parents and children are regularly solicited to cover various common expenses of the school, including festivals, award ceremonies and repairs. These contributions could be in cash, kind and labour, with individual households funding not just direct education expenses for their children attending the school, but also contributing frequently to fund the general expenses of the school. While officially 'voluntary', these contributions create equity issues between families, and in some cases create situations where the schools discriminate against families that cannot pay, potentially leading to student drop outs. It also means that already overburdened teachers have to focus on raising funds rather than focusing on teaching. The government had at one point imposed a blanket ban on parental donations, which in light of continuing funding gaps at the school proved unsustainable.

As parents realise that their children will not pass exams only by going to school, they pay for after-school tuition.[27] This practice has mostly been illegal and for many years the government has tried to crack down on it.[28] However, tuition remains in high demand because of the overcrowded curriculum that cannot be covered in class, an exam system that encourages memorisation, and large class sizes which make it impossible for teachers to provide individual attention to students. Parents also see tuition as an 'investment', making sure that their children get the best possible chance in life. One father in Mon State explained: 'Some parents who are poor, and whose children are weak in studies, have to take loans in order to send their children for private tuition. It is a kind of investment for them.' Also some parents reported that at times exam questions are revealed by the teachers to children taking tuition, giving those children an unfair advantage. In rural settings, parents sometimes find that they cannot help their children themselves. This is especially true for households where parents are either insufficiently educated or are unable to spare their work-day time to help the child after school with homework and lessons: 'When our child is in a grade that is higher than I have studied, then I have to send them to a tutor who is more educated than me.'[29]

Teachers of course also provide tuition to supplement their meagre incomes.

> The nation's more than 226,000 teachers, like other civil servants, are poorly paid. Public service salaries were drastically increased in January 2010; nevertheless, according to MOE data, a primary school teacher's pay still averages only 47,000 kyat ($58) per month, a secondary school teacher's pay averages 53,000 kyat ($66) per month and a high school teacher's pay (upper secondary) averages 59,000 kyat ($73) per month. [...] According to

interviews carried out in some of Myanmar's border areas, the attrition rate of trained teachers is at times as high as 90 per cent. (Mehta et al., 2014: 85)

UNICEF's Mon Situational Analysis (SITAN) study (Mehta et al., 2014) found that the use of after-school tutoring services has been the most significant form of non-formal education accessed by households. It has been used by families from all walks of life, rich and poor, urban and rural, students in all grades from grade one through primary and secondary school, for all subjects, no matter if these students go to 'high' or 'low' quality schools. The MoE has tried to ban public school teachers from providing private tuition,[30] however, the ban seems to have simply driven the practice into a shadow market, where parents confirmed that they were still paying for the service, whilst teachers would not confirm they were providing tuition.

Most households worry about the future of their children, so knowing that it is the matriculation grade that will determine a child's entrance to university and the subject that their child can study, parents invest in these supplementary classes, no matter what the government says. However, tuition in the end might compensate a little for those who can afford it, but ultimately it substitutes for rather than complements what happens in the classroom.[31]

Conclusion

It has been seen in this chapter that the quality of education in Myanmar has declined over the decades. Despite the government committing to the MDGs, EFA and publishing education development plans, these have remained theoretical documents, not resulting in much change on the ground. The presence of systemic bottlenecks at both the macro and micro level have created severe resource, capacity, information and incentive problems that in turn have weakened the ability of the education system in Myanmar to address the various deprivations and inequities experienced by children and school communities.[32] There has been a large variation in the extent and mix of deprivations experienced across the different states, townships, schools, even across basic education grades. Overall, the presence of widespread poverty and a stagnant economy were key factors affecting education services and the experience of children within schools. The UNICEF funded SITAN study (Mehta et al., 2014) conducted and written before the reforms started, and looking at the situation for children across Myanmar, summarises the issues as follows.

> The immediate causal factors hampering children in Myanmar from realizing their right to education are the limited quality of education services and the high actual and opportunity costs of education. Quality is impaired by insufficient infrastructure, insufficient teachers, outdated teaching methodologies and large teacher-pupil ratios. Although no fees are levied in primary education, there are multiple charges that families must pay in order for their children to access it. This burden is heaviest for the poorest families. Tuition fees are charged for both middle and higher secondary schools. Nearly 30 per cent of school-aged children not attending school in 2009 did not do so because of the cost burden. Parents also have to consider the opportunity cost of keeping their children in education, both for themselves and their children; many feel work is a better option for them than education. Parents' appreciation of the value of education and their willingness to support it for their children is strongly linked to their own educational experience (or lack of it). But even where children do attend school, parental involvement in their education is limited.
>
> Underlying causes for the failure of children in Myanmar to realize their right to education include structural factors undermining service delivery, a lack of options in non-formal basic education and language barriers. The former includes lack of funding for the education sector as well as limited policy development and planning, limited quality of teacher training, sector-level management failings and inadequate monitoring and assessment. The current provision of non-formal or alternative primary education for children who have dropped out of school is very limited in coverage. Despite the country's very complex linguistic diversity, Myanmar language is the sole language of government, public affairs and public education. The 'language barrier' is a significant factor for children from non-Myanmar ethnic groups dropping out of school. Three focus areas of education reform in Myanmar are quality, equity and sector capacity.[33]

It became increasingly clear that government education needed a major overhaul.

Notes

1. It is interesting to note that even eminent western historians of Burma, such as John Furnivall, did not mention these lay schools. The reason for this was arguably because they focused on the education of girls and were not considered worthy of much notice.
2. The State Law and Order Restoration Council (SLORC) changed its name to the State Peace and Development Council (SPDC) in 1997. See Tonkin for more on the 1990 elections, (Tonkin, 2007).
3. In the late 1980s and early 1990s as China withdrew its financial support, the BCP splintered into various ethno-nationalist EAOs.
4. More on this in Chapters 6 and 7.
5. More on this in Rose Metro's thesis: 'The rhetorical aspect of myanmafication was heralded by the "Adaptation of Expressions" law of 1989, which altered the name of the country in non-Burmese languages from "Burma" to "Myanmar," ostensibly in order to correct the misapprehension of colonists who had labelled the country by its spoken name rather than by the more formal term by which it had been known since the dynastic era – *myanma naing-ngan*. The law also claimed that *báma* – what the British had rendered as "Burma" – was not and had never been a nation, but was instead one of the ethnic groups that made up *myanma lu-myò* (previous usages of *myanma lu-myò* to describe the majority ethnic group went unexplained)' (Metro, 2011: 54).
6. In school textbooks, Nick Cheesman found, 'People dressed as Bamar are seen as individuals or in family units, engaged in community celebrations or household tasks. Non-Bamar are usually lumped together in contrived groups displaying standardised national costumes, rather than simple day-to-day scenes' (Cheesman, 2002: 157).
7. Anawarahta (1044–77 CE), Bayinnaung (1551–81 CE), Alaungpaya (1752–60 CE).
8. Any mention of Aung San would remind people of his daughter Aung San Suu Kyi, held by the SPDC under house arrest at the time.
9. Metro traces the process of 'ethnification' of Burmese/*myanma* identity over the past two centuries by examining the continuities and changes in the way schoolbooks portray one king, Kyansittha (Metro, 2011). By investigating Kyansittha's appearances in dynastic, colonial, nationalist and socialist era textbooks, she accounts for his transformation from a universal monarch in his own court inscriptions into a *myanma* king in current textbooks, in line with the military regime's post-1988 project of 'myanmafication' (Houtman, 1999: 26–27) of Burmese identity.
10. See, for example, the Government of Myanmar's (2014a) National EFA Review.
11. This includes a range of government organisations: The MoE leads the literacy programme along with the Myanmar Education Research Bureau (MERB), in 2004 re-named the Department of Myanmar Education Research (DMER); The Ministry of Social Welfare, Relief and Resettlement; and the Ministry of Progress of Border Areas and National Races and Development Affairs (MPBND). The Ministry of Information has established township libraries that are used as Community Learning Centres for Literacy and Continuing Education.

    NGOs: Myanmar Literacy Resource Centre (MLRC), Myanmar Women's Affairs Federation (MWAF), Myanmar Maternal and Child Welfare Association (MMCWA), and Young Women's Christian Association (YWCA). All are providing libraries, CLCs and reading circles for literacy and continuing education.

    International agencies: United Nations Development Programme (UNDP) and UNICEF both support literacy programmes and World Vision and Save the Children have assisted programmes that include literacy development.
12. One slide states: Human Rights Education was first introduced in school curriculum Grades 6–10.
13. Myanmar NFE records, DMER publication (2006) cited in unpublished advisory document to the MoE 2010.
14. Cited in unpublished advisory document to the MoE (2010: 33).
15. Cited in unpublished advisory document to the MoE (2010: 40).
16. This has to remain anonymous as this document was shared in confidence.

17 Anecdotal interview evidence over a decade shows that respondents do not necessarily know that CCA stands for child-centred approaches to teaching and learning. They do know, however, that it is the opposite of teachers lecturing to a class.
18 These were mostly government schoolteachers, although two monastic schools and one private school also took part in the study.
19 Tahnee Wade, personal email to Dorothy Guyot, 22 August 2016.
20 In January 2005, the author met a businessman who had set up a school which was teaching in English. The school was at primary level only and meant as a supplement to regular state school teaching after official classes had ended. The school was located in the businessman's house in a residential area in central Yangon. It emerged over the next few meetings with other education specialists that such schools were common, but that there was no official data as to how many there were and what they taught. Interviews revealed that many taught only English, but an increasing number of schools offered broader curricula, some even employing English-speaking foreigners on an unofficial basis. A visit around 6 months later revealed that there had been a 'crackdown' on such schools and that they were now only allowed to teach English and computers/ IT. The government was also trying to regulate this new market by dictating what fees the providers could charge. It emerged from interviews that especially in secondary supplementary schools, under the heading 'English', a number of social sciences such as history were being taught, and that IT often meant maths and science. In this way, a fuller curriculum could be maintained. Official fees, of course, could be supplemented through black market cash payments (Lall, 2009).
21 This was common knowledge across the education community at the time but not spoken about. The proof came out much later in what Guyot et al. (2016) call the 'President Thein Sein effect'.

	2011	2013
International Schools	10	57
Kindergarten, Primary, Secondary	25	13
Preschools	219	188
Total Private Schools	254	258

'In just 2 years how could anyone transform small schools serving 3–5 year olds into full, multi-grade international schools? Look at the total number of schools. It increased by only four. Thus, the net disappearance of 31 preschools and the disappearance of 12 other schools may make up the bulk of the international school growth. We believe that many preschool owners had been quietly growing their schools for years, just the way ES4S had. […] Excitement was in the air about the forthcoming private school law. We suspect that the vast majority of owners of the 47 new international schools announced their school's existence because they trusted that President Thein Sein's government would welcome their efforts.'

22 Interview with Ko Tar, owner of one of the new private schools in 2005 and again in 2006.
23 'International Language and Business Centre (ILBC) has classes in Taunggyi and Lashio (Shan States). According to the Managing Director, the ILBC, which has the most branches of private schools across the country and is based in Yangon, opened new branches in two cities, Taunggyi and Lashio in the Shan States. They will accept preschool students up to GCE 'O' for summer course and for regular classes. ILBC is the first among the private schools in Yangon and has three branches in Yangon (Bahan, Tarmawe and Thingangyun) with a total of 450 students (*Khit Myanmar Weekly*, 2006: 3).
24 For most of the 2000 institutions could not call themselves schools – however, some institutions did manage to circumvent government rules. (*The Voice Weekly*. (2007) Vol. 3, No. 30, 7 May 2007, 8). This article is not available online.
25 Over the past decade and a half, I have met with several thousand parents across the whole country.

26 Schools also solicit contributions from donors and 'well-wishers' whereby schools receive funding from better-off members within the local community through the institution of the School Board of Trustees.

27 See Bray et al. for more information on tuitions and the education shadow market (Bray et al., 2019).

28 Private subject tuition was investigated in the 2006–7 school year. This was announced on 9 May 2006 by No. 3 Basic Education Department under MoE. The township chief education officer was to instruct those providing tuition to apply to get permission to open the tuition class. The township chief education officer had to report the tuition classes which were eligible within the rules and regulations of the above department. If some problems occurred and if he did not report them, he had to take responsibility for all problems. The teachers from these tuition classes would be investigated too. If a school runs without permission, it would be terminated in accordance with the law of 1984 Rules and Regulation of Private Subject Tuition. (*Living Color Magazine*. 2006 'Private subject tuition investigated', 132 (July), 18).

29 Author's notes, interview with Rural Mothers, Mawlamyine, 2013.

30 'Order banning private tuition is "not fair"'. *Eleven Media*, 14 October 2013 reported that the: 'Ministry of Education has issued an order to teachers not to give private tutoring but the directive doesn't seem to have much effect as the practice continues unabated.' https://www.nationthailand.com/noname/30217080.

31 Concerns that this system creates incentives for teachers to shirk their primary teaching responsibilities within school hours have led MoE to ban the supply of tuition by public school teachers. The ban, however, proved to be both unsustainable and counter-productive – driving the practice into the shadowmarket and making it even more difficult for poorer children to access after-school support.

32 Conclusion drawn by Mehta et al.'s 2014 UNICEF-funded Mon SITAN study. This conclusion can be drawn for the whole country at the time.

33 Mehta et al.'s 2014 study conducted for UNICEF also points to the following disparities that will be explored in more depth in the next chapter. **Primary schooling** Disparities exist: in terms of regions [...] Tanintharyi (98 per cent) had the highest rate of primary education participation and Rakhine (75.8 per cent) the lowest; there was a slight bias towards urban schooling – 93 per cent compared with 89.2 per cent in rural schools; it was much higher for children from the richest quintile (94.9 per cent) than those from the poorest (81.4 per cent). Enrolment of disabled children is particularly low. Ministry of National Planning and Economic Development, Ministry of Health and UNICEF (2011) 80: '[...] Despite official whole township enrolment drives undertaken since 1999–2000, the MICS 2009–10 data show that only 77.3 per cent of 5 year olds attended school. This increased to 95 per cent for 7and 8 year olds. Given the 117 per cent gross enrolment rate in primary education in 2008 and that 11.9 per cent of children aged 10–15 in 2009–10 were attending primary school, these figures indicate that many over-aged children are enrolled in primary education. Again, there are significant disparities. As much as 19 per cent of 10–15-year-old children from the poorest households were still in primary school, but only 5 per cent from the richest. The rich-poor contrast is more marked when the status of 9 year olds is assessed: only 31.2 per cent of 9 year olds from the poorest households were in the last year of primary school, compared with 78.7 per cent of those from the richest. Regional disparities are prominent: just 31.7 per cent of 9 year olds were in the last year of primary school in Rakhine State, compared with 72.3 per cent in Tanintharyi, and UNICEF (Ministry of National Planning and Economic Development, Ministry of Health and UNICEF, 2011: 80-1) '[...] The net completion rate for primary school was only 54.2 per cent (children of primary school completion age attending the last year of primary school) in 2009–10. The same significant disparities are seen based on socio-economic status (78.7 per cent richest quintile, compared with 31.2 per cent poorest quintile), rural–urban division (49.6 per cent, compared with 66.6 per cent)...' (Ministry of National Planning and Economic Development, Ministry of Health and UNICEF, 2011: 81). **Secondary schooling** Participation rates in secondary education are increasing but still low and inequitable. The gross enrolment rate for secondary education was estimated to be 53 per cent in 2008, a significant increase from 34 per cent in 1999. (Global Education and Monitoring Report Team, 2011: 82–3.) '[...] The recent MICS also found that the rural–urban difference

in secondary school attendance (75 per cent versus 52 per cent) was far more pronounced than for primary school attendance. So too were the disparities based on socio-economic status: only 28.2 per cent of children from the poorest households were in secondary school, compared with 85.5 per cent from the richest households. Regional disparities were also greater (figure 29): the secondary school attendance rate was 74.7 per cent in Yangon but only 30.9 per cent in Rakhine, low rates were also found in Shan State'.

2
Education reform and effects on basic education

Introduction

This chapter starts with a description of the state of education prior to 2012, and introduces the education reforms that were engendered in the second half of 2012 under President Thein Sein's government with the CESR, and the role played by the aid agencies. The chapter engages with the tensions between the various stakeholders including the MoE, the CESR team, the Parliamentary Committee lead by Daw Aung San Suu Kyi and the NNER, a civil society-led consortium campaigning for more radical education reforms. It explores the competing reform initiatives and explains why President Thein Sein brought in EPIC to side-line the influence of the international development partners, and how all of this resulted in the NESP[1] and the New Education Law.[2] The chapter also looks at the student protests of 2015, their demands based on social justice and their engagement with the government leading to limited changes in the New Education Law (2014, amended 2015).

The second part of the chapter discusses the challenges faced by the NLD government after taking over in 2015 in trying to meet Myanmar's international commitment to EFA. Education has been a key priority of the NLD government, and the education sector needed further reform after the initial changes that had been initiated by the Thein Sein government. This section engages with the NLD government's development of the education reform process, including the continuity of policy by largely accepting the NESP unchanged. Priorities remain access, quality, curricular reforms and teacher training reforms, thus addressing a few issues in education faced by Myanmar's poor, yet still not addressing the issues of ethnic and linguistic diversity that have resulted in a largely inequitable education system. The chapter engages with the role of the development partners, the structural changes at the

MoE and the curricular reforms of the primary level, including changes that make the content of that curriculum marginally more inclusive. The chapter ends with the mid-term review (MTR) of the NESP that was conducted in the summer of 2019 and made public in the spring of 2020.

Background

At the time of writing in 2020, the Myanmar government educates 9 million children in 45,600 schools with 320,000 teachers. It is the largest education provider across the country, although it is estimated that around 300,000 students study in monastic schools and another 300,000 are provided for by ethnic systems (MIMU, 2017), which are covered in subsequent chapters. Within the government system, there are four types of schools: approved schools where teachers are appointed by the government, branch schools established near an approved school, affiliated schools and self-help schools. The government appoints the teachers once a particular threshold of students is registered at a particular school. Affiliated schools and self-help schools, each of which is administratively attached to a main school, have to prepare and manage all school facilities and teacher arrangements by themselves, while students in these affiliated and self-help schools are reported as students of the main schools, where they also take their exams. In these schools, most of the expenses, including the cost of teachers' salaries, is borne by the entity that established the school – mostly communities or monasteries (JICA, 2013: 25). This, in effect, means that in many places in Myanmar, it is the parents, not the state, who bear the brunt of education expenses. According to the UNICEF Mon Situational Analysis (SITAN) mentioned in Chapter 1 of this volume, community funding of education is estimated at 70 per cent of total education expenditure (Mehta et al., 2014).

Although the Myanmar Government has started to increase government expenditure on education, public education expenditure as a share of Gross Domestic Product (GDP) has traditionally been lower than the ASEAN average. According to official data, government investment in education was 2.1 per cent of GDP in 2013–4 and 2.2 per cent in 2018, a substantial increase from the 0.7 per cent in 2010–1, but still low compared to the region. For example, Malaysia and Vietnam spent 6.3 per cent in 2013 and 2012 respectively; Laos PDR 4.2 per cent in 2014 and Indonesia 3.4 per cent in 2013.⁵

Government data shows that expenditure on education in fiscal year 2015–6 was four times that of fiscal year 2011–2. This rapid rise in government expenditure can also be seen in a comparison between fiscal year 2011–2 and fiscal year 2012–3, during which it more than doubled.[4] In 2015–6, spending on education was around 7 per cent of the government budget (Min Zaw Soe et al., 2017: 11) and in 2018, the latest official figures available, it had risen to 7.75 per cent. The largest expenditure of the government budget is salary payments, estimated at around 90 per cent, leaving little for maintenance and goods and services that schools need to function. There is a separate capital expenditure budget where construction expenditures account for over 90 per cent, leaving little for equipment. Since school budgets are centrally determined based on uniform formulas, they do not meet actual school needs. Although some of this is now slowly changing, TEOs and head teachers have traditionally had little or no discretion over school budgets, making them reliant on community funds to deal with any emergency and even standard expenses. Schools have been given some limited autonomy through the school grants programme that is covered later in this chapter. At the time of writing, the teacher hiring system was being reviewed to allow TEOs some say in what was, until now, a highly centralised system of teacher placement conducted by the MoE in Nay Pyi Taw (NPT), something which will have longer-term effects on budgets. The centralised system has resulted in teacher shortages in rural and primary schools, disadvantaging schools that are already serving the poorer sections of Myanmar society.

The status of education before the reforms started

Chapter 1 of this volume has already offered a snapshot on the education issues Myanmar faced before the reforms began in 2012, while 2010, the year of the elections, is the year against which the success of the reforms will eventually be compared. Using the Integrated Household Living Conditions Survey in Myanmar (IHLCS) (2009–10) that had been conducted by the UN and the Ministry of National Planning and Economic Development based on data from the 2009–10 school year, JICA published a report (JICA, 2013) that established somewhat of a baseline for the subsequent education reforms with regard to access and retention. The JICA report concluded that in 2010, the gap of the Net Enrolment Ratio (NER) between children from poor and non-poor households was around 10 per cent at primary level, widening to around 24 per cent at secondary level. They estimated that this was due to the financial constraints on poor families as secondary education was not free.[5] Interestingly, there was only a slight difference between urban and rural areas for the primary level enrolment rates (3 per cent), whereas the difference became more pronounced at the secondary level (around 30 per cent). More than 90 per cent of pupils at the primary level resided within an hour's walk to school (i.e. within 1.23 miles) but at the secondary level (Grade 6 and above) only 60 per cent of students who lived in urban areas and 24 per cent of students who lived in rural areas were within this distance, suggesting a lack of schools. This is compounded by transport being harder to arrange in rural areas, especially in the rainy season (JICA, 2013: 29). In 2010, almost a quarter (23 per cent) of students dropped out in the last year of primary school – i.e. Grade 5. The drop-out rate reached more than 18 per cent in Grades 8 and 9. More worrying was the high drop-out rates in Grade 1, which was identified as resulting from difficult access to primary schools in rural areas, as well as a 'lack of readiness'[6] of Grade 1 entrants to study in primary education, along with the cost to parents of uniforms, books, exercise books and other expenses.[7] Parents also need to pay a Parent Teacher Association fee and athletic, stationary and library fees from middle school onwards, resulting in more drop outs of poorer children.

The results of the JICA report (JICA, 2013) are confirmed by an analysis of the same data set aggregated with the MoE's EMIS in addition to data collected by a survey of 786 schools (all different types) offering secondary grades, and distributed nationwide during the CESR process with the help of the Asian Development Bank (ADB) (which supported the CESR Team in conducting broader statistical analysis).[8] The analysis of this data concluded that in the school year 2009–10 at higher-grade level and age groups, gross and net enrolment ratios (GER and NER) dropped, the share of out-of-school youth rose, and the gap between GER and NER suggested many children were over-age. The disaggregated analysis showed that overall there is gender equity, but there are large gaps across urban–rural, states–regions, and access to preschool was limited to mostly urban areas. These disparities in access are sizeable in primary education, yet these become much more marked at the secondary level. The data also confirmed low drop-out rates through to Grade 4 – about five-sixths of youth finish primary level; however, nearly a quarter of primary completers never entered middle school, and less than half finished middle school. The drop-off at the transition from primary to middle school is likely to exacerbate inequality, as prospects for entry into middle school appear to be weakest for disadvantaged groups (for example, ethnic group students from remote rural areas) who may also have weaker academic preparedness, increasing their risk of drop-out if they do enter secondary education (CESR, 2014). The EMIS cohort analysis concluded that there are at least 1.1 million new entrants to Grade 1 each year but only around 300,000 reach Grade 11, and two-thirds fail matriculation every year, leaving only around 110,000 finishers out of 1.1 million starters, leading to high levels of repetition in Grade 11 as well. These estimates are fairly consistent with Census tables released in 2014, where the disaggregated analysis showed sizeable gaps between urban–rich and rural–poor. As Figure 2.1 shows, rural schools have few facilities and are much poorer than their urban counterparts. For example, four-fifths of urban children finish middle school, versus less than one-third of poor children; poor girls are worst off: among poor households, the gender gap is widest at Grade 6, meaning that poor girls are least likely to enter middle school. It is well known that the disparities across states and regions and between affluent and poor areas are stark. The ADB data indicate the following (Sy, 2013: 59):

> An NER in Yangon of roughly 74.7 per cent versus only 30.9 per cent in Rakhine: more than four-fifths of children age 10–15 in Yangon are in school (at least in primary), while more than half (52.9 per cent) in Rakhine are already out-of-school. In terms of gender, while a marginally larger share of girls (58.6 per cent versus 58.3 per cent of boys) age 10–15 are in secondary school, the share of girls out-of-school is also slightly larger (30.5 per cent, versus 29.8 per cent for boys).

The ADB data (Sy, 2013: 58–9) also show the following:

> The relationship between wealth quintile and share of 10–15 year olds who are out-of-school youth (OSY) is dramatic and strikingly linear, confirming that enrolment and dropout are strongly affected by socioeconomic status. Moreover, poverty appears to more strongly affect female dropouts: with the exception of the richest quintile, the gender gap in shares of OSY is roughly inversely related to wealth quintile, and for the poorest quintile, the share of OSY girls is 7 percentage points higher than for boys. The share of girls who are OSY is also slightly higher in rural areas and marginally lower in urban areas. These gender dynamics are much sharper for children of secondary school age (10–15 years old) than those of primary school age (5–9 years old).

For non-entry and drop-out during primary level,[9] the IHLCS responses suggest direct cost is the main factor, but among students exiting

Figure 2.1 Rural government school, 2014. Source: Author.

during the secondary level, the number one reason is reported as lack of interest[10] and the opportunity cost that parents have as they need the children to work, especially in agricultural communities. The analysis of IHCLS dataset shows that the largest share (about 42.5 per cent) of household expenditures on education go to private tutoring, which is higher in urban areas, but still large (i.e. more than a quarter of education spending) among poor households. The ADB data (Sy, 2013) maintain that regression analysis suggests high school (not university) is the most costly level per enrolee.

This is the picture two years before the reforms began and against which Myanmar needs to measure its progress. It shows that there are structural issues that perpetuate cycles of inequality and injustice that the reforms needed to address. At the time of writing – 10 years later – access has improved, however, drop-out rates remain high, particularly in Grade 5 for children from poorer households and overall around 2.7 million children remain out of school.[11]

The role of the 2008 Constitution

The 2008 Constitution describes the obligations and duties of the Union with regard to education, and the right of all Myanmar citizens to education. In Chapter 8, Article 366: 'Citizens, Fundamental Rights and Duties of Citizens' describes its obligation to citizens regarding their right to education, and stipulates the following:

> Every citizen shall, in accordance with the educational policy laid down by the Union: (a) have the right to education; (b) be given basic education which the Union prescribes by law as compulsory; and (c) have the right to conduct scientific research, explore science, work with creativity and write, to develop the arts, and conduct research freely with other branches of culture.[12]

In Chapter 1, Article 28, the 2008 Constitution[13] also describes the obligations of the Union in respect to the provision of education and health as follows:

> The Union shall: (a) earnestly strive to improve the education and health of the people; (b) enact the necessary law to enable the Nation's people to participate in matters of their education and health; (c) implement a free compulsory primary education system; and (d) implement a modern education system that will promote all-around correct thinking and a good moral character, contributing towards the building of the Nation.

The aim of the Constitution seems at least in theory to promote and support aspects of social justice with both the right to education and basic education being compulsory. The state here is responsible for providing this service, with a duty to improve the lives of its citizens. There is, however, also the note that education is to promote 'correct' thinking and that this will lead to citizens contributing to nation building – in a way closing the circle of the reciprocal social contract, albeit still reflecting some of the themes of nationalism discussed in Chapter 1 of this volume. Meeting these provisions after decades of military rule meant that the whole education system needed to be overhauled. It is, therefore, in light of this constitution that the education reforms finally began after the 2010 elections had put Myanmar's first civilianised government into office since 1962 (Lall, 2016a).

The start of Myanmar's education reforms and the engagement of the development partners

When power was handed over by the SPDC to the new government in 2011, President Thein Sein's[14] Government developed a 10-point education policy and a 20-year plan called the Basic Education Sector National Education Promotion 20-year Long-term Plan 2011–2031. The new plan was in line with the previous 30-year Basic Education Plan, but was more specific on policy measures that would improve access to education, for example, a stipend programme for students from disadvantaged families In addition, the first ever schools grant programme was proposed. The 10 points would form the basis of what was to come over President Thein Sein's following four years in office.

Education reform was President Thein Sein's fourth priority after national reconciliation with the NLD, peace with the Ethnic Armed Organisations (EAOs) and economic reforms (Lall, 2016a). In February 2012, a Conference on Development Policy Options with Special Reference to Health and Education Sectors was organised by the government and development partners. As a result of this conference, the CESR was launched in July 2012.[15] UNICEF led the education consortium, working together with the Multi-Donor Education Fund (MDEF). The MoE invited all interested development partners to take part, and many, in particular the Australian government (AusAID – now the Department of Foreign Affairs and Trade (DFAT)), the EU and the WB, took the opportunity to engage with the MoE for the first time. The CESR's responsibilities encompassed all sectors of teaching and learning, from early childhood education to HE and involved a wide range of ministries and departments that had a stake in education. The focus of the CESR was on reviewing the formal state education sector around the country in four stages. After the first phase of work (entitled 'Rapid Assessment'), proposals under consideration by the CESR included increasing basic education from 11 to 12 years, and changing the teacher career structure – two major structural changes that would mean all other areas within education would have to adapt. The former aimed to resolve the time pressure that teachers faced in covering the curriculum, the latter to make sure there were enough teachers for primary level education. The latter is particularly important as teachers who wanted promotion moved to the secondary schools, resulting in large teacher-to-student ratios in primary schools with the least experienced teachers teaching these classes. The CESR also reviewed language policies (including the teaching of English) and recommended the translation of textbooks into ethnic languages.[16] Phase 1 of CESR's review was completed in early 2013, followed by CESR Phase 2 (entitled 'In-Depth Analysis'), where more detailed work was conducted resulting in detailed reports for each of the education sectors. Phase 2 of CESR's review promised to put equity at the heart of its mandate. Its website stated the following:[17]

> All the Phase 2 components will look at options for increasing access to education for all groups in society, as well as improving the quality and relevance of education at every level. Recommendations for improving management, planning and monitoring will also be a key feature. As a guiding principle, all the studies will look closely at issues of equity. This will involve:
>
> - analysing how policies, programmes, practices, organisational processes and institutional structures impact on different groups and individuals
> - making recommendations for policies and actions to improve positive impacts so that all groups can benefit equitably
>
> Dimensions of equity which the studies will consider are:
>
> - Gender;
> - Ethnicity/language background;
> - Economic status/poverty;
> - Geographic location (e.g. urban, rural, remote), by State/Region/Township;
> - Disability;
> - Other vulnerabilities, for example, post conflict and migrant communities, impact of HIV/AIDS etc.

Phases 1 and 2 of CESR provided a much clearer understanding of the status of the education sector, including recent achievements and priorities for continued reforms and investments. Phase 3 focused on the costings covering fiscal years 2016–20 of what would be required to make the changes across the sector, and this was later followed by Phase 4, the writing of the National Education Sector Plan – later renamed the 'National Education Strategic Plan'.

The role of donors and development partners

The development partners welcomed the CESR and took the opportunity to engage in Myanmar's education sector – many for the first time. Rather than focusing on issues of social justice (which the CESR emphasised), their views were based on human capital theory – that Myanmar needed to reform education in order to modernise its economy, create graduates that could find jobs and subsequently join the more developed and developing nations. Their views are best summarised by the ADB in one of their final reports on supporting the CESR (ADB, 2016):

> Recognizing the need for an educated population and workforce is essential for sustained economic growth and poverty reduction, in 2011, the Government of Myanmar redoubled efforts to strengthen the education sector, reflected in a doubling of the education budget between fiscal year FY 2011–2 and FY 2012–3. However, a dearth of data posed a key obstacle to education sector reforms, perhaps particularly in the Post-Primary Education (PPE) subsectors – the Secondary Education Subsector (SES), Technical and Vocational Education and Training (TVET), and the Higher Education Subsector (HES) – which involve multiple ministries and linkages to the labour market, and had received little DP organization support.

In order to support education, development partners had come together previously – pooling some of their funds – as the MDEF. Between 2006 and 2011, they had funded the Quality Basic Education Programme (QBEP), led by UNICEF, the only international agency apart from JICA able to work directly with the MoE. UNICEF's work had been limited by government controls, although this was set to change with the announcement of the CESR. After 2012, the MDEF increased its support with UNICEF, EU, AusAID, DFID, Denmark and Norway, being joined by the ADB and the WB (JICA, 2013). The 2012–5 funding was aimed at rolling out QBEP Phase 2, which quickly became linked to the CESR (more on QBEP 2 below). Many others that were not part of MDEF nonetheless committed to supporting education in Myanmar, including bilateral agencies such as the German Corporation for International Cooperation (GIZ) and JICA, multilateral agencies such as UNESCO, and International Non-governmental Organisations (INGOs) such as the Nippon Foundation, the Open Society Foundation, Save the Children, and the BC. In order to coordinate funds and programmes across the development partners, the Development Partner Coordination Group (DPCG) organised regular coordination meetings and established communication and coordination among development partners through a mailing list. In order for development partners to communicate with the government, the Joint Education Sector Working Group (JESWG) was officially formed as a policy dialogue mechanism (JICA, 2013: 3). It was through these mechanisms that the development partners became increasingly involved in the CESR and the wider reform processes. However, as shall be seen below, this was not necessarily welcomed by all.

The battle over education: President, parliament, civil society and students

The CESR had a significant mandate, but at first little political support. Not knowing where the reforms were going to lead and how stable the Thein Sein Government would be in the long run, even Dr Mya Aye, the Minister of Education[18] remained uninvolved, ostensibly leaving the running of the CESR to more junior staff. Daw Tin Tin Shu, head of the CESR, was left to coordinate with the development partners and to fend off criticism that came from all quarters, including from inside the government and the opposition parties. The opposition NLD was at first categorically opposed to the CESR. Shortly after the start of the CESR, the NLD and associated civil society and activist groups started to undertake a national education review of their own led by the NNER and Dr Thein Lwin.[19] Their argument was that the MoE did not have the moral authority to lead the education reform process, that everyone knew what was wrong with the education system (and, therefore, no review was needed), and that a bid to reform needed to be inclusive of all groups, including ethnic education providers.[20] Although the NNER was more inclusive in its approach, allowing for voices from ethnic education systems to be heard, ethnic education groups also found that the NNER had a particular agenda and that inclusiveness did not necessarily mean that other viewpoints were taken on board.[21] The NNER proposal focused mainly on free education, decentralisation and freedom of institutional decision making. Many of their very progressive ideas were impossible to implement given the state of education infrastructure, the lack of teachers and the cost of fixing basic faults within the system, along with the available funding.

Initially, the CESR process and the NNER operated in parallel and without much contact, but after a few months there was some limited collaboration as each review team invited the other to attend events and share (limited) information. This was largely due to the great diplomatic skills of Daw Tin Tin Shu, who was open to suggestions and ideas from all quarters. However, in the end the NNER officially declared that it had lost faith in the government and in the MoE's reform process. The relationship between the NNER and the NLD soured and Dr Thein Lwin, who had led the NNER since its inception, was removed from the NLD in February 2015. The NLD released a statement saying that neither he nor the NNER were speaking for the party and threatened legal action against him as he had violated party rules by not seeking permission from the committee to become involved in a separate organisation.[22]

Subsequently, other matters further complicated the working of the CESR. Given that the CESR was the main window through which the development partners were able to exert influence on the thinking around education reform, the process quickly became dominated by the various aid agencies sending in experts for areas close to their hearts. The BC, for example, paid for a specialist to advise on English language teaching in schools, and others such as AusAid (now DFAT) and the EU also sent in their own people, specialists in various education sectors, to help with issues ranging from early childhood development to HE. Whilst the help and good intentions were appreciated, the CESR was largely over-run by foreign experts. There was only limited time available for the actual review and to construct a coherent education plan, so the MoE officials were rather overwhelmed. This also led to criticisms from inside the government. The development partners were seen as too influential in setting the course of education reforms. The situation was not helped by the fact that the two resident experts in the posts coordinated by UNICEF to help run the CESR (technical adviser and coordinator) kept changing. None of these experts had any prior experience of Myanmar and whilst they had worked on education reviews and reforms in other countries previously, each new appointment took a certain time to catch up and understand the workings of the CESR and the complicated political context in which it was evolving. While this was certainly a strain on the CESR team,[23] they continued functioning and produced a second set of reports to conclude Phase 2, largely on time in early 2014.[24]

Finding that the CESR process was taking too long to feed into the legislative process, and wanting to secure a set of education laws well in time for the 2015 elections, the President's Office constituted EPIC. To the surprise of all the development partners who were called at short notice to NPT on 7 October 2013, the Office of the President convened a National Seminar on Pragmatic Reforms for Education announcing that this new body would take the lead on education. The development partners were assured that this was not to replace the CESR, nor to do similar work twice, but that EPIC and the CESR were complementary to each other. In reality, however, this was a move to retake control of the process without having to shut down the CESR or make the development partners' prior work redundant (Lall, 2017). The EPIC team took up residence only a few hundred metres away from the CESR in the Diamond Jubilee Hall on the Yangon University Campus. The three components included a task force of deputy ministers from the 13 ministries directly involved in education, supported by their director generals, an advisory group consisting of retired MoE officials, academics and other national experts, and 18 working groups covering specific areas of education reform, with two co-leads – one from government and one from the group of experts totalling over 200 people. Its 18 thematic working groups were tasked with formulating policies and plans for pragmatic education reforms. The EPIC team had limited contact with the CESR teams and the involvement of development partners was severely reduced, not least because all meetings were held in Burmese. Whilst the main task of the CESR was to develop recommendations for the reform of the education system, the main purpose of EPIC was to draft policies for the implementation of educational reform, with both organisations coming together in Phase 3 when costings had to be developed (Min Zaw Soe et al., 2017). The EPIC reports were submitted by the end of January 2014. They were clearly supported by the President's Office and were the answer not only to what was seen as an inefficiently led MoE process subject to too much international interference, but also as a riposte to the Parliamentary Education Promotion Committee (PEPC) that had been promoted by the speaker of the parliament, Thura U Shwe Mann and Daw Aung San Suu Kyi. The PEPC was comprised of 10 Union Solidarity Development Party (USDP) members, three NLD members and two MPs from the Shan Nationalities Democratic Party and had been tasked with developing an overarching education 'mother law' to provide a framework for education reforms. The powerful speaker of Parliament, Thura U Shwe Mann, had teamed up with Daw Aung San Suu Kyi to push the legislative process in Parliament (held quite separate from the CESR work). Parliament had started to challenge government ministries, and parliamentary committees quickly learnt to use their new authority to summon officials and hold ministries to account. Thura U Shwe Mann and Daw Aung San Suu Kyi started by calling the acting Minister of Education and other officials in November 2013 to criticise the pace of the education reforms and demand a greater involvement of the Parliament in the process. The Parliamentary Guarantees, Pledges and Undertakings Vetting Committee then also criticised the MoE for failing to deliver on 220 of its commitments (Pyoe Pin, 2014). As a result,

Thura U Shwe Mann and Daw Aung San Suu Kyi decided to take the lead in the Parliament with regard to the education reform process and a power struggle erupted between the processes led by Parliament and those affiliated with the President's office.

In the meantime, the President's office also tried to remain in control of the legislative process by removing 'hardliners', and putting presidential allies in place. Key actors of the executive branch in education included the Vice President Dr Sai Mauk Kham (who allegedly was close to EPIC and attended many of the policy planning sessions, and the Ministers of the President's office – also known as the 'super cabinet' – mainly U Tin Naing Thein, who was responsible for social affairs). Other advisors included Dr Aung Tun Thet, a former lecturer at the Yangon Institute of Economics and former Director General in the Ministry of Health and Dr Yin Yin Nwe, a former Country Representative for UNICEF and a former geology lecturer at the University of Yangon.

The education law and student protests

The process inside EPIC went on largely unperturbed by the power play on the outside, and in March 2014, EPIC drafted the National Education Bill that was then submitted to Parliament in July 2014. It needed presidential approval, and President Thein Sein sent the Bill back to Parliament with 25 suggested changes. On 30 September 2014, the law was enacted, accepting 19 of the proposed changes.

During the whole process, momentum for protest increased; civil society organisations and student and teacher unions accused the Government of excluding them and not taking into account the advice from the relevant stakeholders. The NNER held meetings that decried the law as cementing the centralisation of Myanmar's education system. The meetings resulted in a set of detailed suggestions that were submitted to Parliament.[25] The main issues that sparked unhappiness included the lack of teaching of ethnic languages and cultures at universities, the lack of independence of universities, and the legality of students taking part in political activities.[26] The Action Committee for Democratic Education (ACDE) – comprising members of the All Burma Federation of Students' Unions (ABFSU), the Confederation of University Student Unions and University Student Union – began to campaign for the amendment or redrafting of the National Education Law. Demanding a quadripartite meeting between ACDE, NNER, the Government and Parliament, they held a demonstration between 14 and 17 November

2014 at various locations in Yangon and other parts of the country, and threatened nationwide demonstrations if the government did not respond within 60 days. Once the 60 days expired, more than 100 people started to march from Mandalay to Yangon, commencing on 20 January 2016. Other protesters joined the march from across the country, including from Pakokku, the Delta, Dawei and Mawlamyine. The 11 points issued by the ACDE on 24 January demanded a meeting with the Government and for the law to be amended. The Government agreed to meet with the students in February to discuss their demands. Three quadripartite meetings took place during which time the student protests continued. As Dr Thein Lwin had been expelled from the NLD, the NLD was not seen to be on the side of the NNER and the students. Students maintained that their protests would only stop after the new or amended law had been passed by the Parliament. At the last meeting, an agreement was struck, with the Government promising to take into account the 11 demands. The Government repeatedly asked the students to suspend their protests, and even a head monk endorsed this position requesting the students 'to go back to their studies'. However, the tensions grew and as police tried to prevent the protesters from marching onto Yangon from Latpadan, the protests became violent. Solidarity protests by students and civil society organisations near Sule Pya in Yangon were violently broken up by the police in March 2015. Figure 2.2 shows protesters running away from the police. The Government not only used police to control the protesters and manhandle them, but civilian thugs, who were recruited from poor areas, or who had recently been released from jail.

Figure 2.2 Education protests, 2015. Source: Author.

The riots resulted in the arrest of 127 students and students being beaten in the streets.

On 26 March 2014, the Upper House voted to accept amendments to the National Education Law, however, it did not agree to all of the changes that the students had demanded.[27] For example, whilst the students had insisted that 20 per cent of national spending should go to education, the law vowed to increase spending year on year, yet without the 20 per cent explicitly guaranteed. Part of the problem in agreeing the amendments of the law were the various competing drafts of the law that had been sent to Parliament. The students accused the Government of dishonesty as a draft that had allegedly been discarded at one of the quadripartite meetings was presented to the legislature. In June 2015, just 5 months before the elections, the revised Bill was voted into law, leaving many disillusioned and disappointed as they felt the Government had broken its promise.[28]

Key problems that were left for the NLD Government: Decentralisation

The CESR and the education law writing process did start to address some of Myanmar's main education issues, however, the Thein Sein Government was not able to deal with all problems, leaving some key issues unfinished and to be dealt with by the incoming NLD Government. One of the most important issues was decentralisation.

Myanmar's 2008 Constitution indicates that some level of decentralisation was to be expected, however, the legislative side of decentralisation in the education sector remained ambiguous, even after the reform process had started During the Thein Sein Government, there had been some announcements about re-distributing decision-making authority to the local, state and township levels, but these were ad hoc, incomplete and tentative. In education, there were some policy directives relating to decision-making capacity being placed at the local level: local setting of curriculum, hiring of primary school teachers, role of the newly appointed district education officers and responsibility for school construction contracts. A new administrative layer of District Offices was created, yet without clear directives as to how they would contribute to decentralisation. Conversations in 2014–5 with local officials across the country showed that no one at the local level seemed to be confident as to what these transfers of power actually meant and preferred not to 'rock the boat' lest they be punished by someone higher up for being overly ambitious. This was a key problem which was handed to the NLD.

The Framework for Social and Economic Reforms (FESR), the first document that gave some indication of a possible decentralisation framework, had indicated that the Government of Myanmar planned to work with a distributed (or de-concentrated) model of education management, albeit retaining: 'the budgetary controls over health and education expenditure for transitional adjustments, which may be a future subject of decision for fiscal decentralisation' (MoE, 2012: 34). At the time it was also unclear how far the de-concentrated education management model envisaged a role for non-state actors and stakeholders in achieving the government's key goals in basic education, despite the actual reality that non-state education was in effect already delivering education services in remote and conflict-affected areas (MoE, 2012: 29 – see also Chapter 7 of this volume):

> While the Government of Myanmar strengthens regulatory policies to streamline various private and community-run educational programs, it is also moving ahead with the decentralization of education management in line with the requirements of the Constitution by integrating locally-designed teaching curriculum as well as non-formal programs in basic education system. This reform policy and strategy will focus on the need to expand the system of basic education from eleven to twelve years, on child-centred teaching methodologies, upgrading teacher training and other curriculum reforms necessary to enhance the quality of basic education, on teacher remuneration and broader issues of education financing, on establishing a rigorous system for education quality assessment and performance, and on further reforms in the management of basic education including the importance of active engagement in the process by the parents themselves. In addition, the Government of Myanmar will also pay attention to other supportive measures that can address high drop-out rates and out of pocket cost burdens on families.

During the Thein Sein administration, the budgetary process proved to be an impediment to decentralisation as the funding made available to each school, and the control of expenditure, continued to be decided at ministerial level, regardless of local circumstances or needs. This tradition had led to a unique and strange situation where schools had to rely on local communities to provide the bulk of resources for financing expenditure within a centralised public school system.

Schools grants and stipends programme: The first step to autonomy for schools

One way forward towards limited decentralisation or 'de-concentration' was the establishment of two Union Government-funded direct-grant programmes to schools: the Student Stipends and School Grants, initiated in the 2012–3 school year. The key feature of this programme was that money was allocated to schools on the basis of a simple but transparent formula. The grants were required to be administered locally, and TEOs and head teachers were expected to take local decisions. The School Grants Programme aimed to improve the education quality, to reduce the amount of resources needed to be raised from communities, and to create a better teaching and learning environment for schools. This was to be done by creating a reliable and transparent flow of resources to schools, building capacity in schools to prepare budgets and develop school improvement plans, and to strengthen community participation in schools.

The first set of school grants, however, were provided to schools with defined expenditure categories, and the TEOs' responsibility was to audit these, potentially restricting the development of local decision-making capacity. Research in 2014 showed that schools could not necessarily meet their actual needs with the new money, although many hoped that in time things would become more flexible. Given that these direct grant programmes were the first foray of the Government of Myanmar into decentralisation, the WB decided to get involved in supporting, expanding and deepening the programme.[29]

The second programme for stipends was small both in terms of financing and the number of beneficiaries, although it was rolled out across the country. The aims of the stipends were to increase the rates of completion by levels of basic education, transition from primary level to middle school level and transition from middle school level to high school, and to reduce drop-out rates by offering stipends to students who found it difficult to continue their schooling. The beneficiary population was about 11,000 students nationally, only 2–6 students per township.[30] At the start, the stipend amounted to only USD 5 per month over 10 months for primary students, USD 6 per month for lower secondary students and USD 8 per month for upper secondary students. Schools were asked to select one or two of the poorest or most disadvantaged students in their school and submit these to the township education office for final selection. Priority was given to orphans or children who only had one parent who was not able to work. Conversations with head teachers in the first year of the project revealed how frustrating some of them found the process as it was a lot of paperwork for a very low chance of their students actually receiving the money. They felt there were many deserving students that should qualify and that the money on offer was simply inadequate. In fact, the Year 2, Phase 1 and Phase 2 Qualitative Assessment of the Myanmar School Grants and Stipends Programme showed how the roll-out of the programme had raised new issues at schools, many of which were related to equality and social justice. For example, in one area there were questions at the stipend training regarding whether the younger students of parents and older students who were White Card holders[31] were entitled to receive a stipend. Stipends were only allowed for Myanmar nationals, but given the ambiguous status of White Cards, the TEOs were uncertain and could not provide a definitive answer as to whether White Card holders were eligible or not. In one township, the TEO team decided all poor students should receive a stipend and did not exclude White Card holders. In other townships, the TEO teams asked the State Education Office (SEO) for further guidance, but received no reply. Subsequently, these TEO teams decided not to provide the stipend to the students whose parents were White Card holders. There were similar issues with regard to religion. In a township where approximately 30 per cent of the people residing in a particular ward identified as Muslim, and with approximately the same ratio of Muslim children in school, no student was selected to receive a stipend. Teachers attempted to explain that they were not eligible since most of them did not have a National Registration Card,[32] and those who did were not perceived as poor. Despite explanations of the rationale behind the selection process, most of the families felt dissatisfied with the whole process and thought it was simply a case of discrimination (Myint Zaw Soe et al., 2017: 13). The review of the programme also linked the inadequate staffing levels of TEOs to some of the issues faced by the programme, as staff did not feel they had enough time to work on the programmes due to this having been added to their already heavy regular workload (Myint Zaw Soe et al., 2017: 15). In addition, instructions from the central level to the township were often unclear or delayed (Myint Zaw Soe et al., 2017: 22): 'The lack of clarity was instrumental for confusing and/or delaying many aspects of the programs (e.g. participation in training, reimbursement of allowances, school grant transfers to monastic schools, delay in stipend fund transfers etc.)'

Despite all the issues noted above, it was the very first time that schools, head teachers and TEOs were able to take some limited decisions without ministerial approval, and this in itself felt like some (limited) empowerment. It should be remembered that both the school grants and the stipend programmes had come out of President Thein Sein's 10 points for education, with a view to improving matters related to disparity, poverty and social injustice. In actual fact, rather than doing much for the most disadvantaged and their schools, the programmes became the first vehicle for some form of decentralisation.

The WB has continued to support both direct grant programmes by channelling the funding through government coffers. In 2017, the Government invested USD 100 million in the school grants and stipend programme. School grants rose to a minimum of 800,000 MMK, equal to nearly USD 700 per school, and student stipends also increased. There was also an extension to the scholarship programmes, and to the scouts and girl guides programmes (Myint Zaw Soe et al., 2017). Today both the school grants[33] and the stipend programmes have expanded exponentially and the WB claims that some of the inequity issues seem to have been resolved.[34]

The NLD's 'new' education policy: How the NESP remained the NESP

Education policy under the NLD Government has really not changed much from that of the previous government, and is reflected in the National Education Strategic Plan (NESP) of 2016, launched by the NLD Government in February 2017, that is based on the previous government's draft National Education Sector Plan (NESP), that in turn had come out of the CESR. The main focus of the NESP remains on access, completion, quality and transparency and the main aims are 'equity, quality and relevance'. In order to achieve this, the plan proposes nine transformational shifts that are to be driven by the MoE (MoE, 2016).

Even the 'new' NESP has not been without its local critics. In a widely circulated letter entitled 'Comments on the National Education Strategic Plan (2016–21) of the Ministry of Education, Myanmar', Dr Thein Lwin, head of the NNER, lamented the fact that his organisation had not been invited to participate in the process of drafting the NESP 2016–2021, despite being part of the four-party meeting with the government in 2015 (Thein Lwin, 2017).[35] In fact, he reminded the Government that the original amendment of the education law had been achieved as part of this four-party meeting between the Government, Parliament, the Boycott Committee for Democratic Education and the NNER. The four-party group meeting had happened because of the students' protests for the amendment to the law. Dr Thein Lwin argued that: 'Since these events mark the historic movements in the history of Myanmar education system, the Ministry of Education should not ignore or overlook these historical events whether it likes or not.'[36] The NNER claims that it had no knowledge of the NESP 2016 until a consultant[37] to the Global Partnership for Education[38] met with the NNER in January 2017. Dr Thein Lwin's detailed analysis of the NESP focuses on how the planned reforms are unlikely to result in greater social justice for the broader Myanmar population and provides an excellent running commentary to main issues presented by the policy document. The NNER priorities remain the aims of the SDG 4 and the Indigenous Peoples' Rights to Education. Dr Thein Lwin argues[39] that the peace process and the education reform process need to be linked so that ethnic nationality communities (or indigenous people as he calls them) have a right to self-determination and their education systems – mainly organised by the EAOs – should be recognised:

> Myanmar has been one of the signatories to the United Nations Declaration on The Rights of Indigenous Peoples since 2007. As per the Declaration, it is a prerogative to recognize the schools established by the Indigenous Peoples, their local school curriculums, teachers and students. Since there is no recognition from the government, the students of the indigenous schools face difficulty in studying in the government's schools and national universities. (Thein Lwin, 2017: 2)

A third critique regards the need to develop a local curriculum rather than that solely developed by the central government, arguing that the cultural diversity of Myanmar can only be served if local curricula are included at school so as to reflect the local context:[40]

> Since the curriculum used in all the regions of Myanmar is made and produced by the central government alone, the curriculum is inordinately influenced by the culture and values of the curriculum developers. As a result of this curriculum, many students in the ethnic regions are not happy in the schools and leave before they complete the primary levels. (Thein Lwin, 2017: 2–3)

As before, the NNER also argues for MTB-MLE to improve achievement and attendance of ethnic children, as well as asking the government to teach ethnic languages during the school hours for equity reasons and so that families see that the government takes ethnic languages as seriously as other subjects. The commentary argues that leaving ethnic languages as after-school subjects results in poorer children, who have to help their parents, missing these classes.

> For those that fear 'which language to choose out of 135', there are ways and means to overcome this. In rural areas and hill regions, people of the same language mostly live together in the village. The language most familiar with children and used in the village can be used as the Mother Tongue, thereby Mother Tongue, Myanmar and English may be used as the medium of teaching in the school. Since children in the cities are familiar with Myanmar language, they may be taught in Myanmar language as Mother Tongue. For instance, if there are Karen and Burmese in one of the wards of Insein Township, children in their primary school can be taught in a tri-lingual education system in which Myanmar as Mother Tongue, Karen as second language and English as third language may be used (Thein Lwin, 2017: 3–4).

In addition, the NNER commentary complains that the examination remains summative, and that the curriculum method of teaching and examination all need to be changed. The document also reviews issues with teacher autonomy, the fact that students' unions are not yet allowed, and that children with disabilities do not yet have an equal right to education, as even with special provisions planned in certain areas this will not allow disabled children to study anywhere they want. Dr Thein Lwin concludes that whilst quality of education is the driving force of the NESP: 'the quality set by the Center (*sic*) is not in line with the needs of local context, people and individuals' (Thein Lwin, 2017: 6).

The chapter now turns to the changes made by the NLD Government in education based on the NESP, exploring if Dr Thein Lwin's assessment is correct.

New and revised structures to support the MoE in the reform process

In February 2016, the NLD Government set up two new parliamentary committees to support Education. The Pyithu Hluttaw Education Promotion Committee (Lower House) was set up to provide support for the following:

> ... to develop the education promotion function; to support to improve public education and to support to implement modernized education with right concept, good behavior and critical thinking to contribute in the state building process.[41]

The Amyotha Hluttaw Education Promotion Committee (Upper House) had the same responsibilities but additionally included the following:

> ... supporting every child to complete basic education and lifelong-learning process, supporting reforming pedagogy system of teacher, supporting reforming curriculum and examination systems, supporting to make sure sufficient school infrastructure, teaching aids and deployment of teachers and supporting teachers to access sufficient social welfare.[42]

It is unclear why the Upper House Committee has responsibilities that have some bearing on social justice, such as supporting all children to complete their education and supporting teachers to access social welfare, when the Lower House of Parliament has a more limited brief.[43]

Part of taking over the government meant that the NLD had the freedom to revise ministerial structures. In education, they did this by merging the MoE and Ministry of Science and Technology in August 2016. This resulted in the establishment of a new Department of Alternative Education; merging other departments to create a new Department of Education Research, Planning and Training (DERPT) and abolishing the Department of Teacher Education and Training – the responsibilities of which will be split between the DERPT and the Department of Higher Education. According to a recent report, the MoE has an estimated 670,000 positions with up to 55 per cent of total allotted staff member positions remaining unfilled (MoE and Quality Basic Education Programme, 2016). The report also showed a disparity between male and female employees: 'While females make up 61 per cent of the sampled workforce, they currently occupy 25 per cent of filled executive level positions' (GoM and DFAT, 2017: 11).

The MoE was also able to create new structures and institutions as had been laid out in the National Education Law 2014 and the 2015 Amendments. The National Education Policy Commission (NEPC) was established first in September 2016 as a statutory body to provide education policies for 'the promotion of national development'. The NEPC has 21 academic and educationist members from various education sectors to provide practical education policies for the attainment of the national education objectives, to advise on how to achieve quality education accessible to all, and to provide policy recommendations so that Myanmar can achieve 'international standards and develop human resources for a knowledge based economy and society'. The NEPC was designed to have an executive role in advising and coordinating HE policy and legislation in the form of Myanmar's 30-year Long-term Education Development Plan as well as coordinating with development partners (Channon, 2017). The NEPC also oversees the National Curriculum Committee (NCC), the National Accreditation and Quality Assurance Committee (NAQAC) and the Rectors' Committee (RC)

The NCC was formed in November 2016 with 15 members to develop and review curricula so that they met international standards. The NAQAC, formed in January 2017, is composed of 20 members focusing on developing and implementing a comprehensive quality assurance system as well as assessing and providing accreditation to educational institutions and programmes. Finally, the RC, formed just over a year later in April 2018, has as members all rectors and principals of public HEIs. It also has a Central Committee of 44 members and a Central Executive Committee of 15 members elected from among its members. It is meant to coordinate the affairs of HEIs, help to enhance the quality of teaching, research and management in HEIs, give guidance to HEIs in the transition to autonomy and provide advice to HEIs for increasing revenues to support their development.

These four institutions are meant to support the MoE in delivering the reforms by bringing in non-ministerial experienced staff, but the MoE remains the main government institution that is responsible for delivering the nine transformational shifts on which the NESP is based.

Role of the development partners and aid money post-2015

With the NLD government in power after 2015, the role of the development partners was to change. Under the Thein Sein Government, the primary guidance for the development partners' aid had been the FESR, which framed the government's priorities across the whole economy. The new government, however, did not adopt an overarching framework for the country's development, and focused instead on defining strategy at the sectoral level. The NLD started to reorganise donor structures to provide more effective support to the reform processes. In the first instance, the Education Sector Coordination Committee (ESCC) developed Terms of

Reference (ToR) to clarify memberships of the various working groups and their roles and responsibilities, in order to better align with government policies. The ToR specified that it was for the government to lead on the reform agenda, and that the government owned the change process. The ToR also noted that there needed to be systematic measurement and accountability for results, inclusive partnerships with stakeholders at national, sub-national and school/community levels, greater transparency, knowledge sharing and learning, and sustained emphasis on capacity building at all levels of education service delivery. The ESCC started to meet in February 2017. Other development partner-related structures included the JESWG, the Education Thematic Working Group (ETWG) and sub-national education coordination groups. The JESWG had been in existence since 2012 and remained responsible for high-level dialogue between government and development partners, and included government, INGO and representatives of development partners. The ETWG that had existed since 2009 was named as an inclusive and neutral forum for consultation and advocacy, providing technical and policy expertise with over 400 members from government, CSOs and NGOs. At the time of writing, the ETWG had eight sub-working groups. The sub-national education coordination groups that had been in place since 2015 were now there to promote coordination between the government, development partners and non-state actors at sub-national level (starting in Mon and Karen states).

This was also the time that UNICEF's Quality Basic Education Programme – QBEP Phase 2 – started to come to an end, changing the relationship between development partners and the government as UNICEF was no longer to hold the monopoly on coordinating education reform programmes. Phase 2 of QBEP, mentioned at the start of this chapter, was a 4-year (2012–6), USD 76.6 million joint Myanmar MDEF[44] and MoE effort to strengthen the provision, quality and administration of government basic education. The QBEP programmes supported education reform before the NESP brought in the nine transformational shifts. This included capacity building and providing direct education services in 34 selected disadvantaged townships (UNICEF, 2017) including a programme for in-service teacher training based in schools (SITE) that is reviewed in Chapter 5 of this volume as well as Child Friendly Schools and the Language Enrichment Programme, discussed briefly below.

As the development partners remained involved, their role and their influence started to change. One of the new priorities has been the support of development partners to help transform the MoE. As has been seen above, the MoE's ways of working have been defined by decades of centralisation, with officials not empowered to make their own decisions. In order to transform Myanmar's education system, a change in working style and structure is needed. As part of supporting this aspect of the process, different development partners have offered targeted support to the MoE to try to change the ways in which the Ministry and its staff work. In October 2017, the MoE established a Capacity Development Fund (CDF), in partnership with DANIDA (the development arm of Denmark's Ministry of Foreign Affairs) to strengthen MoE systems and build human resource capacity. The key challenge that was identified was the limited professional training programmes for new and existing staff that were needed to strengthen human resource development. In order to enhance capacity of senior managers to be able to support the NESP implementation, as well as strengthen the effectiveness of existing systems and procedures at national and sub-national levels, the CDF project put in place an 'Education Management Training Programme' that included critical thinking and management seminars, as well as the development of a Diploma in Education Management to be delivered by the Yangon University of Education (with the support of the University College London's Institute of Education). Figure 2.3 shows some of this training in NPT. The idea behind this project was that senior staff of the

Figure 2.3 Leadership and management seminars for informed decision making for the Ministry of Education, 2019. Source: Author.

MoE, including Director Generals (DGs) and Deputy Director Generals (DDGs) would get the kind of training required that would not have been available previously from Myanmar's un-reformed HE system. The CDF and others also arranged for ICT and English training for more junior staff as part of a general capacity building programme.

In May 2018, the Government joined the Global Partnership for Education (GPE), which supports countries in the drafting and implementation of quality sector plans, and has a particular focus on equity, learning and efficiency. In line with GPE requirements, the MoE and development partners commissioned an independent appraisal of the NESP. The appraisal identified a number of areas for improvement, including further work in developing and implementing the NESP monitoring and evaluation (GoM and DFAT, 2017: 10). The MoE has traditionally been focused on numbers rather than outcomes or standards, and monitoring and evaluation are relatively new concepts. Monitoring and evaluation has now been formalised at the MoE through a dedicated department, which has, however, struggled with its mandate.[45] Australia's DFAT-funded 'My-Equip Quality Improvement Programme'[46] is the programme that aims to support the MoE in developing systems to measure education quality and evidence-based planning. As a part of this, it supports the Monitoring and Evaluation Department to develop and implement an education quality improvement system that assesses performance of education services against indicators and quality standards, produces outputs to inform decision making, and enables learning and continuous improvement in the sector. The aim is to fill knowledge gaps – including quality assurance, monitoring, evaluation and research. The project's focus according to DFAT is on building capacity, systems and a culture in which decision makers are empowered to make decisions within their level based on evidence (GoM and DFAT, 2017). Linked with this is the UNESCO-supported MoE's EMIS, including work on data collection and reporting systems. The UNESCO Cap-Ed programme[47] also provides broader capacity development training and support on education sector planning and budgeting.

Other large development partner projects include UNESCO's Strengthening Pre-service Teacher Education in Myanmar (STEM), discussed further in Chapter 5 of this volume. A new national Teacher Competency and Standards Framework had been written in 2016 as part of STEM. The Teacher Competency and Standards Framework has articulated for the first time what is expected of teachers in their professional practice at various stages in their professional development. The work of STEM is continuing with a focus on teacher empowerment through the UNESCO pre-service teacher education project by developing the curriculum for the new Early Childhood degree. This work has been on-going since 2015–6, starting with a review of the curriculum used in education colleges and the subsequent development of a curriculum framework for a competency-based curriculum for a four-year degree programme, with primary and middle school teacher specialisation tracks.[48]

In the summer of 2019, DFID began the five-year Myanmar–UK Partnership for Education (MUPE) programme that addresses some of the interrelated issues in the education reform process. The five components focus on strengthening English and teacher education, assessment and education reform support, education provided by monastic and ethnic education providers, and education in conflict-affected areas, including Rakhine.

The development partners agree that the whole education system needs a quality shift and are pouring support directly into the MoE and developing large programmes that feed into the NESP priorities. However, at the time of writing, the various departments of the MoE no longer seem to have the capacity to absorb more funds and training, in part, because there are not enough staff, but also because too much is being done at the same time and everyone is attempting to work on everything simultaneously.[49]

Reforms to basic education

The reforms to basic education (from KG to Grade 11) are numerous and complex. They include access (including through alternative education for out-of-school children), formalising a KG year and moving to 12-year schooling. The new basic education structure of KG+12 (kindergarten plus 12 years) was introduced for the Academic Year (AY) 2016–7. The previous education structure (5–4–2) (Grades 1–5 for primary level, Grades 6–9 for lower secondary level and Grades 10–11 for upper secondary level) was transformed into the KG+ (5–4–3) structure with an extra year of schooling for upper secondary level. Under the Thein Sein Government, the number of schools and students had increased dramatically: rising from 39,398 basic education schools and 7,776,148 students in the AY 2007–8, to 43,181 basic education schools and 8,597,348 students in the AY 2013–4.[50] As more schools have opened around the country, more teachers have been appointed to reduce the teacher-to-student ratio In rural and remote areas, university graduates who were residents of these regions were appointed as primary school teachers in 2013 and 2014: 53,975 more basic education teachers, 2,233 more HE teachers and 534 more teacher trainers were appointed in the AY 2015–6 than in the AY 2011–2. Some teachers for government schools were also recruited from the monastic schools as they had classroom experience.

In 2016, a development partner meeting[51] reviewed the results of the massive new hiring of teachers that had resulted in them making up around 40 per cent of all the primary school teachers. Most of the new teachers had been hired as Daily Wage Teachers (DWTs) but were then converted to permanent staff after a month's training. The new teachers had strikingly different background characteristics compared to experienced teachers. The (unpublished) data reported at the meeting noted that only 32 per cent of new teachers had an education degree or higher, compared to 96 per cent of experienced teachers; 21 per cent of new teachers had DWT diplomas and 8 per cent had no teacher training qualifications which means that across the board they had limited pedagogical training. However, a large number of new teachers had the one-year Certificate of Education offered by the education colleges, which qualified them to teach at primary level. The new teachers tended to work in the most remote schools where they had limited access to support and other professional development.[52] They were also much more likely to be obliged to teach multi-grade. This is a unique disadvantage in terms of teaching workload and pedagogical difficulty, especially in challenging areas. A further study into the effects of DWTs entitled: 'Having at least 5 teachers at every school' revealed that the hiring of DWTs at primary level had improved the teacher-to-student ratios. Traditionally teacher-to-student ratios were lower in urban areas and larger in remote and rural areas, and that the large number of new teachers did improve numbers around the country. However, the study alleges that the hiring of DWTs allowed more experienced senior teachers at primary schools to move to the centre of townships or allowed them to transfer to middle school and high schools where the numbers increased to 12,103 (17.4 per cent) and 4,741 (16.4 per cent) respectively (Muta, 2015). So while the massive input of DWTs in 2014 diminished the regional disparity in the teacher-to-student ratio, the disparity in the teachers' quality remained unresolved. Even though DWTs are supposed to have a bachelor's degree or matriculation pass (depending on the state/region), they have not had adequate pedagogical training and in general they do not have experience as teachers. They are expected to be trained by senior teachers on the job, so if there are only a limited number of senior teachers in the school, such training is impossible and the only teaching method new DWTs can rely on is to repeat what they observed when they were primary school students.

The reforms also include overhauling the curriculum and the examinations system as well as training teachers in a new pedagogy to be able to deliver the new curriculum and prepare the students for the new examinations system in order to improve quality.[53] This is bound to be complex – the QBEP 2 evaluation of the Child Friendly Schools and the Language Enrichment Programme reminds us that many elements need to fall into place for teachers to be able to change their practice. In the QBEP final evaluation, Emily Stenning (UNICEF, 2018) concludes that there are three main reasons teachers did not change their behaviour and these are as follows:

- The training is not long or frequent enough, with teachers not being able to practice to make behaviour change sustainable.
- External, environmental factors have not been taken into account and pose significant barriers. These can include infrastructural constraints such as partitioned rooms (noise), immovable furniture, crammed classrooms, insufficient teaching aids as well as socio-economic constraints such as language barrier (multi-lingual classes), parental resistance and large teacher-to-student ratios.
- System constraints included teacher transfers and lack of time.

The QBEP programme did not seem to have resulted in sustained change, and therefore the next phase of reforms would require some joined up thinking across the MoE and development partners.

Most at the MoE will agree that the quality shift expected by the NESP is substantial. The issue is that some of the changes have been hampered by the interrelated nature of the system; for example, to implement a more child-centred approach to education requires both different teacher training and a reformed examination system that does not rely on rote learning – as well as more teachers teaching smaller class sizes in better equipped classrooms.[54] This is why the lessons learnt as part of the QBEP evaluation are so important.

One of the main reforms to basic education are the changes to the curriculum and textbook content, led by JICA under the 'Project for Curriculum Reform at Primary Level of Basic Education (CREATE)' that began in May 2014.[55] This has been the first major curriculum revision in 20 years and involved 40 Japanese and overseas curriculum experts as well as over 60 Myanmar academics. The textbooks were reviewed and approved by the National Curriculum Committee. The new primary education curriculum now comprises nine subjects: Myanmar, English, mathematics, science, social studies, morality and civics, life skills, physical education and arts (performing arts and visual arts). In 2017, the new Grade 1 curriculum and its textbooks, developed jointly by the MoE and JICA, were introduced into schools. The announcement by the Ministry of Foreign Affairs (MoFA) stated that: 'approximately 1.3 million new Grade 1 primary school students across the country will learn with the new textbooks. [...] The textbooks are colorful with many pictures and designed in a way that learning is fun and linked with students' life' (JICA, 2017a). The project also developed a detailed teachers' guide for each subject that helps teachers move away from using rote learning. In preparation for the introduction of the new Grade 1 curriculum, JICA supported a series of cascade training courses, which were conducted by the MoE for education officers from townships, districts and states/regions, as well as ministerial officials from the concerned departments at the central level. Following this, nationwide in-service teacher training (INSET) was conducted to introduce the new curriculum to teachers and JICA claims that through the INSET, all primary teachers who teach Grade 1 from all schools, including monastic schools, private schools and other schools that use the government curriculum were trained (JICA, 2017a). The JICA CREATE MTR acknowledges the 'hindering factors' (Mizuno et al., 2019: 15) that included the role of teachers and the difficulties faced by them. It states that although head teachers were recognised as key in supporting teachers in rolling out the curriculum and materials, some head teachers did not attend the introduction training. This was particularly the case for head teachers of the high and middle schools with primary level sections, as the training clashed with the Grade 6 training for secondary schools. The JICA report also states that teachers complained of a number of barriers in using the new curriculum. These included insufficient time to prepare the lessons, teaching subjects they had no training in – such as performing arts, especially playing the flute and singing songs in front of their students, and visual arts 'because teachers by themselves are sometimes poor in drawing and painting'.[56] But the main issue seems to have been the cascade training (Mizuno et al., 2019: 16), where the lower the cascade, the thinner the transmission of the concepts required for the new curriculum, with teachers struggling to understand and use the new materials.[57] Interviews conducted by JICA with teachers revealed that some head teachers were not supportive, specifically with regard to preparing the new lessons and that teachers worried about less able students falling behind in the group work. They also felt the level of the Grade 1 maths textbook was too high for some students who were unable to read it. (Mizuno et al., 2019: 18–21) This presumably means more time is spent for the teacher to make sure all students keep up with the work.

In its review, JICA did not look at the effects of the new assessment system. The Oxford Policy Management (OPM) team conducted the only review of how the new formative and summative assessment system is affecting teachers (OPM, 2019). The head teachers and serving teachers were affected differently with head teachers questioning 'the presence of a coherent strategic vision and plan' and the lack of clarity with regard to the roll-out of the new examination system causing confusion (OPM, 2019: i–iii). It seems that rapid changes have resulted in parallel systems in the same school, which means that some teachers are teaching both the old and the new curricula with both pedagogies depending on which class they were teaching. The head teachers confirmed that teachers did not have sufficient training to implement the new skills that were required both with regard to teaching and assessment and therefore rote learning prevailed.[58] Large class sizes continued to impede the use of group discussions and other types of child-centred interactions. Other barriers included extra work for teachers to support students who failed Grade 5 exams (that also clashes with the requirement that all students should pass) and the changing of the grading system from percentage scores to grades (A, B, C, D) that do not allow for comparisons between students (and is unpopular with parents). The OPM field notes[59] give an insight into how teachers feel about the new examination system. While many like the new system as it motivates the creativity of students, teachers are worried because they do not feel they have the pedagogical skills to use the new approach. Teachers complained that the training sessions were too short and did not really help them in teaching the new content or teaching in a more child-centred way, especially when they had a large class size. (OPM, 2019: 38). All teachers interviewed by OPM said they needed further training on how to teach the new curriculum courses. The teachers also felt that they were unable to conduct classroom assessment on individual students due to the lack of experience with the new system. 'For Grade 3 and Grade 6 new curriculum teachers, trained skills and experiences are very limited to two-week assignment/project work and so teachers are not able to apply it very effectively in classroom practices. In primary classes, a class teacher is responsible for all subjects and it highlights that a single teacher cannot perform classroom assessment on all subjects for individual students' (OPM,

2019: 42). This points to the problem that teachers have not been trained in how to collect individual student information on achievement in very large classes across various subjects (OPM, 2019: 43). The lack of assessment training also means that teachers have a lack of knowledge on how to develop tests and how to use criteria and standards to evaluate students.

An official at the JICA Yangon office explained that at the base of JICA's overall education strategy for Myanmar was employment,[60] and that foundational capacity development was very important. The overall aim for CREATE was better learning in the classroom along with supporting students to lead a happier life through holistic development. The official explained that it was unusual for JICA to engage with all subjects, as they usually only focus on maths and the sciences. The content development was influenced not only by the Japanese curriculum but also by various ASEAN curricula. The three impact surveys that were shared showed improvements in learning, especially in mathematics, but parents apparently are complaining that children no longer recite what they have learnt in school and so they are worried that they are not learning anything. This shows a move away from the scourge of rote learning – a positive improvement if this can be sustained, but it also means that parents need to be brought on board to support the changes and make them sustainable. The effects on parents, how they view the reforms and what barriers they might experience do not seem to have been examined systematically. Clearly, a longer school path of 12 years will increase expenses. Presumably, the new curriculum and assessment system will also mean a change in the parental role as parental involvement in education will become more important than previously (exacerbating urban, rural and class divides). Parents, especially those from disadvantaged backgrounds and less educated, do not get involved in homework or in supporting their children's learning. Parental involvement in Myanmar is primarily about parents supporting the school materially if something needs to be fixed. The OPM report 2019 explains: 'Parents can help or hinder the transition. They express support for the aims of developing higher order skills, but are not engaged properly on issues of teaching methods and they can often be reluctant to risk poorer grades for their children by trying new things' (OPM, 2019: ii). Parents do seem mostly positive as they reported that they hope the new curriculum will allow their children to choose a career path based on their interests but some were apprehensive that those children that did not master reading and writing in KG would face difficulties in all subsequent years. The OPM research team also spoke to students who reported that teachers and parents still encouraged rote learning and teaching and assessment remained textbook based.

Rote learning, formative assessment and parental involvement are not Myanmar's only problems with the new curriculum. Issues of discriminatory content *vis-à-vis* different ethnic groups was discussed in Chapter 1 of this volume and it would be interesting to see if the curricular reforms have altered the content with regard to identity, equality and citizenship. The first study on this was undertaken by Rose Metro who examined the KG–Grade 3 textbooks and compared them to the previous curriculum, and shared her findings at a conference in NPT in 2019.[61] Metro argues that the reforms were an opportunity to rethink how national identity is defined in Myanmar: 'who is at the center, who is on the periphery, and where the boundary falls between national races and foreigners'(Metro, 2019: 1). Whilst arguing that there is now a more inclusive focus on non-Burman and non-Buddhist groups in the new textbooks, the Burman Buddhist identities still remain at the centre of what is taught as Myanmar's national identity. As before, all the heroes in the social studies books remain Burman Buddhist military men. Metro points out that they are referred to as 'Myanmar', which 'is supposed to include all the Eight National Races, but in practice it is often used to mean Burman'(Metro, 2019: 7). Metro reports that there has been some progress in 'Morality and Civics' texts (Metro, 2019: 8–9):

> Although light-skinned Burman Buddhist military leaders are centered in the curriculum, they are situated within a discourse that purports to be inclusive. First, offensive content – for instance, a poem insulting people of 'mixed blood' (Su Myat Mon, 2019) – is not present. Second, children are often instructed to tolerate each other's differences. For instance, they are told to accept people of any ethnicity, religion, or place ('*lumyo batha neya*'.) (Third Grade Morality and Civics, 38). One poem compares the national races to 'blood relations' (Third Grade Morality and Civics, 56). In a notable and welcome departure from previous textbooks, children are even asked open-ended questions that allow them to self-identify and identify the ethnicities of others: 'Who are the ethnic groups in your area?' (First Grade Morality and Civics, 59). Finally, science textbooks do mention that human skin tone and hair texture vary (First Grade Science, 23), and a poem cautions against discrimination based on skin color (Third Grade Morality and Civics, 3).

Nevertheless, non-Burman ethnicities are never the protagonists and remain on the periphery as they are only mentioned when they support the Burmans. Metro points to a few instances of inclusivity where the Pwo Karen language is mentioned, or a church or a Kachin Manao pole is shown in a picture (Metro, 2019: 10). Individual ethnic groups are not mentioned, only the term Myanmar is used. This, however, also erases the independent histories of other groups and more importantly whitewashes ethnic conflict: 'King Bayinnaung fights against nameless enemies (in fact, the Mon) at the Battle of Naungyo' (Third Grade Social Studies, 57, as cited in Metro, 2019). 'By leaving out ethnic identifiers, in what may be a well-intentioned attempt to downplay conflict, history is sanitized in a way that glosses over the contributions and histories of non-Burmans' (Metro, 2019: 11). Outsiders, such as people of Indian or Chinese origin who have lived in Myanmar for generations are still not mentioned (Metro, 2019: 12).

Whilst the changes with regard to national identity are a positive step, they do not yet seem to go far enough. There is also a question of the role of the teachers and how far the changes in teacher training will address such issues – something which remains unclear (see Chapter 5 of this volume). As Higgins et al. found, teachers sometimes view the exclusive and sectarian approach of identity as normal, as that is what they were taught: 'Aligning with such viewpoints on the function of history, teachers implicitly present themselves as guardians of their culture' (Higgins et al., 2016: 121). Civil society groups have also voiced concerns. In December 2018, more than 120 civil society groups sent an open letter to President U Win Myint to urge a review of the curriculum for primary school civics classes, claiming that it supported ethnic and religious discrimination (Su Myat Mon, 2019). The letter claimed that the civics education curriculum seemed to be an: 'attempt to indoctrinate the innocent minds of children with discriminatory practices' and contradicted Section 348 of the 2008 Constitution, that prohibits discrimination on the grounds of race, birth, religion, official position, status, culture, sex and wealth. According to an interview conducted by the newspaper *Frontier* anti-hate speech campaigner Ma Zar Chi Oo, the discriminatory language she had heard was not in a student textbook but came from a guide for teachers which had been read to the class. She suggested that this was deliberate, to make it harder to prove what was being taught to the children was questionable. It is clear that curricular and textbook content reforms still have some way to go to be truly inclusive of all groups so as to underpin a more equal society.

NESP mid-term review

The NESP, as has been established above, has been the guiding policy document of the education reform process. Reaching its half-way point in the summer of 2019, a MTR was undertaken to allow for a re-prioritisation and some streamlining of programmes within the MoE. A data gap analysis workshop was conducted by UNESCO to inform the MTR in April 2019 prior to its start, and officials from each MoE Department at the Union level and all State/Regional Departments contributed to this workshop. This gap analysis focused on all nine transformational shifts, identifying if data was available to establish how far the 93 outcome indicators outlined in the NESP were progressing. The MoE Data Gap Analysis report established that: '… in many cases, even where implementation has significantly progressed, information to measure outcome level indicators may not be available to provide evidence of achievement'(MoE, 2019a: 5). Part of the exercise was to shift the MoE from looking at what had been done to what had actually been achieved. However, the lack of baseline data meant that it was difficult for the MTR to show what progress had been made over time (MoE, 2019a: 54). Another issue raised at the workshop was that of responsibility and data format: 'In many of the discussions with departments, it was not clear with whom the responsibility for monitoring activities lie. […] In some cases, monitoring does take place, but the data is often not in the correct format to review progress' (MoE, 2019a: 55).

An MTR reference group that included development partners (chaired by Dr Aye Myint), a MTR team and a ministerial MTR team were established. Independent consultants organised by DFAT reviewed the work of the various departments in light of the NESP, focusing on what had been achieved at the mid-way point. The process nevertheless remained led by the MoE. Interviews with the development partners and the MoE in September 2019 showed that a rift had started to emerge, with development partners getting increasingly frustrated at their lack of influence. One issue was the late submission of the inception report by the MoE that did not allow development partners to comment in time before the actual MTR process started.

Amongst the development partners' respondents there was some concern as the MTR was not seen as a research-driven process and they expected it to be more anecdotal as opposed to data driven. One of the Australian consultants complained[62] that she was given no access, not much information, and then told that the site visits she undertook could not be used in her report. She felt the MTR was a checklist of activities that had been undertaken rather than a report of what progress these activities had contributed to. It seems that the MTR went off track because it was initially not meant to be an evaluation, rather a way of establishing areas that the MoE needed to focus on, although in the inception workshop the issues of efficiency and effectiveness emerged. The MTR inception report (MoE, 2019b: 10) notes that: 'the MTR will examine the NESP against the standard criteria associated with relevance, effectiveness, and efficiency. It will validate and supplement the data collected from key informant interviews and focus group discussions, observations, literature review, and a Strengths, Weaknesses, Opportunities and Threats (SWOT) analysis'. In that same report, the main purposes of the MTR were described as follows:

> ... management – to enable the MoE to make evidence-based decisions on priorities, resources, direction, and strategy going forward; accountability – to ensure alignment with relevant policies, procedures, programming decisions, expenditure, and to ensure these are clearly understood by funders and relevant stakeholders; and learning – to learn about what has worked well and less well and how to improve the implementation of the NESP. (MoE, 2019b: 10)

The MoE respondents interviewed in 2019 insisted the process had been data driven, not least through the submission of the Annual Progress Reviews (APRs) and other data that had been requested by the consultants that they say they provided. In fact, the increased use of data does need to be commended. The new department responsible for monitoring and evaluation led by Director General Dr Sai has produced two APRs for 2016–7 and 2017–8, the first of their kind.[63] According to the APR 2018 text, the MoE has developed a new management system called the 'Annual Planning and Budget Estimate Cycle' to provide senior ministry officials with more accurate and timely performance to inform decisions on priority activities for the next ministry annual budget (MoE, 2018: 8). In addition, departmental monitoring and evaluation plans, annual budgets and outputs, evaluation reports and performance reports all feed into this new annual publication. Dr Sai said in an interview[64] that the APR reports allow the MoE to share education information widely across the various stakeholders at state and region level, making them a bigger part of the reform process. These two reports are indeed an impressive achievement, especially in a country where previously such data was not available.

The MTR inception report states that the MTR is also due to review issues of inclusion and equality to see if: 'the MoE and its key stakeholders are doing the right things and doing things right' within the context of the SDGs' (MoE, 2019b: 7). The section mentions both the economic disparities between communities as well as the effect of conflict on ethnic children as follows:

> ... the impressive conditions of the economy and improvements in living standards mask deep fissures in terms of inclusion, equity and vulnerabilities between urban and rural settings, across regions, and along ethnic lines. The Multidimensional Index of Disadvantage records stark spatial diversity of disadvantage, exemplified by nearly two thirds of households in Rakhine and Kayin being disadvantaged in at least five different aspects of disadvantageousness; intra-state variations in disadvantage at Township levels; rural populations being more than twice as likely to experience multiple disadvantages as compared to urban populations; and 84 per cent of the population experiencing disadvantage in at least one indicator. [...] Ongoing conflicts and ethnic tensions have led to displacement of the ethnic populations and economic disenfranchisement, and have severely impacted the peacebuilding processes ushered in with the National Ceasefire Agreement (NCA), signed between the government and the Ethnic Armed Organisations. Significantly, the persistence of conflict has disrupted education opportunities for children in these areas. (MoE, 2019b: 6)

The report goes on to acknowledge the real progress that has been made across the country with primary enrolment rates at over 90 per cent, but notes the following three challenges (MoE, 2019b: 7):

- Most children are under-prepared for school, with only 20 per cent having access to early childhood education prior to enrolment in primary school, and this under-preparedness has an early impact on learning and an early educational divide.
- Low quality of primary provision with under-resourced schools and low-paid teachers utilising outdated teaching methods.
- Extremely low transition rates from primary to secondary school, with only 10 per cent of children who commenced primary school successfully completing upper secondary education.

The MoE recognises that the low transition rates result in children not in school needing different pathways to complete their education, and has made this a priority as part of the equitable educational access for all (MoE, 2019b: 8). Other aspects showing an awareness of inclusion in the MTR process was the addition of gender[65] as a category beyond the adopted Organisation for Economic Cooperation and Development (OECD) evaluation framework,[66] and an adequate coverage of rural areas across the two data collection phases including district and township level stakeholders in Sittwe, Mandalay, Lashio, Myitkyina and Mawlamyine (MoE, 2019b: 14).

The MTR final report that was circulated in February 2020, covers all the main chapter headings of the NESP.[67] It explains that the reforms to basic education are complex and ambitious, because they involve many large-scale activities occurring simultaneously including infrastructure projects and the development and roll-out of the new curriculum, as well as changes to pedagogy and assessment, underpinned by reform in teacher capacity building. 'At the time of this review, it is difficult to gauge the overall effectiveness of these profound changes to embed and systemise new educational practice and improve student learning. Each intervention is interrelated requiring sustained investment and time before systematic gains in student learning are evident' (MoE, 2020: ix). The new curriculum moves Myanmar teaching away from rote learning and hopes to increase student engagement and performance, but requires teachers to have the capabilities to deliver this. 'The new curriculum also reflects society's need for citizens capable of learning how to learn, applying critical thinking, communication and creativity and possess a core of knowledge and skills in technical and academic areas' (MoE, 2020: ix). It was expected that the MTR would allow the MoE to focus on priority areas rather than trying to change everything at once; and at the same time allowing the MoE to reflect on which departments need what kind of support and perhaps engage with the development partners in a more strategic way. The MTR final report's list of priority recommendations for basic education in the NESP 2019–21 does not really do this, but recognises that more time is needed for the transformational shifts to embed. 'The combined reform across all the Basic Education Transformational Shifts is planned to be implemented over a period of at least 10 years in order to become fully established in schools across the country' (MoE, 2020: xii).

Conclusion

Returning to Iris Young's framework of social justice discussed in the Introduction, and reviewing how far the education reforms at the MoE and within basic education are allowing the Myanmar government to deliver on its manifesto promises, it is crucial to mention that the policy documents all engage with issues of marginalisation and inclusion. This includes the NEP MTR final report that acknowledges: 'There is a lack of awareness about inclusivity combined with limited capacity to implement inclusive practices at the school level' and 'Limited quality data to understand and address equity and inclusion issues' (MoE, 2020: viii). The MTR includes a full chapter on disparities and specifically mentions rural poor populations, children living in conflict affected areas, children with disabilities and children whose mother tongue is not Burmese as particularly disadvantaged, especially with regard to access to education. The MTR acknowledges that Gender Equality and Social Inclusion (GESI) has not been integrated across all nine Transformational Shifts of the NESP. To remedy the disparities and shift attitudes, the MTR suggests collaborations across ministries and with civil society organisations to develop targeted interventions and awareness campaigns at school and community levels. However, it is unclear how the MoE is to take these suggestions forward.

The emerging problem is not a lack of understanding of Myanmar's social justice issues, rather it seems to lie in the policy–practice gap, raising questions as to why what is acknowledged in policy fails to translate into planned changes on the ground. This is particularly the case with regard to the reforms of the curriculum content where there is improvement, but as of yet cultural differences are erased rather than supported, and where equality between the national races is not yet part of the education discourse, certain forms of 'cultural imperialism' remain. Structures are a key part of the problem; the lack of decentralisation means that schools, teachers and other education workers remain powerless, and dependent on the MoE decisions in NPT. It seems that part of the problem are the hierarchical structures, cultural traditions and the top-down nature of the reforms that do not allow the stakeholders to question or shape the changes, in effect, reinforcing rather than resolving inequalities. The relationship between the MoE and the development partners is also increasingly problematic, and it is unclear in how far rolling out the reforms promote mutuality, recognition and respect between stakeholders.

Notes

1. Renamed 'National Education Strategic Plan' (still 'NESP') by the NLD government after 2016. Under the President Thein Sein Government until 2015 it was the 'Sector Plan' and under the NLD after 2016 it became the 'Strategic Plan'. But the acronym remains NESP.
2. The author was special education advisor to AusAID in Myanmar at the time, therefore accessing both the MoE–CESR staff as well as the international agencies.
3. See: World Bank, 2018a. Government expenditure on education, total (% of GDP) – Myanmar 2017. According to the WB (2018a: 2): 'Public funding for education significantly increased in recent years, going from MMK 310 billion (about USD 200 million equivalent) in 2011–2 to more than MMK 2,177 million (about USD 1.4 billion equivalent) in 2018–9, but remains considerably lower than in neighbouring and comparator countries […] as a percentage of GDP (at around 2.2 per cent)'.
4. Under President Thein Sein (i.e. between 2012 and 2015), teachers received a pay rise and more teachers were recruited from the monastic sector to make up for teacher shortages, accounting for much of this expenditure increase.
5. The poverty line was defined as 376,151 MMK/year (1,030 MMK/day) in 2010 (IHLCA Project Technical Unit 2011: 6).
6. This probably includes language issues for ethnic children who do not speak Burmese.
7. IHLCA Survey responses (2011) suggest at least 12 per cent repetition in Grade 1.
8. All figures are from a MoE document by U Ko Lay Win and Chris Spohr (no date). Myanmar's Comprehensive Education Sector Review (CESR): Statistics for Evidence-Based Policy and Planning. Unpublished.
9. Data provided by UNICEF at a meeting the author attended on 10 September 2015, showed: 35.72 per cent of children aged 5–17 do not attend school. This is the equivalent of 4.5 million children nationally.
10. Families never have a 'lack of interest' in education. They only say they are not interested if they do not see any point in getting educated – i.e. if the pathways to a better life through employment are in effect not determined by staying and doing well at school.
11. Background information from DFID (no date). Terms of Reference – Burma UK Partnership for Education (BUPE): Component 5 – Evaluation, Evidence and Learning Component (EELC).
12. https://constituteproject.org, no date. Myanmar's Constitution 2008: 99.
13. https://constituteproject.org, no date. Myanmar's Constitution 2008: 12.
14. President's 10-Point Education Policy, announced by President U Thein Sein at the Parliament in March 2011, as follows:

    - To implement a free, compulsory primary education system.
    - To increase the enrolment rate in the basic education sector.
    - To nurture new generations as intellectuals and intelligentsia in the human resources development.
    - To improve capacities of teachers in both basic and HE sectors
    - To utilise teaching aids more effectively.
    - To upgrade the quality and the socio-economic status of educational personnel.
    - To provide scholarships, stipends and awards both locally and internationally.
    - To promulgate relevant laws for the participation and contribution of private sectors in education services.
    - To collaborate with international and local organisations including the UN, INGOs and NGOs.
    - To upgrade education standards to an international level.

15. This was the second time a CESR had been formed; the first was in 1992 (Min Saw Zoe et al., 2017).
16. For more on the issue of ethnic languages, see Chapter 6 of this volume.
17. See: http://www.cesrmm.org/phase-two.
18. He died at the end of 2013 and was first replaced by an acting minister and later by Dr Khin San Yi who became Minister of Education in February 2014.
19. Dr Thein Lwin, the founder of the Thinking Classroom Foundation became the head of the NNER movement. He was a member of the NLD executive committee until 2015.

20 Conversation with Dr Thein Lwin, 2013.
21 Conversations with various ethnic education stakeholders 2013–4.
22 http://www.irrawaddy.org/burma/nld-distances-leading-voice-education.html. More on this is in the final part of Chapter 4 discussing student protests.
23 Confidential interviews with the CESR team in 2014.
24 It is interesting to note that UNICEF takes credit for much of the CESR because of the QBEP support through these advisors to Daw Tin Tin Shu's team. For more on this see the QBEP final evaluation (UNICEF, 2016). While UNICEF certainly was a key partner in the CESR, it should not try to claim credit for what was essentially a MoE-run review, that received funding and specialist support from a number of development partners. The actual credit for the CESR and its success should unequivocally go to Daw Tin Tin Shu and her team, who put in the hard work.
25 http://www.burmapartnership.org/updates-national-education-law-student-protest/.
26 https://www.mmtimes.com/national-news/11994-student-unions-vow-to-continue-protests-against-education-law.html.
27 http://www.irrawaddy.org/burma/upper-house-approves-education-law-amendments.html.
28 http://www.rfa.org/english/news/myanmar/reform-06192015175225.html.
29 World Bank, 2013. 'School grants and student stipends'. Unpublished WB documents.
30 The numbers were later increased.
31 White Cards were identification (ID) cards that denoted people whose citizenship status was ambiguous. In Rakhine, many Muslims had White Cards. These cards were eventually abolished prior to the 2015 elections, making their holders in effect stateless.
32 That denotes Myanmar citizenship.
33 Now called the 'School Improvement Support Program' (SISP).
34 'School Improvement Funds (SIFs), amounts having gone from between USD 250 and USD 500 per school for small, medium and large schools in 2013–4 to between USD 400 and USD 15,000 in 2017–18' (World Bank, 2018b: 3). On stipends: 'The program is: (a) now operating in 55 townships (including two townships in Rakhine State – Manaung and Gwa) (b) provided (*sic*.) monthly transfers to more than 192,000 poor and at-risk students in 2017–8; and (c) follows clearly defined program parameters and processes laid out in OGs, which are updated and revised yearly according to lessons learned from the field and distributed to selected school heads and education officials during training. Recent analysis of quantitative survey data (schools, households, and students having applied to the programme) indicates significant and positive impacts. First, the selection processes appear to be implemented mostly as instructed, and the programme is generally successful in reaching the poorest and most 'at-risk' students. Second, outcomes such as drop-out, transition, and attendance of stipend recipients appear significantly better than non-recipients' (World Bank, 2018b: 4).
35 Letter from Dr Thein Lwin (NNER), dated 10 March 2017.
36 Letter from Dr Thein Lwin (NNER), dated 10 March 2017.
37 Mr Mathias Rwehere, according to the letter.
38 A partnership that supports close to 70 developing countries in achieving quality education.
39 As the author of this book has argued since 2012, including submitting a brief to this effect to President Thein Sein in 2013.
40 More on the Local Curriculum as later developed by the government in Chapter 6 of this volume.
41 Mann Win Khaing Than, Speaker of Parliament. 'Letter: 100/Ah Ma La/1-3(Committee) 2016 (74)'. Date: 19 February 2016.
42 Mann Win Khaing Than, Speaker of Parliament.
43 It has not been possible to find out what these committees have actually done between their inception and 2020.
44 Australia, Denmark, the European Union, Norway, the United Kingdom and UNICEF.
45 Expressed by many participants at a training seminar for monitoring and evaluation held in January 2019.
46 GoM and DFAT 2017.
47 See: https://en.unesco.org/themes/education/caped.
48 More on this in Chapter 5 of this volume.
49 Personal experience in delivering capacity development programmes at the MoE between 2016 and 2019. These insights are supported by a My-Equip Organisational Capacity Analysis conducted in 2019, which is elaborated on in the conclusion of this volume.

50 All references here are from: MoE, 2014. National EFA Review Report, March 2014. Data on AY enrolments etc., are on page 12.
51 Preliminary results for a Myanmar School Survey presented at a WB-sponsored development partner meeting on 10 May 2016.
52 Preliminary results for a Myanmar School Survey presented at a WB-sponsored development partner meeting on 10 May 2016. The data showed that 83 per cent of all new teachers were in category C, D and E schools. In contrast, 41 per cent of teachers with more than 3 years' experience were in category A schools (Note: A and B are urban while C, D and E are rural).
53 The new curriculum, along with its relevant textbooks and training for Grades 1, 2, 3 and 6, started in the 2018–9 and 2019–20 academic years. The new curriculum for Grades 4, 7 and 10 is currently planned for 2020–1, and the complete textbooks and training for all 12 Grades will be in 2022–3. The curricular reforms for the primary level are led by JICA and are detailed further below.
54 This is presented as a 'new' issue, yet was highlighted in the pre-CESR review by Lall et al., 2013. The problem was also detailed in a review of CCA in monastic schools by Lall, 2011, where teachers said CCA was impossible if the examination systems did not change and if they had between 50 and 100 children in a class.
55 In education, JICA is also involved in enhancement of engineering education at HE level. This year, JICA will expand their assistance to the TVET sector. (Interview with a JICA official, Yangon, September 2019.)
56 As a solution to the problem 'A Facebook page among primary teachers has been established voluntarily to share their experiences in the new curriculum. In the Facebook page, primary teachers enable to access practical videos which show how to play the misvial instruments and to practice PE activities introduced in the new textbooks.' (Mizuno et al., 2019: 19).
57 Most of the issues related to in-service training are dealt with in the next section on teacher education.
58 'The new curriculum is accompanied by a clear ideal of the approach that teachers should take. Teachers should use the ITPR (Introduce, Teach, Practice, Review). This includes methods such as story-telling, discussion, question and answer, group work, interactive approaches, peer learning and self-study. The teachers who are teaching old curriculum courses draw the lesson plans based on memorization of facts, concepts and mastering. Group work activities are rare in old curriculum courses and students are not able to promote the soft skills 5Cs.' 'All teachers, and teacher educators, in the study have substantial knowledge of the revised Bloom's taxonomy, but there was no evidence that they can link it to their teaching practice.' (OPM, 2019: Executive Summary).
59 Report on Field Study by Dr Khin Thuza Saw and Dr Kyaw Zan Hla in the OPM, 2019: Annex.
60 Personal interview, September 2018.
61 See Metro, 2019.
62 Interview over Skype, autumn 2019.
63 At the time of writing, it is understood that the third APR for 2018–9 was being compiled.
64 September 2019.
65 The MTR will explore whether the MoE has effectively developed and delivered education strategies and services to meet the NESP's stated gender and inclusion priorities (MoE, 2019b: 11).
66 The OECD's Development Assistance Committee's (OECD/DAC) evaluation criteria are based on the concept that evaluation is an assessment: 'to determine the relevance and fulfilment of objectives, efficiency, effectiveness, impact, and sustainability' (OECD, 1991: 10).
67 As such, the MTR is discussed in three chapters in this volume, covering basic education, HE and teacher education.

3
The alternative: Monastic education

Introduction

Myanmar's education system has historically been closely linked with Buddhism and Myanmar culture incorporates the traditional Buddhist value of service to the community. Society supports monks and monasteries through donations as part of their religious duty, and monasteries have been the main vehicle for inclusion in education by offering schooling to poor and disadvantaged children. This chapter considers the role of monasteries in bringing about change in the classroom, a change which occurred before state education reforms had begun. Whilst monastic schools have always catered to the poorest and the most disadvantaged members of society, their relative independence and status outside of the direct purview of the MoE allowed them to pioneer CCA in the classroom. Phaung Daw Oo, the largest monastic school in the country, based in Mandalay, is led by Sayadaw U Nayaka who can be credited with bringing large-scale change to teaching methods across all monastic schools through founding a centre for monastic teacher training that was supported by local donors as well as international aid funding. Drawing on original interview and focus group data from monastic teachers collected in 2010 and 2014, the chapter examines how CCA spread across monastic networks, and the role of both local and international teacher training agents across the country in this. In the end, it was monastic schools that led the way in reforms that affected teaching methods, especially the introduction of CCA in the classroom, which the state sector emulated a few years later. The chapter discusses how children from the most disadvantaged background ultimately had access to better teaching practices than those at government schools as a result of the work pioneered in Phaung Daw Oo. The chapter also draws on original focus group data with parents whose children attended these schools, so as to portray their views on the role of monasteries in education in Myanmar. Finally, the chapter describes the role of monasteries in maintaining ethnic nationality languages and culture, especially in Mon, Karen, Shan and Pa-O societies through their summer school language and literature programmes, a theme that will be further examined in Chapter 6 on ethnic languages.

Background: Buddhism and education, monastic schools in history

The history of monastic education dates back over 1,000 years to the Bagan era (1044–1287) when King Anawrahta first established Theravada Buddhism in what is today lower Myanmar. Evidence suggests that the origins of monastic schools go even further back to a Mon-dominated kingdom in the south some centuries earlier (Kaung, 1963). Monasteries were the only education providers during the rule of the Burmese kings,[1] and, therefore, educational control rested with the Sangha.[2] The focus was on learning Buddhist texts, and boys started their education at the age of eight (Cheesman, 2003: 48). This free monastery-based education was possible as monasteries were supported by the local community in the villages where they were located, and other, more wealthy donors undertook the responsibility to feed the monks, as well as funding the construction and maintenance of schools (Aung-Thwin, 1985: 175). The monks themselves were generally from the same background as the community in which they were situated (Kaung, 1963: 20).

When the British arrived in Burma they encountered a society that already had an education system, however, most colonial administrators dismissed monastic schooling as inadequate, believing that this type of religion-based education was unsuitable for the modern era (Cheesman, 2003). The introduction of a British secular education system in the colonial days led to a decline of the monastic system; by removing the King and changing the Burmese social structure, the Sangha no longer had its traditional support base (Cheesman, 2003). The more 'modern' alternative education system was at first not readily adopted. As Furnivall points out, although: 'the people acquiesced perforce in the desertion of the monasteries and the degradation of their own system of education', they were relatively uninterested in the new schools (Furnivall, 1938: 81–2, cited in Cheesman, 2003: 50–1). In the end, those Burmans who wanted to advance socially embraced British education (Cheesman,

2003), relegating monastic education to the poor, thus resulting in a two-tier education system where monastic schools were seen to cater to the poor and disadvantaged, a view which persists to this day. During colonial times, the British administration viewed the monks and their monasteries as antiquated, not in line with British colonial objectives, and thus were not supportive of the parallel education that the monasteries provided (Cheesman, 2003). Zoellner describes how the widespread demand of a distinctively Buddhist education as opposed to the British secular system became a significant part of the nationalist movement and the anti-colonial struggle (Zoellner, 2007).

After independence in 1948, Burma's socialist government centralised schooling and made it dependent on state funding (MoE, 1953). The new education policy recognised a role for religious instruction: 'The five elements essential to a sound educational tradition were identified as religion, discipline, culture, athletics and service' (Cheesman, 2003: 54). As Burma's post-independence years were characterised by instability and civil war, society increasingly attributed rising anti-social activities and crime to the perceived inadequacies of secular schools.[3] According to Smith, a powerful association of monks in 1959 demanded a reversion to monastic instruction at primary school level in order to prevent a nationwide breakdown (Smith, 1965: 178–9). In 1962, after the military coup and the advent of the 'Burmese way to Socialism', schools were: 'subject to unambiguous directives that emphasised military-style "socialist" prerogatives' (Burma Administrative and Social Affairs, 1963, cited in Cheesman, 2003: 55). Despite the central control held by the military, the monastic system did nevertheless experience a limited revival under Burmese socialist party rule. Although all schools had been nationalised, the government system could not reach across the whole country and monastic schools began to fill the gaps. The state, nonetheless, made sure that the Sangha was controlled through a system of registration and supervision that tightened over the mid-1960s through to the late 1970s. Cheesman explains that the introduction of the first Basic Education Law in 1966 continued the trend towards tighter supervision of schools, including monastic schools (Cheesman, 2003). The monastic schools were overseen first by the Ministry for Social Welfare (MSW), later by the MoE, and after 1988, the responsibility moved to the Ministry of Religious Affairs (MoRA). Cheesman writes that after the uprisings in 1988 and 1990, the relationship between state and Sangha was remodelled to resemble the earlier regal system of patronage, albeit with the state firmly in control and the Sangha having no means to undermine the government (Cheesman, 2003).[4] It was also at this time, possibly because the under-funded state education system could not meet the needs of all families, that more monastic schools were encouraged to open and allowed to register so as to gain a certain legal status, which consequently allowed some of the bigger monastic networks to establish themselves.

Since 1992, all registered monastic schools have used the national curriculum as prescribed by the MoE. Up until the turn of the twenty-first century, monastic education was largely perceived as 'non-formal' education until the government realised that in order to meet its responsibilities under the 'Education For All' declaration that it had signed, the children in monastic schools needed to be counted and included.[5] Monastic schools were suddenly seen as part of the solution to provide education across all sections of society and across the country (Lall, 2011). Consequently, monastic schools today are in a more prominent position than at any time since independence. Any monastic school can register with the MoRA, and there is now a formal structure in place with monastic school committees at township, state/region and national levels.

Zobrist describes the institutional framework for monastic education as being tripartite, including two government ministries (the MoRA and the MoE) and the state *Saṅgha Mahā Nāyaka* Committee where the MoRA takes the administrative lead, defining rules and regulations, and is responsible for school registrations (Zobrist, 2015). Within MoRA, monastic education is the responsibility of Domestic Religious Affairs under the Department of Promotion and Propagation of Sasana.[6] The MoE is not responsible for monastic schools but prescribes the curriculum and assessment. The state *Saṅgha Mahā Nāyaka* Committee is the supervisory body for monastic education and there are Monastic Education Supervisory Committees (MESC) at central, state/region and township levels.[7] There are now regular monastic education conferences bringing the heads of monastic schools together. The first was held in 2014 and they are funded through donations and managed by a group of head monks who are engaged with MoRA and MoE.[8] The conferences are hosted in a large monastic school called Naung Taung Monastic School in Ho Pone, Shan State. One of the key outputs of the second conference in 2015 was a series of eight resolutions[9] for the monastic education system which are now the basis of a monastic school policy.

Over the last 80 years, the number of monastic schools has fluctuated significantly. In 1932, there were 928 schools. By 1958, this had risen substantially to 5,545. Then after the 1962 military coup, most were officially disbanded. After monastic schools officially reopened in 1992, the number of schools rose and by 1996 there were 1,507. The number of students enrolled, however, was only 30 per cent of today's enrolment figures (Ohnmar Tin and Stenning, 2015: 11–12). In 2005, it was estimated that the same number of 1,500 monastic schools catered for 93,000 children (Achilles, 2005). According to data collected by MoRA, in 2010 there were 196,458 children enrolled in registered monastic schools across the country (Lall, 2011).[10] There could be more with those in non-registered but affiliated monastic schools, as there was no accurate data concerning how many monastic schools registered, so that the only official data available is from registered schools. The major incentive to register today is to receive government subsidies (Zobrist, 2015; 15–6). This has become increasingly more important as monastic schools traditionally rely on donations. Since 2013–4, the government has started providing some financial support to registered monastic schools, specifically subsidising teacher salaries based on the number of enrolled students. According to Ohnmar Tin and Stenning, the government subsidises the cost of one teacher for the first 20 students, then subsidises further salaries for every additional 40 students (Ohnmar Tin and Stenning, 2015: 22). As of 2015–6, the government also included registered monastic schools in their school grants programme. Despite this recent support from the government, the issue of funding continues to be problematic, especially with regard to teacher salaries, which are significantly lower than government schoolteachers, and some monastic schools have no other option but to ask parents to contribute towards fees. Some monastic schools have now started to explore how they can initiate effective 'Income Generating Activities' (IGAs) in order to provide greater job security for their teachers.[11]

According to analysis by MIMU of the five-year period between 2012 and 2013 and between 2016 and 2017, 303,061 students attended registered monastic schools across Myanmar in 2016 (MIMU, 2017). Of these, 12 per cent were young novices and nuns and 88 per cent were ordinary boys and girls, with marginally more boys than girls (51:49), and many more novices than nuns (65:35). Officially, monastic schools can only provide primary (Grades 1–5) and post-primary education (Grades 6–8), although there are a small number of middle schools and an even smaller number of high schools.[12] Other secondary monastic schools have found a way around this by affiliating with a government school (Zobrist, 2015: 17). In monastic education, 72 per cent of children are at primary school levels between Grades 1–4, and there has been a 22 per cent increase (53,823 more children) in the number of children enrolled in monastic education between 2012 and 2017 (MIMU, 2017). Children from monastic schools who want to remain in education are expected to transfer to government middle schools – the monastic system is not intended as a parallel education pathway. Transfers are simple as the head monk only has to issue a transfer certificate in Grade 5 that is then endorsed by the local TEO and then given to the middle school head teacher.[13]

Monastic schools today: A social justice agenda

The two-tier system mentioned above means that those who cannot afford to go to state schools go to monastic schools or forego their education altogether. Monastic schools clearly cater for the poor and disadvantaged. At the time of writing, monastic schools are the most important civil society institutions that bridge the accessibility gap to the government education system. While public schooling is not available in many rural, remote or conflict affected areas, there is a monastery in nearly every village.

A study by the Burnet Institute Myanmar (BIM) and the Monastic Education Development Group (MEDG), that reviewed 127 monastic schools, provides a snapshot of the state of monastic schools, including structural issues such as water supply, sanitation and hygiene (BIM and MEDG, 2014). According to this study, most monastic schools are managed by monks, sometimes supported by school committees. However, only 49 per cent of schools had a staff member trained in school administration. Although school committees or PTAs were present at 67 per cent of these monastic schools (usually made up of the principal, teachers, monks, parents and other community members), they did not meet very often. Their main functions were to support the monastery with fundraising, school maintenance, coordinating parental involvement, supporting the building of new infrastructure, encouraging out-of-school children to go to school, and hiring new teachers. All in all, the monastic school is very much a community responsibility.

The classroom environment is often problematic, with 75 per cent of schools in the BIM and MEDG study conducting multiple classes in one large room. Teaching space is a major issue and monasteries often cannot offer more than one large hall. In some cases, however, the building has been provided by the government but the monastery (and by extension, donations from the community) has to pay for a teacher. This is especially the case in more remote areas (Lorch, 2007). The hygiene condition of many schools is also a problem: only 37 per cent of schools in the BIM–MEDG 2014 study had a good waste disposal system, not all schools had access to clean water (58 per cent of schools had tube wells), the majority of schools (59 per cent) had poor water drainage systems and a few schools (6 per cent) did not have any toilets, while girls had separate toilets in only 47 per cent of schools. Hand-washing facilities were only noted in 67 per cent of the schools and most had no soap. The environment is a result of what the local community can afford and what the head monk manages to raise in donations.

It is clear that those attending monastic schools are usually those who would otherwise not attend school at all, making monastic schools a critical piece for inclusion in Myanmar's education system. The cost of education to families is the main issue. In all studies conducted on Myanmar's monastic schools (Lall, 2011 and 2016b; Zobrist, 2015; BIM and MEDG, 2014; Ohnmar Tin and Stenning, 2015) parents say that they simply cannot afford the hidden fees of the government system. Most parents are agricultural workers, migrant workers or small-scale vendors with very low, often daily wage, incomes. There are nevertheless other reasons for choosing a monastic school including safety and distance, in some cases preference for values-based education, familiarity with the abbot and teachers, and the school's flexible schedule that allows children to work to support their families. In some cases, disability or disease means that students are barred from government schools but accepted in monastic education centres.[14] With regards to students with disabilities, interestingly, UNESCO (cited in Zobrist, 2015) reports that 45 per cent of all students with disabilities attend monastic institutions. Since monastic students represent only 3 per cent of the total student population, it is significant that these schools absorb such a high percentage of students with disabilities despite no direct investment from any ministry for the provision of services, and no capacity to offer specialised help for disabled children. In certain cases, monastic heads show flexibility when children do not have the required official documents (birth certificates, citizenship registration cards, etc.)[15] In other cases, school heads allowed over-aged students to enrol or held special evening classes for older children who had to work, something which is impossible at a government school. Often monastic schools will also cater for ethnic minority students (Zobrist, 2015; Ohnmar Tin and Stenning, 2015), albeit teachers teach in Burmese and have no training in multilingual education.

Teachers and training

Across both state and monastic schools, the quality varies tremendously. Monastic teachers do not come from the same pool as those who teach in the state system. Head monks usually prefer to employ university graduates[16] as teachers but often have to compromise and accept the most qualified local staff. Most are female, live locally and many are very young. In Phaung Daw Oo, there is a preference to employ their own graduates after they have finished Year 11. There is no formal pre-service training and many, especially in the rural areas, have no more than the 11 years of basic schooling. Some schools have benefitted from in-service teacher training funded by international organisations such as JICA or UNICEF. There is also a MoE annual two-week in-service teacher training course that many monastic teachers are allowed to attend, although some have reported that it is difficult to access the training location. In some very rare cases, schools or particular teachers (often head monks) have had access to an Open Society-developed programme entitled 'Reading, Writing and Critical Thinking' (RWCT), a programme funded out of Thailand.[17] But many monastic schools have had nothing at all and teachers teach as they were taught when they were children.

Some larger schools such as Phaung Daw Oo have started to use teaching assistants, especially in very large classes where space allows. Classroom observations showed that the coordination between the main teacher and the teaching assistant is still something that needs to be learnt, as the mechanisms did not seem to have been fully worked out in some classrooms. However, teaching assistants are crucial in settings with over 80 or 100 students in a class if the teaching method is to go beyond simple rote learning.

Phaung Daw Oo is often represented as the country's model monastic school. Teachers there have received more training than in most other monastic school settings, starting in 2005 with specialist CCA training provided in Thailand (Lall, 2010). Teachers there have also received mathematics, English and subject-specific training as well as RWCT training. The Head Teacher of Phaung Daw Oo explained (Lall et al., 2016):

> In 2006, there was one month self-awareness training from Thailand. Teachers could not go home during that training. The middle school teachers have received gender training. The government also organizes life skill trainings. The new teachers receive TOT[18] training from the teachers at this school.

Since Phaung Daw Oo's Grades 9 and 10 are linked to a government school, each subject dean also receives subject-specific training from the government that includes lesson planning, curriculum development and management. It should be remembered that most monastic schools are not like Phaung Daw Oo, yet all have an important contribution to make, as is described by the parents below.

Parent views on monastic education and social justice

Studies conducted by the author across monastic schools in 2010, 2015 and in 2016 reflect much of what other research also discussed. Students were from poor and very poor families living in the local areas, and in some cases were orphans or ethnic minority students living as boarders in the monastery (Lall, 2011, Lall, 2016b; Lall et al., 2016). One monastery had built a special shelter for the children who had fled from cyclone Nargis in 2010 and who either had no family left, or whose families could no longer feed them. Generally, there were 80–100 students in each class and the benches and rooms were overcrowded. In most schools, multiple classes were held in one hall. Figure 3.1 shows a typical monastic hall. Both in urban and rural areas, classes had varying age groups with some students having started education late. In general, boys and girls learnt together but in some schools they were seated separately. Apart from one very large school located in the Delta which was perfectly disciplined,

Figure 3.1 Monastic school, 2010. Source: Author.

order and adherence to rules was better in smaller schools and in the larger schools there seemed to be utter chaos most of the time.

The choice of school for most parents was based on the fact that the school was free and that they were poor. Many parents explained that their daily wage was not enough to pay for the extra costs of the local government school. Many parents, especially in the rural areas, also said that the school was close and that their children could easily and safely walk to school alone. There was an implicit trust in the teachers and the head monk that the children would be treated well and protected. 'The teachers treat our children like their own' was a refrain often heard. Beyond free education, the monasteries also often supported the families by other means, such as meals or snacks for the children, and this was mentioned as an important factor.

The parents interviewed were all very interested in their children's education but many said they were unable to help or felt incapable of taking part in the education process either due to time constraints (most families live hand to mouth and have a hard time putting one daily meal on the table) or because they were not educated themselves. All parents also said that they wanted their children to become 'civilised' and that the school was the best way for this. Discipline and order was something the teachers could impart and this would make the children good adults, with Buddhist values and respect for their elders and wider society. In the discussions, there was no critique of the schools whatsoever. In fact, many parents said they felt the schools were 'perfect' and there was a wide sense of gratitude towards the head monk and the teachers. Only when prompted markedly did they have some suggestions for improvement. Mostly, these consisted in wanting the school to expand (to have more space) or the school becoming a middle or high school. The parents know that they will not be able to send their children to the government middle or high schools due to the costs of uniforms and books. They also feel that it would be nicer for their children to remain in the same environment until Grade 11.[19] Many parents also appreciated the vocational classes or the courses in sustainable development, and although not asked about them made it a point to mention how helpful these were. Invariably, parents hoped that their children would take on work in which they were interested, and without exception the parents wanted the children to have better employment than themselves and saw education as the only means forward. Monastic schools are, therefore, a key part of Myanmar's Buddhism social justice fabric, offering an educational path to the most disadvantaged. This path is by no means perfect, not least because it mostly offers education only to the end of primary school, but it does allow some to escape from the grinding poverty of their parents, and improves literacy levels across the country.

Phaung Daw Oo is exceptional and its parents know how lucky they are to get their children admitted. It is not only a monastic school that offers 11 years of schooling up to the metric exam, but it is also a school that has pioneered new teaching methods of CCA (see next section) and even offered fast-track classes where the curriculum is taught to smaller groups of students in English.[20] The head monk, U Nayaka, explained that these classes were for any gifted child at his school. However, upon closer examination, it turned out that the children in the fast-track section had parents largely emanating from the middle and lower middle classes. These parents praised the system for not requiring extra tuition they felt they would have had to provide to their children in government schools. It meant that some poorer students were able to mix with middle class peers, but it also shows that middle class parents will send their children to a monastic school if that school provides better quality education than the local government alternative.[21]

Phaung Daw Oo is also the only monastic school with a reasonable number of computers. They use technology regularly and find that the students who board are more familiar with IT than those who go back home in the evening, as they do not have access to computers at home. One teacher, however, mentioned that there were potential issues with online resources (Lall, 2011)

> Although there are good things about Facebook, there is too much hate speech which is disappointing so I don't use it much anymore. I use the computer more for presentations, downloads and scholarship information.

Given the issues that have developed across the country with regard to growing Buddhist nationalism and discrimination towards certain religious minorities, it was heartening to hear this from the leading monastic school in the country.

Developing child-centred approaches in education in monastic schools

Child-centred approaches in education arrived in Myanmar through INGOs such as UNICEF and JICA in the late 1990s and early 2000s, and was later adopted by local NGOs. Child-centred approaches are government endorsed, and both UNICEF and JICA, which had the first Memoranda of Understanding (MOU) with the MoE, worked with the teachers' colleges to train state sector teachers in CCA methods. However, evidence suggests that the methodology was rarely, if ever, applied in government schools, largely because of the examination system being based on the chapter-end test, which required children to regurgitate what had been rote learnt in the preceding weeks.[22]

Around 2003–4, Pestalozzi Children's Foundation, an INGO, started to offer training to teachers in the monastic sector, including those from Phaung Daw Oo monastery. Since 2005, there have been a number of CCA training providers who have worked with monastic schools, including Hantha educators, Yinthway Foundation, the Asia Peace and Education Foundation (APEF), Shalom (Nyein Foundation) and Save the Children, amongst others. Some of these are local NGOs (with and without international support) and some are international charities (such as Save the Children). The international response to Cyclone Nargis in 2010 increased funding in the education sector and brought with it an expansion of teacher training provision and funding for further training, which in turn allowed for this new 'sector' to develop.[23] The training provided in the monastic schools that were visited in 2010 and 2016 has often been a mix of diverse approaches – some teachers have had one set of training by one provider, others have been on multiple courses run by external providers, and some have been trained by in-house trainers as well as attending training sessions outside. The length of the training sessions also varied considerably from a few days to several weeks. Not all training provided follow-up sessions and the cascade model used by many assured large numbers of trained teachers, but with no quality assurance as to how much of the method was actually being retained, passed on and utilised. Discussions with teacher trainers revealed that there was a wide disparity in quality and the understanding of training methodologies. The lack of coordination between the training providers is one of the main issues as schools literally accept any training offered, but this approach lacks the possibility of building on what has been previously learnt. There has also been an issue with certain teachers believing that since they received training as trainers in a cascade model, they were in effect qualified to train the teachers of their school. Not only did this create new hierarchies and associated intercollegiate problems, those assigned to train other teachers could not clearly explain their own efforts at training. The issue of quality assurance of the various training methods is thus quite central. Additionally, training often occurred outside the school away from the teachers' home schools, so presented difficulties in ensuring the application of the newly learnt techniques once teachers returned home. Only one training provider made it a point to train teachers within their own classrooms.

The main training providers are linked to each other and to a number of nodal monastic schools with whom they collaborate through a complex network web (see Figure 3.2).[24] It is interesting how some organisations and names seemed to be at the centre of the web and at the base of the often used cascading model – through which trainers were trained and then went on to train more trainers as well as teachers.

Overall, the objectives of all the programmes are the same as they aim to train teachers or teacher trainers to develop a child centred approach in the monastic school classrooms. Their definition of child-centeredness is also essentially the same. There were differences in that some providers focused more on lesson planning and classroom management, while others focused on teaching techniques and the types of teaching exercises that can be done with students. However, the manuals reviewed[25] had different approaches in securing the objectives, and training techniques varied. One training manual in particular was extremely theoretical and did not bear much connection to the local context. Some training providers were more technical than others; some had simpler and shorter approaches; some, especially those developed locally, were also more adapted to local circumstance.

Teachers had no difficulties explaining what they saw as the main elements of CCA and what they believed the benefits were. In focus groups (Figure 3.3), many explained through examples what methods they used in the classroom, and classroom observations showed that CCA practices were indeed being used in many (not all) classrooms, especially for the younger children and in schools where some teachers had received training in focus group discussions. The most commonly used approaches included group and pair work, student presentations in front of the class, getting more able students to teach others in small groups, the use of teaching aids such as flash cards and pictures (especially in mathematics, Myanmar and English), role-play, singing songs and reciting poetry (sometimes together as a whole class), drawing pictures, using pictures to illustrate body parts, plants or other objects and using jigsaw puzzles and storytelling. Since classrooms often did not have walls (at times only one big hall with small partitions), students' work was displayed only occasionally. Furthermore, given the cramped space, teachers could not grow plants in the classroom (or keep an

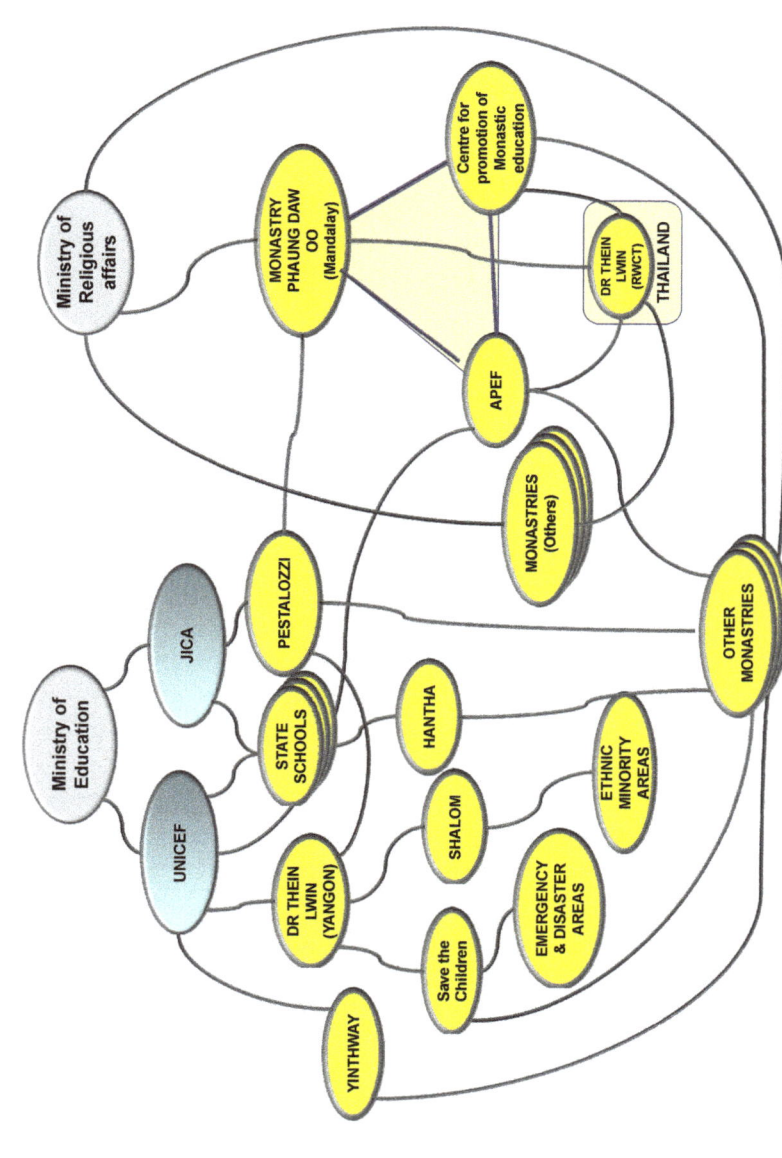

Figure 3.2 Monastic teacher training: Network of child-centred approaches (CCA) trainers, 2010.[26]
Source: Author.

Figure 3.3 Phaung Daw Oo Monastic School, 2010 teachers' focus group discussion. Source: Author.

aquarium as one American educationist suggested). Despite the limitations, teachers spoke of taking the children outside and showing them plants and objects so they could learn through observation. Some teachers brought in common household items such as jars and bottles and used these as teaching aids. Assessment practices had also changed quite radically for those who applied CCA. Unlike their colleagues, who mainly used written tests, more CCA teachers used a form of oral assessment by asking questions.

The teachers themselves spoke of the benefits they experienced when using CCA. They felt that they learnt as well – and had more fun with the students; some felt that CCA also gave them a closer relationship with the students. They would immediately know if one student was not following the topic, or had difficulties understanding. They also felt that it improved relations between the students as group work ensured the stronger students helped the weaker ones. It should be noted that not all teachers were equally enthusiastic, and in general CCA was more easily adopted by the younger women. Based both on classroom observations and interviews, it seemed that some male teachers seemed resistant to changing their ways stating that: 'some subjects are suitable for CCA teaching and some are not' (Lall, 2010). There were more female teachers overall, and they were mostly responsible for the younger classes, making the adoption of CCA methods not only gender dependent but also related to the age of the students and the level of the class. Younger women spoke frequently about how they had fewer problems in the changing hierarchies where students feel free to ask questions and where the traditional silent respect for teachers is eroded. They understood that the method would improve their teaching but were outside their comfort zone in using it. As one of the head monks said, 'If they cannot understand the new method they do not dare let go of the old method' (Lall, 2010).

In all monastic schools visited, the rote method of learning was still applied, especially with older students, by teachers who had had no training and in those classes where due to the cramped conditions moving about between benches was impossible. One of the head monks said that he felt times are changing and teaching methods also have to change accordingly (Lall, 2010). This was echoed by teachers and trainers who emphasised that Myanmar had to dispense with the strategy of rote learning in order to raise standards across the country. Since government schools were unlikely to take the lead in this, it was left, ironically, to the age-old monastic school tradition to lead the way. All were aware that this would meet with resistance, not least from parents who were wondering what was happening in classrooms if the children did not bring home something written in their notebooks, or if they could not recite the phrases learnt at school back at home. Resistance also came from the monasteries themselves as monks, used to silence and respect, suddenly had to deal with noisy children in and outside the classrooms. The issue of respect and how the students view teachers and

Figure 3.4 Monastic school Yangon Region, 2010 parents' focus group discussion. Source: Author.

parents or other elders remains central as many see a major difficulty in how to balance the new 'modern' and 'Western' approach with traditional Myanmar culture. Parents who took part in focus group discussions (as seen in Figure 3.4) were especially worried that children would become too disrespectful and reject traditional hierarchies at home.

However, there was a general understanding by all stakeholders – including the parents – that the children taught with the new methods could apply what they learnt in the classroom to the outside world and to everyday life. Teachers also felt they had to learn more themselves to adapt lessons to the real world, and this in turn had benefits for their own understanding of the world.

Despite all their misgivings, parents and teachers interviewed spoke about how the teaching methodology had changed children's attitudes. Children were seen to be more engaged and happy to come to school. Parents in particular mentioned how children were excited by the prospect of going to class in the morning. Teachers mentioned fewer absences and drop-outs as proof that children were more engaged. In the classroom, the teachers said that the children's confidence was up and many were no longer afraid to ask questions: 'they feel they [the children] can say what they want to do and feel more able to do things by themselves' was a commonly echoed refrain (Lall, 2010). Children were also more curious, interested and keen to explore. Many female teachers also spoke at length about the new 'bond' they felt children were developing and that generally this meant they had a closer relationship and that classroom relations were no longer based on fear. The absence of corporal punishment in all classes visited contributed to that bonding process. Some (predominantly male) teachers, however, felt that this closer bond also eroded the traditional respect children had for teachers, and some parents also expressed worries to that effect. 'Children become noisy' was seen as a discipline problem at home and at school as well as by other monks in the monasteries where the schools were located (Lall, 2010). Conversely, parents found that children were more willing to do homework at home. Overall, teachers, parents and head monks all agreed that the changes witnessed in the children affected by the new teaching methods were positive and outweighed the problems of discipline and respect.

Child-centred approaches was often seen as a 'foreign' or 'Western' way to teach. In the long discussions about Myanmar's transition into 'modern' times and how children should be equipped for life outside the school and the home, it was often suggested that there was a need for a Myanmar-centric CCA which would encompass Asian – and in particular local – values. One training provider mentioned how CCA can be compared to Buddha's teaching – a warm relationship but with respect, and that teachers had to know how to cultivate the respect for teachers, parents and other elders. Child-centred approaches could reflect Buddhist values if teachers were properly trained and had a deeper understanding of their own culture. It did not necessarily mean the loss of boundaries even if the child was at the centre and even if the child was able to ask questions. Clearly, this is a very fine balance to strike and most engaged in this conversation tended to say that they were not sure how to do it. Only one other teacher trainer spoke at length how the image of Buddha and his teaching had to be used as an example for the classroom, and that CCA was not incompatible with the Myanmar culture, but rather that the old style of teaching was what was incompatible with a Buddhist way of teaching and learning.

However, a number of issues were raised – including first and foremost the extra work required to apply CCA in the classroom. Most teachers were familiar with lesson planning but a CCA session requires careful thought as to what aids are needed and when, so that classroom preparation also meant time management. Since teaching aids were often not readily available, teachers would either have to think of an easily obtained substitute from their home, or construct and build props themselves. Given the paucity of materials such as colour pens and glue, this was not always easy and required more than just good ideas and creativity. One training provider had developed teaching aids from recycled materials and showed teachers how to make their own, but in some very poor areas even these materials might not be available, and at times teachers were seen struggling with just a blackboard and a few pieces of paper on which to draw pictures.

The time factor was mentioned many times as teachers felt that they could not necessarily cover the required lesson in the time allocated, especially in classrooms with too many students. Giving individual attention to small groups of students not only ate into the allocated time but also meant that in some cases the rest of the class then posed a discipline issue, as students would start to run around and disrupt the learning environment. In these cases, at least one teaching assistant would be required, and this again would mean extra work as teaching would have to be coordinated. Yet, far more worrying for the teachers than the issue of time and discipline, was the fact that many felt they might be asked questions they would not be able to answer. In a culture where the respect for teachers is so deeply ingrained, some felt that having an 'ignorant teacher' could fatally undermine their position. In order to avoid this potential scenario, teachers said they would have to read much more. This again was extra work and often there was no means to acquire this extra knowledge (limited access to the internet, few if any books, etc.). Head monks, trainers and teachers all agreed that teachers still needed to learn and practice the CCA methods, and that the teachers were not used to the self-reflection and collaborative procedures which underlie such teaching. Those who had successfully mastered the method (very few felt this way) said that teaching had become easier due to the changed attitudes of the students. But some, mainly the males and teachers of older classes, felt that the new methodology was not necessarily appropriate across the board and that CCA should be used only for 'some subjects' or for the younger classes.

Aside from the extra work and time required, there were logistical difficulties in applying CCA in the schools as they are currently built and equipped. All complained about class sizes and teacher-to-student ratios – often at 100 students to one teacher. This was generally compounded by the lack of space. One classroom visited was so full that the teacher had to climb on the benches where students were sitting to get from the first row to the back of the classroom. The space was so tight that a stray dog entered and hid behind a bench and could not be chased out.

The teacher-to-student ratio did not seem that important when there were teaching assistants or second teachers present, and when there was enough space to form small groups of students to work together (i.e. if furniture could be moved). Often, the lack of space affected teaching in other ways as well. Not often mentioned but still important is the fact that many classes take place in one room or hall with few if any partitions, so that those classes engaged in CCA type exercises will often disturb each other. In one school, CCA methods were restricted to three hours a day so that everyone 'would have their turn' in the hall. Linked to the large classes is the issue of managing to cover the lesson in a certain amount of time. With a small group, the teacher could spend time with each child, however, with large numbers of students, some groups received little attention or were left out altogether. Teachers also frequently grumbled about the lack of time to get through a lesson.

A number of the schools visited had double shifts of classes. The teachers all taught both shifts, which meant an early start and an 11-hour day, with no time to prepare lessons and even less time to construct teaching aids. Sometimes, there were libraries where teachers could get extra information – although the books contained therein were often of limited value to a CCA curriculum. Only one school visited had useful materials for both students and teachers.

The teachers interviewed mentioned that in many schools where they had colleagues, the principal was unhappy with any change of teaching methodology. If the principal or the head monk of the cluster was not supportive, teachers would encounter difficulties. This was compounded by monks who felt that their environment should not be disturbed by noisy children all day long (a particular problem for the double shift schools with a 6 a.m. start). See Figure 3.5 for children leaving a monastic school after class. The fact that parents were hard to engage (mostly because of their living hand to mouth) also meant that it was more difficult to get them to understand and support what the children were doing at school.

Clusters and networks

Across Myanmar, the monastic schools often operate in a cluster, with networks assisting each other. Zobrist discusses how abbots and head nuns have a wide-reaching network through which they support one another and discuss education and school management topics (Zobrist, 2015).

Figure 3.5 Monastic school in Mandalay, 2010. Source: Author.

The creation of the Monastic Education Development Group (MEDG)

The Monastic Education Development Group (MEDG) was established in 2011 in order to improve the quality of monastic education. The group was initiated by the chairs of the state and regional MESC and was accredited by MoRA in 2014. It had 11 elected head monks and was led by the head monk of Phaung Daw Oo, U Nayaka (Ohnmar Tin and Stenning, 2015: 19). The MEDG office is based at the Phaung Daw Oo monastery. In some ways, MEDG followed from the Phaung Daw Oo's 'Centre for the Promotion of Monastic Education' that U Nayaka created to coordinate CCA training across monastic schools over a decade ago. Its mandate is to support teacher training, systems development and improvement to the school environment. The group is meant to be both a national level coordination body and implementation provider.

More recently, teacher training has been one of the activities spread through the monastic networks. The cascading methodology of a number of training providers means that teachers at monastic schools get trained as trainers and subsequently train the teachers in their own school, and later the teachers in the affiliated schools. Teachers and head monks frequently cited Phaung Daw Oo as the source of information on training opportunities and often, the location of training courses.[27] In 2012, a learner-centered competency-based teacher training for the monastic system was developed with support from Pyoe Pin.[28] Now distributed through the Yaung Zin teacher development group, the Yaung Zin 'Competency-Based Teacher Training Programme' for primary teachers was designed for Myanmar non-state schools (primarily monastic and community schools). The programme aims to improve the development of teachers and students in the non-state education sector where many teachers are untrained or undertrained in their roles of teaching and facilitating learning. It consists of 8 modules that can be completed in 31 days, and teachers who complete the programme receive a certificate of completion.[29] Interestingly, the Yaung Zin programme includes mentoring to ensure that newly trained teachers have proper support to implement what they have learned in the training back in their classrooms – something that was lacking in most of the other CCA training. The MEDG now accredits the Yaung Zin programme and offers it to new and untrained monastic teachers across the monastic networks. If the teachers are successfully assessed, they receive the Yaung Zin Certificate of Competence.[30]

Beyond supporting teacher training, the MEDG offers administrative training. By 2015, they had trained about 600 staff in 300 schools (Ohnmar Tin and Stenning, 2015: 20). Between 2013 and 2015, the MEDG developed a 'comprehensive school approach' to develop capacity in leadership and management, teacher education, school environment (including a Water, Sanitation and Hygiene – 'WASH' – programme), and parent and community engagement in 100 model monastic schools in order to support the delivery of quality basic education.[31]

The role of donors: The Myanmar Education Consortium (MEC)

Monastic schools are mostly supported by their local communities. In some instances, there are foreign donors, either through small foundations or through occasional visits. Some international aid organisations became involved in monastic education through the delivery of CCA training described above. As this engagement increased, and as the government wanted the education reforms to include hard-to-reach children and young people who are often unable to take part in mainstream schooling, donors decided to pool their funding. In 2012, in order to streamline funding to the monastic and ethnic education sectors, the United Kingdom and the Australian Governments established the Myanmar Education Consortium (MEC). According to MEC's advocacy strategy (MEC, 2015), it has the overall goal of increasing the number and proportion of children in Myanmar accessing and completing quality basic education: 'In particular, MEC aims to increase the quality of and access to complementary (non-government) education including early childhood, primary and non-formal education programs.' MEC also has a role advocating for the involvement of the Myanmar Government in supporting civil society engagement in education. Compared to the role of donors in other education sectors, monastic schools get rather less attention and money, despite educating over 300,000 of Myanmar's children.

The role of monastic schools in maintaining ethnic languages and culture

Monastic schools also have a role to play in the maintenance of ethnic languages and cultures, especially for the Buddhist ethnic nationalities such as the Mon, Karen (70 per cent of whom are Buddhist), Shan and Pa-O. Their role is largely one of supporting the communities through summer schools, and the degree to which monasteries and monastic schools are involved varies considerably from state to state. In some cases, the monks will be responsible for training the teachers; in other cases, they will simply offer the space for communities to organise the summer classes. They do not usually teach the regular government curriculum in an ethnic language – with a notable exception described below.

Taungalay Monastic School

Just outside of Karen State's capital Hpa-An is the State's largest monastic school, which offers schooling from KG to Grade 10. The Taungalay Monastic School provides accommodation for 150 boarders (who have travelled from as far away as Ye and Dawei), out of a total of more than 500 students, nearly all of whom are Karen.[32] As well as the main school, there are six associated satellite schools in nearby Karen villages, illustrating the far-reaching influence of the head monk. In an interview in 2016, he confirmed that he has good relations with the SEO and has received help from a number of NGOs and agencies, such as the Adventist

Development and Relief Agency (ADRA), the Karen Development Network, Thabyay Education Foundation[33] and Yinthway Foundation.[34]

The school trains its own teachers, many of whom are their own graduates who have returned. To help the students matriculate, government school teachers volunteer to teach in Grade 10. Although the school follows the government curriculum, this is offered in Pwo Karen with some form of transfer to Burmese at post-primary level. They also cater for Karen children whose families live outside Karen State. In an interview in 2016, the head monk reiterated that this means that girls were especially safe whilst growing up. They accept transfers from the KNU and schools on the border.

The Taungalay Monastic School also provides Pwo language teaching after hours, and in the summer holidays. Taungalay is, therefore, an exception in that the regular government curriculum is available in an ethnic language. In Mon State, a few Mon national schools 'converted' to monastic schools around 2009–10 when the existing ceasefire was under threat. However, in contrast to Taungalay, they were not run by the monastery, instead they used the monastery as a location to run a school that had until then been managed by the Mon National Education Committee (MNEC), the New Mon State Party's (NMSP) education department. Many of these schools have now officially reverted back to MNEC control. This will be considered further in Chapter 7 of this volume.

Summer language and culture programmes

In ethnic areas, especially Mon and Karen States as well as the Pa-O Self-Administered Zone (SAZ) in Shan State, monastic schools are active in culture and language summer schools. The programmes differ from state to state and between ethnic groups, however, they usually emanate from collaboration between the ethnic Literature and Culture Committees (LCC) and the Sangha (monks), offering training programmes for volunteer teachers who then are able to teach children enrolled in Myanmar state schools (where Burmese is the language of instruction) in their mother tongue.

Mon monastic summer school and literacy programme

In the 1990s, and particularly after the 1995 NMSP ceasefire, monastic education initiatives expanded considerably. Before the ceasefire, Mon monks had for many years been conducting various forms of language and culture teaching, particularly in the school summer holidays (March–May), but these activities were not systematically coordinated until after the ceasefire. In 1997, Mon Literature and Culture Society members, including students and graduates of Mawlamyine University, in partnership with some progressive monks, began to organise Mon Summer Literacy and Buddhist Culture (MSLBC) training in a number of monasteries. By 2010, there were 310 monasteries across 16 townships (in Mon and Karen States, and Tanintharyi, Bago, Yangon and Mandalay regions) taking part.[35] While the extent of MSLBC training activities has expanded as a direct result of the increased space created by the NMSP ceasefire, Mon armed groups were not directly involved in these initiatives. Although NMSP leaders have occasionally attended MSLBC closing ceremonies, and sometimes attempted to co-opt this movement into the Mon armed nationalist cause, the summer training remains largely independent. They are based in and 'owned' by the monastic and lay communities, and have been, therefore, less susceptible to suppression. This characteristic was illustrated by the fact that after foreign funding was withdrawn in 2010, the MSLBC training continued in nearly all of the monasteries in which it had previously been conducted. Township-level examinations also continued, where prizes were awarded for outstanding students. However, the withdrawal of external funding did undermine Mon educators' ability to conduct all-Mon region examinations, or to provide incentives for outstanding students and teachers (Lall and South, 2013a and b).

Pa-O monastic summer school

The Pa-O monastic summer school has been in operation for over 37 years. The length of course depends on the village, but usually varies between 10 and 15 days, although some villages offer month-long courses. Some courses are for adults and some for children. Monks give annual teacher training for five days every year and every village sends two people to be trained, who then go back and deliver the course. When the programme started, they had between 200 and 300 teachers, but now there are over 4,000 teachers teaching around 10,000 people every year. According to the Pa-O National Organisation (PNO), it is compulsory for all young people between the ages of 20 and 25 to attend. The teachers are offered certificates after the training. The PNO's Parami Development Network, the Pa-O literature and culture organisation, and the Sangha work together to make sure the summer school takes place every year during Ta Baung (around March) either in private houses, village halls or monasteries.

Monastic-based language and literature programmes like the Pa-O and Mon summer schools are supported by the community. Volunteer teachers in the Pa-O system only need support in kind during the one-week training phase, as they then return home and teach in their own villages. Head monks raise the necessary money for books and graduation ceremonies from well-wishers and local donors. This is similar for the Karen, Kachin, Mon and Chin teachers, although some programmes require the community to support the volunteer teachers whilst they are teaching, especially if they are not from that village.

Conclusion

Iris Young's framework indicates that monastic schools are a key mechanism in Myanmar's education system to combat marginalisation, and aim for the inclusion of the poorest in society. By ensuring that the monastic schools and teachers are supported through donations from society, monastic heads undermine the exploitative relationship of the tuitions system within the government education system to which poor parents are subject. Monastic schools contribute to supporting ethnic minorities as well, but (as shall be seen in Chapter 6 of this volume) only a small number are able to deal with the lasting disadvantages that come from the dominance of Burmese as the language of instruction. This is more so in ethnic areas such as Mon and Shan State, where monastic schools provide 'summer schools' that use the medium of ethnic nationality language, thus counteracting the 'Bamar' cultural imperialism promoted through the government schooling systems.

Phaung Daw Oo in particular has been a beacon for the various monastic networks in raising the profile of the work done by monastic schools. Well before the 2012 reforms, Phaung Daw Oo was able to improve teaching methods in the classroom despite the lack of resources that characterise the monastic education system. It was largely through the efforts of Phaung Daw Oo's abbot, U Nayaka, that monastic schools formed networks enabling international donors to not only engage with Myanmar's education system (when government schools were in effect closed to donors – apart from UNICEF), but also to support the cascade of more proficient teaching to many schools across the whole country. In a reverse of fortune, the poor children attending monastic schools often had access to better teaching pedagogy before better-off children in government schools.

The Myanmar Government in the meantime has recognised the importance of monastic schools in delivering education where the government system might be unable to reach. The relationship between the government and the monastic sector is now based on recognition and respect, whilst monastic schools in turn reduce the powerlessness of the poorest sections of Myanmar society.

Notes

1. The word for 'school' in Myanmar language is the word for 'monastery' (*kyaung*).
2. 'Sangha' is the term used to denote the community of Buddhist monks.
3. The corresponding decay of the monasteries' schools was described in at least one government report as a 'national calamity' (Report on the Public Instruction, 1954 16, cited in Cheesman, 2003: 55).
4. This was a dramatic contrast to the Sangha's historic role: 'where under certain circumstances its power and resources could become so great as to overwhelm a kingdom completely, and lead to its demise' (Aung-Thwin, 1985, cited in Cheesman, 2003: 57).
5. Interview: Yangon, 8 June 2010.
6. There are three departments under Ministry of Religious Affairs: Department of Religious Affairs; Department of Promotion Propagation of Sasana; Department of International Theravada Buddhist Missionary University.
7. Although the responsibilities for each entity is clearly defined, as is the relationship between the three bodies, Zobrist (2015) notes that head monks do find that communication between them is not always what it should be and that there is at times confusion about who is responsible for what.
8. Apparently, the MoE declined the invitation to attend.
9. The eight resolutions are as follows:

    1. Quality assurance for monastic education.
    2. Implementation of integration of Myanmar educational activities and international practices.
    3. Find ways and means for sustainability of monastic education.
    4. Inclusion of environmental, moral and civic education in the curriculum.
    5. Making effort for establishment of monastic teacher education colleges and monastic education universities.
    6. Implement the 24 points of Chapter 9 of the Monastic Education Policy, which was agreed and adopted in this second monastic education seminar.
    7. Experience sharing among monastic schools.
    8. Making effort to upgrade monastic schools from primary level to middle school level to high school level.

10. This means that there could be well over double that amount in the non-registered but affiliated monastic schools, and even more children when border areas are taken into account.
11. Ohnmar Tin and Stenning note that many monasteries have already established small IGAs such as water purification and brick making (Ohnmar Tin and Stenning, 2015: 23). Shine Hope, one of the corporate donors, originally gave money to subsidise salaries. Recognising that they were creating dependencies and in light of the recent government salary subsidies, the profits donated are now used to conduct sewing training and provide technical support to introduce a micro credit system. At the 2nd Monastic Education Conference (May 2015), there was a workshop specifically to discuss ideas on how to sustain monastic schools. Part of the impetus for this workshop came from a Mandalay-based businessman who wants to support a nationwide monastic school social enterprise. The premise is that working as a collective they would have better market access for their product.
12. Phaung Daw Oo, described later in this chapter, is one of the two permitted high schools.
13. Theoretically, the certificates should be recognised by all government schools. There are, however, reports that as the endorsement is at the discretion of the TEO, it can depend on the relationship between the head monk and the TEO. In some middle schools, they also ask the students to sit a placement test before confirming their place. There is no recognised transfer certificate for middle and high school so any student continuing to monastic middle school

can only continue their education in the monastic system. If a monk or nun wants to complete middle and high school in a government school they have to re-enter lay life (Ohnmar Tin and Stenning, 2015: 24).
14 Interviews by the author with monastic heads. Zobrist also discusses HIV status students in monastic schools (Zobrist, 2015).
15 Interview with an abbot who had many children of Indian origin in his school in 2016.
16 Interviews with monastic heads in 2011 and 2016.
17 'Thadama Zawtikar Yone, with a near 50 per cent drop-out rate, has a young head monk in his early thirties who has received 2 months training in Chang Mai on the RWCT (Reading, Writing and Critical Thinking) course run for Burmese teachers by "Education Burma". This situation of a young monk who has received educational training abroad is very rare within the monastic community. During our interview, we learnt how keen he is to experiment with more practical teaching approaches, often applying the "observation method" (one of the 21 methods of the CCA, which requires outdoor activities). The monastic school also possesses a newly constructed library (also unusual within the monastic community).' From: Peace Interfaith Initiative Myanmar, 2009.
18 Training of Teachers (TOT).
19 Myanmar had only 11 years of schooling at the time of the fieldwork.
20 The differential teaching system (fast track versus normal) creates difficulties between students as those in 'normal' classrooms would have wanted to have the same number of hours of teaching in the preferential circumstances of their peers. In that school, the normal sections of primary and middle schools receive 3.5 and 4 hours' instruction in Myanmar in classes of around 100 students each. The fast track sections receive 5 hours in English with a max of 30 students in each classroom.
21 This was also before the expansion of the private schools in Mandalay – so some parents might have now chosen the private school option where teaching and learning is also in English.
22 See preceding chapters of this volume for more on the issues of rote learning and exams.
23 **Hantha** trainers developed in 2005 with the help of a former state school teacher who started to facilitate former government teachers becoming 'teacher trainers'. They are using a cascading cluster system and are active across monastic networks. The centrepiece of their model is that they train teachers in the classroom. They have developed their own training manual in Burmese and also showcase a number of teaching aids for teachers that are made out of local and recycled materials and are easy to copy and reproduce. **Shalom** (Nyein Foundation) has specialised in training teachers in the ethnic minority areas since 2005. They have worked with Yangon-based consultant Dr Thein Lwin to train their master trainers who have cascaded the model to 60 other teacher trainers. **Yinthway** started teacher training in 2008 and has come to CCA through their programme on early childhood development and early childhood books. They developed a relationship with UNICEF and then developed three model schools in Yangon, Lashio and Mandalay. They have been funded by INGOs and work with local partners on the ground that include Christian organisations in ethnic minority areas and monastic schools. **APEF** was built up after Cyclone Nargis (2008) and based its method on the training offered previously by UNICEF. The programme is linked with Phaung Da Oo monastery, which has established the Centre for the Promotion of Monastic Education (CPME) that has in-house trainers who help train teachers across the wider network linked with this monastery. In 2008, 150 teachers were trained to become independent trainers and 50 of these were taken over by Yinthway as facilitators for their own programme. APEF also recruited some of these trainers and APEF's teacher training programme began in earnest in March 2009. They now have 12 master trainers who work in different areas of the country and train teachers across monastic networks in the Delta and Yangon division. They have also developed their own training manual in Burmese. **Save the Children** came in with teacher training after Cyclone Nargis and brought with them a methodology designed for areas in conflict and crisis.
24 The diagram was constructed on the basis of the interviews conducted with the training providers (Lall, 2011). It refers to CCA training only. The MoE manages its own teacher training in its teaching colleges. However, it relied on UNICEF and JICA to provide CCA training for the government teachers.
25 The author was given access to a few full training manuals and overall some form of materials related to teacher or trainer training by five organisations.
26 Reproduced from Lall (Lall, 2011: 227).

27 This is, however, only the case when the head monk or principal of the school is willing to propagate the new teaching method. In a number of monasteries there is resistance to new teaching methods as hierarchies change and the children become noisier. Even a head monk with 'a vision' can find battling the traditional monastic community difficult at times.
28 The course was developed on the back of the needs assessment and report on CCA in monastic schools conducted and written by the author. Pyoe Pin was a British Council programme that later registered as a local NGO.
29 According to the MEDG website, training may be undertaken in two lots of four modules or teachers may do all eight modules in one programme. The modules which comprise this teacher training programme are as follows:
- Learning needs and learning styles
- Teaching and learning strategies
- Classroom management
- Teaching and learning aids
- Assessment
- Lesson planning
- Professional development and the reflective practitioner
- Working with parents and the community.
30 This assessment usually takes place about four or five months after completion of the teacher training. Success in this assessment indicates they are able to apply their Yaung Zin learning effectively in their classroom (MEDG website: https://www.medg.org/about-us/our-approach).
31 MEDG website: https://www.medg.org/about-us/our-approach.
32 Students were reported as 90 per cent Pwo, 5 per cent Sgaw and 5 per cent non-Karen.
33 Thabyay's programmes are designed to support students and key community and civil society workers: 'We help them to acquire the skills, knowledge, networks and assistance to foster self-directed, sustainable development in their communities and the wider society.' http://www.thabyay.org/.
34 'Yinthway is a local NGO whose goal is to promote and support the holistic development of children in communities in Myanmar.' http://www.yinthway.org.
35 Data from Mon education CEOs interview with Nai Soe Than in Moulmein in 2011.

4
Higher education: Towards international standards in a neo-liberal world

Introduction

The quality of higher education (HE) has deteriorated sharply in Myanmar since independence when Rangoon University was seen as a leading HEI in the region. Today, HE is seen as a key part of the education reform process as well as a driver for future change with regard to employment and Myanmar's desire to catch up with the ASEAN region. HE can have a catalytic role in recovery and development of conflict-affected societies (Milton and Barakat, 2016), as seen in post-Soviet countries (Fullan, 2001) and in periods following regime change (Couch, 2019; Esson and Wang, 2018). However, evidence demonstrates that reform strategies need to account for economic growth, human rights and national identity to support national development (Couch, 2019). Therefore, a balance needs to be struck between engaging with international organisations to link with global scholarship (Altbach, 2009) whilst accounting for local contexts and conditions (Naidoo, 2007).

This chapter reviews how the reforms have impacted Myanmar's universities across the country, starting with a snapshot of Yangon and Mandalay Universities in 2005 and 2006, when the author was teaching there during the summer months. The chapter then moves to the main HE reform agenda including the development of the National Institute of Higher Education Development (NIHED)[1] that has started training senior academic staff across the HE sector, as well as other new HE-related structures that have been put in place by the NESP. The chapter engages with the vexed issue of decentralisation, including the rotation of staff appointments, the changing role of research and how universities are starting to engage with issues of access, quality and designing their own curricula. At the time of writing, HE, though almost free and despite there being over 150 institutions across Myanmar, is only accessible to a small number of mostly middle class students, with the poorer students enrolling in one of the world's largest, but possibly also worst, distance HE systems.[2] The chapter discusses the inequalities, particularly the issues of limited access of ethnic minority young people due to a severe language disadvantage[3] that emanates from their lack of access to basic education. Unless engaged with, this is likely to lead to long-term structural inequity problems. As observed by the ADB in an analysis of the financing of HE in Asia: 'Any higher education system that fails to cultivate the breadth of talent in society – men and women, rural and urban, rich and poor – is sacrificing both quality and efficiency' (ADB, 2016). The risks of ignoring inclusive growth could lead to a long-term stalling of the reforms, lower growth and rising inequalities that could result in socio-economic tensions, including armed conflict. However, Myanmar's HE reform is driven first and foremost by the desire of policy makers to regain international respect for the Myanmar universities, which means that issues of inclusive growth and inequalities are seen as less important than creating an elite system with the support of international universities and a new drive for top universities to look for partnerships as part of their internationalisation process.

Background

Modern HE came to Myanmar through British colonialism. Rangoon College was opened as an affiliated college of the University of Calcutta in 1878. It became 'University College' in 1920 shortly before being amalgamated with the Baptist Judson College to form Rangoon University. Mandalay University was added in 1925. Further teacher training, medical and agricultural colleges were added to Rangoon University between 1930 and 1938, although during World War II, the university was shut down. A year after independence, in 1949, the Burmese Government re-opened Rangoon university by bringing together relatively autonomous colleges and making them into university faculties. Mandalay University was established as a separate university in 1959, and both Yangon and Mandalay Universities were placed directly under state control in 1963 soon after the Ne Win military coup. A year later, the technical faculties of education, engineering, economics and medicine were removed from both Yangon[4] and Mandalay Universities, given degree-awarding powers as separate technical and professional institutions, leaving both universities with the liberal arts, science and law. In effect, the amalgamation of previous years was reversed, creating a larger number of smaller, specialist universities, akin to the system India was also developing. The 1973 University Education Law consolidated the new division between arts and science universities and technical institutes (CESR, 2013: 4). The same University Education Law explicitly deprived HEIs of financial autonomy. As with other state institutions, universities had their budget estimates approved by the state and had to ensure that all expenditures were consistent with state-approved norms (CESR, 2013: 7). In 1982, English was re-introduced as the official medium of instruction.[5]

1988 and the student protests

Student protests in the 1980s and 1990s resulted in the closure of universities for extended periods. In Yangon, universities were closed for 10 of the 12 years from 1988 to 2000. In light of the protests, the government decided to relocate much of the country's undergraduate provision outside of the urban centres, making it harder for students to engage in politics and protest. A number of these institutions were new HEIs registered with other ministries. Mandalay and Yangon Universities lost their undergraduate programmes (CESR, 2013: 5).[6] Needless to say, universities that had been isolated from the rest of the world throughout the 'Burmese way to Socialism' years became even more isolated after the protests. Myanmar academics had very little opportunity to go abroad and foreigners were not allowed on any of the campuses. Only a few academics received scholarships to complete doctorates, mainly in Japan, returning to teach in the Myanmar system upon return. Without access to international research, new books, journals and the internet, Myanmar's HEIs simply became a form of schooling that used set textbooks and rote learning without any research input or innovation. Laboratories were under-resourced, libraries stocked materials that were obsolete and out of date and teaching spaces were old and dusty. The universities therefore deteriorated rapidly.

The universities in 2004, 2005 and 2006

In the early 2000s, there were hardly any academic links between Myanmar universities and international HEIs or foreign academics, especially from the West. Limited contact continued through doctoral scholarships with Japanese HEIs. All contact between university staff and foreigners was tightly controlled. Myanmar academics needed approval from the MoE for any travel abroad and permission to invite any foreigners onto their campus. The only programme to support Myanmar academics in the social sciences was set up by Dr Kyaw Yin Hlaing, a Myanmar academic who had completed his PhD at Cornell University in the US, and was at the time based at the National University of Singapore. With financial support from the German political foundation Konrad Adenauer Stiftung (KAS), whose regional headquarters were in Kuala Lumpur, Malaysia, he developed a programme to enable foreign (including Western) academics to come and teach intensive courses to Myanmar junior academics at Yangon University. After lobbying helpful regime contacts, Dr Kyaw Yin Hlaing and Professor Robert Taylor, a long-time Myanmar specialist, managed to get permission from the government for foreign academics to teach at Myanmar universities. The programme ran for the first time in the summer of 2004 with academics mainly based at National University of Singapore, a few of whom were American citizens. In the summer of 2005, the programme was again conducted, and this time included an academic from the University of London[7] and one from the Hiroshima Peace Institute in Japan, with the team being allowed to teach not only in Yangon University, but also in Mandalay University. These academics between them offered 'updates' in anthropology, international relations, political economy, history and research methods, and despite being recorded, they could say anything and teach what they wanted. Money from KAS was used to purchase suitcases full of books to bring into the country, and these were then left for the university libraries. Most of these books would have been photocopied and passed on amongst academics, as it was impossible at that time to purchase books from the outside (Lall, 2016a). The programme ran again in 2006, although only in Yangon and only for Yangon University academics, with an even wider variety of subjects and international staff, one of whom had travelled from the US. In the summer of 2007, the teaching programme ran into some trouble as the permission to teach at the university was withdrawn at the very last minute, after the academics had arrived in Myanmar.[8] The experience was eye opening to those who had come from outside Myanmar, in that many of the young university teachers were completing their PhDs with little or no access to contemporary or up-to-date materials in their subjects. Staying in touch post-programme was also challenging, as their email communications were monitored. The experience was eye opening for the Myanmar colleagues too, as they heard about the transformation of the universities in the West, the competition for research funding, the pressure to publish, etc., none of which they were familiar with.

Higher education today

At the time of writing, there are 174 HEIs in Myanmar (MoE, 2016) under the jurisdiction of eight different ministries and these fall into two broad categories: arts and science universities and the technical and professional universities. In 2012, there were only eight universities permitted to award doctorates.[9] At the time of writing, all the HEIs are state-financed and accept students after matriculation, depending on their grades. The HE GER is low, at 15.96 per cent (UNESCO, 2019a). In 2018, arts and science universities had 266,833 registered students, technological universities had 75,455 registered students and the recently added teacher education colleges (dealt with in Chapter 5) had 20,069 registered students bringing the grand total to 362,357 students (MoE, 2019c). Those who cannot afford to live away from home access the very poor quality distance education programme that serves around 500,000 students. The total number of students enrolled increased by 14.5 per cent from 2016–7 to 2017–8 (MoE, 2019c: Fig 2.6.2, 52) and the total number of foreign students in the country was 425 in 2017–8, alongside 176 foreign experts (MoE, 2019c: Fig. 2.6.5 and 2.6.6, 54) with 62 per cent of those from China (MoE, 2019c: Fig. 2.6.10). There are 13,610 teachers in HE (MoE, 2019c: 147–8). According to the CESR, 82.6 per cent of academic staff and 60 per cent of students in 2012 were female (CESR, 2013).

To date, Myanmar's universities have operated quite differently from most other HE systems in the world. Everything is very centralised and the universities have hardly any autonomy.[10] The curriculum and the assessment are set by the MoE. The hiring of staff is also coordinated by the government and most staff are rotated every two to four years to universities around the country, making the setting up of research teams almost impossible. The centralised 'command and control' system has resulted in strict hierarchies with many senior academics worried about taking decisions that might be counter to the ministry's wishes. Although the elite universities have been promised limited autonomy from the education reform process – such as being able to hire local staff and choose their students – the fact that the government controls the budget means that the reality of university governance is severely limited. There are large differences between regional universities in remote areas, especially in ethnic states, and urban institutions. For example, universities in ethnic states will often have some local staff, who will not necessarily be rotated as part of the national system.

University-led research in Myanmar

There has been no systematic research culture at Myanmar universities for a number of decades. It is true that even today after almost eight years of education reform, academics at Myanmar universities are not research active in the same sense that Western universities would understand the term. There are multiple reasons for this – not least the job rotations every few years where academics are assigned to a new university anywhere in the country. This makes developing a personal research portfolio challenging and it is almost impossible to develop a stable research team. In addition to this, the process of getting permission to undertake research is complex and as with everything else in Myanmar, is a top-down process with little input from the bottom. There is no incentive for academics to add to what is already a very full workload of teaching and administration. Research is not only inadequately supported, but does not count formally in the promotion structure (CESR, 2013: 32). This, however, does not mean that research is not taking place at universities. Senior staff of 11 universities from around the country[11] took part in a one-year HE leadership and management programme, entitled 'Transforming Higher Education in Myanmar', set up in partnership with the MoE in Myanmar, the Irrawaddy Policy Exchange (IPE) and the BC and run by the UCL Institute of Education in 2018 (Figure 4.1).[12] As part of the programme they were asked to present one research project of their institution that either had been published or was going to be published. The results were surprising in the diversity and depth of what was presented. Some research was part of newly established international collaborations, other research was led by individual academics, other research again focused on improving the teaching and learning experience of their students. The research projects were later presented at Myanmar's first HE conference attended by Dr Myo Thein Gyi, the Union Minister for Education (Figure 4.2). Linking research to community benefit and teaching is new and still in the very early stages, however it is clear that given the space, academics will want to undertake research. According to the CESR, centres of research excellence were just beginning, but these were: 'still not well benchmarked

Figure 4.1 Transforming Higher Education Programme, senior management from 11 universities, 2018. Source: Author.

Figure 4.2 First National Higher Education Conference with Minister of Education, 2018. Source: Author.

against international standards, and funding arrangements for them are unclear' (CESR, 2013: 32). This development means that it is likely that elite universities will start to develop a more sustained research culture, most likely with the help of some of the internationalisation processes and links with international universities (further discussed below).

Teaching and learning challenges

Higher education curricula and subject syllabuses are out-dated because teaching is not linked to research, and because Myanmar HEIs have not had access to international content, models and standards for a number of decades. The ministry has traditionally set what is taught, including choosing textbooks. Students are expected to learn content by heart and demonstrate their 'knowledge' of the subject in an exam. The teaching methodology, which resembles the rote learning or ordinary school classrooms, is part of the problem. This means that students are not expected to use what they have learnt to solve problems or demonstrate independent critical thinking skills. The CESR Phase 1 Report on Higher Education (CESR, 2013) pointed out that no feedback on either the curriculum or teaching and learning experience is collected from students, and that employers and industry have no opportunity to contribute to curriculum development, making graduates woefully inadequate for the labour market.

To start to address this, the BC funded a short programme to help improve HE teaching methodology. It was offered both in Yangon and Mandalay Universities in 2017 and the report on the programme concluded that: 'The workshops proved without doubt that there is an appetite for changing professional practice in HE and that once new practices have been modelled with participants they are adopted enthusiastically' (Wright and Stoakes, 2017: 5–7). It was reported that the staff who took part were interested in receiving more staff development so that their practice would be closer to what is practiced internationally. The report also explained that part of the problem was that university teachers had had no pedagogical training, and whilst they knew their subject, they were used to teaching from the textbook. The experience is similar even at very senior levels. Many of the university staff such as rectors, pro-rectors and heads of department who took part in the 'Transforming Higher Education in Myanmar' training mentioned above, also expressed a great desire for more autonomy in the classroom, on what to teach and how to teach it – especially those from the elite universities who now have increased access to resources. Things are even more difficult in universities in remote parts of the country where there is little internet access and where books and materials are still out-dated. However, two (both located in ethnic states) of the 11 participating universities undertook a project on student experience and changing teaching methods as an experiment to see how this would affect students. The feedback they received showed that the more interesting classes resulted in reduced student absenteeism. This was also reflected in the earlier BC study that focused on teaching methods, where HEI teaching staff had come to the conclusion that in many cases the reasons for absenteeism was the lack of motivating classes, often due to the textbooks but also the lack of teaching skills and the failure to constructively align the teaching, learning and assessment: 'If the mode of assessment is usually an end of year/semester exam which asks students to memorise knowledge from the textbook, there is little reason to attend the classes' (Wright and Stoakes, 2017: 23).

The NESP does put the issue of quality at the heart of HE reform, linking its problems to the centralised model of governance, the inadequate infrastructure and the lack of staff training in 'experiment-focused' methodologies. However, the NESP also explains that: 'University education is criticised for too much emphasis on a rote-learning culture and not providing students with knowledge and skills relevant to Myanmar's societal and employment needs' (MoE, 2016: 55). This means that teaching methods need to improve and university staff need support at different levels. For example, class sizes, access to the internet, up-to-date materials and the assessment system are all barriers to improving the teaching and learning experience at Myanmar universities. A key part of the problem also relates to the language of instruction being English, when so many Myanmar students leave school without a decent grasp of the language, and while so many university teachers also lack fluency.

A report on the workshop on the issue of English as the university language of instruction, organised by the British Academy and *École Française d'Extrême-Orient*, notes that national law allows individual universities and departments to choose their preferred language of instruction, either English or Burmese or some combination of the two, but that in practice Myanmar universities have adopted a policy whereby English is used as the sole medium of instruction with explanations of terminology or concepts in Burmese if necessary (British Academy and *École Française d'Extrême-Orient*, 2015). The policy emanates from the perception that English is important for the students to master and that any quality international HE system needs to be conducted in English. In 1962, the Ne Win Government had overseen a 'nativisation' of university materials, many of which were translated into Burmese in order to remove what was perceived as the 'colonial legacy' of the British from Myanmar's education system.[13] However, this period is also associated with poverty and economic decline, and consequently, Burmese language is associated 'with economic failure and insularity' and people 'think of the Burmese language as somehow not sufficient' (British Academy and *École Française d'Extrême-Orient*, 2015: 6). Consequently, in 1985, English textbooks were reintroduced into the universities and by 1990 the use of English at universities had become the norm. In light of this, it is interesting to note that before the 2015 election, the NLD suggested that the: 'Medium of instruction shall be decided independently by each university (for example, English, Burmese, etc.)' (Mackenzie, 2013: 16).[14]

In practice, however, it is clear that many of the academic staff tasked to teach in English have not mastered the language well enough and that students do not understand sufficient English to follow classes either. This became apparent when, at the BC–IPE-funded programme of 'Transforming Higher Education in Myanmar', a translator was required to summarise all English lectures by the visiting international staff to make sure that all senior academics were able to follow the proceedings. There is also a discrepancy between staff in Yangon and Mandalay Universities and staff in universities across the country. Therefore, the adoption of English as the language of instruction is highly problematic and makes university education even less accessible to ordinary Myanmar citizens, especially those of ethnic backgrounds whose mother tongue is not Burmese and who have struggled to understand their Burmese-speaking teacher at school. This language disadvantage, discussed in detail in Chapter 6 of this volume, remains one of the biggest barriers for ethnic students to access HE.

Higher education in reform

Higher education reforms began in 2012 just like the reforms of the other education sectors under the CESR. However, the first indication of the changes that were to come was during Vice President Dr Sai Mauk Kham's visit to Mandalay University in July 2011 (*New Light of Myanmar*, 2011). His address included the message that an educated society was needed to: 'lead the establishment of a modern and developed nation' and that whilst the government had spent a lot of money on establishing HEIs and there were more and more graduates, the quality of the graduates was 'lower gradually' and 'the qualification of faculty members is also declining'. This was the first time such a senior member of the Myanmar Government admitted that Myanmar's HE system had quality issues. Dr Sai Mauk Kham, himself an ethnic Shan, also referred to inclusive and equitable HE (*New Light of Myanmar*, 2011: 16): 'University is a garden where students like colorful flowers blossom. Faculty members are like gardeners. Only when over 100 species of flowers blossom, will it be a beautiful garden.'

These concerns were reflected in the CESR reports, but were largely absent from the new law. A key part of the reforms was the drafting of the National Education Law in 2014 that defined the key issues facing HE in Myanmar as: university autonomy, the right to form unions and the right of universities to formulate their own curriculum (Kamibeppu and Chao, 2017). The National Education Law (2014, amended 2015) was not without controversy; as mentioned in Chapter 2, student protests occurred in the streets of Yangon and other cities in Myanmar. As discussed earlier in this volume, student protests have been part of Myanmar's political scene since independence, but tight controls meant that hardly any protests took place between 1990 and 2014.[15] Rose Metro argues that student protests are linked to the country's history as students have protested for decades not only on education issues, but also on social and economic issues (Metro, 2017). After the new National Education Law was made public, the students organised themselves under the banner of the 'Action Committee for Democratic Education' (ACDE) and went back onto the streets (*The Irrawaddy*, 2015).[16] Some of their 11 demands[17] were framed in terms of equity and social justice. This included the demand about equality for students with disabilities and the inclusion of ethnic languages in HE so that ethnic students could more easily take part. Other demands focused more on issues of governance and autonomy, in particular, the freedom to establish student and teacher unions, as well as the inclusion of teachers and students in HE policy making. Metro argues that the National Education Law makes it clear that the three governments – the SPDC (1988–2010), the Thein Sein USDP-led government (2011–5) and the NLD-led government (2015–onwards) – have very similar conceptions of 'democratic education' and want to centralise control of HE and HEIs (Metro, 2017: 211). She argues that the autonomy promised to universities by the National Education Law is largely symbolic, as the NEPC will retain control over the curriculum. '… the law functions like an elaborate shell game, in which autonomy is promised to regional and local authorities, but actual decision-making power remains in the hands of the central government' (Metro, 2017: 213). Students felt this way as well, and the initial student protests began in May 2014. These were followed by a 4-day march in November 2014 and a 60-day ultimatum to the government to organise a quadripartite meeting that was to include the student leaders, the NNER, members of parliament and the government. The Minister of Education, Dr Mya Aye, urged the students to meet with EPIC. When the students' ultimatum expired, protesting students from around the country went on a 404-mile march. The first quadripartite meeting took place in February 2015. At the start of that meeting, the NLD issued a statement that the leader of the NNER, Dr Thein Lwin, who had until then been an NLD central committee member, did not represent the party, disowning him and the NNER movement completely. This came as a shock to students who could not understand why the NLD would not support them at such a crucial time. It also showed that the NLD would side with the government rather than the protesting students when it came to governance, centralisation and control issues. The quadripartite negotiations did not reach a satisfactory conclusion and student protests continued. In March 2015, the government used force, cracking down on the students, beating them with batons in the streets and arresting them.[18] Ultimately, the contentious National Education Law was revised in 2015, but there were only minor concessions from the government and it remained largely as it had been originally drafted.

The National League for Democracy's (NLD) higher education reform project

Education has remained a key priority of the NLD Government. Former Rector of West Yangon University, Dr Myo Thein Gyi, a hardliner during the 2014 student protests,[19] was appointed Minister of Education by Daw Aung San Suu Kyi.[20] Since 2016, he has headed the education reform process focused on delivering the priorities as defined by the NESP.

Three strategies for HE reform are identified in the NESP (MoE, 2016), based on the National Education Law and the CESR. These are: 'to strengthen higher education governance and management capacity; to improve the quality and relevance of higher education; and to expand equitable access to higher education'. The NESP expects universities to gradually become more autonomous. Whilst devolution offers universities the opportunity to take control, the biggest hurdle remains the centralised budget that does not allow individual institutions to make their own decisions. Universities will, therefore, face challenges to develop their own research agenda. Curricula that have traditionally been passed down from the MoE to teach subjects will have to be revised, and courses supplemented with new and relevant material for which individual universities and not the MoE will be responsible, without much in the way of resources for making such changes. For the first time, universities will have to engage with issues such as ethics, student engagement, international engagement and at high-level meetings new ways of funding are being discussed which could mean significant changes for the way universities operate.[21] The first steps in this direction have been taken with Yangon and Mandalay Universities being allowed to select their students, and it is expected that as a next step they will be allowed to hire some of their own staff,[22] with this being a test case for granting autonomy.

The NLD's focus has been on the historical flagship of Yangon University, with Daw Aung San Suu Kyi pushing to restore it to its former 'glory' as one of Asia's leading universities. She personally asked both Britain and Australia to support Yangon University's development. In fact, Yangon University was expected to become the first autonomous arts and science university, although interviews at the MoE in September 2019 showed that the MoE planned to have 14 universities reach autonomy across two clusters – Yangon and Mandalay – by the end of 2020.[23] In his early assessment of Myanmar's HE system and the potential for reforms, Professor Kenneth King had noted that academic freedom was key to some, but less so to others whose priorities were more around a more balanced teaching schedule:

> Academic autonomy meant different things to different people. Academics were in fact civil servants and many were not in fact anxious to change this status. For others, academic freedom meant a change to the situation in which they had almost no free time. For staff in regular arts and science universities there were major demands on their time from the several cycles of assessment, and intensive 10-day preparation, related to the requirements of the distance university students. This was compulsory for them, so their concern was not so much academic freedom, but they had almost no free time at all during the year. (Mackenzie, 2013:16)

Before coming to power the NLD had promised: 'educational freedom in order to increase opportunities for learning, raise the secondary school completion rates and the quality of education' (Thein Lwin, cited in Mackenzie, 2013:16). The recommendations go on to promise: 'There shall be academic freedom in research and freedom to publish the findings. Universities shall have the freedom to engage with different universities and institutions around the world for educational purposes' (Thein Lwin, cited in Mackenzie, 2013:16). The BC report points out that: 'the same "Recommendations" suggest that although different university departments should write their own curriculum, they also say that the university's council should compile a draft curriculum, and then send it up to the Universities Central Council for approval' (Mackenzie, 2013:16), so it is unclear how much autonomy and academic freedom will actually be given.

Yangon University's test case shows how the top-down nature of education reforms is likely to impact universities in a rather more cosmetic than substantive way. Drawing on Arnhold et al.'s educational reconstruction conceptual framework (Arnhold et al., 1998), Esson and Wang analysed the reform process of Yangon University in 2013 and argued that efforts have failed to consider the ideological and psychological reconstruction of the university within the reform process (Esson and Wang, 2018). Esson and Wang describe how, in November 2012, a special parliamentary committee personally chaired by Daw Aung San Suu Kyi was formed to oversee the reform of Yangon University. Once Yangon University was designated as a 'Centre of Excellence' and given priority to upgrade its facilities to international standards, the physical reconstruction began with (in 2012–3) a budget of MMK 6446.6 million (approximately USD 7.2 million) – just in time for President Obama's visit. Government funds were supplemented by a donation of MMK 500 million (approximately USD 555,000) made by Yangon University alumni. According to Esson and Wang, the money was spent mostly on cosmetic changes such as painting and decorating while the staff and students would have prioritised upgrading basic facilities such as water and electricity supplies (Esson and Wang, 2018: 1184–90).[24] Esson and Wang go on to describe how a library officer complained that despite the reforms: 'both of the main libraries still do not have a computerised search facility, and people still have to use manual card-catalogues for book searches' (Esson and Wang, 2018: 1190). In keeping with the traditional top-down way of implementing change, policies have been implemented with little or no consultation with staff and/or students (Esson and Wang, 2018: 1192). The article does describe other positive changes that have emerged as part of Yangon University's change in status – one being that staff are now allowed to engage internationally and enter into international collaborations, principally with the aim to facilitate staff capacity building. More on this is detailed below.

Myanmar's new higher education institutions

The NESP requires new HE coordinating bodies to be established to underpin the change process in HE. This includes the NEPC in 2019, NIHED and the Rectors' Committee (established in 2018). The NEPC is the overarching body, independent from the MoE, and focused on the formulation and implementation of the reform of education policy. It was designed to have an executive role in advising and coordinating HE policy and legislation in the form of Myanmar's 30-year Long-term Education Development Plan as well as coordinating with development partners (Channon, 2017). At the time of writing, the NEPC comprises three committees: the National Curriculum Committee, the National Accreditation and Quality Assurance Committee (NAQAC), and a Rectors' Committee, as well as an affiliated National Institute for Higher Education Development.

The Rectors' Committee was established in March 2018 with representatives from 173 of Myanmar's public universities. It is a coordination, collaboration and negotiation body that is supporting universities with reform, and is meant to guide the process leading to autonomy, starting with limited decentralisation. It is expected to become the collective national HE governance body representing and taking collective responsibility for a system of autonomous universities.

NAQAC is responsible for quality policies for the entire education sector. Currently, NAQAC is focusing on developing standards and guidelines for accreditation and quality assurance for Myanmar's HEIs, based on the relevant ASEAN instruments. At the time of writing, it is unclear how institutions will relate their own governance and quality structures to NAQAC.

NIHED was established: 'to improve higher education governance and management' and 'build individual skills and strengthen institutional capabilities'. Its mandate included supporting policy makers through research and supporting HEI senior staff through training so as to sustain the reform process. The BC–IPE-funded programme of 'Transforming Higher Education in Myanmar' was tasked with training the senior trainers of NIHED and co-constructing part of a leadership and management curriculum with them.

These new administrative structures are meant to support the HE reform process and move universities towards more autonomy, yet in many ways they maintain traditional hierarchies. Structural change is also not sufficient in achieving what is a monumental shift. The sectoral needs assessment undertaken by the Leadership Foundation (UK) in 2016-7 suggested that senior HE staff needed training at three levels – system, institutional and personal. This included training in funding, quality assurance, institutional accountability, information management, planning and reporting, governance frameworks, leadership behaviours, institutional strategy development and how quality systems can be set up to improve research, teaching and assessment. It also included practical management skills such as leading and managing change, motivational skills, stakeholder management (including with potential international university partners), analysis and critical thinking and effective decision making. The main challenge for the university staff is how to work in an increasingly autonomous system, rather than take orders from above. At the moment, it looks like the NEPC may simply replace the MoE in the top-down role it has played, unless the academic staff receive relevant training to change ways of working across the system. To remedy this, the Leadership Foundation suggested that development for rectors and pro rectors: 'should focus on strategy, quality assurance, management information and sources of funding' and that: 'training for administrative Heads and Registrars should focus on data, governance and strategy issues' (Leadership Foundation for Higher Education, 2016: 17).

Distance education: Increasing access?

There are a number of reasons why Myanmar hosts one of the world's largest (but also possibly worst) distance education systems, with around 500,000 part-time students. In part, distance education offers access to the poorer sections of society, where students can study part time whilst still working and living at home. It also received state support as a result of the 1988 and 1990 student protests – students who are not living together in university residences are less likely to get involved in national protests. The current system is coordinated by two distance education universities, Yangon University of Distance Education (YUDE) for Lower Myanmar, and Mandalay University of Distance Education (MUDE) for Upper Myanmar. There are 19 bachelor-level courses delivered by 35 learning centres (15 for YUDE and 20 for MUDE) in day universities providing national coverage (Fawssett and Gregson 2016: 3). However, teachers have not been trained to deliver courses appropriately through a distance learning pedagogy. Distance education arts students attend the day university twice a year, once to enrol, between January to March, the other time for 10 days to prepare for and sit the exam at the end of the academic year (October–November) for what is in effect a cramming session that covers the same material as what is usually delivered over four months for full-time students. Science students are additionally required to attend 12 weekends over the year for practical sessions. There are no dedicated distance education staff. All sessions are delivered by day university teachers[25] mostly in Burmese – something they have to do on top of their regular workload of teaching day students. Since the exam preparation cramming sessions cover the same material the students have been asked to learn at home, students do not always attend for the whole 10 days although it is compulsory (Fawssett and Gregson, 2016: 20–1). Some teachers also offer private tuition for both full-time and distance students, which allows students to engage with the teachers directly. Most people in Myanmar are aware of the low quality of the distance education system, yet interestingly research by the Open University found that employers (that were interviewed for that research) said they did not distinguish between distance education and full-time HE degrees, rather employment depended on the skills of the candidates (Fawssett and Gregson, 2016: 27).

Inclusive higher education?

Given that HE is almost free and there are over 150 institutions around the country and a large distance education system for those who have to work or cannot live away from home, one could imagine that Myanmar has an inclusive tradition of HE. Yet the CESR Phase 1 Report on Higher Education quotes that only 11 per cent of Myanmar youth are able to access HE (CESR, 2013). Entrance to university depends on students' scores in the matriculation exam, taken in Grade 10 at the age of 16.[26] According to the MoE, 35 per cent of those sitting pass the exam, and of these 40 per cent are from urban areas, 32 per cent from rural areas, and 21 per cent are from poor families (MoE, 2014: 21). There are important regional differences, with Chin State having the lowest matriculation pass rate at 17 per cent. It is clear that students from urban areas are almost twice as likely to go to university as poorer students from rural areas, who would additionally have to bear the cost of boarding, a major disincentive for poor families.[27] The fact that there are few scholarships, and those that do exist are so low (sometimes just a few hundred MMKs a month) that they barely warrant the effort of the application compounds the problem, so it is not enough that fees are low.[28]

There are also substantial gender differences in HE. Girls overall tend to do better than boys although rural girls are still at a disadvantage.[29] In fact, superficially, the gender disparity seems to go against boys and men with significantly more female students enrolled than male students. This is even more pronounced in the arts and science HEIs. There are also more female university teaching staff – mirroring the imbalance of female–male teachers in schools, largely because the low salaries make the profession unattractive to men. Disaggregated figures for HE are not available, however the IHLCS shows that, for the overall education sector, employment represented 1 per cent of the overall male workforce, compared with 4.9 per cent for women (Mackenzie, 2013: 27–8).

Traditionally, the main focus of 'inclusion' in education in Myanmar has been on poorer sections of society through donations to monasteries to support monastic schools (as seen in Chapter 3), rather than equality and equity pertaining to the unequal access to education of different ethnic groups.[30] This inequity has been brought to the fore through the incomplete peace process that has run in parallel with the wider education and other reforms (Lall and South, 2018). It is generally recognised that ethnic students have had less access to education as a whole, and HE in particular, largely because of lasting disadvantages due to the language barrier at primary school level. Currently, there is no ethnic breakdown of participation of ethnic students in HE.[31] The CESR Phase 1 Report on Higher Education had already identified this gap, saying it was unclear how Myanmar's wide ethnic diversity was represented in HE (CESR, 2013: 1). Equity in this report is represented in terms of a traditional belief in: 'the five pillars of Myanmar society – farmers, workers, students, monks and the military' and the need to unite them (Channon, 2017: 22). This is to foster an atmosphere of: 'empathy and trust … in the pursuit of a common goal which is posited as: 'the development of the nation' (CESR, 2013: 22). The difficulties involved in achieving this are acknowledged and inequality and poverty are cited as major obstacles. Two recommendations in this CESR Phase 1 Report on Higher Education included, first, to support modelling exercises designed to determine the relative costs and benefits of widening access to HE, including the option of raising fees; and second, to develop an index of minimum quality using teacher-to-student ratios. In comparison with the CESR Phase 1 Report on Higher Education, which identified barriers to access on the basis of ethnicity as a key priority (explicitly referencing the Rohingyas), the CESR Phase 2 Report (Brady and CESR, 2014) shied away from explicitly addressing exclusion resulting from ethnicity, gender, religion, language or disability (Channon, 2017). Emerging out of the CESR reports, one of the NESP strategies for the reform and development of the HE sector is to expand: 'equitable access to higher education'. It is unclear who is included in this definition of 'equity' but one can deduce from the wider text that the prime focus is on the poor as opposed to those from minority backgrounds, especially those whose first language might not be Burmese.[32] The recommendations include creating a good learning environment (including good dormitories for those coming from distant locations) and promoting student support programmes so that students from disadvantaged backgrounds can access and complete their studies. This last NESP component is rather thinner than the others and the language is significantly watered down from the original CESR Phase 1 Report on Higher Education.

Senior MoE staff are aware of the issues of inclusion, widening participation and inequity between ethnic groups and regions. This was evident when a member of the NEPC gave a presentation at the second National Conference on Higher Education in October 2018 in Yangon's Diamond Jubilee Hall. His presentation entitled 'Equity in Myanmar's Higher Education: Opportunities and Challenges', emphasised that engaging with these issues was still a major priority of Myanmar's HE reform.[33] Explaining the disparities across Myanmar society based on geographic regions, ethnic groups (in this case, based on numbers of people living in ethnic states as opposed to an ethnic breakdown),[34] socio-economic status, disability and gender, he held that increased disparity would widen the social divide, gradually leading to social unrest, and conflict and chaos in the society. Therefore 'equity interventions' were needed to reduce disparities and include marginalised groups to ensure social justice, and facilitate social cohesion, peace and prosperity of the whole society. Based on data from the 2014 census, examples of inequity presented included the higher urban rates of education completion, much higher numbers of urban female than male students enrolled in HEIs, and 68 per cent of young people from the richest quintile attaining education levels beyond secondary education versus only 1.2 per cent of those from the poorest quintile going beyond secondary education. Although not explicitly expressed, it was acknowledged that rural-based ethnic young people are, therefore, least likely to achieve similar education outcomes to their Bamar[35] urban counterparts.

Referring to the relevant policy texts of the 2008 Constitution, the 2014 and 2015 National Education Law, the 2015 Law for Protection of the Rights of National Races and the 2015 Law on the Rights of Persons with Disability, the senior policy official explained that Myanmar, as part of its reforms, had made commitments to reduce inequity from a legislative perspective, but that programmes were needed to put these into practice. One way forward, he suggested, was to establish more HEIs across the country to address the imbalanced distribution reflected in too many students (60 per cent) enrolling in the low-quality distance education programmes. The urban and rural divide is also seen in the allocation of resources, reflected in regional universities having much worse teacher-to-student ratios than urban institutions, with a teacher-to-student ratio of 1:5 in Yangon University but 1:29 in Kalay University in the west of the country. The key challenge that emerged from the conference keynote was that of balancing equity and inclusion on one hand, and quality and excellence on the other, captured through the phrase 'Inclusive Excellence'. Figure 4.3 shows the follow-on session where participants were asked to think about how to work on inclusion at an institutional level.

Figure 4.3 Second National Higher Education Conference, 2018: Building Quality and Equity in Higher Education. Source: Author.

This policy perspective is supported by Lynne Heslop's interviews of two MoE officials, who saw the government's efforts towards peace-building reflected in the opening of universities in rural and ethnic areas to enable greater access and participation of marginalised and conflict-affected communities (Heslop, 2019). One of them is quoted as saying: 'We would like to consider the inclusive and equitable access for the education, because Myanmar has very diverse ethnic groups. That's why in every region and state there are universities for social science, science and engineering and computer universities' (Heslop, 2019: 184–5). Heslop argues that, on the one hand, the opening of more universities in ethnic states can be seen to contribute to a more equitable access to HE, but that on the other, keeps ethnic intellectuals separate from the Bamar majority areas, to possibly counter student activism and possible challenges to the state.

Competing with the region and international collaborations

As mentioned in the introduction, Myanmar's HE reform has been driven by the desire to catch up with the rest of the world and to give students suitable skills for the job market. Much of what is happening in HE is, therefore, being contextualised within ASEAN and Myanmar's desire is to adopt ASEAN standards as benchmarks for its own reform goals. The CESR Phase 1 Report on Higher Education also saw adapting to ASEAN benchmarks as a way to engage with Myanmar's issues of wider societal inequalities and social justice (CESR, 2013: 2):

> Myanmar's Human Development Index (HDI) remains low in comparison with those of its Southeast Asian neighbours. Income distribution remains unequal, with significant disparities evident between rural and urban incomes, and geographically. A Gender Inequality Index (GEI) of 100 is higher than neighbouring ASEAN member states. Rates of poverty declined from 32.1% in 2005 to 25.6% in 2010 – but these figures do properly reflect the extent of the poverty gaps between rural and urban populations, ethnic groups, and combinations thereof. The UNDP's Human Development Report for 2011 showed over 23% of the population suffering multidimensional poverty, 13.4% of the population as being vulnerable to poverty, and 9.4% of the population as being vulnerable to extreme poverty. HDI scores, though up from 0.30

in 1990 to 0.48 in 2011, remain the lowest for Southeast Asia. Myanmar's global HDI rank is currently 149, of a total country count of 187. These circumstances impact directly on educational participation and progression.

It is clear that the current state of Myanmar's HE system compares unfavourably with its neighbours in the region in terms of investment in education, research output, knowledge economy indices and enrolment ratios. The government has recognised that alongside the need for infrastructure development to match modern universities in the region, there is also a need for capacity building in teaching, administration and research quality as significant priorities if Myanmar is to be comparable to its neighbours and wider afield. In fact, the evidence from the CESR and the NESP suggests that Myanmar wishes to align its HE system with its neighbours in order to move to become a world-class HE system that can enter global university rankings. Multiple interviews with the Department of Higher Education at the MoE have shown this to be a prime motivator and that both the MoE and the senior staff of the NEPC want to see Yangon University listed in a recognised rankings system. In order to do this, Myanmar HEIs have begun the process of integration into the ASEAN University Network Quality Assurance Framework (AUN-QA).[36] The aim is not solely academic – adapting to shared and recognised frameworks is also driven by the concern to develop a recognised qualifications system that will promote greater workforce mobility. Human capital creation and a qualified workforce is part of NESP's mission statement (MoE, 2016: 188): 'to produce graduate human resources who possess the required qualifications for the construction of a new, modern, developed, disciplined, democratic nation', requiring graduate qualifications to be accepted outside of Myanmar. This is also why Myanmar is taking part in the EU-funded SHARE programme that focuses on quality assurance and transferability of degrees.[37] SHARE's overarching objective is to: strengthen regional cooperation, enhance the quality, competitiveness and internationalisation of ASEAN HEIs and students, contributing to an ASEAN Community beyond 2015'. SHARE activities build on the related ASEAN Qualifications Reference Framework (AQRF) Task Force that is being developed by the ASEAN–Australia and New Zealand Free Trade Area (AANZFTA). Part of the work is also to develop a credit transfer system that aims to facilitate student mobility, that in turn is supported by intra-ASEAN and ASEAN–EU scholarships.

International engagement and international partnerships

Funding to HE by international donors and agencies has been limited – in fact, Heslop argues that HE has been largely neglected by development partners and international aid agencies (Heslop, 2019). A range of short-term capacity-building programmes have been funded by UNESCO, the BC and the Open Society Foundation. While Australia, the UK, Japan and China offer scholarships, JICA is the only development partner that has a sustained programme of support for some of Myanmar's technical HEIs, in particular, Yangon Technological University and Mandalay Technological University. The representative for JICA in Tokyo mentioned that their particular focus is on engineering, the medical and agricultural sectors. Overall, JICA is collaborating with six technical universities in Myanmar, including establishing labs at Yangon Technological University as well as sending academics in residence to Yangon Technological University and Mandalay Technological University to help enhance research capability and the quality of undergraduate teaching. Beyond this, Japan is supporting 26 Myanmar HEIs by strengthening the Engineering Education ASEAN Network (Phase VI, 2018–21). Aside from offering scholarships for 44 doctoral students at Japanese universities, JICA also supports HE by linking HEIs with industry, sending university students to companies for internship in Thilawa SEZ, which is largely run by Japanese companies.[38]

Most of HE's international engagement seems to be through university partnerships where Myanmar universities have signed MoUs with international counterparts. At the start of the reforms, in 2012, such MoUs were signed without much thought of how to leverage them to the advantage of the Myanmar HEI. In 2014–5, the MoE reported 102 MoUs and MoAs with foreign institutions, falling to 51 and 29 in the subsequent 2 years (MoE 2019c: 53, Fig. 2.6.4). Many ended up in a filing cabinet without much follow up. Most international universities have been particularly interested in engaging with Yangon or Mandalay Universities as opposed to regional universities, or technical specialist universities in Yangon and/or Mandalay. Esson and Wang describe how Yangon University has developed its programme of internationalisation through: 'visiting academics programmes with the Open Society Foundation, two centres of excellence – one in collaboration with the University of Cologne (Germany), and the other a joint venture with Johns Hopkins University (USA) and Chung Aung University (South Korea), and the e-Tekkatho project (an on-line and off-line library database project) with the University of Manchester (UK)' (Esson and Wang, 2018: 1191). These collaborations have not been without challenges and whilst staff and students in Esson and Wang's research hope that such exposure will serve as a catalyst for change, all those taking part still face the challenge that any fieldwork that might be required still has to be authorised, and are subject to 'long standing and ingrained attempts to control academic freedom' (Esson and Wang, 2018: 1192). Their research shows that academics in the sciences had more freedom to conduct the research as they wished compared to those in the arts and social sciences.[39]

Lynne Heslop's doctoral work examining the international collaborations of four Myanmar HEIs (three government universities and one private HEI) with British institutions, shows that the benefits of such collaborations are also limited for the Myanmar partner universities. Her study exposes the injustice in the HE international interactions as well as how the internationalisation processes that are supposed to help build the capacity of Myanmar HEIs actually end up: 'entrenching inequalities in the global circulation of knowledge production, perpetuate the epistemological subordination of Myanmar researchers, and create or maintain economic, cultural and political hegemonies in resources and power, reproducing the dependencies of Myanmar public HEIs and privileging Northern HEI partners' (Heslop, 2019: 5). Her work, focused on answering the question in how far HEI partnerships could improve social justice in Myanmar, concludes that these kinds of interactions do not in general allow for greater social justice within Myanmar or between Myanmar and the wider world of global academia.

Mid-Term Review of the NESP

As already discussed in Chapter 2, in the summer of 2019, the NESP reached its mid-point and the MoE organised a MTR (MoE, 2019b and 2020) to establish if the reforms were 'on track'. For HE, this meant reviewing the three drivers for change.

With regard to 'Strengthening Management (including autonomy)', the MTR reports that the Rectors consider 'Autonomy' the highest priority reform. While the NESP does not envisage full independence of HEIs, it was envisaged that they should have autonomous decision making over elements such as: governance and management; academic profile and curriculum; external and financial partnerships; and research. The MTR reports that the Department for Higher Education has increased technical support to an initial lead batch of (no more than eight) HEIs: 'to make integrated progress with establishment of new arrangements for autonomy, piloting of new admissions process, piloting quality assurance processes, providing management and leadership support to Rectors' and HEI management' (MoE, 2020: xiii). Autononomy was officially granted to 16 HEIs in September 2016.

In regard to the driver of 'Quality and Relevance', which includes developing a quality assurance framework for all sub sectors so as to provide a framework for, and assessment of, the achievement of quality of education against standards, with the aim of sustaining the reforms over the long term, the MTR reports that: 'Progress has been made: an external quality assurance system for Higher Education is in development' and due to be implemented in 2020 (MoE, 2020: x–xi).

There is less of a review of what has been achieved in relation to 'Equitable Access'. The MTR reviews distance education and concludes that it is: 'widely available but needs significant improvement' as the number of students accessing this system of HE: 'is now approximately equal to the number of students attending university'. The MTR seems to conclude that least progress has been made in this area as: 'There appears to be little investment in the development of online resources or the development of dedicated delivery platforms. There was little investment in developing quality face-to-face events to supplement the individual, home based learning' (MoE, 2020: x–xi). No more is said on how to rectify the inequities within the system.

Conclusion

As Myanmar embraces a globalising world, HE in Myanmar is poised for a deep transformation. Developing indigenous HE systems has been a pathway out of dependence on colonial powers (Castells, 1994). However, neo-liberal policies can function to recreate dependent relationships, especially if international standards become the domestic benchmarks and links with global universities are the main medium for quality enhancement. The international markers for success may need to be adapted with new criteria and incentives (Naidoo, 2007).

As discussed by Kandiko-Howson and Lall, there are possibilities for developing countries such as Myanmar to showcase models for excellence that build on traditional values, notably inclusion, care for the environment and more sustainable ways of living (Kandiko-Howson and Lall, 2020). However, while the pathway of internationalisation that Myanmar's HE system has chosen might take it out of international isolation, there is a risk of creating new exploitative relationships (through the MoUs universities are signing that benefit the international partners more than themselves). In order to become 'recognised', the universities in Myanmar have to accept international practices. Some of these will improve the quality of their research and teaching, others, such as competition for funding, will just reproduce neo-liberal policies that are failing in other countries. The desire to promote (and to financially support) developing competitive research-intensive universities places pressure on flagship urban institutions to work towards international levels of research and publications, whereas regional universities are not brought into this discourse. This is likely to increase stratification of the system, exacerbating the urban and rural divide and subsequent consequences for equity across the country. For example, a neo-liberal push for international collaboration with urban flagship universities is at odds with local needs for HE to promote integration and social justice across ethnic regions and conflict-affected regions within the country (Heslop, 2019). Domestically, it is clear that a tiered – perhaps even three-tier system – is being proposed, with Yangon and Mandalay Universities at the helm of an elite system, and regional universities in ethnic states at the bottom of the pile, not being given the required autonomy, and not benefitting from greater investment. This, in turn, will embed the disparities between ethnic students who manage to get into universities close to home, compared to the Bamar students accessing urban HE provision, in turn, exacerbating the already existing social inequalities. What is proposed is a system that will not be able to increase social justice. Second- and third-tier universities, their staff and students are unlikely to receive the same recognition and respect as their elite counterparts. The NESP MTR already shows that issues of equity and access are not the sector's top priority.

Notes

1 The author was part of a small team training the NIHED senior trainers and supporting NIHED in its first HE training of 11 universities.
2 There are over 500,000 students at the University of Distance Education (Yangon) that serves Lower Myanmar and at the University of Distance Education (Mandalay) that serves Upper Myanmar. The largest Open University in the world is India's Indira Gandhi Open University with around 4 million students, however, it offers both distance and face-to-face education.
3 This is a double disadvantage as HE is supposed to be in English, and the books are in English, even if the actual teaching is in Burmese. Many ethnic nationality students are unable to matriculate because of their poor levels of Burmese, making it impossible for them to access HE. Those who do make it then find that following course materials in English presents a double challenge.

4   Renamed when Rangoon was renamed Yangon.
5   Having been replaced in 1962 by Burmese.
6   This has recently been reversed as part of the education reforms with both universities now having resumed undergraduate provision.
7   The author was the academic from the University of London.
8   U Than Aung was the Education Minister with whom Professor Robert Taylor and Dr Kyaw Yin Hlaing negotiated the first few teaching programmes at Yangon and Mandalay Universities. He was replaced by Dr Chan Nyein who cancelled the programme for the MoE, so it was arranged to move the teaching to the Myanmar Fisheries Federation (MFF) and the students came from Union Solidarity and Development Association (USDA). More on the role of MFF in Lall, 2016a.
9   'Yangon University, Mandalay University, Yangon Institute of Economics, Yangon Institute of Education, Mawlamyine University, Monywa Institute of Economics, Meiktila Institute of Economics, and Yangon University of Foreign Languages. About 2,000 candidates were enrolled in PhD programmes across these eight institutions – but this figure may not be entirely reliable. Possibly, as many as one-half of these candidates were enrolled at the University of Yangon' (CESR, 2013: 8).
10 Universities have: 'no authority on appointments, travel, research, promotion, curriculum development, disciplinary association conference, even the planning of a golden anniversary university conference' (senior staff comment). Another rector noted that there was 'no authority to appoint even lower order maintenance staff, even a window-cleaner. Everything had to go up 'through proper channels'. 'Even when a member of staff is invited to a prestigious conference in the region, the conference date may have passed before any decision is taken "on high". If someone is allowed to travel to a meeting, their passport has to be returned afterwards.' [...] HEIs have been formally without financial autonomy since the 1970s. However, from 1998, there has been the possibility of a measure of income generation through what are termed Human Resource Development (HRD) courses in most if not all HEIs under the MoE. These often take place early in the day, before regular working hours, or after work. As the CESR notes, the scale and the income associated with what are in effect parallel courses are not well known. But in at least one major university, the HRD numbers in masters and diploma courses are almost 50 per cent of the entire university enrolment. Also, CESR notes that the total number of HRD courses are 195 as compared with regular courses which are 215 (CESR, 2013).
11 Yangon University, Yangon Technological University, Yangon University of Education, Yangon University of Economics, Medicine 1 (Yangon), Mandalay University, Mandalay Technical University, Yezin Agricultural University, Taunggyi University, Sittwe University and Myitkyina University.
12 The BC-funded training focused on managing change and engaging senior staff with issues pertaining to developing their own curricula and assessments, and developing a research strategy as well as developing international partnerships with foreign universities. The author was part of the training team.
13 Burmese – which is the official language – is the native spoken language of approximately 30 million people out of a total population of over 53 million (British Academy and *École Française d'Extrême-Orient*, 2015: 5).
14 But presumably not including any ethnic languages.
15 There were some protests in Yangon in 1996, but they were put down very quickly.
16 Discussed also in Chapter 2.
17 The 11 demands are as follows:

- Inclusion of representatives of teachers and students in legislation process of education policies and laws, by-laws and other related laws
- The right to freely establish and operate student and teacher unions and legal recognition for them
- Establishment of National Education Commission and University Coordination Committee mentioned in the approved National Education Law
- Self-determination and self-management on educational affairs of individual state/regions and schools
- Modifying current examination and university matriculation system

- Modifying teaching methods to such that ensure freedom for thinking and self-studying of students
- Inclusion of a provision in the National Education Law that ensure freedom for the practice of ethnic languages and mother tongue-based multilingual education for ethnic populations and tribes
- Inclusive education for all children including children with disabilities
- Resumption of enrolment for students previously expelled from schools due to the student uprisings
- Allocation of 20 per cent of national budget for education
- Regulating of free compulsory education up to middle school level rather than primary level

18 BBC News. 2015. 'Myanmar riot police beat student protesters with batons'. 10 March 2015. https://www.bbc.co.uk/news/world-asia-31812028.
19 https://www.mmtimes.com/national-news/19825-opposition-builds-over-ministers.html
20 Daw Aung San Suu Kyi had appointed herself Minister of Education before the new role of State Counsellor was created for her.
21 https://www.universityworld-dnews.com/post.php?story=20190604151019822.
22 This of course is bound to create a difference between locally hired staff attached to individual universities versus staff hired by the MoE, who rotate between institutions and have government employee status. Whilst the universities are aware that this will create issues, at the time of writing, no solutions have been proposed.
23 In September 2020, 16 universities were granted autonomy.
24 Sanchez, J. (forthcoming). Blinded like a State? Urban sanitation, improvement and high modernism in contemporary Myanmar. *Political Geography*.
25 There is a system of rotation (Fawcett and Gregson, 2016: 8).
26 University entrance is being changed as part of the ongoing curricular and examination reforms process. It is unclear at the time of writing if the matriculation will stand, and be taken in Grade 11 or 12, and/or if universities will offer their own entrance exams (as in Japan).
27 Comprehensive Education Sector Review (CESR, 2013). According to a preliminary analysis of data from the IHLCS (IHLCS, 2011: 9) in Myanmar in 2009–10, the net enrolment rate of young people aged 18–21 in HE was 10.6 per cent, but with some marked disparities between different groups of young people. Among urban households, almost 30 per cent of 18 and 19 year olds were enrolled in HE, compared with about 9 per cent for rural households, and less than 5 per cent for poor rural households.
28 '[…] in the interests of equity, tuition fees are kept low, with 20,000 MMK (USD 23.50) commonly cited. A policy of having low tuition fees is very much in accord with regional initiatives to move towards more inclusive HE models, which do not discriminate against the poor, rural dwellers, women and ethnic minorities. In HEIs managed by the Ministry of Defence and all students are employees and have military ranks, no fees are applied, a practice that, according to one Rector allowed these HEIs to ensure that perhaps half their intake came from rural areas, with another 30% coming from poor families'(Mackenzie, 2013:18).
29 To remedy this, the pass mark for university entrance for boys has dropped (Fawssett and Gregson, 2016: 8).
30 Myanmar has 135 recognised ethnic groups and seven ethnic states that have a majority of ethnic residents. More on this in Chapters 6 and 7 of this volume.
31 The 2014 Census shows the break-down of people whose highest education attainment is post-secondary education by state, but not by ethnic group. In any case, the percentage of those having completed tertiary education in ethnic states is lower than the national average of 9 per cent (GoM, 2017: 56).
32 And who are therefore disadvantaged for life as they will have done less well on the school matriculation examination that to date is the entrance exam for all universities.
33 See Kandiko-Howson and La l, 2020 for more detail.
34 The ethnic breakdown figures in and outside the ethnic states collected in the 2014 Census remain unpublished. See Chapter 6 in this volume for more details.
35 Bamar (Burman) are the dominant ethnic group.
36 http://www.aunsec.org/aseanqaadbproject.php.

37 https://www.share-asean.eu/activities?_ga=2.36418528.1937099769.1565585196-933614781.1565585196.
38 Interview with Tokyo- and Yangon-based JICA staff on the HE reforms in 2018 and 2019.
39 One head of department based in the arts explained that all research proposals have to be submitted to the MoE not only for funding, but general approval, and the Ministry does not approve research topics deemed 'politically sensitive' (Esson and Wang, 2018: 1192–3).

5
Teacher education and training: Is changing practice possible?

Introduction

The chapter focuses on the reforms and the restructuring of teacher education and training in light of the issues faced by student teachers and teacher educators. Drawing on original survey data collected across 20 education colleges[1] in the midst of the reform process in 2015 and 2016, it engages with the views, hopes, challenges and fears faced by those who want to become teachers. As teacher training is being revised at the time of writing, the chapter can only reflect the realities as they are in the midst of flux, rather than discuss any tangible results of the reforms in this part of the education sector. What is clear throughout the process, however, is the lack of attention paid to the issues of inequalities inherent in the teaching profession as it stands.

The chapter also engages with a number of additional teacher training programmes supplemented by development partners, in particular, the more recent engagement of the BC-funded 'English for Education College Trainers' (EfECT) project that focused on upgrading teacher educators' English and teaching methodology; and the UNESCO 'Strengthening Teacher Education in Myanmar' (STEM) programme that is responsible for the review and upgrading of the pre-service teacher education curriculum. The chapter discusses how this teacher education curricular review is not in sync with the curricular reforms of basic education (discussed in Chapter 2 of this volume), as they are supported by different aid agencies with little communication or coordination. Teacher education is, therefore, another example of the tensions that arise from these uncoordinated efforts to improve education across Myanmar.

The issues relating to teacher education are complex, shaped by cultural gender politics and inequitable structures that result in many more female teachers in the system, yet with more of their male counterparts reaching positions of power by becoming TEOs or SEOs. Issues with ethnicity and language, specifically the special challenges faced by the few ethnic nationality student teachers who manage to get into the education colleges, are touched on and expanded upon in Chapter 6.[2] While the lack of ethnic teachers is a real issue for ethnic nationality children who cannot understand Burmese, this chapter focuses on gender inequities and discusses how reformed teacher education might become a key part of sustaining peace and social justice across the country.[3]

Background on teacher training

Until the 2012 education reforms, Myanmar did not have a comprehensive teacher education policy. Consequently, there was no framework for pre- or in-service teacher training and none for the professional standards the various education stakeholders were supposed to meet. According to a JICA report, pre-service teacher training had stopped in 1971 but was re-instituted in 1998 when five teacher training colleges (TTCs) and 14 teacher training schools (TTSs) were upgraded to education colleges (JICA, 2013). The system that is being reformed today has, therefore, been in place virtually unchanged for around 20 years.

Teacher trainees, known in Myanmar as student teachers, are required to have graduated with matriculation from upper secondary school. The main way of becoming a teacher has traditionally been to take the Diploma in Teacher Education (DTEd), a two-year post-matriculation course. Previously, there was a one-year certificate qualification route to become a primary school teacher, but the new pre-primary teacher training (PPTT), a four-month course for graduates to become primary teachers, has now replaced this. The DTEd allows teachers to teach at middle school level, although they will start as primary assistant teachers when they graduate, and then move up to middle school after five years when they can become junior assistant teachers (JAT). Under this system, if teachers wanted to become secondary school teachers or move on to administrative posts in education, they needed a Bachelor of Education degree that could be acquired at the Institutes of Education in Yangon or Sagaing, for those in Lower and Upper Myanmar respectively.[4] The whole system is being revamped as the new teacher education curriculum is being upgraded to a four-year degree level course, further discussed below.

The traditional basic career path of a teacher was linear, from primary assistant teacher (PAT), to junior assistant teacher (JAT) through to senior assistant teacher (SAT) and above. By gaining years of teaching experience and upgrading teaching certificates and degrees, teachers advanced in their careers and increased their salaries, moving from primary schools to secondary schools as they became more experienced. Due to the ascending linear salary system, once a teacher started their career, they started looking for a better position in a higher level school. It also meant that the most inexperienced teachers were serving at primary level, often in the most difficult and remote parts of the country, and the more experienced teachers were in secondary schools in urban areas. As discussed further below, this linear model is also being changed as part of the reforms, so that student teachers train towards a level (primary or secondary) and a specialisation.

At the time of writing, there are 22 education colleges and two institutes of education that produce around 10,000 teachers annually.[5] In the 2019–20 academic year, education colleges admitted 3,343 first-year student teachers (1,676 female and 1,667 male), for the new four-year degree programme (May San Yee, 2019). These numbers are lower than those for previous years, presumably, to ensure manageability for education colleges in the roll-out of the four-year degree programme. The four-year degree programme discussed further below was rolled-out in December 2019 for first-year student teachers while the second-year courses continue to follow the previous two-year curriculum.

To date, the Institutes of Education in Yangon and Sagaing approve any changes to the curriculum and ensure consistency across the board of the education colleges. The curriculum is quite demanding: 17 subjects are covered in the first year and 14 in the second year, including the following (UNESCO, 2016):

- Subject content knowledge: knowledge and understanding of school subjects in the basic education curriculum (referred to as academic subjects). The subject textbooks are all in English, which creates issues.
- Pedagogic content knowledge: teaching methods and ways of assessing learning related to specific subject areas, and how these are matched to the capabilities of learners (referred to as 'methods' courses).
- Professional studies: understanding how children learn; knowledge and skill in classroom management and pastoral care; knowledge of effective techniques to promote learning; acquisition of professional identity as a teacher; and awareness of relevant educational legislation, responsibilities, etc.

- A short 9-week teaching practicum referred to as block teaching.
- Co-curricular subjects include music, art, agriculture, physical education, domestic science, and industrial science. These courses, on the whole, appear to be considered the bottom of the 'curricula hierarchy'.

Classes in ICT are offered in all education colleges. The ICT teacher educators teach basic Microsoft programs with training handbooks that are often out of date. Student teachers have access to computers during these classes although they often have to share. The lack of reliable electricity supply and non-functioning computers mean that practical 'hands on' training is not always possible. According to a UNESCO site visit, the teacher educators are also responsible for fixing the computers when they break and supporting the education college staff to do their own computer-related work (UNESCO, 2016: 12–3).

Teacher educators use a combination of methods that include demonstration, whole-class teaching using question and answer, lecture and some simulation. However, the main emphasis is on theoretical knowledge about teaching and not on demonstrating how to teach or using learner-centric approaches so that student teachers experience the teaching methodology they are supposed to apply. The academic subject textbooks serve as 'manuals of instruction' for activities that are to be conducted by the teachers. Despite the fact that many teachers will face challenges that include language barriers as well as multigrade teaching during their posting, the diversity of potential learners and their different abilities are not addressed by the pedagogical approaches that are taught at the education colleges.

Anecdotal evidence[6] shows that different education colleges do use different teaching strategies, sometimes including storytelling, observation, demonstration and role-play. Demonstration lessons include one demonstration for each subject the students will have to teach – including maths, Myanmar language, English, science, geography and history. The student teachers are then asked to give feedback. There is also 'peer teaching' that involves groups of student teachers making lesson plans, which are delivered to the other student teachers and the education college teacher educator, who then gives feedback. It seems that this strategy is practiced before the 'block teaching'.[7] However, discussion as well as question-and-answer sessions appear to be the most commonly used methodologies, emphasising the passive methods that predominate in the classrooms across Myanmar. It seems that teacher educators and their students predominantly apply the method in which they have been taught when they themselves are teaching.

During the nine-week block teaching where student teachers practice in schools, they often find themselves left to their own devices, barely supported by the already overloaded local head teacher or the teacher educators. Feedback on a recent project spoke of 'surviving' rather than 'learning' on the job.[8] Many student teachers found that the theory they have been taught is quite different from the practice they have to apply, leading to confusing situations. As a part of the block teaching students are now encouraged to conduct basic action research under the heading of 'lesson study'. This includes choosing a classroom action research theme, designing the lesson plan, being observed using observation tools and checklists and receiving constructive feedback. Clearly, for this to work well requires the support of peers and the head teacher, which is not always readily available.

To date, the education colleges have been perceived as second-class institutions within Myanmar's educational hierarchy. The education colleges have extremely limited budgets, out-dated curricula and textbooks, and inadequate teaching and learning resources.[9] The teacher-to-student ratio is supposed to be 35–40 students per teacher educator, although there is evidence of larger classes with up to 55 student teachers.[10] Teacher educators are considered overworked, not only because of the time spent teaching, but because they need to prepare classes, mark correspondence work from in-service teachers and manage continuous professional development (CPD) activities for in-service teachers (UNESCO, 2016: 12–3).

It is notable that despite this structure for training teachers, there are still a large number of untrained teachers serving in government schools, especially in the remote and conflict-affected areas. An often cited figure from the McE in 2000 states that approximately 57 per cent of primary teachers, 58 per cent of middle school teachers and 9 per cent of high school teachers had never attended any teacher training (Thein Lwin, 2000). These figures are 20 years old, but the recent recruitment of daily wage teachers by the government to increase overall teacher numbers might have increased these numbers.

The reforms

When the 2012 reforms started, the MoE was in the midst of implementing its 30-Year Long-Term Plan for Basic Education 2001–31, one of the priority areas being teacher education and specifically the reduction of in-service uncertified teachers, ensuring full strength of teaching staff for basic education schools in border areas and improving the quality of teacher education (JICA, 2013). These aims were overtaken by the NESP reform priorities for teachers that include the following three priority areas:

- Strengthening teacher quality assurance and management, including the introduction of teacher competency standards, deployment and promotion mechanisms.
- Improving quality of pre-service education using the recently developed Teacher Competency Standards Framework (TCSF) as a driver for improvement.
- Improving the quality of teacher CPD including access to a coherent system with basic recognised qualifications and mentoring, and targeted training for the new basic curriculum.

Section 50 of the revised 2015 National Education Law stipulates the following:

Teachers shall:

a) be allowed to research freely without impact to the national benefit
b) be allowed to choose methods which are relevant to the curriculum freely for the development of learning
c) have the opportunity to continue to learn internal or in foreign for improving quality of teaching
d) be allowed to apply to their desired schools or regions freely

To meet the legal and NESP goals, teacher education requires an overhaul.

A new teacher training curriculum and degree

To meet ASEAN standards, the teacher education system is preparing to shift to a four-year degree, a basic pre-service qualification that will replace the two-year DTEd. The teacher education curriculum requires new content so as to link in with the new basic education curriculum (JICA's 'CREATE' project).[11] A new curriculum is being developed by technical experts including education colleges' teacher educators and coordinated through UNESCO's 'Strengthening Pre-Service Teacher Education in Myanmar' (STEM) project, covered in more detail below.[12]

The first-year curriculum was introduced in December 2019. STEM's focus has been to ensure that student teachers master the competencies – a combination of content knowledge, skills and attitude needed to produce effective learning for pupils in a classroom – shifting from the way they were taught themselves (by rote) to the new student-centred way. The training approach is changing in that teachers no longer only receive the theoretical knowledge to teach, relevant in a content-based curriculum, but receive training in the ability to teach through a competency-based approach. A validation survey for the TCSF is currently being piloted by the MoE before national implementation.[13]

No publically available study has collected data on how education colleges, teacher educators and student teachers are managing with the new curriculum and the new teaching method or what challenges they face in understanding and implementing these. According to a consultant from TREE, feedback collected for STEM revealed that teacher educators struggled with new subjects, the number of activities that have to be conducted in limited time, and understanding some of the learning outcomes. Some teacher educators complained that the English curriculum was dense, the Myanmar translation confusing and the education colleges lacked resources to support lesson planning.

Part of the change in qualification and coursework has been the development of a TCSF between 2017 and 2019 as a set of written standards underpinning ambitions for the creation of a teaching workforce with the: 'professional knowledge, understanding and skills associated with the role and duties expected of Myanmar's teachers and the process of teaching' (MoE, 2019d: 5). The TCSF was developed by a core working group led by Dr Aung Min, retired Rector of the Yangon University of Education, supported by Dr Aye Aye Myint, Acting Rector of the Yangon University of Education, and included members from the Yangon University of Education (YUOE), the Sagaing University of Education (SUOE), the University for the Development of National Races (UDNR),[14] as well as invited representatives from Yankin, Thingangun and Hlegu Education Colleges.[15] Technical assistance was provided by UNESCO's STEM project.[16]

The field testing of the framework by the TCSF working group in 2016 involved 76 test sites that included education colleges as well as schools. Data was collected from student teachers and teacher educators as well as serving teachers, head teachers and principals of education colleges. The report documents that those interviewed understood the intent of the framework but that the technical language made it difficult to use and respondents felt the language needed to be simplified. Stakeholders also had concerns on how the framework would be implemented, especially for those teachers with less experience (Aye Aye Myint and Myo Win, 2016: 21–2). This conclusion is supported by UNESCO's report on STEM and the TCSF that found the introduction of generic international standards to Myanmar creates challenges: 'Likely issues include difficulties in understanding the language in these products, in transitioning from current to new practices, and difficulties around a lack of knowledge in skills required in using the products' (UNESCO, 2019b: 21).[17]

Dr Aung Min, the retired Rector of YUOE writes in the foreword to the TCSF (MoE, 2019d: 2) the following:

> In Myanmar's tradition, it is believed that "Knowledge is treasure; Teachers matter and teachers are at the centre of the learning process." In Myanmar society, teachers are regarded as one of the "five gems" (Buddha, Dhamma, Sangha, parents and teachers). While remaining in this highly respected position, we must recognize that, as education moves towards a learner-centred approach, the role of the teacher is changing to that of a facilitator. (…) At present, our teachers need to be equipped with the teacher competencies necessary for them to move from a teacher-centred approach, in which teachers engage in purely direct instruction as the sole source of knowledge, to a learner-centred approach, in which the teacher provides guidance and support, coaching and facilitation. In a number of different countries, competency-based teacher training programmes are based on the following categories: knowledge, skills, and attributes or values. (…) The content of each category has been aligned with the Myanmar context.

The standards are not only going to be used to assess and train student teachers at education colleges, but will also form the basis of their professional development throughout their teaching career. The draft document states the following (MoE, 2019d: 3):

> As Myanmar raises the quality of the education system, through reforms to the basic education curriculum and structure of schooling (Kindergarten to Grade 12), it needs teachers with the right values, skills and knowledge to be effective practitioners. To achieve this objective, Myanmar needs a strong system of teacher education (pre-service and continuing), with programmes that

provide the theoretical foundations to produce graduates and a quality teacher workforce with the kinds of professional knowledge, understanding and skills associated with the role and duties expected of Myanmar's teachers and the process of teaching.

As part of the reformed system, teachers will now train for a certain level: KG, primary, lower secondary, upper secondary plus a subject specialisation of their choice. The complete set of competency standards includes teaching competence – the role of the teacher in the classroom, directly linked to the act of teaching (pedagogical content knowledge) as well as teacher competence – the wider systemic view of teacher professionalism including the role and responsibility of the teacher as an individual, within the school, the local community and as a participant in professional networks (MoE, 2019d: 9).[18] With an interesting nod to the international community and the development partners involved in the education reform process, the document emphasises that the framework: 'is grounded in the culture of the country' (MoE, 2019d: 7) and demonstrates: 'values and attitudes consistent with Myanmar's tradition of perceiving teachers as role models' (MoE, 2019d: 17). Whilst not explicitly mentioned, this seems to be a reaction to the various programmes such as the Western CCA pushed upon Myanmar teachers in the years preceding the reforms.[19]

Promotions and transfers

Changes to the promotion and transfer system are also planned, but are currently quite unclear. Teachers are all civil servants, and major reforms are under way as detailed in the Civil Service Reform Strategic Action Plan.[20] According to JICA: 'the civil service personnel management system is not administered consistently ... [and] nepotism and bribery are still common practices for recruitment, transfer and promotion' (JICA, 2017b: 1). President Thein Sein brought in significant wage increases for teachers to relieve issues created by corruption and the tuition business, without which teachers could not survive. According to the WB, the whole wage bill of all civil servants had therefore increased quite dramatically.[21] As of 2013, annual pay and allowances have also been increased whereby all civil servants receive a monthly bonus. A new 'hardship pay' was introduced for civil servants (including teachers) who serve in 'hardship' areas, mainly remote border areas, to incentivise them to work there.

With the new qualification being a university degree, the implementation and management of pre-service teacher education has been shifted within the MoE from the Department of Teacher Education and Training (DTET) to the Department of Higher Education. In-service teacher training, however, will go on under the DEPT.[22] While teacher educators become academics teaching towards a four-year degree, it is unclear if they will have to rotate from one campus to another, as their peers at universities do. A new points-based system is being put in place where teacher educators can accrue points according to a number of criteria – qualifications, research output, departmental activity, seniority and other activities. Panels, including members from the MoE, unions and departmental staff, will then make recommendations on appointments. The Department of Higher Education is encouraging teacher educators to undertake research and is disbursing grants for this purpose.[23] The structure of the education colleges is likely to change significantly as the curricular reforms progress. For education colleges to be able to confer degrees, they must have powers equivalent to universities. Options for status change of education colleges are already being discussed and the Higher Education Bill is likely to describe the final decision, but integrating education colleges with existing universities was one possibility being discussed.

It is unclear how the new system will affect the appointment and deployment system for basic education teachers, although a more devolved approach is being considered: 'Since 2013–4, state/region education officers can make some decisions about teacher deployment, including daily wage teachers' (MoE, 2016: 40). However, to date, the collaboration of education colleges and TEOs is limited to attending graduation ceremonies at education colleges and coordinating practicum placements for education college students,[24] rather than becoming involved in deployment of teachers to areas of need.

Teachers: Needs and supply

The issue of deployment links in with the problem of teacher needs and teacher supply. Every year, teacher vacancies are reported by all the TEOs and, based on this available data, teacher posts are compiled into a list by the DBE by 1 March every year, from which requests for the new teachers are sent to the DEPT. The DEPT then provides a new teacher list and the DBE forms the educational committee chaired by the director general to deploy newly certified teachers from education colleges and institutes of education. JICA's report maintains that new teachers are considered depending on their specialised subjects and native hometown, but evidence on the ground does not bear out the claim that consideration of mother tongue and cultural background are linked to new posts (JICA, 2013). Exact data on the supply and demand of teachers does not seem to be available publically, although conversations with state education officers across four states and regions in the past few years point to the fact that the supply of teachers is insufficient to meet the demand, especially in remote areas.[25]

Problems and challenges with teacher education

The current realities of teacher education include a long list of challenges that include the following issues: the teaching at the education colleges, the practicum, ICT, CPD, along with the uncertainties of the changed degree structure. The existing practicum system does not prepare student teachers for the real world and the student teachers do not get adequate support or feedback. This often means they are unable to use a student-centred pedagogy as they face overcrowded classes, classroom management issues, resource shortages and at times language difficulties. With regard to access to computers and the internet during training, the education colleges have few computers (more likely to be desktops than laptops), and these are often located in administrative rooms. Student teachers tend to use their personal phones to access the internet, and instruction on how to use ICT in teaching is not a systematic part of their training.

Even if student teachers leave the education college reasonably well prepared, it is not easy for them to develop their skills further later in their careers. This will be a particular problem as those who have taken the two-year diploma are likely to be seen as second rate to those completing the future four-year teaching degree. There is no systemic CPD framework in place and principals do not see this as their responsibility. Most CPD consists of one-off workshops, or a series of workshops as the current mode of CPD.[26] Other recognised CPD options include Master Degrees and PhDs, and there are also 'National Competitions for Teaching Aids and Action Research' held twice a year, as well as informal CPD programmes at some colleges where short refresher courses are available. Although it is being reformed, the teacher education curriculum does not prepare teachers for the realities on the ground such as multigrade teaching, the short supply of ICT and other teaching resources, large classes and language difficulties (Stigler and Hiebert, 2007). These issues reflect the study on student teachers (Lall, 2015 and 2016b) that is detailed in the next section of this chapter.

Views from 20 education colleges in 2015–6

In 2015 and 2016, the first ever study of student teachers was conducted as part of the British Council funded EfECT project (discussed further below). The survey was distributed to 100 students in each one of the existing 20 education colleges by British Council staff during the academic year of 2015, and repeated in 2016. It is unclear how the responding students were chosen.[27] However, the study was able for the first time to reveal who in Myanmar chose to go into the teaching profession, for what reasons, and what challenges they faced. The study also serves as a baseline for teacher education before the NESP reforms really began to affect Myanmar school education.

In 2015, there were 2,003 respondents, 1,005 in their first year of study and 969 in their second year of study. There were 29 respondents who did not specify which academic year they were in. Of the 2,003 respondents, 791 (39 per cent) were male and 1,196 (60 per cent) were female and 16 did not specify their gender. As would be expected, the majority of students were between 17 (37.7 per cent) and 18 (42.69 per cent) years of age. However, there were 3 per cent of younger students at 16 years of age, and a few older ones between 19 and 23. In the first year of study, there were 764 and in the second year there were 725 Bamar students, with 241 (year 1) and 244 (year 2) identifying as ethnic students. Just under 93.5 per cent self-identified as Buddhists, with 108 (5.4 per cent) Christians and only 17 Muslims (< 1 per cent), signalling a sharp lack of religious diversity.

The survey was repeated in 2016 and there were again 2,003 respondents, 951 in their first and 1,050 in their second year of study. There were two respondents who did not specify which academic year they were in. There were 796 repondents who took the survey for the second time; there were 460 male and 479 female students (year 1) and 466 male and 580 female students (year 2). For this survey, there was a higher male representation with 47 per cent male respondents compared to 39 per cent male respondents in 2015. The increase in the number of male respondents was due to the increase in those belonging to the non-Bamar ethnic groups. However, overall, the intake of men in education colleges is much lower than women, as teaching is seen as a less attractive profession for men, although once in the system, male teachers tend to move up the ranks more swiftly than their female counterparts. Similar to 2015, the Bamar ethnic group constituted 74 per cent of the total respondents. Almost 25 per cent of the respondents identified themselves as members of ethnic groups, and only four respondents did not specify their ethnic group. Almost 93 per cent of respondents identified themselves as Buddhists, 6.2 per cent as Christians and 0.7 per cent as Muslims. As would be expected, the majority of the students were between 17 (35 per cent) and 18 (44 per cent) years of age. Again, there were about 3 per cent who were younger (16 years of age) and there was a similar proportion of older students between the ages of 19 and 23.

In year one of the research, the survey did not ask about matriculation marks, however, upon requests from a number of donor agencies, this question was added in 2016. The self-reported matriculation marks of the respondents in 2016 suggested higher performance among the Bamar ethnic group, with a majority of the respondents scoring in the range of 400–99. The performance of the non-Bamar ethnic groups was in the lower range between 300–99. Women performed higher than their male counterparts. The difference between ethnic groups was not unexpected as pupils for whom Burmese is not a first language struggle to follow the lessons in Burmese at government schools, and generally lag behind Bamar students throughout their academic careers. This has always resulted in a lower numbers of ethnic teachers, so that that the cycle of ethnic underperformance repeats itself – an issue elaborated upon in Chapter 6 in this volume.

Being a teacher in Myanmar is a challenging profession. Despite the respect bestowed by society, salaries are low and, as civil servants, teachers are sent where the government deems it needs them. Younger teachers are often sent to remote areas, where life is especially hard if they do not speak the local language. Mairead Condon's Masters dissertation revealed that many women who entered the teaching profession felt it was impossible to marry. They were often posted away from their families, and husbands unable to move with them might not accept this kind of an arrangement – a situation her respondents found deeply unjust (Condon, 2017). It was, therefore, interesting to find out more about the motivation of the students in wanting to become a teacher. In both years of the study, around half the students said they wanted to serve their country or contribute to society. The second most important reason was a stable job and a regular salary – although it is not high, at least it is guaranteed. A small percentage cited love for children or parental expectations. The numbers of those responding that their 'parents pushed them' can probably be attributed to the young age of respondents. Only very few said that they did not want to become a teacher and had no choice. The main significant difference between male and female students was with regard to a stable and regular salary, with more women choosing that option as motivation. Given the social and economic changes in Myanmar that include rampant inflation, a stable government job can be attractive. Whilst the teaching profession has traditionally been badly paid, this – as mentioned above – changed with the Thein Sein government (2011–5) increasing pay for public servants and teachers, and offering a bonus for those working in remote and conflict-affected areas.

Respondents were asked where they wanted to teach once they were qualified and they were asked to choose between where their family was located and where the government needed them or would place them. Reflecting the motivation of wanting to serve their country, around two-thirds were happy to accept the government's choice. This seems related to a great sense of nationalism and personal responsibility towards the development of their country.

In both years, career goals were fairly evenly distributed across the sector. Very few respondents wanted to join a private school or envisioned a career outside of the education system. Looking in more detail at the responses, and adjusting for sample size differences between men and women, it became clear that for those who expressed their career goal as being a teacher at secondary school, women were 50 per cent more likely to state that as a goal. Women were also a third more likely than men to pursue the goal of becoming a teacher educator or a head teacher. Men were 50 per cent more likely to state their desire of becoming a township education officer as a driver for being a teacher, and a quarter more likely than women to state their desire of becoming a state education officer as a career goal – posts that hold real power compared to head teachers in schools. This is reflected in Myanmar's administrative reality where women are more prevalent in the teaching profession at every grade (including head teacher) apart from senior administrative posts such as township education officers or state education officers, which are mostly held by men. For those who expressed their career goal as moving on from teaching as a profession (which has an impact on attrition), men were one-and-a-half-times more likely than women to state that goal *before* completing their training, possibly because of salary issues.

One of the main issues the survey endeavoured to uncover was the challenges student teachers expected to face in the classroom and how their training prepared them for these issues. Student teachers, recently having left school, understand the issues of the education system both from the student as well as the teacher perspective, making them the ideal respondent to review the state of education across Myanmar. Responses to the question about what challenges the student teachers expected once they became teachers were incredibly varied and detailed. Student teachers gave very frank and very personalised answers, revealing anxieties and worries in commencing their profession. The answers fell into several categories that included: lack of classroom experience, a real worry of implementing CCA, infrastructural issues that include everything from lack of transport to too many students in class, dealing with parents, living far away from home, being sent to a remote area, language issues and confronting student and family poverty.

The quotes below are samples from a very rich set of responses that was given across the 4,000 plus surveys. Very few said that they expected to face no problems, or felt confident enough to deal with whatever arose. However, in the section asking them how prepared they felt to start their career as a teacher, the student teachers mostly said that they felt prepared enough to teach children at school. Two major issues that emerged across the two years were classroom experience and CCA. The qualitative data pointed to a marked lack of confidence, as student teachers felt they did not have the practical, in-classroom experience that they would need to be able to apply what they were learning at the education colleges. Some spoke of their shyness and their fear in dealing with students for the first time. A few also mentioned that children might have a better understanding of the new technologies than their teachers and they might not be able to respond to all questions, something which made them particularly nervous as it would erode respect for them. Responses by students included the following (Lall, 2015; Lall, 2016b):

- 'The difficulties are having little classroom experience and not being friendly with the students, being at the start of the career and being worried, and being tired of doing the teaching and admin stuff.'
- 'When I become a teacher, I'd be younger than other teachers, so the students might not show respect. I'm worried that I can't overcome the new experiences and I can't put the teaching theories into practice. But I'll try.'
- 'Technology has improved now. The children are curious and inquisitive. I suppose only if teachers know about everything, they

will be able to answer the children's questions. The children will expect teachers to be aware of the development changes.'
- 'The problems that I might have when I become a teacher is how to control and manage students. As I am the only son in my family and I don't have any siblings, I have never done baby-sitting. So it would be difficult for me to manage and monitor students. Teaching knowledge is pretty good through the training at this college. However, we still need to know how to monitor students.'
- 'Limited classroom experience, large number of students and too many lessons to cover in limited period.'
- 'Inexperience in teaching, weak in classroom management, numerous students to handle and unfamiliar with the lesson.'

The fear of using/practicing CCA is directly linked to a lack of classroom experience and the fact that often the student teachers themselves are not taught with this methodology. In addition, teachers expressed the fear of being overtaken by student knowledge. The student teachers point to the fact that CCA requires them to have a lot of knowledge, as students would expect them to answer questions on everything under the sun. They also pointed to the practicalities of overcrowded classrooms, short periods, lack of teaching aids and not enough time to cover all the material on the syllabus. Lastly, they were aware that school cultures, older teachers and parents might not be supportive of what is a relatively new teaching method in Myanmar.

- 'If CCA is used, I need to have a lot of knowledge to be able to answer the students' questions so I think I have to read so many books. I also need to guide them [the students] to develop right attitudes so that the standards of the education system of Myanmar will be upgraded.'
- 'There might be delays in lessons because of not having enough time if we use CCA; we might not complete the lessons in time because individuals need to think and answer. These problems are more common in schools where there are many students and just a few teachers.'
- 'I will face difficulties in the rural areas because Myanmar is a developing country and so there aren't enough classrooms and teaching aids; [in those circumstances] I will have difficulty in teaching. Plus, there are not many schools that use CCA and it's difficult to use it.'
- 'Approaching CCA can be difficult as it is a new methodology and not widely used in Myanmar. I might not be able to answer the students' questions because of my inadequate general knowledge.'

- '[I] won't be able to use CCA when we are in rural areas because of [constrained] classroom space and other conditions.'
- 'Problems with parents, colleagues and the education staff because of the difference in teaching techniques and not all the teachers use CCA.'
- 'There are difficulties in accomplishing CCA [objectives] because most students are used to rote learning and are not good at thinking on their feet.'

These responses reflect issues that had been uncovered in previous research where teachers find CCA impossible to administer due to overcrowded classrooms, time and material constraints as well as the chapter-end tests that dominate the pace of the syllabus (Lall, 2010, Lall 2011; Lall et al. 2013). Since student teachers are aware of the realities of the classrooms where they themselves have been taught not that long ago, they cannot see how – without significant structural transformation of the system – the teaching method can be successfully changed.

Other difficulties included the exam system, the problems in the classroom (the result of the lack of preparation), tuitions (most teachers give priority to tuitions), the need to deal with the parents (some parents are likely to offer bribes), and private schools, regarding which one respondent commented: 'those schools spoil the teachers and just focus on making their school famous'. Some further comments of note were as follows (Lall, 2015; Lall, 2016b):

- 'In G4 and G8 exams are held for students by the government. If I am responsible for grade 4, when students fail the government exam, I have to explain why this has happened to the superiors. That is why, starting from grade 1, students are allowed to pass exams only if they are qualified.'
- 'Having lots of students, heavy workload and the exam system. As I can't pay full attention to the students, it leads to rote learning.'
- 'The system today is exam-oriented so we can't provide the knowledge they need ... there is little time to teach all subjects. We can't help students reach their true potential.'

Infrastructure as a challenge was a broad category and referred to inadequate textbooks, too many students in a classroom, a lack of teaching aids, too little time to get through the materials, but also practical considerations such as issues with public transport both for the students and themselves. Some further comments were as follows (Lall 2015; Lall, 2016b):

- 'The textbooks are not up to date, so I will have difficulty in adapting the text to the outside world, e.g. Science and Geography subjects are not practically useful subjects, they [the students] can't make a living with those. For the students, earning is more important than learning. I'll also face difficulty in using teaching aids.'
- 'The difficulties are having too many students and too many lessons to teach in a short time. The teacher will be stressed when the number of students and teachers are not balanced. If there are many lessons to finish in a short time, there won't be any preparation time and we can't focus on teaching the key concepts.'
- 'Because I want to teach in rural areas, the difficulties are with transportation, food and accommodation, teaching, managing language and social dealings.'
- 'Because the number of classrooms and the number of student numbers are not matched, too many students gather in one classroom. This makes it difficult to teach them, to guide them and to teach them with the CCA approach.'
- 'Transportation can be a problem. Although urban areas are very modern and developed, there are many children who are living in very far places and poor regions. It could be difficult to educate these children.'
- 'There will be problems with the school building, toilet, pure water, living and food.'
- 'The problem with living, water, electricity, teaching aids, and having not enough teachers are prevalent in remote areas.'

Communication, social structure and hierarchy issues that included worry about lack of respect, social communication with parents who are less educated and the fear of communication with superiors, were other prominent themes. It showed that the student teachers were very aware of how important communication issues are, and that they felt unprepared to deal with this particular aspect of the job. Many had problems of self-confidence, and some were afraid of students and superiors alike. The status of a teacher is crucial, as they feel they will be young and inexperienced, yet expected to live up to a professional ideal by colleagues and parents alike. Some comments were as follows (Lall, 2015; Lall, 2016b):

- 'I will have social problems with the senior teachers and difficulties in the workplace because of my lack of experience – and I'm still learning.'
- 'Firstly, teachers must deal with students' parents. Then, they have to associate with people from the community. As the social status of being a teacher is so high, teachers need to be very careful how to behave in society. When we meet naughty students, it is our duty to train them very well.
- 'As I am an ethnic person and a small and short person; I think I could face difficulties in getting respect from the children and to communicate well with children.'
- 'If I've got my position in a very far place, I'll have the usual problems like communication. It's hard for me to take responsibility for students. I'm not sure that students will understand my teaching.'
- 'When I become a teacher, I may face the problems of having less experience, social problems and dealing with my superiors.'
- 'Problems with parents, colleagues and the education staff because of the difference in teaching techniques and not all the teachers use CCA.'

Parents were also seen as a challenge for the student teachers. In Myanmar, parental involvement in education is rare, and usual only amongst the middle classes living in urban areas. Student teachers understand that in rural areas parental priorities will be different, and whilst all parents want their children to be well educated and do well, parents might not always be able to support their children adequately. In addition, becoming a teacher gives the young student teachers a respected social status that can complicate relations with parents. Some have prejudices towards rural populations referring to parents as 'less intelligent'. Some comments were as follows (Lall, 2015; Lall, 2016b):

- 'If I become a teacher, the difficulties are having problems with the parents. In some places, the parents have little knowledge and so they can't train their children. So the children might be spoilt; their thinking might not be creative and they might not listen to the teacher.'
- 'The difficulty is that the village people don't encourage education since the parents dropped out from their middle school and there are no graduates.'
- 'I need to understand the parents because they want their children to be educated and they rely on us for this.'

- 'I have to face the problem of lack of trust of students' parents and [constant blame on teachers for student's performance] because most of their parents think that teachers are greedy.'

Living away from home and far away from parents was less prominent than the other issues detailed above, but it did worry quite a number of student teachers. Most are very young, and until now have been able to rely on their families for help and support. The first posting is likely to be in a remote or rural area, far away from home where they have no support networks. Some comments were as follows (Lall, 2015; Lall, 2016b):

- 'The difficulties are having to work in a remote area because my parents are old now. Plus, I'm the youngest in the family and I won't be able to take care of my parents if I have to work in far away places.'
- 'My parents will feel very sad if I'm away from them because my father loves me so much and he doesn't eat well without me, even when I'm studying in another town near to my place.'
- 'The problems related to transportation, teaching and living associated with remote areas … the need to choose the right methods and the security issue.'
- 'Difficulties in food and accommodation due to being away from home.'

Being posted to a remote area, that could be a 'black' zone or conflict area was also a fear expressed by a large number of student teachers. They worry about shortages of water and food, not being used to local food and customs, lack of transport and not having family support. Serving in a school located in such an area also means that there is a shortage of teachers, resulting in multigrade teaching and that sometimes students cannot attend class due either to having to help their families or due to the on-going conflict. Some comments were as follows (Lall, 2015; Lall, 2016b):

- 'The difficulty is food and accommodation because if I need to go to a remote area, there are no relatives, no place for me to stay, and if I have to stay in someone else's house, I won't be comfortable.'
- 'In remote areas the students can't attend the classes regularly and I need to do lots of duties because there won't be enough teachers.'
- 'If you serve in far-away places, it can be difficult to live and adapt to a different society.'

- I have to face issues such as no electricity, poor telephone network, food availability in a remote area.'
- 'The problems with transportation, water shortage, parents, children from the different backgrounds, and having to work in brown areas.'

Language is another overarching theme, often linked to being posted in a remote area where students do not speak Burmese. There were some respondents who were worried they would not be understood and then there were those who were more worried they would not be able to understand the students (or parents) where they were posted. These challenges were more prevalent with student teachers who were being trained in ethnic states, but they were not often mentioned by respondents in Bamar-majority regions. A few student teachers voiced their fear of not being able to speak English well enough to teach at higher levels. Another set of student teachers said they were shy and therefore their voice did not carry, their language was not clear and that this frightened them. Some comments were as follows (Lall, 2015; Lall, 2016b):

- 'I will have difficulty with the language, for instance, if I have to work in some states with ethnic groups, we might face the problems of not understanding each other's language.'
- 'There will be difficulty in teaching English because it is not our mother tongue and there will be difficulty in pronouncing it correctly.'
- 'The difficulties are with languages in the border areas, if there are so many people who don't understand Myanmar, the teaching won't be effective.'
- 'The government does not know how to assign teachers to several provinces. If you are wrongly assigned to work in a place speaking a different language, you have to manage to speak in a different language and to predict how children feel. All these are hardships faced by a teacher.'
- 'The problems with dialects and people living there, because of living in remote areas, they might not understand Myanmar language.'
- 'Problems with the dialect, having not enough contact with the students and students might not understand the classroom language when teaching English.'

Very few respondents thought poverty of the resident population at their posting was another problem they might face. Those who did worried about not being able to solve the problems that the children and their families faced and somehow felt responsible. This links in with the status of the teacher in Myanmar society, who are seen as natural leaders in society representing wisdom and, therefore, possibly expected to solve community issues.

Some respondents tended to see students as part of the problem, saying that they were dirty, rude or less intelligent. Some comments were as follows (Lall, 2015; Lall, 2016b):

- 'I'm worried about whether I could manage a large number of children since in some schools a large number of students are stuffed in one classroom like the schools I went to when I was young. I also find it annoying if the students do not care for personal hygiene.'
- 'The students might be dirty, rude and they don't understand my language.'
- 'To face the parents of the students because now, government has a rule that we are not allowed to strike children if they become rude. If we strike them for their rudeness, parents will send a complaint letter to officials; in addition, if we can't teach those rude children, the parents will blame us.'

Some respondents were even afraid of children, but interestingly, these were not the ones who admitted that they did not want to become teachers. Some comments were as follows (Lall, 2015; Lall, 2016b):

- 'I am so afraid of the children that I don't dare to face them. When I am in front of the classroom, I may be shaking. I don't like to be blamed. I am worried if the children will understand my teaching because I don't have enough experience.'
- 'The problem is that I am afraid of children. Because of the fear of children, it could lead me to put in less effort in teaching comprehensively.'

The fewest responses came from those respondents who did not see the challenges or problems ahead, and those who felt that they would be able to manage whatever came their way. Some comments were as follows (Lall, 2015; Lall, 2016b):

- 'If I become a teacher, I don't think I will have difficulties because I will teach my students with as much effort as I can. Plus, I will have prepared for the lessons.'

- 'If I become a teacher, I believe that there will be almost no difficulties because I have confidence and a strong personality and I am interested in teaching children as well as training them to be decent. However, many challenges there are, I wouldn't give up this job for the sake of the children and their parents.'
- 'The problem just depends on my attitude; I will try to find solutions to all those teaching problems because I have this desire to do my job for the best.'
- 'A teacher needs to manage different students from different backgrounds, so we need to learn teaching and also to fulfil the needs of the students who have different natures and personalities. I'm confident enough as I am now in the second year at this Education College and I've learned the methods of teaching, those of motivating the students, and of tackling the difficulties from subjects like Psychology and Education Theories.'
- 'There won't be big problems because I'm willing to serve my country. But I'll have a problem with my family because they aren't supporting my career choice.'
- 'I chose a career in teaching to support and serve the State. […] There are difficulties in any jobs. But I am ready with the spirit of teacher [to face] whatever problems I meet because my hobby is exactly the same as my career.'

The overall findings from the two-year study (Lall, 2015; Lall, 2016b) concluded that, at the time of writing, teacher education does not include sufficient practical classroom experience as an integral part of the training, and teacher training methodology is teacher centric and not learner centric. Students find it difficult to apply child-centred methods themselves as they have mostly not been taught this way themselves. It also concluded that newly qualified teachers are not supported in the early years of their training and that young teachers and student teachers are worried as to how to stay on top of new or changing knowledge and how to answer student questions. It also concluded that there is insufficient IT access and training at the colleges that can lead to a gap between teachers and students, especially in urban areas; and that no ethnic language training is made available for those who will (or want to) be posted in ethnic or remote areas.

Over recent years, development partners have started to support the education colleges' reforms to improve teacher education, most recently as part of the NESP

Development partners supporting teacher education and further training

One of the main early projects supporting teacher training was JICA's 'Strengthening of Child Centred Approach' active from 2004 to 2011. In addition to training, the project also proposed concrete descriptions of teacher competencies. In the 2000s, the MoE requested JICA to help develop a teacher's guide to new textbooks that they had published in order to support teachers' understanding of child-centred approaches. A number of workshops and seminars were conducted by JICA to introduce CCA to the education colleges and improve teacher training. They also developed model lesson plans for active learning, and introduced peer review of lessons (British Council, 2016: 17). Other CCA programmes developed in parallel, but many focused on teachers in the monastic or ethnic systems, which were easier to access than government schools.[28]

The three major programmes run by development partners that engage with teacher education and teacher training include the UNICEF's School-based In-service Teacher Education (SITE) project and competency frameworks, TREE under the DFID-funded Myanmar UK Partnership for Education (MUPE) programme (the former BC EfECT programme) that focuses on English and teaching methods of teacher educators and UNESCO's STEM. There are a few other smaller programmes as well, such as UNICEF's head teacher training that is offered to 5,000 head teachers in 34 townships, focusing on management and instructional leadership. The programme is delivered through a cascade model of training and includes school assessment tools, advice on planning and how to mobilise the community and, most importantly, the head teacher's role in teacher development and CPD for staff. This programme, although helping to develop school leaders, has limited effect on the education of student teachers or early career teachers.

Supporting UNICEF's in-service and teacher education for teacher educators (SITE)[29]

UNICEF's SITE was funded by a consortium including the British, Australian, Danish and Norwegian aid agencies and was part of QBEP 2.[30] The SITE project piloted a programme of school-based professional development for existing primary teachers in Mon State in 2012. This included teachers in government, monastic and ethnic/community schools. The project was based on a series of ten self-study distance learning modules, allowing teachers to draw on their classroom experience and helping them collaborate with other teachers in inter-school clusters (Higgens et al., 2016: 109). The focus was on the development of pedagogical skills and reflective, child-friendly teaching practices. Since teachers did not leave their schools for training, the learning was grounded in the reality of the teachers' individual classroom realities. Experienced teachers are meant to support younger, less experienced colleagues and the head teacher has a mentoring role. Capacity building included a programme for in-service teacher training based in schools (SITE) that a local network of state-level training staff, including teacher educators at education colleges, and TEO staff provided through cluster-based, in-service training sessions and monitoring visits. Head teachers were offered a five-day course to help them in their role to provide guidance to teachers during SITE activities. Part of SITE also included working with the BC to produce competency frameworks for teachers, teacher educators, head teachers and TEOs. The integrated nature of the programme, allowing teachers from different sectors to work on these CPD modules, has been one of the very few instances that the 'silo-ed' sectors of Myanmar's education system has been broken down.[31] However, the independent final evaluation showed that in order to change their behaviour, teachers needed more training in interactive approaches and how to include discussions and dialogue in their teaching, as well as opportunities for peer-to-peer support (Stenning, 2018: 11). At the point of the final evaluation, no questions were asked as to why teachers were not doing these things or what the barriers were. Issues raised included the lack of an initial needs assessment and the top-down nature of the project (UNICEF, 2016: vii, 21–2).[32] One of the main issues at the time was that the SITE CCA approaches were not supported by the examination system. Another significant factor hindering SITE activities were transfers and promotions. For SITE to work, a 'critical mass of teachers' were needed, without which other teachers lost motivation (UNICEF, 2016: 32).

The English for Education College Trainers (EfECT) Project – now replaced by Towards Results in Education and English (TREE)

The EfECT project was initiated in 2013 when former President Thein Sein asked the UK Prime Minister during a state visit to provide expatriate teacher–trainers to work in Myanmar's education colleges to support teacher educators with English proficiency and teaching methods. This became a GBP 4.5 million DFID and BC-funded project that deployed 50 expatriate staff (half taken from the BC and half from the Voluntary Service Overseas) across 20 education colleges and two institutes of education to work with 2,200 teacher educators.

In response to the failure of CCA in government schools, EfECT developed a teaching methodology course which combined learner-centred approaches with the use of direct instruction, and which emphasised developing critical thinking and building on prior knowledge throughout (Clifford, 2016). According to Ian Clifford, who headed the programme and whose MA dissertation examined how EfECT impacted teacher agency: 'teachers have traditionally had few opportunities to make choices and realise their agency as professionals. [...] If a pedagogy which encourages autonomy in students is to be promoted then teachers themselves must be enabled, and given the tools, to make choices about their subjects, careers and methods' (Clifford, 2016: 32). Because of decades without much autonomy, teachers and teacher educators had little confidence in using different approaches and teaching methods. Teacher educators cited a range of structural constraints to the use of alternative methodologies including time, assessment, class sizes, classroom layout, levels of student teachers' motivation, training, and fears around the perceptions of teacher educators. Clifford's findings showed that the programme offered a range of methods to teacher educators, including some support for promoting more teacher-directed whole-class teaching such as direct instruction, and that they felt empowered to choose the type of method that was appropriate in different circumstances.

The focus of the programme, however, was in the first instance the use and quality of English. According to the EfECT needs analysis (British Council, 2015), around a third of teacher educators are expected to teach their subjects with English as a medium of instruction. In reality, Burmese is used, as neither teachers nor students are proficient enough in English. In fact, the levels of English of the teacher educators was found to be very low (British Council, 2015).[33] Drinan, who was engaged by the BC to undertake two studies to support the work of the CESR in 2013 commented on this as well: 'Instructors teaching English sometimes teach in English but more often in Myanmar. This is because students enter the college with low matriculation results and low levels of English language proficiency. Those spoken to felt most of their students were elementary level at reading and writing. Their speaking and listening is even lower. Very few enter the education colleges at an intermediate level and those who do are probably graduate educators from university. Therefore, the translation method is used in teaching and students "learn" through memorisation' (Drinan, 2013: 31).

Overall, EfECT was deemed to have had a positive outcome as teacher educators improved their English and increased their confidence. Simon Borg, who undertook the final evaluation of the programme commented: 'Relative to their position at baseline, TEs across Myanmar made measurable and visible progress in their English proficiency, knowledge of teaching methodology, confidence, teaching skills and basic reflective competence. Their entry levels of English were particularly modest, and the fact that they performed as well as they did over the two years on a programme taught entirely in English is further evidence of EfECT's achievements' (Borg et al., 2018: 84).

Towards Results in Education and English (TREE) 2019–24 builds on EfECT and aims to improve the quality of teaching of teacher educators and academic oversight of management staff in teacher education institutions (Myanmar Teacher Education Working Group, 2019). There are four integrated workstreams: CPD; English proficiency and pedagogy; systems strengthening through practicum and partnerships; and inclusive practices and disability. These workstreams will integrate two cross-cutting themes – educational technology and research and monitoring – which develop over three phases: Foundation, Consolidation and Continuation. At the time of writing, TREE is in the process of deploying 50 trainers to work in the education colleges and use education technology in order to support the workstreams (DFID, 2019). TREE is supported by DFID with GBP 12 million (DFID, 2019).

UNESCO's 'Strengthening Pre-Service Teacher Education in Myanmar' (STEM) project

The UNESCO's 'Strengthening Pre-Service Teacher Education in Myanmar' (STEM) project is funded by DFAT, the Australian bilateral development agency. There are a number of programme elements that relate to teacher education and the management of education colleges. In the first instance, STEM is focusing on the reform of the teacher education curriculum over a five-year period that will transform the teacher education curriculum in the education colleges to degree level. STEM also aims to improve the ICT equipment for the education colleges, with teacher educators being trained in how to use ICT, and STEM developing a curriculum module around ICT for teacher educators to deliver to student teachers.

STEM was originally conceived of as one component of the multi-donor 'Quality Basic Education Programme' (QBEP). QBEP consisted of three components, with UNICEF having responsibility for Output One (policy), while UNESCO had responsibility for delivering Output Two (curriculum/pedagogy) and Output Three (management) (UNESCO, 2016: 14–5). Under the QBEP, STEM was initially intended to focus on four pilot education colleges. However, the MoE felt that all education colleges needed to be involved. In 2014, Australia decided to directly fund the partnership with UNESCO for the implementation of STEM, independent of the QBEP programme (UNESCO, 2016: 14–5). STEM Phase One (2014–7) focused on three outcome areas: teacher policy, curriculum and pedagogy, management and ICT. According to the curriculum review report (UNESCO, 2016: 14–5; DFAT, 2017), STEM had successfully worked on the following outputs:

- the current curriculum at ECs has been reviewed and a new two-year diploma curriculum has been proposed
- the curriculum framework for a four-year degree programme for basic and middle school teachers has been drafted
- a teacher-competency framework has been drafted using a participatory process
- an ICT subject has been developed and is being delivered in all education colleges, each education college now has two to three ICT tutors and the programme is continuing to support the capacity building of ICT teachers through training, the installation of internet infrastructure in all education colleges and the development of an e-portal.

The Draft Education College Curriculum Framework is at the heart of the most important change as it will require teachers to be educated to degree level. UNESCO says that the focus is to ensure that student teachers master the competencies (a combination of content knowledge, skills and attitude) needed to produce effective learning for pupils in a classroom. The training approach is changing in that teachers no longer only receive the (theoretical) knowledge to teach – relevant in a content-based curriculum – but receive training in the ability to teach through a competency-based approach. The Draft Education College Curriculum Framework is linked to the TCSF discussed above, which describes the minimum competency standards a teacher should be able to demonstrate (UNESCO, 2016: 16). The new proposed modules include the following:

1. Educational Studies: that focuses on the ability to teach rather than just being knowledgeable of teaching.
2. Curriculum and Pedagogical Studies: an integrated approach wherein the underlying educational theory and knowledge required is learned through practicing real teaching and applying concepts in the classroom. Academic subjects are to be taught in conjunction with how they need to be taught in either primary or middle school.
3. The Practicum: extended from the current curriculum, monitored and supported to contribute to learning from feedback and practice.
4. Core skills: communication, use of language, additional English, and ICT have been added as new core skills.
5. Self-study and reflection: ensuring time for investigation, self-study and reflection, especially online as connectivity improves. (UNESCO, 2016: 16)

While the changes seem to address some of the shortcomings of the current structure, there seem to have been insufficient links between the teacher education curriculum to the new basic education curriculum. JICA's CREATE MTR (Mizuno et al., 2019) confirmed that there had been a collaboration mechanism between CREATE and UNESCO–STEM to link the new primary school curriculum with the new education college materials (lesson plans, lecture notes and student handouts) and that 'Grade 1–3 training modules for education college teacher educators was developed and distributed at the time of the Central Training.' (Mizuno et al., 2019: 11) But it also seems that not all CREATE materials were introduced to the teacher educators and student teachers in education colleges because the timings of the two projects were not coordinated. In the event, some of the materials provided by JICA to UNESCO arrived too late to be included in the training materials.[34] This does not seem to be seen by JICA as too much of a problem because it has produced detailed teacher guidebooks, which allow even less well-trained teachers to deliver the class with CCA elements. Each chapter has detailed suggestions on activities, questions with the relevant answers (so no teacher loses face in front of the children) and an explanation on how to achieve the required learning outcomes. There seems to be a fundamental disconnect between what UNESCO has in mind for the teachers, and what JICA is designing for the classroom, showing how poor the development partners' coordination is.

STEM has also been working on the management of the 22 education colleges in light of the changes brought about by the NESP. The UNESCO management review report (UNESCO, 2016) explains that the new organisational structures of the education colleges are not clear to education college staff and that education college staff, including managers and administrators, are not clear on the roles and responsibilities of each position in the new education college structure. To UNESCO, this indicates a need to review existing guidelines for the management of education colleges, and the development of policies and guidelines in areas where they have not yet been developed (UNESCO, 2016: 6–7). The UNESCO report also recommended that ICT needs to be mainstreamed as an integral part of efficient education college management and will require more ICT equipment, software and training. In addition, the report mentions the need for a systematic training programme for education college staff, including management staff, such as a human resource development programme. While education colleges have college management boards, these do not have the decision-making authority to propose necessary posts or adjust the number of staff and how these are allocated. UNESCO suggests that the development of an online sharing platform for education colleges could facilitate greater learning and collaboration between teacher educators at the different education colleges, which could enhance their professional development (UNESCO, 2016: 24). Given that education college management is centralised at MoE department level, the management issues are likely to remain challenging.

The Australian Government reports that STEM has operated in a difficult environment and that problems included the restructuring of the MoE following the 2015 elections, and policy decisions being deferred until after the establishment of the NEPC in October 2016. Nevertheless the programme continues – STEM Phase Two (2017–20) started in January 2017 and builds on STEM Phase One, adding a fourth output related to human rights, equity and promotion of gender equality.[35]

The National Education Strategic Plan (NESP) Mid-Term Review on teacher education

The MTR Inception report (MoE, 2019b) reminds the readers that the NESP had promised an integrated approach in order to reform both teacher education and management. The report however finds that: 'the emphasis on reforming teacher management is either overlooked, de-emphasised or not yet actioned' (MoE, 2019b: 45). Nevertheless, the MTR acknowledges that progress has been made with regard to the Teacher Competency Standards Framework: 'The standards, elements and indicators of the Teachers Competency Standards Framework (TCSF), Beginner level, have been developed and piloted and NEPC has provided feedback on this. The TCSF aligns with the learning outcomes of the four-year competency-based teacher education programs, which are to be implemented throughout Myanmar from 2020' (MoE, 2019d: 46). In line with the four-year degree structure, the MTR Inception report warns that there could be a lack of teachers between 2021 and 2023:

> 'To fill this gap MoE has introduced six-months teacher training programs for graduates and has proposed the reintroduction of Daily Wage Teachers. While these may be short-term solutions to maintain teacher strength in the near future, the potential risks of reintroducing Daily Wage Teachers (such as increase in the number of teachers who apply for promotion to teacher higher grades) need to be mitigated, such as through defining a clear time period for their deployment' (MoE, 2019b: 47).

The final MTR report (MoE, 2020) acknowledges that reform mechanisms for teachers have been slow and that there still is no Teacher Task Force to support an effective teacher management system (MoE, 2020: vii). The final report reiterated the issues of a potential lack of teachers between 2021 and 2023 due to the four-year degree programme (MoE, 2020: ix). A masterplan to support recruitment, training for teacher educators, building of classrooms and expanding provision of accommodation on campus has been developed. Despite this, there may still be a shortage of teacher educators and teachers.

With regard to the priority recommendations for NESP 2019–2021, the MTR suggests: 'Assign high priority to development of strategies for the retention of quality teachers through better mechanisms for teacher recruitment, deployment, career pathways, and promotion' (MoE, 2020: xiii) in addition to addressing the other issues promised by the NESP such as the Teacher Task Force and expanding the TCSF at beginner level across all schools. The MTR also recommends that it is a priority of education colleges to ensure the effectiveness of the new four-year programme as well as the student-centred pedagogical approach.

Conclusion: Teacher education and social justice

The system of teacher education and the teaching profession is inherently inequitable. Not only do teachers face their own social justice challenges partly due to material constraints, and partly due to the local cultural outlook, but teacher education is instrumental in reproducing the same social justice issues again and again. The main issues are around gender and ethnicity. According to JICA, more than 80 per cent of teachers are female. However, only 60 per cent of female teachers become head teachers and fewer make it to TEO positions, something reflected in the expectations of the student teachers surveyed between 2015 and 2016 (see Lall, 2015; Lall, 2016b). Serving in conflict-affected areas and deployment to remote areas favour men getting quicker promotions because they are able to serve in difficult areas, unlike their female counterparts. Recent reforms have tried to address the gender imbalance by raising salaries and lowering the selection criteria for men, not something that the higher-achieving women are likely to find fair.[36] However, the issues are more than just salaries. Teaching is seen in Myanmar as a service profession where the teacher serves society and is a role model to the community in which they work. The transfers often mean that female teachers cannot marry, as their husbands might not be able to find a job where they are posted. Mairead Condon examined how teacher educators felt empowered by their position, finding that teacher educators often chose not to marry, both because of society's expectation and to be 'free from family' and able to dedicate their lives to their profession (Condon, 2017). She explained how many of the younger women coming to the profession thought these expectations were unfair and that men would never behave in this way (Condon, 2017). It can be argued that the structure of the teaching profession, as well as the teacher educator profession, is in fact exploitative of women and that they do not receive the same recognition or respect as their male counterparts.

Marginalisation is rife, and remains unaddressed in teacher education and the teaching profession. There are fewer ethnic minority teachers in schools than their Bamar counterparts,[37] in part because the matriculation exam is offered only in Burmese, which is not the mother tongue of the ethnic students.[38] The Ministry of Border Affairs runs the University for Development of National Races (UDNR) located in Ywathitgyi, Sagaing Region, that focuses on educating ethnic groups in the border areas (JICA, 2013). For decades this has been seen as the answer to 'ethnic teachers', but the system is in effect discriminatory.

The lack of ethnic teachers perpetuates the problem of more ethnic students not making the matriculation grades that would allow them then to become teachers themselves.[39]

Recent changes in the 2017–8 academic year suggest access to education colleges appears now to have become more equitable and inclusive. According to Salem-Gervais and Raynaud, the MoE now has a township-based enrolment policy for the DTEd teacher-training pathway, which means that every year a number of places in the education colleges are reserved for candidates in each of the townships of the state/region (Salem-Gervais and Raynaud, 2020).[40] Therefore, applicants in remote, rural, ethnic or poor townships no longer have to compete with those in townships with better education and economic opportunities or with a predominantly Bamar population. Previously, applicants from the majority group Bamar could apply to education colleges in ethnic states. As many of them usually performed better in matriculation examinations than ethnic students did, they were admitted to education colleges at the expense of ethnic applicants.[41] This policy is indeed progress, but will take time to feed ethnic teachers through the system, balancing the numbers with the Bamar majority. Certain ethnic groups from remote areas might remain unrepresented, especially if their performance is below that of other candidates. Salem-Gervais and Raynaud report that the director general in charge of the education colleges in the MoE's higher education department believes that 'compromises are needed between at least three imperatives: (1) the necessity to train more teachers to keep up with the recent progresses in access to schooling and efforts to diminish student/teacher ratio; (2) decentralization and the training of more local teachers; and (3) maintaining the education standards of the teachers' (Salem-Gervais and Raynaud, 2020: 109).

Despite modest improvements, education colleges still need to proactively ensure their progress towards equitable and inclusive HEIs in all their practices including preparing student teachers to be able to apply inclusive pedagogy, for instance, in ensuring learning achievement of ethnic children who will have to learn in the Myanmar language. According to TREE, reflecting other conversations with SEOs, TEOs and teachers over the past decade it was striking that many teacher educators and heads of departments seemed to have neither awareness nor interest in ethnic culture and language issues for teachers or students. This was something they were not preparing student teachers for, possibly due to lack of practical experience in local classrooms, and as most teacher educators were Burmese, possibly lacking sensitivity around language and cultural needs.

The importance of the fear of language barriers is reflected in the views from the 20 education colleges in 2015 and 2016 as detailed earlier in the chapter. TREE also questions the wisdom of 'partner schools' clustered around the education colleges envisioned by the four-year degree course that is in the making, which will mean that student teachers are not exposed to the areas where most of the ethnic nationality groups reside, institutionalising the discrimination further. TREE found that in certain cases, the limited scope for shaping policy was used positively by local SEOs and TEOs:

> For example, in Kayah State the State Ministers of Social Affairs, with the support of the Minister of Ethnic Affairs, developed and implemented what amounts to a policy of positive discrimination/ affirmative action for accepting ethnic Kayah students into Loikaw's new education college. As a result of the Minister's formal request to the Union Minister of Education, the education college can now apply criteria including completion of Grade 10 in Kayah State or a Kayah ethnicity stated on one's national registration card.[42]

However, in essence, this requires leaders to have a view that differs from most others. The fact that teacher educators, teachers and student teachers do not question issues around ethnicity and language makes them complicit in the reproduction of dominant hierarchies that reinforce marginalisation (Metro, 2019) and forms of Bamar 'cultural imperialism' as ethnic differences are not affirmed. Teachers have been accused of a failure of promoting critical thinking and not deviating from textbook content. Higgins et al. go as far as to say that the: 'pedagogy is seen as reproduction of violence – rewarding obedience and replication'. (Higgins et al., 2016: 92). Their research shows that teachers within government and ethnic systems were aware of the potential of history to contribute to peace building, but felt constrained by existing curricula frameworks. However, the problem goes further in that the teachers' own sectarian approaches to history 'undermined their commitment to exploiting the subjects to contribute to social cohesion' (Higgins et al., 2016: 123).

Education colleges have made some progress in inclusive access in terms of gender, yet according to the NESP MTR (MoE, 2020: 48) the numbers of female student teachers still far exceeded those of male student teachers from 2014–5 to 2017–8.[43] The root cause of the disparities remains fundamentally structural and the education reforms are not engaging with the structures that recreate the inequity and social justice challenges. The full new teacher education curriculum cannot yet be judged. However, given that the changes to the basic education curriculum do not address gender and ethnic disparities in a systematic way, it is questionable how far the new education college degree will engage with social justice issues that are so engrained in Myanmar's culture and society.

What the reforms do offer is an increased level of monitoring through the new teacher competency framework. It is unclear how far this new system of accountability will focus on the teaching and learning process, promote equity in the classroom and the staff room, and/or be used as a tool to control. Technical monitoring might not engage with the actual learning happening in the classroom, but rather focus on indicators that can be easily measured, ranging from number of students and teachers, to other materials they find present in the school (Higgins et al., 2016: 97). So while there is an urgent need to reform teacher education, what is on offer does not at present engage with the structural inequalities of the system. The question remains as to how far the additional interventions in teacher education and training offered by development partners are able to engage with these issues.

No donor/development partner-led work seems to directly engage with the inherent issue of gender disparity, however, Higgins et al. claim that conflict, peace and by extension ethnic issues are being considered (Higgins et al., 2016). The Research Consortium on Education and Peacebuilding looked at teacher education interventions and development partner support through a 'peace promotion lens'. Their premise is that teachers are a critical component for the peace process to be successful and sustainable. Teachers they spoke to agreed, for example, stating the following:

> ... They are the medium connecting, like improving the youths, for students to understand the country, to understand each other and the foundation of the country in every sector. So the teacher is very important, the teacher needs to understand contemporary issues and conflict issues and needs [to be] more proficient in their language, their subjects. (Higgins et al., 2016: 98)

However, teachers' primary role as expected by parents and the MoE is not to promote peace, but to complete the curriculum so as to prepare children for exams. Examining four development partner programmes,[44] they concluded that all programmes had: 'frequent implicit and indirect approaches to enhancing the peace building role of teachers.'[45] The team claims that teachers to whom they spoke understood that the pedagogical and managerial skills they were given through the training was relevant to their roles in the classroom, especially to establishing peaceful relations at their school, but this did not necessarily reflect on the wider issues of ethnic relations, conflict and peace across the country. However, the emphasis on demonstrating respect, a lack of bias when dealing with student diversity, critical thinking, and using problem-solving techniques do teach students different approaches to solving issues without violence. How difficult all of this is will be made clear in the next two chapters of this volume that engage with education issues faced by the ethnic nationalities across Myanmar.

Notes

1. At the time there were only 20 education colleges. There are now 22.
2. Chapter 6, dedicated to language, looks in more detail at the alternative teacher education college that was set up by the Pa-O to specifically train those ethnic nationality candidates that failed to get into the education colleges.
3. Language issues are dealt with in Chapter 6 of this volume.
4. In 2013, and as a part of the education reforms and a way to increase the number of teachers in schools, uncertified teachers who have been working at monastic or private schools have been allowed to join government schools under a special scheme. These teachers receive a month of training and are then employed at a lower salary and without benefits. After a year, they can become permanent staff. 'Since the start of the policy an additional 72,000 teachers (representing nearly a quarter of all teachers employed) had been recruited and deployed in this way' (Unpublished WB report on impediments to effective teaching, Yangon 2015). The new teacher hiring policy means that it is now much easier to join the profession. This also means that state education officers and township education officers now have a greater say in which teachers they wish to hire or fire, which previously was the prerogative of the ministries in NPT.
5. The education colleges in Chin and in Kayah State were opened very recently.
6. Informal discussions with EfECT tutors.
7. A nine-week practicum in schools.
8. Informal discussions with EfECT tutors.
9. The curriculum is being revised – more on this later in this chapter.
10. Informal discussions with EfECT tutors.
11. For more on CREATE see: https://createmm.org/en. At the time of writing, Grades 1–3 and Grade 6 textbooks are already in use.
12. See for example: http://www.ibe.unesco.org/en/news/strengthening-pre-service-teacher-education-myanmar.
13. The purpose of the survey is to ascertain the extent to which teachers understand education reform, awareness of the TCSF and whether the TCSF captures effective teaching practice in Myanmar. Efforts have been made to disseminate the first level of the TCSF and seek feedback; some stakeholders view the TCSF to be over ambitious and catering to the most capable teachers. The survey was not accessible for review.
14. A report for the British Council 2015. 'English for Education College Trainers' (EfECT) Project Needs Analysis, 15. There is also a smaller teacher training system run by the Ministry of Border Affairs to place assistant teachers from Myanmar's ethnic groups in border areas where Myanmar is not the main language spoken. The Ministry of Border Affairs runs the University for the Development of the National Races which conducts five-year courses to train teachers from minority groups through a similar curriculum but with additional 'special co-curricular' subjects such as traditional medicine, martial arts and military training.

15 Specialised advice provided by three national advisers Dr Khin Zaw Dr Htoo Htoo Aung, Dr Myint Thein and U Zaw Htay retired Director General of the Department of Higher Education.
16 Funded by the Governments of Australia and Finland.
17 Other issues include: 'The context of the relative status, remuneration and profile of current teachers across Myanmar (mostly under-qualified women with variation in skill between locations) is absent. This detail would clarify the means or resources, incentives and barriers to skills upgrading for this group, and for the reform of education colleges. It would also test the feasibility of certain delivery platforms such as distance learning for teachers in rural locations. The documents do not convey the ethnic diversity of Myanmar and the fact that teachers will likely need competencies in multilingual, multicultural classroom management.' (UNESCO, 2019b: 21–2).
18 There are four domains: Domain A: Professional Knowledge and Understanding; Domain B: Professional Skills and Practices; Domain C: Professional Values and Dispositions; Domain D: Professional Growth and Development.
19 For an analysis of the issues surrounding CCA in Myanmar schools, see Lall, 2010 and Lall, 2011.
20 The operation and legal framework of Myanmar's civil service is described in a number of related laws, namely the 2010 Union Civil Service Board Law, 2011 Union Civil Service Board Rules, 2013 Civil Service Personnel Law and 2014 Civil Service Personnel Rules.
21 'Specifically, during the period 1972–2013, nominal wages were only increased six times.' Unpublished WB report (2015) on the impediments of effective teaching. The wage structure was fixed in nominal terms during the following periods: 1. 1972–88; 2. 1989–93; 3. 1993–2000; 4. 2000–6; 5. 2006–9; 6. 2010–3; and 7. 2013–4.
22 The 'TREE Political Economic Analysis' is not in the public domain but was shared with the author. (TREE Political and Economic Analysis: 9)
23 Discussion with the Director General of the Department of Higher Education in September 2019.
24 While assistant township education officers (ATEOs) cannot monitor the student teachers during their practicum period, ATEOs instruct the respective head teachers to supervise and mentor the student teachers (Thornton and Tolmer, 2017: 17).
25 The demand for teachers will also increase across the system as the school years are expanded to include KG plus 12 years of schooling, and the transition from a two- to a four-year teacher education course slows the production rate of new graduates.
26 A four-year School Mentoring and Cluster Programme has recently been put in place aimed at: 'Providing in-service continuous professional development to the approximately 90,000 primary school teachers'. 157 mentors were trained in 2016 in 50 townships, and each month a mentor would do 3 weeks of mentoring and have approximately 30–40 mentees with which to work. Mentors are trained by a core group consisting of professors from YUOE and some education college educators who provide training twice a year for 5–7 days. Mentees are teachers with no teaching certificate or unfinished qualifications and with less than three years' teaching experience. 'Myanmar Additional Financing for the Decentralizing Fund to Schools Project (P157231) Community Participation Planning Framework (CPPF), DRAFT, 2016–2017' – cited in Drinan and Zin Zin Win 2017: 24.
27 Neither the BC nor the author had any input into which student teachers took part.
28 See Chapter 3 on Monastic Education for more on CCA programmes
29 The final evaluation was conducted by Montrose in 2016. It is unclear how much of the programme has continued since then.
30 Quality Basic Education Programme (QBEP) was a four-year (2012–6), USD 76.6 million joint Myanmar Multi-Donor Education Fund (MDEF) and MoE effort to strengthen the provision, quality, and administration of government basic education. The QBEP programmes supported education reform before the NESP brought in the nine transformational shifts. This included capacity building and providing direct education services in 34 select disadvantaged townships.
31 The Myanmar MoE has provided in-service training for government and Mon National Education Committee (MNEC) teachers together, but this was not deemed a success by the MNEC teachers. For more on MNEC, see Chapter 7 on EAO education provision in this volume.
32 Final Report Dr Mike Thair (Montrose).

33 The Report found that levels of English of the teacher educators was low, with 75 per cent having a level lower than B1 on the Common European Framework (i.e. 75 per cent lower than the intermediate level teacher educators might be expected to have).
34 'UNESCO with Montrose has applied *some parts* of the materials provided by the project to develop textbooks and teachers' guides.' (p.11 italics added) 'CDT (Curriculum Development Team) and TET (Teacher education team) as well as UNESCO officers explained that it varies between subjects but about 50% of materials provided by the project (CREATE) were integrated into the Year 1 textbooks and teachers' guides partly or as a whole. [...] In some subjects, because the new curriculum materials from the project were provided after the UNESCO STEM project had developed the draft of textbooks, it was too late to reflect those materials from the project into EC curriculum.' (Mizuno et al., 2019: 13).
35 The project is being implemented with approximately USD 7.1 million funding support by Governments of Finland, Australia and UK provided in varying timeframes (UNESCO, 2019b).
36 According to JICA, 2013, one institute of education has now fixed percentages at intake (60 per cent male and 40 per cent female).
37 There is no hard data on this. According to the JICA report (JICA, 2013), course completion data suggests that between 1964 and 2010, only 12,493 ethnic teachers have been deployed in the system.
38 And there is no offer to lower entrance requirements for ethnic students as has been done to increase numbers of male students.
39 This is further discussed in Chapter 6 on language in this volume.
40 Criteria include the overall capacity of the local education colleges and the student population in each township of the state/region, of course, but also the gender of the candidates (a 50/50 ratio) as well as their subject stream ('30 per cent arts, 30 per cent science and 40 per cent "mixed"). (Salem-Gervais and Raynaud, 2020: 109).
41 Information from informal conversation with staff working for TREE who met with education college staff in ethnic states.
42 From an unpublished report for TREE.
43 For example, 39,249 female and 8,821 male students in 2017–8 academic year (MoE, 2020: 48). According to a conversation with the staff working for TREE, some education college staff believed that selection criteria for male applicants were relaxed in 2019–20, in order to increase male teachers and improve the gender ratio among schoolteachers.
44 The BC's EfECT; UNICEF's SITE; UNICEF's HT; and Monastic Education Development Group's Yaung Zin modules (Higgins et al., 2016: 112–3).
45 'However, some interventions did explicitly engage with the peacebuilding agency of teachers. For instance, the addition of "Conflict Sensitivity" to UNICEF's head teacher training addresses issues of conflict resolution. This emerged out of a recognition within aid agencies and amongst recipients of initial training for head teachers that handling conflict and building peaceful relationships between students, staff and the wider community was a key aspect of the school leader's role' (Higgins et al., 2016: 114).

6
Ethnic education: Language and local curriculum issues

Introduction

Despite the reforms, education has remained highly centralised, with only Burmese language being allowed as the official means of instruction. Policy under the NLD Government has not changed much, although ethnic minority languages are now allowed as 'classroom language' to help explain concepts when necessary,[1] mother tongue-based multilingual education (MTB-MLE) is not presently Myanmar education policy, marginalising ethnic hopes and concerns.[2] The only concession from the government has been the introduction of a 'local curriculum' (LC) of one period a day for the first three years of education that is locally developed and can be taught in an ethnic language.[3] The development of this LC and its roll-out is haphazard and uneven, privileging larger, more organised ethnic groups. This chapter engages with the often overlooked voices of minorities within minorities relegating their views on language, education and language of instruction (LoI), and how this shapes their relationship with both the more dominant ethnic groups as well as the ruling Burman majority. All these minorities work hard to preserve their ethnic language and culture, and depending on where they live and how many other minorities are in the same area, have varying views on what the LoI for their children at school should be. Despite the prevailing view that most ethnic families want their children to learn in their mother tongue or ethnic language, there are some who want Burmese to remain the LoI. Many who took part in the 2018 fieldwork in Shan and Rakhine States emphasised that Burmese was the essential language for their children to be able to get good jobs and bring their families and communities out of poverty.[4] Not all communities, therefore, support an MTB-MLE system, and some say they prefer multilingual local teachers who can explain and still use the Burmese textbooks with their children. This chapter looks at the issue of ethnic language, education and how different ethnic groups want the government to deliver a more socially just education system that allows their children to compete with their Bamar peers, rather than facing a life-long disadvantage that begins in primary schools.

Background on Myanmar's ethnic diversity and languages

Myanmar is divided into seven states (populated mostly by ethnic nationality communities)[5] and seven regions dominated by the majority Burman (*Bamar*) ethnic group. Demographic statistics remain contested, despite a census – the first in 31 years – held in 2014 which calculated the population at 51.4 million people (GoM, 2017).[6] It is estimated that non-Bamar communities make up around 30–40 per cent of the population, including Shan 9 per cent, Karen 7 per cent, Rakhine 4 per cent, Chinese 3 per cent, Indian 2 per cent, Mon 2 per cent and other 5 per cent.[7] The official categories of 135 'national races' (*taingyintha*) recognised by the government are deeply problematic, representing arbitrary and often imposed identities (Cheesman, 2017). Although ethnicity is fluid, subject to re-imagination over time and in different contexts (Anderson, 1983), in Myanmar, it has become a fixed category and a key element in leveraging access to political and economic resources. Ethnic communities, however, are rarely homogenous in terms of ethno-linguistic orientation or policy preferences, and the ethnic diversity extends to intra-group dynamics. Furthermore, in many parts of Myanmar, larger ethnic groups such as the Karen, Kachin, Rakhine and Shan co-exist with smaller minority communities like the Pa-O, Danu, Lahu, Lisu, Wa, Htet, Dainet, etc. This diversity also translates into a linguistic challenge with over 100 languages spoken throughout the country (MEC, 2017).

Nicolas Salem-Gervais explains in the first of his three-part series on ethnic education on the 'Tea Circle' website, that some ethnic languages are spoken by millions, others by thousands, or only hundreds (Salem-Gervais, 2018). Some are spoken in limited areas whereas others are spoken across different states, and sometimes across the border in China, Thailand or India as well. Some are very similar to the national language Burmese, others belong to completely different ethno-linguistic families. Some are relatively homogenous, while others have numerous sub-dialects, which are not necessarily mutually intelligible (like Naga). Some have one script whilst some have no script – and others have several. This is not an uncommon situation across Asia or even other parts of the world, however, in Myanmar, it has meant that under military rule the Bamar majority has used this diversity as an excuse to impose its language and culture, a process referred to as 'Burmarisation', allegedly to keep the country united. Burmanisation started in the early 1960s after Ne Win's military coup.[8] As explained in more detail in Chapter 1, the main precepts of what was in essence an assimilation policy, included all ethnic groups needing to accept the majority Bamar cultural norms, reinforced by the army with regard to any ethnic separatist movements. Burmanisation included Buddhism being made the official state religion, and Burmese ('*Bama saga*' the only official language of the Union, including being the official LoI at all government and monastic schools. This deliberate process in turn contributed to the birth of individual ethnic consciousness (Kheunsai, 2017) and has been key in sustaining the ethnic armed organisations for over half a century of armed ethnic conflict. Since then the suppression of minority languages has been one of the main grievances of ethnic nationality people, as a unitary language policy was a key pillar in the military regime's Burmanisation of national culture (Houtman, 1999; Callahan 2004). This policy resulted in the jailing of ethnic language teachers and ethnic nationality citizens were forbidden to use their language in public. The imposition of the policy varied from place to place, with some communities continuing to use their ethnic language, which was often easier in remote places, where even the government authorities were represented by ethnic people (Jolliffe and Speers Mears, 2016).[9] In response to Burmanisation, ethnic nationality elites developed alternative non-formal, mostly after-school systems through the civil society sector, and in particular faith-based (Christian and Buddhist) associations to maintain their languages, scripts and culture. Some larger ethnic communities built their own schooling systems complete with education departments and teacher training facilities, run by Ethnic Armed Organisations (EAOs), CSOs or the communities themselves (Lall and South, 2018; South and Lall, 2016a, 2016b and 2016c; Lall, 2016a). These separate education systems that are based on the mother tongue are discussed in Chapter 7 of this volume. This chapter engages with the issues faced by ethnic nationality groups who have struggled to keep their language and culture alive without having access to EAO-run schools. In particular, it focuses on those smaller ethnic nationality groups who have battled against the odds of dual discrimination – that of larger Bamar majoritarianism as well as larger ethnic groups that dominate the state, often because they are represented by an armed group.[10] These smaller groups have generally not had access to any mother tongue or mother tongue-based multilingual education systems, and more often than not are dependent on Burmese government or monastic education provision supplemented by summer schools, community teacher support and/or after school language provision.

Minority languages, education reform and the peace process

One of the key challenges facing the government since the reform process started in 2012 has been to reach a consensus on language education policies that meets the diverse needs and hopes of all groups and can help promote social cohesion, ensuring that all children have an equal opportunity to learn effectively across the country. The education reform policies discussed earlier aim to meet the government's stated commitments to EFA as outlined in the 2016 NESP, and promise to improve quality of education, including for ethnic nationality citizens and marginalised communities in remote conflict-affected areas. This is a key social justice issue for the affected communities. As discussed in previous chapters of this volume, the five main aspirations of the NESP are quoted as access, quality, equity, inclusion and efficiency (MoE, 2016: 57). As such, the reforms represented a window of opportunity to reverse decades of Burmanisation by engaging with the needs of the ethnic nationality communities. This should have been a priority given the historic disparity of achievement of ethnic children in government schools, largely due to the language gap that children face when having to learn in Burmese despite their mother tongue being quite different. In the first study of its kind in Myanmar, research by Shalom (Nyein Foundation, 2011) shows that ethnic nationality children, especially in remote and conflict-affected areas, cannot read or write Burmese at the same speed as their Bamar peers, and subsequently often drop-out of school (Nyein Foundation, 2011). Testing a total of 474 students across Grades 2–5, they found that ethnic students who were able to read a whole passage took between three and four times as long as their Bamar counterparts. Of those surveyed, 15 per cent could not read at all and 18 per cent could not read the whole passage.[11] Research conducted on language in Chin State showed that students:

simply cannot always understand their lessons. They are thrown into a curriculum which presupposes they can speak the language and are familiar with the orthography, and with teachers who often cannot speak additional languages other than Burmese. They are not being taught from the perspective of needing Burmese as an additional language. Many participants described not being able to understand anything at school. For example, one participant explained that he had memorised everything but he had 'nothing in his head'. Learning is reduced to 'decoding' and rote memorisation rather than learning. (Edwards, 2018: 5)

This created lifelong and insurmountable disparities between these ethnic children and their Bamar peers. Those who do stay in the education system are often unable to join university due to poorer matriculation marks, resulting in a cycle of lifelong disadvantage for the individual, their family and the whole community. These research findings are born out in the 2014 Census data that shows how children and families in ethnic states are less literate, access fewer schools, and are less well-off than those living in the Bamar dominated regions. This disparity is aggravated for those in rural areas which are remote and conflict affected, where there are few if any Bamar residents, and where government education often cannot reach. As discussed later in this chapter, the 2014 Census also masks disparities between ethnic groups and especially the intra-state disparities of the smaller ethnic groups that make it impossible to know how 'minorities within minorities' are faring.[12]

The peace process and the NESP

Despite ethnic aspirations to see their languages recognised and used in the formal education system, neither the peace process nor the education reforms have delivered. Part of the problem has been the separation between the education reform process and the peace process. Ethnic language provision was largely absent in the formal nationwide ceasefire negotiations and the subsequent broader peace process from 2012, as these focused in the first place on securing and monitoring ceasefires. The nationwide political dialogue that was planned following the signing of the NCA in 2015 was expected to include multiple stakeholders (government, parliament, Tatmadaw,[13] EAOs, ethnic civil society, etc.) and would focus on these 'softer' issues. Interviews in 2014 and 2015 with key EAO leaders (Aung Htung and Lall et al., 2015) showed that even the ethnic leaders were not raising issues of education and language as their focus was on getting the terms of the ceasefire right, a negotiation process between the Thein Sein Government and the EAOs that would take several years, culminating in the November 2015 'nationwide' ceasefire agreement that ultimately only eight of the EAO groups signed.[14] The political dialogue process has stalled since 2015, and the on-going negotiations still fail to address issues pertaining to education and ethnic language. Ethnic nationality representatives at the various twenty-first-century Panglong conferences run by the NLD confirm that neither language policy nor education is on the 'peace agenda' despite this being a high priority issue for the ethnic communities. The talks in July 2018[15] yielded 14 new basic principles, among which for the first time is a reference to an 'all-inclusive education system', a point which was not further clarified at the meeting (Salem-Gervais, 2018).

The education reform process failed in this regard as well. The CESR that underpinned the creation of the NESP[16] did not engage adequately with issues of ethnic language and ethnic education. There was only one meeting between ethnic education providers and the CESR team in the summer of 2013 (Figure 6.1).[17] As a part of their

Figure 6.1 Ethnic education representatives meet Comprehensive Education Sector Review (CESR) team, 2013. Source: Author.

Peace Building Education and Advocacy Programme, UNICEF-funded Australian education and language specialist Professor Joseph Lo Bianco from the University of Melbourne to advise on issues pertaining to mother tongue and mother tongue-based education. The initiative became part of a multi-country project (also involving Thailand and Malaysia) entitled Language, Education and Social Cohesion Initiative (LESC). The LESC programme in Myanmar focused mainly on exploring the link between language and educational equity, in order to 'encourage national reconciliation and ethnic rights', 'support small minority languages' where there were speakers of a number of different languages, 'improve literacy and education in Burmese' and 'build a culture of dialogue and ethnic education' (Lo Bianco, 2016). Lo Bianco facilitated dialogue meetings, starting with one held in Mae Sot, Thailand in 2014, which resulted in the creation of the advocacy and action group, Myanmar/Burma Indigenous Network for Education (MINE).[18] Later, various meetings held at state and union level with selected ethnic nationality representatives[19] developed the Nay Pyi Taw Principles on Language.[20]

In as far as the CESR was concerned, LESC resulted in the Early Childhood Education team including mother tongue-based education for all children at primary level in their draft bill. The Education Thematic Working Group (ETWG) established an Education and Language Sub-working Group after the ETWG supported a meeting on language and cohesion in September 2014. This piggy-backed on a regional Language Education and Social Cohesion Workshop, supported by UNICEF to consider the next steps for multilingual education for Myanmar. The meeting allowed for 156 participants from government, state and union parliaments, development partners, INGOs, CSOs, universities, private schools and international/national education experts to meet each other and discuss the issue of language and education in Myanmar. The final part of LESC was the International Conference on Language Policy in Multicultural and Multilingual Settings hosted in Mandalay in February 2016. The conference was attended by over 300 participants who discussed both the state of multilingual education and language policy in diverse countries as well as critical issues and development in language policy and planning in Myanmar.[21] However, the ideas of MTB-MLE promoted by the initiative and the conference were ultimately rejected by the government and the MoE. The Peace Promoting National Language Policy for Myanmar was quietly shelved after the NPT policy summit of June 2016.[22]

There was not much change in this regard after the NLD formed a government in 2016. Despite making other changes, language and

LoI policy under the NLD government has not fundamentally departed from only Burmese being allowed as a means of instruction (Lall and South, 2018). The only concession made by the NLD in their revision of the NESP is that ethnic minority languages are now allowed as 'classroom language' to help explain concepts when necessary. However, using any ethnic language in the classroom effectively would require recruiting local teachers, or teachers who have learnt an ethnic language. According to UNICEF, 70 per cent of teachers working in ethnic areas do not speak local languages (Joliffe and Speers, 2016: 37) and although recent interviews conducted by Salem-Gervais and Raynaud suggest that more ethnic teachers are being recruited through a new township priority system (Salem-Gervais and Raynaud, 2019a and 2020), discussed in Chapter 5, there is no official policy or text that bears this out at the time of writing and the effects of this policy are still to be assessed.

Research has borne out that fluency and literacy in the mother tongue are the basis for learning other languages (Ball, 2011; Ball, 2014; Cummins, 2000). Those with a strong foundation in their mother tongue develop stronger literacy ability in the school language with knowledge and skills transferring across languages (Cummins, 2000). The level of competence in the second language is related to the level of competence they have achieved in their first language (Khan, 2014). If children are forced to transition too soon from mother tongue to schooling in a second language, their first language may be attenuated or even lost (Benson, 2004; Ball, 2014). Despite the strong evidence of mother tongue and mother tongue-based education benefits, including fewer drop-outs and better levels of achievement, mother tongue-based multilingual education (MTB-MLE) is *not* presently Myanmar education policy.

Myanmar has been using a monolingual 'submersion' system, where the majority language is used as the sole LoI (Ouane, 2003), an approach that can curtail children's development, perpetuating poverty. Even where students are able to 'pronounce' words in the second language, it may take many years before they understand what they are reading (Kosonen, 2005; SIL, 2018). The problem is particularly acute for children who have no contact with the LoI in the remote communities in which they live. This has impacted on ethnic hopes and concerns about equal access to, and quality of, education for their children (Lall and South, 2018).[23]

The reason is rooted in Burmanisation – the government believes that a unitary language is essential in holding the country together, a belief that is neither unusual regionally, nor likely to change.[24] Research in multi-ethnic environments points to the importance of a common language and comprehensive school system for ruling governments to cement the foundations upon which national states and national identities are formed (Anderson, 1983; Gellner, 1983) Fishman refers to the choice of a particular language as fundamental to the project of national integration and standardisation (Fishman, 1973), and Callahan identifies language as a cohesive factor that helps on the one hand to create alliances for unity and power, and on the other as a divisive and differentiating factor that tends to reinforce conflict and antagonism in Myanmar society (Callahan, 2003 and 2004).[25] The choice, therefore, for the government is greater social justice with equal education and linguistic rights for all citizens, including the ethnic nationality communities versus control of ethnic nationality communities through language, education and ultimately employment opportunities. Given the predominance of Burmese as a marker of power of the Bamar majority, it is, therefore, not surprising that MTB-MLE is not seen by the government as an acceptable option.

Ethnic language teaching in government schools and local curriculum development

Instead of offering MTB-MLE, the diversity of the country is being recognised through the introduction of a LC of one period a day in KG, Grade 1 and Grade 2[26] that is locally developed and that can be taught in an ethnic language. The teaching of ethnic languages in government schools that started in 2013 is different from the development of this LC, a more recent initiative that started in 2016–7, although as shall be seen below the two do overlap. The LC initiative is broader as it encompasses cultural and local content that is relevant at state level.

The formalisation of teaching ethnic languages in government schools started in Mon State, where the state parliament dominated by a Mon party (2010–5) lobbied the central government for the inclusion of Mon as a subject in government schools across Mon State. They were successful and a programme was set up training Mon language and subject teachers across the state, some of which even came from the Mon National Education Committee (associated with the New Mon State Party, the Mon EAO – see Chapter 7 of this volume). The passing of the private school bill in 2011 (Myo Thant, 2011), which allowed the teaching of ethnic languages, showed that the policy concerning government schooling and language was loosening, and that there would be options for ethnic organisations to teach ethnic languages. Some other ethnic communities followed the Mon example, although not in such a systematic manner. In 2013, when the MoE announced it would help train ethnic teachers so that ethnic languages could be taught after school,[27] the practice did not spread widely – possibly because it required communities to organise themselves, and possibly because subjects taught after school and not examined are often seen as an unnecessary extra burden on children.[28] Edwards reports the same issue occurring in Chin state as follows (Edwards, 2018: 3):

> Many parents expressed concern language lessons were being held outside school hours when children might be tired. All parents wanted their children to learn their mother tongue, but they did not agree on how children should access this learning. Some believed that it was enough to learn it within the family and the community, others said that church summer school was sufficient (generally a maximum of two weeks per year), others wanted mother tongue to be taught as an additional subject within the curriculum and others believed mother tongue should be the medium of instruction with a full mother tongue-based curriculum.

The idea of the LC system depends largely on the support of LCCs, local CSOs and in some cases UNICEF. Based on the 2014–5 Education Law (Article 39, f and g), a LC is meant to allow each state and region to introduce locally relevant content, amounting to 14 per cent at primary level, and 10 per cent in middle and high schools (although only 5 per cent is allowed in Grade 12) of the total teaching hours.[29] This means one period a day at primary level, with three of the five periods dedicated to the teaching of the local language, and two are meant to cover general knowledge of the state.[30]

The (re)introduction (Salem-Gervais, 2018) of ethnic languages throughout government schools in ethnic nationality-populated regions is significant in that it allows all ethnic and linguistic groups to see their language, script and culture recognised in the government education system, possibly improving access and commitment from ethnic families who have felt marginalised. According to Salem-Gervais, this recognition will increase the value of the ethnic languages in the eyes of their communities, possibly contributing to their long-term survival. He also believes that the official recognition of these languages may even have some effect on national reconciliation.[31] As will be discussed in more detail below, fieldwork over nine months in 2018 across all ethnic states shows that the development of this LC and its roll-out is still haphazard and uneven, privileging larger, more organised ethnic groups.[32]

According to the MoE in the 2018–9 school year, 54 ethnic minority languages were being taught officially to over 750,000 children, in 12,248 schools, by a total of 28,783 teachers, across all the states and regions. Recent MoE statistics indicate that 64 languages are now being taught in 2019–20 (Salem-Gervais and Raynaud, 2020). However, the situation on the ground is not always clear or consistent, and depends on the attitude of state/region and TEOs, and individual head teachers.[33] There are also challenges regarding which language should be offered at which school, and what to do in multilingual and multi-ethnic schools. Other challenges include teacher training and whether these classes can be held during school hours or only after school. The timing of such classes being particularly important as discussed above, however, in multilingual communities having classes in one language and not in the others means that those not covered during school are forced to take place outside of school hours.

A key issue that has been raised by many stakeholders and respondents who took part in the research is the salary and status of these teachers. Where requested, government funds were raised for a stipend for the teachers, but MMK 30,000 (USD 22) per month for 10 months a year to cover the teaching of one period a day is often insufficient to attract and then retain ethnic language teachers. In Pa-O communities, the classes were not being held between 2016 and 2018 because no teachers could be recruited at this level of remuneration. More recently, in 2019, things on the ground seem to be changing; Salem-Gervais and Reynaud note that 2018–9 MoE data indicates that 47 per cent of the 23,811 '30,000 kyats' ethnic language teachers are in fact government school teachers, teaching ethnic minority languages in addition to other subjects, and receiving this amount in addition to their salary (Salem-Gervais and Reynaud, 2019a and 2019b). The numbers of these teachers are, however, falling (from 10,760 in 2018–9 to 7,080 in 2019–20), in part, because the MoE has found it difficult to verify these classes are taking place, and also because the government is now privileging ethnic teaching assistants (TAs) – a position created in 2017 through a collaboration between the MoE, the Ministry of Ethnic Affairs (MoEA) and the LCCs. The first batch of around 5,200 ethnic TAs was appointed for the 2017–8 school year. Those part-time volunteer teachers who had a bachelor degree and completed training can over time become permanent government staff.[34] The others remain on daily wage salaries at MMK 4,800 a day (USD 3.5), much better than the

30,000 MMK offered per month to the 'volunteer language' teachers. The ethnic TAs are expected to help ethnic children, using the ethnic language as a classroom language and they are expected to teach the LC, especially the ethnic language as a subject. The 'volunteer language' (30,000 MMK) teachers who were trained by the LCCs and who only teach the 20 hours per month in government schools are likely to be phased out as the numbers of ethnic TAs increase.

The LC is not only about teaching the ethnic language – it is meant to include a wide range of subjects that primarily are relevant to the state and can include subjects such as agriculture, local economic activities or computer skills, but could also be used for the teaching of content related to local identities (Salem-Gervais, 2018). Currently, however, content seems to vary since there is not as yet an agreed state-level LC anywhere. According to Salem-Gervais, the development of the LC has resulted in new curricula for the teaching of 25 languages in Grades 1–3, as well as 3.5 million copies of storybooks for KG in the 66 languages being used in government schools (Salem-Gervais, 2018). However, a number of schools implementing the policy are either using books that were developed under the Thein Sein Government (with the help of the UNICEF-led ethnic mother tongue language initiative, LESC, mentioned above) that were usually used outside of school hours, or they are using materials designed for language summer schools, usually developed by the local LCC. State Education Offices have to approve the textbooks that are to be used in these lessons, and LCCs of the different ethnic groups have faced the challenge of standardising materials that had been used across communities in summer or Sunday schools, and which often had different scripts and varied spellings depending on religion and denomination.

This has led to disagreements between community leaders, the splitting of communities and the creation of new LCCs who are in disagreement with each other.[35] Intra-ethnic disputes usually focus on which LCC/language-dialect/script should be used – particularly in towns, as these are more multi-ethnic than most villages. On some occasions, communities split on religious lines as well, especially between different Christian denominations. The Akhas of eastern Shan State, for instance, currently use two different 'common' scripts, the United Akha Orthography (created in 2004) and the Common Akha Orthography (created in 2008), depending on their religious and political affiliations.[36] A Deputy Education Officer in Chin state (a Dai Chin) explained that: 'rival LCCs write to him, asking the MoE to bar other LCCs from teaching in "their" schools villages, and also complain to NPT – which is a headache for him.'[37] Government acceptance of LCC teaching in schools also depends on whether the community in question is recognised as having a script and literature that is linked to the list kept by MoE.[38] Those ethnic communities/languages that are not on the list have added difficulty teaching in schools. The complexity of the politics of language teaching has resulted in the creation of new LCCs, some of which focus on developing new scripts. However, this has also led to pitching intra-ethnic identities against each other, creating new sub-groups with particular political aims. As described by Salem-Gervais and Raynaud: 'They are always defined in contrast to other, neighbouring or encompassing political projects, sometimes even aiming to "purify" their languages by creating words to replace loanwords borrowed from other languages which are, or have been, influencing their own' (Salem-Gervais and Raynaud, 2019a).

Five out of seven ethnic states (Mon, Karen, Kayah, Kachin and Chin) are now working on developing locally relevant content for their state's LC. In interviews in 2018, SEO officials said that the structure of the LC had been prescribed centrally, as the MoE felt that the groups developing it did not have the technical expertise to do so, as well as to avoid any overlap with the national curriculum. Participants invited by the MoE to take part in the LC development included representatives from the local LCCs, technical experts, university professors from relevant departments of the local universities such as agriculture, education colleges, ethnic affairs ministers and NGOs. The role of EAO education departments in the process is problematic and interviews confirmed that EAO representatives who did attend any of these meetings felt their voices and expertise were drowned out by the large number of participants.[39] The role of the SEO seems to vary between states. In one case, a SEO noted that none of his staff were from the relevant ethnic group, and all had been posted to the office and, therefore, they could not contribute much to the LC. In other cases, the SEOs do have local ethnic staff, who are interested in being involved. UNICEF[40] has been acting as a facilitator providing technical and financial support by facilitating meetings at state and at national level.

It seems that the individual state government (as opposed to the SEO) needs to take the lead for LC development and ask for it to commence. This can be problematic as state governments rarely have enough funds, and ethnic languages are not always seen as a priority. Although Salem-Gervais and Raynaud point to some budgets being transferred from NPT to the state administrations, the figures they cite show that much less money is transferred to states (as opposed to regions) and the amounts are quite low overall (Salem-Gervais and Raynaud, 2020). The Shan State Government has not yet asked to take part in the development of their LC, so whilst there is a period for LC in KG, Grade 1 and Grade 2 in every government school for the delivery of this content, it is not being implemented. Respondents from the Shan, Pa-O, Danu, Intha, Khun Tai, Lahu and Wa mostly knew that the ethnic language could be taught outside of school hours as in the Thein Sein Government provision, but *did not know* that this had now been shifted to within school hours as a part of LC. Fieldwork in 2018 showed that LC or ethnic language was *not taught* for any of the groups visited either in Taunggyi Township or Kengtung Township. On the other side of the spectrum is Chin State, ironically the state where there are most languages.[41] According to UNICEF and research conducted by Ashley South,[42] Chin State is probably the most advanced state with regard to developing LC content. The Chin State Parliament passed a policy directive for LC content and they have been establishing MoE-led Township Literature and Culture Committees in each township, with seemingly variable LCC involvement. There are 31 Chin dialects approved by the SEO for teaching in government schools.

It needs to be remembered that despite the LC development being a step in the right direction for the inclusion of the many ethnic minorities in Myanmar, it does not solve the main issue for ethnic children of starting their schooling and understanding their teacher – essential ingredients for children to remain in school and achieve at par with the majority community. The LC is unlikely to solve the main discriminatory issue of understanding and achievement between groups. This is discussed in more detail in the next section.

Census data for key issues highlighting literacy and achievement

The 2014 Census was conducted during March–April, and was the first since 1983. This section draws on some of the key issues in the Thematic Report on Education (GoM, 2017) including literacy, school attendance and school attainment to showcase the disparities between states and regions, which by extension indicates differences between the ethnic nationality groups and their Bamar counterparts – although, as mentioned earlier, the 2014 Census did not release the figures broken down by ethnic group and this masks disparities between and within groups.

Overall, the literacy rate in Myanmar was 89.5 per cent. Unsurprisingly, younger people were more literate than older people, and urban dwellers were more literate than those who live in rural areas (Table 6.1). As shown in the same table, there were wide disparities between states. Shan State had the lowest literacy rates at 64.6 per cent, with Kayin State at 74.4 per cent and Chin at 79.4 per cent. In Kayah, Kayin, Chin, and Mon, the difference between rural and urban was more than 10 age points, and in Shan was as high as 27 points. The lowest 10 districts for literacy were all in Shan State with the lowest in Makman District where adult literacy was just 24.9 per cent (GoM, 2017: 25, Table 3.4).

School attendance up to age of 12 was slightly higher in rural areas, but was significantly lower after that age (GoM, 2017: 34, Table 4.2). Table 6.2 shows the lowest rates are in Kayin (65.2 per cent) and Shan (55.9 per cent).

There were also large differences in the percentages of the population with no schooling between states and regions. Table 6.3 shows that Shan (44.9 per cent), Kayin (31.8 per cent) and Chin (25.8 per cent) had the highest proportions of people who had not had any schooling. Table 6.3 also shows that the proportion with no schooling is consistently much higher in rural than in urban areas.

The 2014 Census had a section on children not in school aged 7–15 of which there were almost 500,000 who had never attended school (GoM, 2017: 43).[43] Non-attendance levels were more than twice as high in rural areas (6.2 per cent) than in urban areas (2.2 per cent), and this was the case at all ages (GoM, 2017: 43, Table 4.7). Table 6.4 shows that the highest proportions of 7–15 year olds who had never attendance school were in Shan State (21.9 per cent) and Kayin State (10.1 per cent). It was also reported that over a third of those who had never attended school were from the lowest wealth quintile 'reinforcing the link between affordability and attendance' (GoM, 2017: 49).

Although there was no specific question on the reason for not attending school in the 2014 Census (GoM, 2017: 46), the CESR, in full swing at the time, found that the reasons for not attending were (in order of importance): high costs; lack of interest; personal illness; agricultural work; and care for family. Drop-out rates are high during the transition from primary to lower secondary, and a language barrier is a significant factor to children from minority groups dropping out of school (GoM, 2017: 46).

Educational attainment is a key variable in indicating disparities and institutional discrimination. Completed level of education of those

Table 6.1 Adult literacy rates by sex, urban and rural areas, states/regions, 2014 Census

State/Region	Adult literacy rate (percentage)								
	Urban					Rural			
	Both sexes	Males	Females		Both sexes	Males	Females		
UNION	95.2	97.1	93.7		87.0	90.7	83.8		
Kachin	94.2	96.3	92.4		90.1	92.8	87.5		
Kayah	93.1	95.9	90.8		78.0	83.9	72.5		
Kayin	93.2	95.3	91.3		68.6	73.2	64.7		
Chin	89.6	95.1	85.2		76.5	86.6	67.9		
Sagaing	96.2	98.1	94.7		93.2	96.3	90.7		
Tanintharyi	96.6	97.9	95.5		91.4	93.3	89.6		
Bago	95.9	97.9	94.3		93.8	96.4	91.5		
Magway	96.1	98.1	94.6		91.6	96.3	87.9		
Mandalay	96.4	98.3	94.9		92.3	96.8	88.8		
Mon	93.8	95.7	92.2		83.6	86.9	80.8		
Rakhine	90.3	94.3	87.3		83.5	91.8	76.9		
Yangon	97.2	98.5	96.2		95.2	96.9	93.6		
Shan	85.2	89.4	81.6		57.9	64.4	51.8		
Ayeyarwady	95.9	97.7	94.4		93.5	95.6	91.5		
Nay Pyi Taw	97.2	98.9	95.9		93.2	97.5	89.3		
Total	9,902,101	4,551,622	5,350,479		20,476,718	9,857,290	10,619,428		

Source: Adapted from GoM (2017: 24, Table 3.3).

Table 6.2 School attendance rates by age by sex, states/regions, 2014 Census

State/Region	Children of primary age (5–9) (%)			Children of secondary age (10–15) (%)			Post-secondary age groups (16–29) (%)			All ages (5–29) (%)		
	Both sexes	Males	Females	Both sexes	Males	Females	Both sexes	Males	Females	Both sexes	Males	Females
UNION	71.2	70.7	71.7	68.0	68.2	67.9	9.9	9.8	10.1	38.8	39.6	38.1
Kachin	77.6	77.2	78.1	81.9	80.1	83.8	17.5	15.8	19.2	49.0	47.8	50.1
Kayah	77.9	77.4	78.5	78.0	76.4	79.5	12.1	10.4	13.6	45.7	44.8	46.5
Kayin	65.2	63.8	66.6	67.0	64.0	70.0	9.7	8.7	10.5	41.8	40.8	42.8
Chin	74.6	74.5	74.7	67.3	67.0	60.0	22.7	25.1	20.7	56.4	59.0	54.0
Sagaing	76.8	76.4	77.3	71.2	71.5	70.9	10.1	10.0	10.3	41.2	42.4	40.0
Tanintharyi	71.4	70.8	72.0	73.6	71.5	75.6	10.1	8.6	11.5	43.6	42.7	44.4
Bago	74.5	74.1	75.0	66.3	66.8	65.8	7.8	7.5	8.0	38.6	39.6	37.6
Magway	75.4	74.9	75.8	71.3	72.2	70.5	10.2	10.5	10.0	40.8	42.8	39.1
Mandalay	74.7	74.2	75.2	68.4	68.6	68.1	10.4	10.4	10.3	37.8	38.8	36.9
Mon	71.1	70.5	71.7	67.0	65.4	68.5	9.8	8.7	10.8	41.7	41.8	41.6
Rakhine	72.9	72.8	73.0	70.0	72.3	67.7	9.3	10.7	8.2	42.2	45.8	39.1
Yangon	70.5	70.2	70.7	68.0	68.7	67.3	11.7	12.1	11.3	35.4	36.8	34.1
Shan	55.9	55.2	56.6	57.3	57.0	57.6	7.6	7.1	8.0	32.0	31.5	32.4
Ayeyarwady	72.5	72.1	72.8	66.3	66.6	66.0	8.1	7.7	8.5	38.7	39.2	38.2
Nay Pyi Taw	76.4	76.0	76.7	75.5	76.0	75.0	10.4	10.5	10.4	41.2	42.3	40.1
Total	3,363,302	1,678,614	1,684,688	3,918,030	1,932,665	1,985,365	1,105,629	507,537	598,092	8,386,961	4,118,816	4,268,145

Source: Adapted from GoM (2017: 38, Table 4.4).

Table 6.3 Proportion of population aged 25 and over with no schooling by sex, urban and rural areas, states/regions, 2014 Census

State/Region	Total (%)			Urban areas (%)			Rural areas (%)		
	Both sexes	Males	Females	Both sexes	Males	Females	Both sexes	Males	Females
UNION	**16.2**	**13.3**	**18.8**	**7.3**	**5.2**	**9.1**	**20.2**	**16.9**	**23.2**
Kachin	12.3	9.6	15.2	8.9	6.3	11.5	14.3	11.3	17.6
Kayah	22.6	16.1	28.9	9.7	6.2	12.8	27.7	19.9	35.4
Kayin	31.8	27.6	35.6	9.1	6.7	11.4	38.8	34.2	43.0
Chin	25.8	14.1	35.7	14.0	6.4	20.4	29.3	16.4	40.4
Sagaing	11.9	8.8	14.4	6.2	3.8	8.2	13.1	9.9	15.8
Tanintharyi	10.3	9.1	11.5	4.8	3.6	5.8	12.3	11.0	13.6
Bago	10.9	8.5	12.9	6.8	4.6	8.5	12.1	9.6	14.3
Magway	19.3	16.7	21.3	7.6	5.5	9.2	21.4	18.7	23.6
Mandalay	12.5	8.8	15.5	6.2	4.0	8.0	15.8	11.3	19.6
Mon	17.2	14.8	19.3	8.3	6.3	9.9	21.0	18.4	23.3
Rakhine	20.2	12.8	26.3	12.2	7.9	15.6	21.9	13.9	28.6
Yangon	5.9	4.4	7.1	4.4	2.9	5.7	9.6	8.0	11.1
Shan	44.9	39.7	49.8	20.6	16.4	24.4	53.4	47.6	59.1
Ayeyarwady	12.3	10.3	14.0	7.0	4.8	8.7	13.2	11.3	15.0
Nay Pyi Taw	8.1	3.9	11.9	3.9	1.9	5.6	10.3	4.9	15.1

Source: Adapted from GoM (2017b: 60, Table 5.7).

Table 6.4 Children aged 7–15 by school attendance, states/regions, 2014 Census

State/Region	Currently attending		Previously attended		Never attended	
	Number	%	Number	%	Number	%
UNION	6,293,585	73.2	1,857,373	21.6	447,091	5.2
Kachin	236,739	84.9	37,385	13.4	4,874	1.7
Kayah	46,221	82.5	8,427	15.0	1,411	2.5
Kayin	221,696	71.3	57,924	18.6	31,254	10.1
Chin	94,967	88.4	8,680	8.1	3,768	3.5
Sagaing	696,881	76.7	193,354	21.3	18,809	2.1
Tanintharyi	224,856	78.2	52,786	18.4	9,721	3.4
Bago	618,429	73.2	204,875	24.2	21,661	2.6
Magway	487,472	76.8	136,115	21.4	11,523	1.8
Mandalay	708,435	74.0	231,463	24.2	17,101	1.8
Mon	281,361	73.0	89,947	23.3	14,316	3.7
Rakhine	312,699	74.7	82,639	19.8	23,014	5.5
Yangon	774,108	72.5	272,430	25.5	21,906	2.1
Shan	649,764	61.0	181,338	17.0	233,553	21.9
Ayeyarwady	789,833	72.7	265,496	24.4	31,013	2.9
Nay Pyi Taw	150,124	79.9	34,514	18.4	3,167	1.7

Source: Adapted from GoM (2017: 46, Table 4.8).

aged 25 and over is significant as those aged 25 and over are likely the parents of current school-aged children. Table 5.1 (GoM, 2017) shows that 0.4 per cent have a postgraduate or a Master's degree, and only 5.2 per cent completed upper secondary, while 61.3 per cent of the population had either completed primary school, not completed primary school or had no education at all. There are large differences in the highest completed level of education between states and regions. Table 6.5 shows that those in Shan and Kayin were the least well educated. In Kayin, over a third of the female population aged 25 and over (35.6 per cent) reported having no level of education, while in Shan the situation was even worse at 49.8 per cent, rising to almost 60 per cent in rural areas of Shan State and over 80 per cent in some districts of Shan State.

The 2014 Census data also show a clear relationship between the level of educational attainment and household wealth (GoM, 2017: 57). Table 6.5 (GoM, 2017) shows the distribution pattern of educational attainment when cross-analysed by the household wealth index. The percentage of the population with no completed level of education was highest in the lowest wealth quintile (30.1 per cent); however, the proportion of those who completed primary school is not significantly different across the wealth index quintiles. There were large differences in the percentages of the population with no schooling between states and regions. Table 6.3 also shows that Shan (44.9 per cent), Kayin (31.8 per cent) and Chin (25.8 per cent) had the highest proportions and that the proportion with no schooling is consistently much higher in rural than in urban areas. In Shan State, more than half of the population aged 25 and over in rural areas reported having no schooling, compared with just a fifth in urban areas (GoM, 2017: 60).

These figures show huge disparities between states in educational provision and attainment. Given that the census was not implemented in some conflict-affected areas, the actual situation on the ground is likely to be far worse for ethnic nationality children in the most remote regions. The lack of information on smaller minorities also masks the pronounced disadvantages that occur for them within larger ethnic groups.

This chapter now turns to the often overlooked voices of minorities within minorities, in two of Myanmar's ethnic states (Shan and Rakhine States) that continue to experience severe education and conflict issues, masking the needs of smaller groups.[44] It discusses their views on language, education and the LoI, and how this shapes their relationship with both the more dominant ethnic groups as well as the ruling Burman majority. Whilst all minorities within minorities that were consulted do work hard to preserve their ethnic language and culture, some argue that

Table 6.5. Percentage of population aged 25 and over by highest completed level of education by sex, states/regions, 2014 Census

State/Region	Completed education (percentage)							
	No education	Incomplete primary	Completed primary	Incomplete secondary	Completed upper secondary	Higher than upper secondary	Other	Total
Both Sexes								
UNION	16.2	22.6	22.5	22.6	5.2	9.1	1.7	100
Kachin	12.3	19.2	19.6	31.9	7.6	8.5	0.9	100
Kayah	22.6	21.7	13.1	25.3	8.5	8.1	0.7	100
Kayin	31.8	25.4	13.1	19.4	3.9	4.5	1.8	100
Chin	25.8	18.6	17.5	23.7	7.9	6.5	0.1	100
Sagaing	11.9	21.5	33.7	19.1	4.0	7.2	2.6	100
Tanintharyi	10.3	27.9	22.7	25.2	5.9	6.8	1.2	100
Bago	10.9	30.5	23.1	23.3	3.8	7.0	1.5	100
Magway	19.3	20.4	29.6	18.9	4.0	6.7	1.2	100
Mandalay	12.5	23.4	24.8	22.5	4.9	10.7	1.2	100
Mon	17.2	28.7	17.8	22.5	5.1	7.6	1.1	100
Rakhine	20.2	30.4	20.9	18.7	4.0	5.4	0.4	100
Yangon	5.9	17.0	14.9	31.9	9.8	19.3	1.0	100
Shan	44.9	17.0	12.1	15.8	3.7	5.1	1.4	100
Ayeyarwady	12.3	25.0	29.2	20.6	3.8	5.5	3.7	100
Nay Pyi Taw	8.1	21.1	22.7	24.6	6.7	14.6	2.1	100
Total (number)	4,369,423	6,093,024	6,067,151	6,085,072	1,412,870	2,446,943	448,790	26,923,273

(Continued table 6.5)

(Continued table 6.5)

State/Region	Completed education (percentage)							
	No education	Incomplete primary	Completed primary	Incomplete secondary	Completed upper secondary	Higher than upper secondary	Other	Total
Males								
UNION	13.3	19.6	22.6	27.4	6.2	8.8	2.0	100
Kachin	9.6	17.1	19.9	36.0	8.2	8.1	1.1	100
Kayah	16.1	22.9	14.5	29.5	8.6	7.6	0.8	100
Kayin	27.6	25.1	13.3	22.6	4.4	4.4	2.5	100
Chin	14.1	17.1	20.0	30.7	9.9	8.1	0.1	100
Sagaing	8.8	17.8	34.1	23.9	5.0	7.5	2.9	100
Tanintharyi	9.1	24.3	22.5	29.6	6.5	6.3	1.7	100
Bago	8.5	26.0	23.1	29.3	4.7	6.6	1.8	100
Magway	16.7	15.7	30.1	24.3	5.1	6.7	1.4	100
Mandalay	8.8	19.5	24.9	28.4	6.1	11.0	1.4	100
Mon	14.8	26.5	17.5	26.8	5.9	6.6	1.8	100
Rakhine	12.8	26.4	24.1	24.7	5.1	6.2	0.6	100
Yangon	4.4	14.1	13.9	36.4	11.5	18.6	1.2	100
Shan	39.7	17.8	13.1	18.5	4.0	4.9	1.9	100
Ayeyarwady	10.3	21.6	29.1	25.5	4.4	4.9	4.0	100
Nay Pyi Taw	3.9	16.9	23.2	30.8	8.2	14.7	2.3	100
Total (number)	1,671,231	2,459,097	2,839,697	3,441,966	779,912	1,108,363	249,021	12,549,287

Source: Adapted from GoM (2017: 56–7, Table 5.4).

they want Burmese to remain the LoI as they see it as the essential language for their children to be able to get good jobs and bring their families and communities out of poverty.[45] Burmese, they argue, provides the various communities in multi-ethnic settings with a level playing field they feel is fairer, than if Burman linguistic domination was replaced with another ethnic language – for example, the dominant ethnic language of the state in which they live.[46] The communities discussed below, therefore, do not support an MTB-MLE system that might see larger ethnic languages replace Burmese, and would prefer multilingual local teachers who can explain the Burmese textbooks to their children. It needs to be recognised, however, that there are other similarly small minority communities that do want MTB-MLE. Research conducted for MEC by SIL showed that Naga, Kayah and some Chin groups expressed the desire to have MTB-MLE (SIL, 2018). The example of the Nagas is striking (SIL, 2018: 22):

> Very few Nagas complete their education as a result of the language barrier in school, the lack of access to school, and insufficient teachers available for rural schools. Those Nagas who do complete their education typically travel to Yangon, India or Thailand. Living outside their home areas and studying other languages may result in weakening their mother tongue proficiency. Many fear that without attention to MTB-MLE the children will continue to grow up with weakening levels of mother tongue proficiency.

Some background on Shan and Rakhine States and the communities that live there

Both Shan and Rakhine States are home to a dominant ethnic minority as the state's majority population, and contain smaller ethnic groups as well as Bamar residents. The Shan people are the country's second-largest ethnic nationality after the Bamar, and their state is the largest ethnic state in the Union. Shan State is also home to many other ethnic groups, including Kachin, Pa-O, Palaung, Wa, Ta'ang, Karen, Lahu, Lisu, Akha, and others (Jolliffe and Speers Mears, 2016). As seen in the previous section, Shan State has some of the most concerning census data related to literacy, education attendance and attainment. In Shan State, adult literacy rate was just under 65 per cent compared to 89.5 per cent nationally (GoM, 2017: 22, Table 3.2) and in rural areas the female adult literacy rate was only 51.8 per cent (GoM, 2017: 24, Table 3.3).

The 10 districts with the lowest literacy rates were all in Shan, including Makman District where only 24.9 per cent of adults were literate (GoM, 2017: 25, Table 3.4). Youth literacy rates in Shan were 76.8 per cent (GoM, 2017: 25). A quarter of households in Shan State (24.9 per cent) were classified as illiterate (GoM, 2017: 29, Table 3.8). The 10 districts with the highest proportions of the population aged 25 and over with no schooling were all in Shan, where in Hopan and Makman Districts over 80 per cent of the population aged 25 and over had no schooling (GoM, 2017: 62, Table 5.8). Whilst the census information does not distinguish between the Shan majority and the other ethnic minority groups, evidence from the field shows that some of the low literacy statistics are due to children not understanding the language the teacher speaks in the classroom. This is also the case for Shan children, but particularly acute for children from the smaller minorities who rarely, if ever, will have a teacher in their class able to speak their language. Drop-outs are often linked to children not being able to understand the government teacher who usually does not speak the local language. Another reason for the low levels of schooling and literacy is that Shan is a conflict-affected state with nine or more armed groups operating in different parts of the state. During 2018–9, over 9,000 people were displaced to 33 IDP (Internally Displaced Person/People) sites[47] due to clashes between the armed groups and the Tatmadaw, and in North Eastern Shan State due to the fighting between two local EAOs – the Shan State Progressive Party (SSPP) and the Restoration Council of Shan State (RCSS) Political wing of a Shan army. These conflicts mean that government teachers mandated to these regions often flee when the fighting starts, and schools cannot operate. Anecdotal evidence collected in one of the conflict areas in South Eastern Shan State shows that locally- and community-recruited teachers tended to stay with their community even through the conflict.

Problems in Rakhine's education sector have been substantially exacerbated by the inter-communal conflict between Buddhist and Muslim communities that has affected the state since 2012, and more recently by the new conflict between the Arakan Army and the Myanmar Tatmadaw (REACH, 2015). Figures differ widely, but in 2015, UNICEF estimated there were 124,000 conflict-affected children aged 3–17 years, many of whom were residing in internal displacement camps and in need of education support (UNICEF, 2015: 27). Whilst some of these camps have now closed and children have been returned to schools, a total of 128,000 people from the as yet unresolved conflict remain in IDP camps.[48] A new conflict gathered pace towards the end of 2018 and affected parts of the state including the Mrauk U area (visited for fieldwork in 2018 before the conflict started), that is home to many minority communities such as Chin, Dainet, Mro and Thet, many of whom live in abject poverty in very remote areas. In 2019 UNOCHA estimated that the new conflict had displaced 30,000 people and it seems this has increased since.[49]

Literacy rates at 84.7 per cent in Rakhine are better than in Shan (GoM, 2017: 22, Table 3.2). However, the rate declines to 76.9 per cent for women in rural areas. The SEO confirmed in an interview (October 2018) that all government teachers speak Rakhine, most are local and are able to use Rakhine in the classroom. However, non-Rakhine minorities will not have teachers who speak their language and face the dual disadvantage of having to engage both with Burmese and Rakhine. Whilst these languages are close, they are nevertheless different enough to confuse children whose mother tongue is somewhat different and who have not been exposed to either Rakhine or Burmese before arriving at school. As with Shan State, the census education data does not distinguish between ethnic groups. The figures for attainment at primary school level in Rakhine are marginally better than in Shan State: 20.9 per cent completed primary versus 12.1 per cent in Shan – possibly because the number of minority children is proportionately fewer. However, only 4 per cent completed secondary education, similar to the 3.7 per cent in Shan (GoM, 2017: 56, Table 5.4).

Minority within minority positions

During field work for research conducted in the summer and autumn of 2018 in Shan and Rakhine States,[50] minority within minority community respondents emphasised that the preservation of their culture and language was important and, therefore, they did want a LC in their language for use in government schools. In many cases, they felt that it was unfair that larger groups had their textbooks recognised for teaching in government schools whilst smaller groups did not. However, the issue they faced was not the fact that their language was or was not being taught in government school (during after-school hours), but rather the fact that they wanted their children to learn Burmese and learn it well so that their community members would be able to join the Myanmar government higher education system and become professionals.[51] 'Since Early Childhood Care and Development (ECCD) the children learn Burmese. The ECCD teachers are Wa, but the community insist on Burmese unless children don't understand. That way the children have less problems later' (Wa LCC. Field notes, autumn 2018). The head of the Wa LCC in Kengtung explained that few Wa had done well historically because of the language barrier. His personal experience was that he had failed when he was young, but then he learnt Burmese and he was able to get a government job. He added that: 'Only when the children are good in Burmese they can get higher education to become government staff. Not enough Wa are working as government staff.' Burmese was seen as more valuable than their mother tongue, as knowing Burmese was seen as a way out of the poverty faced by the whole community, especially those living in remote areas. The fact that government teachers did not speak the local language was seen as a problem, not because they could not teach in the mother tongue, but because these Bamar teachers could not explain Burmese to their children: 'This is not their fault, but they don't see the needs of the community' (Akha leader, head of a boarding house for rural Akha children. Field notes, autumn 2018) (see Figure 6.2).

The Myanmar Government was not seen as helpful in supporting the ethnic communities learn either their own language or Burmese. The 'best way', as suggested by the respondents, was for local bilingual

Figure 6.2 Conversation with the Akha community 2018. Source: Author.

community members to be recruited and trained as teachers so as to be able to bridge the language gap, allowing smaller minority children to stay on in school rather than drop-out due to a lack of understanding. However, few ethnic students make it into the state-based education colleges (Lall, 2015).[52] To fill this gap, the Pa-O have set up their own Teacher Education College for ethnic teachers, which is discussed in more detail below.

A number of ethnic organisations that took part in the research (in this case, the Akha in Kengtung and the Mro in Mrauk U) had set up boarding houses in urban areas for their ethnic children so they can attend better schools, and the children were given remedial Burmese lessons so as to improve their achievement levels and their chance of continuing on into secondary, post-secondary and possibly higher education. These organisations worked on the preservation of their language and cultures as well, but the prime focus was on their children being able to finish school, and move on to secondary school and later higher education. The head of the Akha boarding house explained (Field notes, autumn 2018):

> 15 years ago there were no Akha educated people. [...] Children now learn Burmese in kindergarten. During their time in school they faced problem with the language. [they stay] in village school till grade 5, then they go to the city in grade 6, in the village they spoke only Akha but when they came to the city they have to speak Burmese. [...] At the beginning they face problems, but later the problems get solved. So many learn from Burmese teachers. They learn and then the problem is solved. Last year 280 Akha students passed metric and among them 7 or 8 received distinction in Myanmar language.

This was the pride of the community, and they had kept the newspaper cutting with the names of the Akha students for all to see. One organisation had mobilised its diaspora to provide scholarships for children that managed to gain access to a university. The Danu group had set up a foundation to help students with education-related fees, particularly for higher education.

None of these smaller minorities felt that setting up their own schools using their mother tongue (as has been done by larger ethnic communities such as the Mon, Karen and Kachin) was either viable or desirable, and all were fearful that any system privileging a particular ethnic language in the state as part of the LC would mean that their children would find education even harder. A MTB-MLE system based on the state language[53] was something they definitely rejected, knowing that their community was too small for their language to be accepted as the mother tongue in an MTB system.

There were of course differences between communities in urban and in rural areas. A lack of education and lack of information on laws, policies and rules was seen as an acute barrier for all rural non-Shan and non-Rakhine minority respondents in navigating government bureaucracy. When they came to towns and had to interact with government, they were discriminated against because they did not speak Burmese correctly, or did not understand how they were expected to behave with officials. A majority of the respondents explained that their communities all spoke the mother tongue – so that was not the problem – but the only way for their community to improve their situation was to learn more Burmese so they could understand the laws and communicate with the 'ruling' Burmese. They generally felt that their community remained 'backward' due to the fact that they did not have educated representatives to represent them in dealing with government. 'Ordinary people don't know about the laws or even the amendments. Officials themselves are not clear themselves. So implementation is not effective. Ordinary people lose self-confidence, being not sure what they are allowed to do and what not' (Rural Danu respondent. Field notes, autumn 2018). The Dainet leaders (see Figure 6.3) spoke of the fear that the lack of education and language knowledge created: '[We are] … afraid to go to government office. We can't write a letter, have low education, can't speak Rakhine or Burmese language, therefore [there is] discrimination' (Field notes, autumn 2018). They felt that if as an organisation they were able to have an office in an urban area, they would have more status and it would help the development of their community. Students would also have a place to stay to attend an urban school, starting a cycle that could bring their communities out of poverty.

Lack of education was also related to poverty as some of these communities are located in remote and conflict-affected areas: 'In the villages there are drop outs, the parents take children out after they reach 10 years of age as they need to work in the field' (Akha community leader. Field notes, autumn 2018). Lahu leaders spoke about the same issue: 'The main barrier is when the Lahu come to the urban area, not used to using Burmese. In remote areas how much Burmese do they learn? In the urban areas because of the mixed ethnic classrooms

Figure 6.3 Members of the Dainet community, 2018. Source: Author.

and because they use it outside school, the children learn.' The Thet felt multiple language development was the best way: 'We speak Thet at home. We speak Rakhine and Burmese with outside people, in Maungdaw we speak the forbidden language with our Muslim neighbours' (Field notes, autumn 2018). They claim the children do not have language problems at school as the Thet community lives in mixed villages close to the Rakhine community. Remote areas where there are pure Thet villages and the residents cannot understand Rakhine are of course disadvantaged. A few respondents noted that the Pa-O have successfully overcome some of their marginalisation by improving the education levels of their community through the use of Burmese and by encouraging their children to study to higher education levels. When speaking to the Pa-O leaders a clear strategy emerged. The Pa-O, being a large minority within minority and concentrated in a geographical area around Taunggyi, were particularly clear about what non-Shan minorities in Shan State needed to do.[54] A Pa-O National Organisation (PNO) leader[55] explained that one generation ago, the Pa-O were mainly poor farmers with very few finishing primary school. The Parami Network (a Pa-O civil society organisation, see Figure 6.4) adopted the goal of increasing the number of Pa-O in the Myanmar government administrative ranks, and the key strategy to attain this goal was seen as success in government education. Today, while the older Pa-O generation are still farmers, younger Pa-O have moved to towns like Taunggyi and have white-collar jobs. Research conducted by Celine Margontier-Haynes as part of her MA dissertation on the language and culture of the Pa-O, showed that the younger urban-based Pa-O do not necessarily speak Pa-O to their children, and that with the focus on Burmese many can no longer communicate with their rural relatives, especially grandparents (Margontier-Haynes, 2016). This was seen as a problem by many who felt speaking Pa-O is an essential part of the Pa-O culture, but others felt it was more important for their children to do well and get good jobs by being proficient in Burmese. Yet there was great unhappiness with the government education system, both in rural and urban areas. The Pa-O LCC and parents who discussed these issues in focus groups said that teachers do not teach effectively, and in fact focus on earning extra income through private tutoring.[56] In particular, respondents from the PNO said they were unhappy with the education that the Pa-O children were receiving. The most popular solution was to push for more

Figure 6.4 Members of the PNO, PDN, PWEF and PLCO with Daw Aye Aye Tun, 2016. Source: Author.

bilingual teachers who would be able to explain Burmese school content in Pa-O. This was the underlying motive in setting up their own teacher education college – to train more ethnic teachers for their community and others like them.

Example of a solution: The Pa-O Teacher Education College

The PNO has developed an innovative teacher training system. Finding that an insufficient number of Pa-O ethnic nationals were being accepted into the state-run education colleges, the PNO leaders negotiated with the Shan SEO to open their own teacher education college in 2016 (see Figure 6.5). This followed the same two-year teacher training curriculum as all education colleges, and the students received training from teacher educators employed in the Taunggyi education college. In addition, the college offered extra modules in Pa-O and ethnic languages. The recruits were ethnic nationality student teachers who had applied, but not been

Figure 6.5 Shan State Pa-O Teacher Education College, 2018. Source: Author.

accepted, into the education colleges in Taunggyi and Kayah State. The college opened its doors in January 2016 with 113 student teachers from 10 ethnic nationalities, including Pa-O, Danu, Shan, Kayah and others. The programme was residential and the trainees first lived with local families whilst the dormitories were being built. Although set up privately by Pa-O civil society groups, the Shan SEO recognised the student teachers graduating from this education college, as their own education college did not supply sufficient teachers every year.[57] All student teachers from the first batch graduated in 2018, and all of them were appointed by the MoE as primary school teachers in government schools in Shan and Kayah States (except one who went on to study at the Sagain University of Education). However, rather than all student teachers being sent back to serve in Pa-O-speaking communities (or communities where they speak the local language), those from outside the Self Administered Zone (SAZ)[58] were sent to remote areas in Shan State where there are other ethnic communities, and where they do not speak the relevant language. Although these schools have vacant positions, those were filled by non-Pa-O-speaking teachers or graduates from the Taunggyi government education college. As a result, schools in Pa-O areas in Taunggyi district did not receive Pa-O-speaking teachers, in effect defeating the original purpose of the college.

The ethnic nationality graduates from this college are clearly not enough to fill the required gaps. More teachers, especially from remote areas where there are shortages of teachers, need to be trained so that they can return to their homes and teach. This view is supported by a member of the Pa-O LCC who said that '… for rural areas where there are language barriers we need teachers who can explain things in Pa-O, and qualified teachers who have to be patient to make sure the children learn'. Other respondents have similar views. A member of the SAZ Leading Body said some head teachers do not support the teaching of Pa-O in schools, even if the school serves a Pa-O community: 'However, if there is a Pa-O teacher in the school, then he or she can explain things in Pa-O and teach Pa-O to the children' (Field notes, autumn 2018).

Conclusion: Issues for children and social justice and equality

The government's development of a LC has led to many new questions – including which language should be taught, by whom, and in which schools. Clearly, the MoE is trying to meet the aims of the NESP which emphasises: 'support and promotion of ethnic languages and cultures, including for primary-age ethnic children who speak different languages' and 'prioritizing the needs of schools in less developed areas to make education more accessible to all' (MoE, 2016: 32).

These directives in themselves aim to improve the situation for ethnic nationality children and their families – and especially the smaller minorities who do not have an armed group to represent their views and position. At this point, there is not sufficient decentralisation to allow for the relevant local voices to shape what language they want taught in their schools, or if and how they want to be taught ethnic languages. Beyond education, there is also a need to recognise ethnic languages in the relevant states in areas of public administration and justice (South and Lall, 2016a and b), as languages have to be used and recognised to be deemed of value to any community.

Returning to Iris Young's framework, it is clear that the LC does not reverse the process of marginalisation embedded in the government's education system that impacts so adversely on smaller minority groups (Young, 2005). In fact, rather than greater inclusion, the manner in which it is being developed and rolled-out is sewing division even within the ethnic groups. The respondents interviewed for this chapter believed that in order for their community to be treated with respect, and recognised by the government and wider administration, they needed more access to Burmese – even if this promoted a form of Bamar cultural imperialism. Many felt powerless in light of how the authorities treated their culture, and the lack of materials they had been asked to present to contribute to the development of the LC.

However, the result of the critique also depends on the social justice framework used. If, instead of Young, we use the '4 R framework' of Novelli et al.: redistribution, recognition, representation and reconciliation (Novelli et al., 2015) – also used in Chapter 7 of this volume to explore EAO education systems[59] – and apply it to the issues of language and LC, the Government of Myanmar could argue that they are in fact making significant progress. The MoE is for the first time committing resources to ethnic language education by paying teachers to deliver the LC, and by hiring ethnic TAs. Allowing ethnic textbooks to be used during the school day means the MoE is in effect recognising these languages and the right of the ethnic groups to teach their language and culture to their children. The MoE has also ensured representation from all these groups to co-develop the LC. In doing so, MoE officials have argued they are working towards reconciliation, and even though education is not part of the peace process, they see this as a peace promotion strategy.[60]

The views explored in this chapter nevertheless leave open the broad debate on the teaching of ethnic languages through either a LC or by developing a full MTB-MLE system. The census points to the fact that the lack of MTB-MLE in Myanmar means that the country will retain long-term structural disadvantages for certain groups. There are ethnic armed groups and affiliated organisations that have developed alternative, parallel MTB-MLE systems for their communities and four of these are described in the next chapter. At the time of writing, it is impossible to judge if the children who go to these schools fare better than ethnic children in government schools. In fact, SIL (2018), in their research for MEC write about how the term 'MTB-MLE' has been taken to mean almost any system that uses the mother tongue in the classroom. They argue that MTB-MLE is technically quite specific in the way programmes are structured, so that children can scaffold their learning at the appropriate times and that this is quite lengthy (minimum six years) and difficult to achieve, and not even those systems described next represent complete and full MTB-MLE provision.

Notes

1 Adding the stipulation of ethnic languages being allowed to be used as 'classroom languages' under certain circumstances was one of the very few changes by the NLD government, who otherwise took up the NESP almost unchanged after they took power. However, according to Salem-Gervais and Raynaud, the original version on the 2014 Education Law actually allowed ethnic languages as a LoI and this was changed in 2015 (Salem-Gervais and Raynaud, 2020): 'The second paragraph (b) of Article 43 in the first version (2014) of the Education law included provision for using ethnic minority languages as a medium of instruction during primary and secondary education: (b) If there is a need, an ethnic language can be used alongside Myanmar as a LoI at the basic education level. This paragraph was amended in 2015, after the student demonstrations, in what is in fact a step back in terms of introducing ethnic minority languages in formal education' (Salem-Gervais and Raynaud, 2020: 79).
2 As Chapter 7 of this volume will show, many larger ethnic nationality groups would like MTB-MLE. But even just using an ethnic language in the classroom would require recruiting local teachers, or teachers who have learnt an ethnic language. According to UNICEF, 70 per cent of teachers working in ethnic areas do not speak local languages (Jolliffe and Speers, 2016: 37). More on this later in this chapter.
3 It should be noted that the NESP MTR's recommendations that came out in early 2020 for Basic Education include the surprising suggestion for the NESP 2019–21: 'Promote and implement use of national ethnic languages as the primary language of instruction in initial years of education, and provide language-appropriate curriculum adaptation, learning materials and continue engagement of language assistants.' (MoE, 2020: xii). Given Myanmar's education and language policy to date, it is unclear how this would be implemented. Like many suggestions of the CESR regarding ethnic equality and equity, this recommendation could just vanish and not make it into NESP 2019–21.

4   Those who propagate MTB-MLE emphasise that it allows the children to learn Burmese better if children start in their mother tongue. This might be true, however, for small minorities there is a very real fear that if MTB-MLE were to become Myanmar policy, the larger state languages would become the LoI, making it even harder for their children to learn as there would be two 'foreign' languages involved rather than just one.
5   Ethnic minorities reject the terminology that includes the word 'minority' and prefer to be referred to as 'ethnic nationality communities' or simply 'ethnic', which is respected in this volume.
6   The 2014 Census, designed by the UN Population Fund and conducted by the Ministry of Immigration and Population, was seen as deeply problematic, especially with the way that it allowed respondents to self-identify their ethnic group. In particular, there was no Rohingya category, Rohingya being asked to self identify as Bengali. The 2014 Census was also not held in some conflict-affected areas. Ethnic and religious figures have not been published. For more on this, see https://www.crisisgroup.org/asia/south-east-asia/myanmar/counting-costs-myanmar-s-problematic-census and Callahan, 2017.
7   https://www.cia.gov/library/publications/the-world-factbook/geos/bm.html
8   More detail on how this was propagated through the education system in Chapter 1 of this volume.
9   Although discussions the author held with ethnic nationality respondents in ethnic states and conflict-affected areas in 2011, 2012, 2014, 2016 and 2018 always go back to how repressive the Burmanisation policy was, official policy seems to have been different – at least until the late 1980s: 'According to the official curriculum guidelines, ethnic languages could be taught up to Grade 3, with a maximum of five 45-minute classes a week [in certain areas]' (Thaung Htut, 1980, cited in Salem-Gervais, 2018). Textbooks for several ethnic languages were also produced during the 1970s and 1980s for the teaching of the main ethnic languages (usually those associated with one of the ethnic states). The MoE also compiled detailed reports dealing with ethnic languages during the 1970s – one of their explicit aims being to assess the challenges of teaching Burmese in those regions – and many ethnic languages were taught outside of the schools both by lay and religious organisations (the involvement of the latter helping to mobilise human and material resources while often contributing to decrease the suspicions of the authorities). 'In practice, interviews suggest widely varying experiences from one government school to another, even within the same ethnic group, depending on specific local conditions, such as the proximity to conflict, the benevolence of local authorities, the ethnic composition of the school, the interest of the population and the availability of ethnic language speaking teachers' (Salem-Gervais, 2019). According to Salem-Gervais and Raynaud, under SLORC, ethnic languages were further sidelined (Salem-Gervais and Raynaud, 2020: 41): 'In the early 1990's the official program from the MoE indicated that schools could choose to allocate up to 2 sessions of 30 minutes a week to the subject of ethnic languages on the slot dedicated to physical education and school activities.' This seems to have ceased in the mid 1990s.

In her MA thesis on language in Chin state, Nicola Edwards describes meeting communities with local teachers that had continued to use the ethnic language in government schools until quite recently. Being remotely located meant that the Bamar authorities simply could not control what was occurring (Edwards 2018).
10 It is also important to note that in some instances language persecution of minorities came not only from the central state and the army, but also from local dominant armed ethnic groups (Salem-Gervais, 2018).
11 'Grade 2 ethnic average reading time 208.34 seconds versus Bamar reading time 64 seconds; Grade 3 ethnic average reading time 177.35 seconds versus Bamar reading time 50 seconds; Grade 4 ethnic average reading time 179.94 seconds versus Bamar reading time 68 seconds; Grade 5 ethnic average reading time 65 seconds versus Bamar reading time 20 seconds' (Shalom (Nyein Foundation), 2011 13)).
12 These findings were also discussed by a senior NEPC member in his presentation at the 2nd Myanmar HE conference in 2018, where a senior Myanmar education official gave a presentation on social justice. See Chapter 4 of this volume and for more details, see Kandiko-Howson and Lall, 2020.

13　Myanmar Army.
14　These were: the Karen National Union (KNU)/Karen National Liberation Army (Peace Council) KNLA (PC), Democratic Karen Buddhist Army (DKBA), Restoration Council of Shan State (RCSS), Chin National Front (CNF), Pa-O National Liberation Army (PNLA), Arakan Liberation Party (ALP) and All Burma Students' Democratic Front (ABSDF). Two further EAOs (New Mon State Party and Lahu Democratic Union) signed later under the NLD government.
15　A fourth round of talks was held in August 2020 but no decisons pertaining to education were discussed.
16　The CESR recommendations related to ethnic and mother-tongue education were:

- Develop coordination strategies for networking among ethnic-minority organisations operating in education (for example, Karen, Chin and Mon organisations); the network of monastic education schools; religious, economic and social organisations, as well as organisations focused on gender equality and women's development organisations; and organisations for inclusive education.
- Strengthen direct connections existing between state/division governments and state/division education sectors.
- Use education as a tool to strengthen peaceful coexistence among ethnicities and exchange strategies.
- Encourage more cooperation between the MoE and international/local NGOs in border areas and areas that have no peace. In doing so, the Ministry should first develop trust from the people and then collaborate according to the Nay Pyi Taw Accord.

17　As a part of her work with AUSAID, the author organised the first and only meeting between the CESR team and a large number of ethnic education providers from around the country in July 2013. It had been hoped that a follow-on meeting would be held both with the CESR team in order to bring the education issues into the CESR as well as involving the Myanmar Peace Centre to bring education issues onto the peace negotiation table. Unfortunately, certain groups based on the Thai-Burmese border convinced development partners to hold the next meeting in Mae Sot, Thailand, making it impossible to discuss the education issues with the Myanmar-based CESR and Myanmar Peace Centre (MPC) teams, who were nevertheless the key actors in the reform process at the time. Ethnic education issues, therefore, were left out of both the CESR and the peace process. For more, see Lall, 2016a.
18　Myanmar/Burma Indigenous Network for Education (MINE) called for the following actions to be considered and entrenched in national education policy reforms:

- For the short to medium term at least, maintain existing community and ethnic nationality schools and do not replace them with government schools.
- Encourage collaboration between community and ethnic nationality schools and school systems and the government school system to improve education delivery.
- Recognise and support community, religious and non-state actor-administered schools.
- Allocate budget for teacher stipends and teaching and learning materials for community, religious and non-state actor-administered schools.
- Support for school management and data collection for community, religious and non-state actor-administered schools.
- Support for local mother tongue-based curriculum development.

19　A number of ethnic education groups told the author that they disagreed with LESC and that they were not part of the process that created the NPT principles.
20　Nay Pyi Taw principles:

- Unity: by supporting all to learn Myanmar language and literacy, for common and equal citizenship.
- Diversity: by supporting ethnic and indigenous communities to maintain, enjoy and transmit their languages to their children.
- Cohesion: by promoting inclusion and participation for ethnic and indigenous minorities.

- Education: by improving equitable access and participation, literacy, vocational and life skills, and academic standards.
- Employment: by raising standards in Myanmar, English and mother tongues, where relevant, to help young people enter the competitive labour market including in trades and professions.
- Service delivery: by supporting communication planning to make sure that public administrations communicating effectively with all citizens especially interpreting and translation in health, legal contexts and social services.
- International relations: in order to support trade, diplomacy and travel through widespread knowledge of English, and labour migration in the context of ASEAN mobility, and learning of strategic foreign languages.
- Inclusive communication: by integrating support for visually and hearing-impaired persons, and other citizens with communication difficulties.
- Ethnic rights: by recognising the unique cultures and traditions of Myanmar's indigenous people.

The NPT principles (part of the NPT Accord) and UNICEF's way of working was not accepted by all ethnic nationality education stakeholders, with a number pulling out of the process because they felt their voices were not being taken into account. In the end, one high profile ethnic CSO found their name was used to endorse the UNICEF process at a public meeting in Mandalay without their consent.

21 For more details on the activities preceding the conference, see Lo Bianco, 2016.
22 Myanmar Education Consortium, May 2018, personal communication.
23 Many international treaties and declarations recognise the right for indigenous and ethnic minorities to use and learn their mother tongues including: the International Labour Organisation (ILO) Convention 169 (ILO: 1989: Article 28); the United Nations General Assembly (UNGA) Minorities Declaration (UN, 1992: Article 4); or the United Nations Declaration on the Rights of Indigenous Peoples (UN 2007, Article 14); and at national levels, including in Myanmar, many constitutions acknowledge the right for indigenous and ethnic minorities to use, learn and preserve their languages. These rights however, are not always implemented (Kosonen cited in Benson, 2004; Kosonen, 2017; Kosonen, 2019; Mohanty, 2009).
24 Anonymous interviews with ministry officials including those working on the CESR as well as a Government Minister for Education between 2012 and 2018.
25 The issue of Burmanisation goes beyond language and also encompasses culture. According to Edwards, Cheery Zahau, a Chin politician and political activist, in a public discussion in December 2016 described how the Myanmar history curriculum is 'full of Burmese kings killing people' with no mention of ethnic histories. Beyond historical figures, Buddhist principles are also prioritised in the curriculum: 'For example, Nyein Foundation research showed even grade 2 primary books contain questions about Nirvana and other complex religious concepts which would probably be beyond Christian children in some mountainous villages in Chin State who are unlikely to have ever seen a temple, or monks, or monasteries, or heard about Nirvana. Because the curriculum presumes knowledge of these, and presupposes the learners are native speakers and Buddhists, there is no specific teaching of these concepts to support children's comprehension' (Edwards, 2018: 6–7).
26 Referred to as Grades 1, 2 and 3. Officials said in interviews in 2018 and 2019 that this can be developed up to Grade 9, different states and different communities within states have developed materials to different levels.
27 Reported in the *Myanmar Times* (El Thae Thae Naing, *Myanmar Times*, 2013).
28 Focus group discussion with parents in Mon and Shan State between 2015 and 2018.
29 Although the LC has currently only been developed for the first 2–3 years of education, it is being allocated time in the official curriculum for all grades: 'In primary schools, the LC takes up five periods a week (120 periods per year), over a total of 840 periods in lower primary and 960 in upper primary, equivalent to about 15% and 12,5% of the teaching time respectively) and can include, according to local situations: Ethnic languages and their histories, traditions and cultures, local geography and economic situation, as well as Agricultural businesses.

In middle schools, the LC occupies four periods a week (108 periods per year, over a total of 1080 periods, 10% of the total teaching time). The LC can include: Ethnic language and culture, Career skills, Basic computer skills, Basic information and communication technology, Agriculture and Home management skills. Finally, in high schools, it corresponds to four periods a week (108 periods per year, over a total of 1080 periods, 10% of the total teaching time) for Grade 10 and 11, and only two periods per week for Grade 12 (5% of the total teaching time). Under the current version of the BECF, the possible subjects are identical to those proposed in middle schools.' (Salem-Gervais and Raynaud, 2020: 152–3).

30 The development of the LC is based on two articles of the 2015 New Education Law (amendment): Article 39(g) which says: 'there shall be freedom to develop the curriculum in each region', while Article 44 states that regional and state governments can introduce the teaching of ethnic languages and literature: 'starting at the primary level and gradually expanding [to higher grades]'.

31 According to some estimates, 50 per cent of the world's 6–7,000 languages could be extinct by 2050. While this concern seems less acute in Myanmar, it is still a concern – out of the 119 languages identified by *Ethnologue*, 20 are categorised as 'in trouble' or 'dying' (Salem-Gervais, 2018).

32 The LC is not accepted by all ethnic education stakeholders as the solution to ethnic linguistic and education grievances. As discussed in Chapter 7 of this volume, any larger ethnic groups such as the Shan, Mon, Karen and Kachin would prefer MTB-MLE (Lall and South, 2018; South and Lall, 2016b and 2016c) and those with parallel and separate MTB-MLE systems would prefer to see their schools and teachers recognised and in some cases even supported by the government.

33 In some cases (for example, parts of Mon State), ethnic languages are used during school hours; elsewhere, ethnic language teaching still occurs outside of school hours. This is problematic because pupils are often tired and not motivated to learn if subjects are not included in the regular school day and do not count towards final grades.

Salem-Gervais and Raynaud agree that provision is uneven: 'Different regions and towns present different situations [...] while six languages are being taught in Hpa An township (four Karen languages, Mon and "Southern" Pa-O), there is no schools teaching more than two languages in the city of Hpa-An for 2019–2020. Mon is being taught in about 40 schools of Mawlamyine township, but not in the city itself (where summer classes are available). According to the Regional MoE office's statistics, for the year 2019–2020, over 16,000 children are learning an ethnic language in the Yangon Region, in 284 schools located in 13 townships (out of 2,700 schools in 44 townships). For this year, the languages available (sometimes out of school hours, during the summer break but inside the school premises in some instances) are Sgaw Kayin, Western Pwo Kayin, Tai Long Shan, and Asho Chin. In the city of Taunggyi, Shan State, no ethnic minority languages were taught in government schools at the beginning of the 2019–2020 school year.'(Salem-Gervais and Raynaud, 2019b: 123).

34 https://www.mmtimes.com/news/govt-promote-ethnic-language-teaching-assistants.html.

35 In some cases, community leaders spoke about how the involvement of the Thailand-based Christian Language organisation SIL had resulted in disagreements between community members as they might be working with one group rather than another, or favouring one orthography over another.

36 Salem-Gervais and Raynaud discuss issues arising from language and script standardisation in more detail. They note: 'Some political and linguistic projects have indeed striking similarities with the priority given to the common "Myanmar" (Burmese) language and identity by successive governments over the whole Union. In the case of Kachin State for instance, in the perspective of federalism, a number of political actors would like to promote the "Kachin" (Jingphaw) language – historically, to a large extent, a common language for the various Kachin groups – as an official language for Kachin State and a medium of instruction for primary schools. While some non-Jingphaw Kachin actors do agree with this perspective, most wish to promote their respective identities and languages (at the time of writing, 6 Kachin – Jingphaw, Lacid, Lhaovo, Lisu, Rawang and Zaiwa – and 5 Shan – Tai Leng, Tai Khamti, Tai Leu, Tai Long and Tai Sar – groups are officially recognised by the Kachin State Government)' (Salem-Gervais and Raynaud, 2019a). This reflects what

minority within minority respondents said in the 2018 research in Shan State, as discussed further below.
37 Discussion with Ashley South after his research in Chin State 2018.
38 Sixty-eight languages are currently accepted by the MoE for development of teaching materials.
39 In Mon State, the interview with the MNEC representative on the LC committee explained that there were too many people who did not know anything about either the Mon language or the Mon culture. In Karen State, the KNU's Karen Education Department (KED) refused to take part, as they felt this would endorse a government-led process, without being able to influence it.
40 Between 2012 and 2017, UNICEF developed early learning materials in ethnic languages for KG in 65 languages, along with teaching guides and big books. They expect the Grade 1 curriculum draft to be completed by the end of 2018. They expect that it will then take 2–3 more months to finalise it and provide teacher training before June 2019 when the next school year starts. The timeframe for LC development is not fixed, and depends on how long those involved take to complete the tasks.
41 When talking to government officials about teaching ethnic languages, they always use Chin State as an example, and say that it is impossible to do so because of the large number of languages across the country, and particularly in this one state.
42 Discussion with Ashley South after his research in Chin State 2018.
43 According to a presentation by MEC based on UNICEF and UNESCO data, only 19.35 per cent of rural children and 36.44 per cent of urban children aged four accessed pre-school/ECCD. The overall rate of Out-of-School Children (OOSC) is 12.26 per cent, dependent on wealth/poverty with 17.2 per cent OOSC in the lowest wealth bracket, and 7.3 per cent in the highest wealth bracket. Thirty-six per cent of children involved in child labour are out of school. Highest rates of OOCS were in Rakhine (33.8 per cent), Mon (15.95 per cent), Chin (15.9 per cent) and the lowest rates in Kayah (7.3 per cent), Shan (7.5 per cent), Kachin (9.4 per cent) and Magwe (9.5 per cent).
44 These are two examples that highlight issues also faced in other ethnic states, but are not representative of all minority within minority positions across Myanmar.
45 All respondents were clearly asked if they would prefer MTB-MLE if this were a possibility and they were informed that children perform best in the MTB-MLE system, learning both their mother tongue as well as the Union language. Despite this, respondents preferred Burmese as a LoI. It seems that there is a recognition that if MTB-MLE were to be offered it would not happen in the smaller minority languages and the respondents were especially fearful of their children having to learn the larger minority's mother tongue such as Shan or Rakhine as part of such a system, creating more rather than fewer problems for them.
46 In her research on language in Chin State, Edwards found that: 'Some parents were so concerned about their children struggling at school they explicitly made decisions to speak Burmese as much as possible at home to help their children at home. Others had to learn Burmese themselves to be able to do this.' (Edwards, 2018: 5)
47 UNOCHA. *MYANMAR: IDP Sites in Shan State* (as of 31 January 2019). https://reliefweb.int/sites/reliefweb.int/files/resources/MMR_Shan_IDP_Site_A0_Jan2019_20190221.pdf.
48 https://reliefweb.int/map/myanmar/myanmar-new-displacement-rakhine-and-chin-states-21-apr-2019.
49 https://reliefweb.int/map/myanmar/myanmar-new-displacement-rakhine-and-chin-states-21-apr-2019.
50 The field trip to Shan State focused on Taunggyi and surrounding areas as well as Keng Tung, covering south and eastern Shan State. Overall, 9 key informant interviews and 12 FGD (with 82 participants) were conducted. Respondents included representatives from the EACs, CSOs, ethnic political parties, ethnic Members of Parliament, one ethnic Minister, local thought leaders, LCCs/ Literature and Culture Associations (LCAs), as well as students, parents and school board members. Separate research during that same trip was conducted with the Pa-O in the Pa-O SAZ in Hopong and Pa-O villages around Taunggyi through key informant interviews and FGD. In this research, phase eight key informant interviews were conducted with respondents representing the Parami Development Network, PNO, PNLO, members of the

Pa-O SAZ Leading Body, Pa-O MPs, the Pa-O Education College principal, head teachers in schools serving Pa-O communities, and a Pa-O monastic school head monk and the monk in charge of education there. A total of 6 FGDs were held with a total of 45 participants including the Pa-O LCC, Pa-O political party representatives, Pa-O Education College trainees and Pa-O and Shan parents, most of whom are sitting on school committees or boards. Interviews were conducted in English, Burmese, Shan and Pa-O depending on the respondents with a translator present. In Rakhine, data was collected during a field trip to Sittwe and Mrauk U and a Chin village a few hours up river from Mrauk U. Three key informant interviews and three FGD (with 31 participants) were conducted with non-Rakine ethnic leaders. Two further key informant interviews were conducted – one with the monastic head whose school in Sittwe offered residential education to ethic minority children from remote areas and another with the Rakhine SEO. Interviews were conducted in English, Burmese, Rakhine and other minority languages depending on the respondents with a translator present.

51 This has been confirmed by Salem-Gervais and Raynaud who write: 'Another question, not to be overlooked in the introduction of minority languages in formal education, is the interest of ethnic minority parents and children themselves, who often see languages such as Burmese, English, or those of neighbouring countries (especially Chinese and Thai) as keys to modernity and economic opportunity' (Salem-Gervais and Raynaud, 2019b).

52 As mentioned earlier, Salem-Gervais and Raynaud claim that there are changes afoot to recruit more ethnic teachers to make the 'classroom language' policy possible (Salem-Gervais and Raynaud, 2019a and 2020). There has also been a recent policy change in recruiting ethnic students to education colleges in ethnic states, discussed in Chapter 5.

53 Similar to India's '3 language formula'.

54 Pa-O is spoken by up to 2 million people. Most live in Shan State, with some in Kayin State, Kayah State, Mon State, and the Bago Division. The Pa-O Self-Administrative Zone encompasses three townships in Shan State.

55 Formerly an armed group, the PNO has transformed itself into a political party and contested the 2010 and 2015 elections at different levels. Currently, the PNO has 10 MPs in the two houses of the Union Parliament and the Shan State Parliament. Some of the State MPs are in the SAZ Leading Body, which is a governance mechanism laid down in the 2008 Constitution. The PNO set up a social affairs department, which later was transformed into an NGO called 'Parami Development Network' (PDN). The PNO as an armed group has also become a people's militia (*pyithu sit*), which is under Myanmar Army command, and also under the Pa-O Military Council led by the former PNO leader Aung Kham Hti. The PDN was founded in 1991 when a PNO bilateral ceasefire agreement with the government was signed. Until 2010, the PDN functioned as the social affairs department of the PNO and collaborated with the Ministry of Border Affairs and donors for local development. The PDN has now been registered as an NGO. Their contribution to language and education is through supporting monks, and by the Pa-O LCC organising summer literacy classes every year in the SAZ and other Pa-O villages. The PDN, including the PDN Deputy Chair (a former teacher) has been involved in KG curriculum development (invited by UNICEF). The PDN plays a brokering or facilitating role in the education of Pa-O communities. They have supported community schools to submit requests to TEOs for sanctioning schools to become government schools, following up with District, State and also at DBE levels. They collect data on Pa-O children in government schools in the SAZ and other townships in Shan State to advocate for the SEO to support Pa-O teaching in schools. The PDN also supports the Pa-O Education College, not financially but by helping the education college with student welfare, for example, finding accommodation for students before the dormitories were ready and dealing with safety and protection of students.

56 The LCC saw it as a main issue, perhaps because they are from urban areas where private tutoring is widespread.

57 The Teacher Education College has only been allowed to run for five years by the MoE to meet temporary needs for teachers, despite the fact that there is an increasing need for ethnic teachers. In Taunggyi, the education college can only accept 300 trainees but each education college should be producing 400, so it was agreed that the Pa-O college could train 100. The respondents were upset that despite the government not being able to meet the 10,000 teachers a year quota, this college is supposed to close after 5 years.

58 The Pa-O were given their own SAZ in 2010. The SAZ Leading Body consists of 12 members, including 25 per cent military personnel. The Leading Body negotiated with the Union and State government to open the Pa O education college. One of the members of the Leading Body and also a CEC member is responsible for social affairs, which includes education.
59 The 4 R framework is also used in Higgins et al., 2016. However, the report engages only with the government and the Mon education systems.
60 Informal conversations with senior MoE officials (DGs and DDGs) in the course of 2018 and 2019.

7
Ethnic education: Recognising alternative systems run by ethnic armed organisations

Introduction

The previous chapter engaged with issues of language and education and how issues of language can marginalise entire communities. It also covered the government's offer of 'inclusive' education through the development and roll-out of the LC as well as the views from some of the minority within minority communities that broadly agree with the government that Burmese needs to remain the main LoI. This view, though legitimate, is limited to certain communities, notably some (but not all) minority within minority community respondents in Shan and Rakhine State. Larger ethnic groups, and some smaller ones such as the Naga would prefer MTB-MLE provision (Dekker et al., 2018a). As Dekker et al. succinctly note:

> This is not to say that after-school or other informal interventions are without value; research and experience has shown the benefits of acquiring mother tongue literacy skills regardless of the academic setting. But the dramatic improvements in all subject areas found in true MTB-MLE programs cannot be expected to be achieved through limited mother tongue instruction. (Dekker et al., 2018b: 11)[1]

In fact, good MTB-MLE programmes result in better literacy and numeracy skills in all languages the children learn, giving them a better future within multilingual countries. MTB-MLE exists in Myanmar, but is not offered by the government. Rather, different forms of mother tongue education or MTB-MLE are offered by some EAOs and their education departments, mostly in remote and conflict-affected areas where government teachers are unable or unwilling to serve. These systems, however, are not recognised by the government and are often seen as 'second class', both by the authorities as well as some of the ethnic parents living in urban areas.

This chapter uses the education systems under the authority of four major EAOs to discuss the relationship between ethnic nationality communities and the state. Drawing on data collected between 2011 and 2018, in schools run by the New Mon State Party's[2] MNEC, the Kachin Independence Organisation's[3] KIO Education Department (KIO-ED), the Karen National Union's Karen Education Department (KED) and the Revolutionary Council of Shan State's Education Department (RCSS-ED) as well as their administrations, the chapter discusses the issue of recognition of alternative and separate education systems. These systems have in effect been filling the gap for education provision in remote and conflict-affected areas for the Myanmar government, while at the same time offering education services in the children's mother tongue. It is clear that addressing the language issue is a central part of finding a sustainable resolution to Myanmar's armed conflict. Yet the key issues of conflict go beyond language, and this chapter engages with the core problems of recognition of EAO authority in education in areas under their control, and how the issues of the peace process, language policy and federalism are inextricably intertwined.

Going beyond Iris Young's framework (Young, 2005), this chapter uses Novelli et al.'s '4 R' framework (mentioned in Chapter 6) that examines how ethnic education systems provided by EAOs provide: 'redistribution' (equity and non discrimination, access to resources and equitable outcomes across communities); 'recognition' (accepting and respecting a diversity of identities, including of language and religion); 'representation' (participation of all groups at all levels of the education system), and; 'reconciliation' (how society deals with past injustices and the psychosocial effects of conflict) (Novelli et al., 2015).[4] Given the lack of involvement of the Myanmar government with these education systems, the Young framework is less relevant. The '4 R' framework engages both social and transitional justice approaches, recognising multiple dimensions of inequality and has been used to study education and peacebuilding in various conflict settings across the world.

Background on the ethnic conflict peace process

It will be clear from earlier sections in the book that the Myanmar government education system developed under military rule has considerable shortcomings when it comes to Novelli et al.'s '4 R' framework, especially so in regard to ethnic minority children. As detailed in Chapter 6, Myanmar has suffered from ethnic conflict for over 50 years. Much of this civil war has raged between the Tatmadaw and a range of armed ethnic organisations (EAOs) that have been fighting for autonomy against the militarised central government (Smith, 1999), some since independence. The conflict is ongoing in certain areas and 'reconciliation' (the 4th R), as shall be seen below, has not yet been achieved; there is as yet no peace education and peace is not part of the new curriculum. The 1962 coup engendered a 'Burmanisation' process whereby language (Burmese) and religion (Buddhism) became central pillars of the state, resulting in large-scale marginalisation and a resentment of ethnic groups that remains in place to this day. 'Recognition' (the 2nd R) of the country's diversity of language, culture and religious traditions has not transcended the education reforms. Earlier chapters have dealt with the differentiated achievement and retention outcomes between different states of the Union, and whilst the available data masks the differences between ethnic groups, the reality is that ethnic children do less well than their Bamar counterparts, which shows that 'redistribution' (the 1st R), especially equitable outcomes across communities, is an aspiration that will not be achieved easily as part of the reforms. Lastly, 'representation' (the 3rd R) and the one that underpins lasting change, is largely absent – the issue of adequate numbers of ethnic teachers has not yet been addressed systematically, although some anecdotal research evidence points to the fact that there might be some changes afoot in government recruiting processes. In fact, Higgins et al. explain how the direction of the education reform process might harm rather than resolve Myanmar's conflict situation (Higgins et al., 2016: 11):[5]

> The National Education Sector Plan (NESP) and the Education Law suggest that 'peace building is everywhere and nowhere': everywhere in the sense that there seems to be a recognition of the need to place the education reform process in the actual context of inequalities and frustrations, yet it is nowhere as a peace building logic or language is notably absent from key reforms. The reform and policy direction potentially might do more harm rather than address the root cause that drove many aspects of the conflict in the first place: a lack of fair **redistribution** of resources and opportunities, a reflection of **recognition** of the various linguistic and cultural needs, a sincere **representation** and a participatory process that not only informs but rather engages with oppositional

and minority perspectives to on the long run enable first steps to addressing the grievances expressed through and inflicted by education through **reconciliation** (bold in the original).

Ethnic armed organisations governance and education systems

Despite being weakened after decades of conflict, most armed ethnic organisations still enjoy varying degrees of legitimacy among the communities they represent (Lall and South, 2018). In part, this results from the public services, including education (and particularly teachers and schools) that these EAOs provide in areas which the Myanmar government does not reach. Ad hoc ethnic nationality education systems were developed by some armed ethnic groups during the chaotic early years of the Civil War in the 1950–60s, with attempts to standardise these systems during the 1970s. Since the 1980s, and particularly with an influx of external support across the Thai border following the 1988 democracy uprising in Burma, non-state education systems expanded and formalised. In addition, a wide range of civil society actors also became active in the field of non-state education provision among ethnic nationality communities, including through the implementation of non-formal and part-time programmes.[6] Communities in conflict-affected regions of Myanmar have struggled to provide education to their children, often under incredibly difficult circumstances, and education services have been repeatedly disrupted by the armed conflict.[7] Whereas most schooling is organised and owned by communities with varying degrees of external support, teachers, curricula and funding come from two main sources: the government and EAOs. Many schools and communities engage, often uneasily, with both sets of education actors (Jolliffe and Speers Mears, 2016).

Education: The litmus test

Ethnic education systems vary widely (see Table 7.1). As detailed in an earlier publication (South and Lall, 2016a), in Myanmar the ethnic nationality education system can be seen as a proxy for ethnic relationships with the state itself. These ethnic education activities are representative of broader struggles for self-determination, and serve as a litmus test when analysing the peace process. Attitudes to Burmanisation

Table 7.1 Typology of ethnic schools. Source: South and Lall, 2016c: 1–7.

Type	Characteristics	Examples
Type 1 – Ethnic-input schools	Government-run schools with civil society input.	• Government-run schools, with some teachers (and teaching materials) provided by the local community or civil society.
Type 2 – Mixed schools	Government schools in EAG-controlled and contested areas, with some EAG and/or civil society input.	• Includes schools in remote areas that accept volunteer teachers.
Type 3 – Hybrid schools	Part government, part EAG; sometimes also input from civil society.	• NDA-K schools in Kachin ceasefire areas. • IDP schools in Kachin areas. • Schools which were previously under the authority of EAG education departments, but have now been 'flipped' (or 'poached') by government MoE.
Type 4 – EAG (government curriculum) schools	Schools managed by EAG, with no government teachers, but which use government curriculum (often in translation) and where children can sometimes transfer to the state system, after a test or local arrangement. Curriculum is supplemented by ethnic nationality-orientated materials, especially for history and social studies, but sometimes also other subjects.	• NMSP/MNEC Mon national schools. • KIO schools (teach government curriculum in Jingphaw, etc., and later in Burmese). • Some Karen schools, particularly those supported by the community with limited KNU/KED input.

(Continued table 7.1)

(Continued table 7.1)

Type	Characteristics	Examples
Type 5 – EAG schools	Schools built and run by EAGs and/or associated civil society groups, with separate mother tongue-based curriculum; no recognition/ accreditation or possible transfer for students.	• KED schools, and 'community schools' in areas under KNU authority or influence; refugee camp schools.
Type 6 – Civil society private schools	Separate mother tongue-based curriculum and different teaching methods; no recognition/ accreditation or possible transfer for students.	• Community-supported schools in northern Shan and Kachin States. • Some Karen schools in KNU-controlled areas (sometimes administered and funded by churches).
Type 7 – Foreign curriculum schools	Curriculum developed in/by another country, allowing (some) students to transfer to other schools in that country.	• Schools with Indian curriculum in Kachin; some Karen mission schools.
Type 8 – Supplementary schools	Schools that focus on ethnic language and/or culture/religion, but teach after the government classes are over – either summer schools or afternoon/evening schools.	• Mostly provided by civil society groups; often linked to the *Sangha* and the churches.

and centralisation can be plotted along a continuum, ranging from demands for outright independence from the Union through varying forms of autonomy and decentralisation. In relation to education, separatist agendas can be represented by schools featuring little or no Burmese language teaching, using a mother tongue curriculum (often radically different to that of the MoE), to the promotion of mother tongue-based teaching in schools that also teach Burmese and broadly follow the government curriculum, albeit modified according to local contexts and conditions. In this framing, the MNEC's education provision model (described below) has achieved a fairly high degree of local self-determination in education, while retaining links to the Union (Lall and South, 2013a and 2013b). This was previously also the case with the KIO system which, under pressure as a result of the resumption of armed conflict in 2011, seems to be moving towards a more separatist model, similar to that adopted historically by the KNU. These positions in relation to education and language use can be taken as proxies of different actors' views regarding a broader range of state/society issues, and the distribution of power and resources between the central government and ethnic polities (South and Lall, 2016a). For example, those who seek to use ethnic languages as a primary medium of administration in ethnic states can be expected to adopt strong/maximalist positions regarding the extent to which natural resource revenue and other financial and political goods should be retained at – or redistributed to – the local/state level, and may even argue for complete separation of the ethnic polities from the Union. Moderates may adopt positions according to which ethnic languages are used together with Burmese, or in a supplementary manner at the state level – corresponding to varying degrees of decentralisation or federalism, a key issue in the ongoing peace process (South and Lall, 2016a). These positions are reflected below in the description of the various ethnic education providers.

Effects of the peace process on ethnic education

The peace process in Myanmar has had both positive and negative impacts on ethnic education. There is, as seen earlier, a lack of strategic and policy connection between education issues and the politics of the peace process, with both processes having been kept separate (Higgins et al., 2016; Lall, 2016a). However, the NESP that came out of the education reforms emphasises that the Myanmar government intends to improve equitable access to quality education for students at all levels of the national education system, emphasising the need for education benefits to be shared among broad segments of the population, and for currently excluded groups not to be left behind. Part of this included the engagement with education systems run by EAOs, therefore inextricably linking the required changes to the peace process.

After two years of difficult negotiations, leaders of eight EAOs signed a NCA with the Myanmar government and army on the 15 October 2015 in Naypyidaw. Figure 7.1 shows Chief of Army General Min Aung Hlaing just before signing the NCA. This document has remained problematic and divisive, as indicated by the decision of some 10 EAOs not to attend the event or sign the NCA, and only two other armed groups (the NMSP and the LDU) signing in February 2018. The peace process in Myanmar has undergone further setbacks since (Lall et al., 2020). In December 2018, two signatory armed groups, the KNU and the RCSS, suspended participation in joint aspects of the peace process – meaning that representatives of these groups could not meet officially with the government (a situation not fully resolved at the time of writing). Despite the unilateral ceasefire announced and held by the Tatmadaw between 21 December 2018 and April 2019 (later extended to September 2019),[8]

Figure 7.1 NCA ceremony 2015 with General Min Aung Hlaing on the screen as he prepares to sign. Source: Author.

and a series of unofficial meetings held mostly in China and Thailand between government and EAO representatives, no further progress seems to have been made.

With regard to the NCA and education, Chapter 6 of the NCA acknowledges the roles of signatory EAOs in the fields of education, health, natural resource management and security, and provides for international assistance in these sectors in partnership and cooperation with the government. The government has acknowledged the NCA signatory groups' administrative and service delivery roles, and they are now challenged to re-invent themselves as post-insurgent organisations. Those EAOs that signed the NCA were removed from the Unlawful Associations, making their engagement with international development partners easier. However, the EAOs and their administrations remain in place with no clear pathway for organisational transformation.

While the EAOs might not have changed much, there has been significant change with regard to government access to the conflict-affected areas. The negotiation leading up to the NCA and the signing of the NCA allowed the government to assert its authority in previously autonomous, ethnic nationality-populated areas, including through teacher provision and school buildings (Lenkova, 2015), particularly in Myanmar's southeast. Jolliffe and Speers Mears note how KNU HQs had: 'issued numerous warnings that the government is expanding its presence prior to negotiation through the provision of education support' (Jolliffe and Speers Mears, 2016: 64). They explain that in Kawkareik Township (KNU defined East Daw Na region), 32 schools (of which 29 were KED-only schools) had been offered MoE teachers between 2012 and 2015 and that 13 schools eventually accepted the teachers (Jollife and Speers Mears, 2016: 66).

This has resulted in widespread local resentment of ethnic nationality stakeholders who are concerned that international aid agencies and donors are, perhaps inadvertently, supporting a government strategy of pushing state structures into conflict-affected areas without taking account of existing local activities and services or the impacts on peace and conflict dynamics, thereby placing traditional EAO and ethnic education systems at risk (Lall and South, 2018). These systems are important as they provide services to at least 300,000 children in Myanmar, in schools either directly administered by non-state education departments or in 'mixed' schools, jointly administered by the MoE and EBEPs.[9] Often these schools are located in remote and conflict-affected areas where the government either has no schools, or where government teachers are unable or unwilling to serve. In these areas, EAO schools provide a service to the community and in effect also to the Myanmar government, whose responsibility includes the education of all Myanmar children no matter where they reside.

Four of the most prominent ethnic nationality systems are briefly described below. The chapter then discusses the difficulties the Myanmar government faces in engaging with EAOs (and vice versa), and how the education reforms are changing the landscape of education in remote and conflict-affected ethnic nationality-dominated areas, yet have still not brought about increased social justice for the ethnic nationality communities who live there.

Ethnic education in Mon State: The Mon National Education Committee and the Mon National Schools

The Mon population consists of about 750,000 Mon in Myanmar,[10] with perhaps 1 million people self-identifying as Mon, including people who do not speak the language fluently (South, 2003). The vast majority of the Mon are Theravada Buddhist, and since the pre-colonial period the Mon Buddhist monkhood was responsible for recording and reproducing elements of Mon national and religious history, and transmitting the Mon language in a context where many observers expected this to die out (South, 2003). Under the U Nu parliamentary government of the 1950s, schools in some areas were permitted to teach ethnic languages. However, as described in Chapter 6, school curricula were centralised and the LoI became Burmese across the country following Gen Ne Win's military coup in 1962. Conflict between the NMSP and the government had been raging since independence in 1948. In 1972, the NMSP Central Education Department was established, with the Mon school system being reformed in 1992 with the formation of the MNEC.[11] The MNEC developed an MTB-MLE education system in which Mon is used at primary level, transitioning to Burmese at middle school, and more-or-less following the government curriculum, mostly in translation with additional modules in Mon language and Mon history. Graduates of the MNEC's Mon National Schools (MNS) speak fluent Mon, but the system was designed so that MNS graduates are also able to sit government matriculation exams in Burmese, allowing them to access Myanmar universities (Lall and South, 2013a and 2013b).

Following a ceasefire with the government in June 1995, the NMSP controlled a 'ceasefire zone' where the NMSP exerted varying degrees

Figure 7.2 Mon National School, 2013. Source: Author.

of military and administrative influence in Mon-populated areas of Mon and Karen States.[12] At the time of the ceasefire, the MNS system consisted of 76 schools (including one high school) which were located in the NMSP 'ceasefire zones' and in the three main Mon refugee camps (South, 2003). Research conducted in 2011–2 established that the ceasefire allowed for the Mon education system to spread to the government-controlled zones, with some two-thirds of MNS operating outside of the ceasefire areas (Lall and South, 2013a and 2013b).[13] Figure 7.2 shows a Mon National School in 2013. In 2018, MNEC supported a total of 132 Mon National Schools (including three high schools, 16 middle schools, 91 primary schools and 22 post-primary schools) across Mon State, Karen State and Tanintharyi Region. There are 10,779 students and 787 teachers at MNS in total. The MNEC supports 156 teachers at 92 mixed schools as well.[14]

Whilst there has been an informal system in place for MNS students to sit government exams and to be able to transfer to government schools where there are no MNEC middle and high schools, cooperation between the Mon and the state education authorities is based on personal relationships in the local setting and vary between township, districts and villages. Transfers between the two systems remain a major issue, as the MNEC system is not officially recognised. Stakeholders interviewed in 2018[15] said that the government had made transfers easier as part of the reforms by systematising the tests the MNS students have to take, as they were trying to recruit Mon students to their system. Others disagreed, claiming that transfers had been made harder as students had to take an exam in Math, Burmese and English in order to be allowed to transfer, whilst previously, transfers were locally arranged between head teachers of the different systems. Some parents interviewed in 2018 also alleged that in some government schools the head teacher asked the transferring student(s) to take an exam in each and every subject, not only in the three required ones, so as to block the transfer.

Since the mid-1990s, Mon has also been taught as part of the curriculum in just under 100 'mixed schools'. These institutions are government-run schools, where the MNEC provide (and usually support financially) one or more Mon-speaking teachers, and also have some input into the syllabus, especially for history. Collaboration between the two systems has been on the increase, including more meetings between SEO officials based in Mawlamyine and MNEC representatives, largely due to a forward-thinking head of the MNEC. This started with a UNICEF-organised workshop in September 2013,[16] and was followed by some joint in-service teacher training. The increased collaboration was made easier by the fact that the NMSP system used the government curriculum in translation. Yet despite this, the collaborative efforts have not all been happy experiences, with many NMSP teachers feeling they were treated like 'second class teachers' when taking part in these activities, and not being allowed to wear their national school uniform (which differs from the government teachers' uniform).[17] The increased ethnic language provision and the development of the LC, described in Chapter 6, in government schools has also complicated matters, with Mon language teachers who had previously worked in mixed schools not being appointed to teach the Mon language as part of the officially sanctioned ethnic language provision in their school and being replaced by another LCC-provided teacher.[18]

Reverting to Novelli et al.'s '4 R' framework, the MNEC education provision offers 'redistribution' in that it gives access to non-discriminatory education and helps Mon children with equal outcomes by providing an MTB-MLE education framework. In not denying the communities access to Burmese as the official government language, it fulfils the requirement of (reverse) 'recognition'. By allowing its teachers to get trained with government teachers, and supporting a mixed school system in government schools where Mon parents and teachers have equal say in their children's education, it also supports 'representation'. Therefore, it can be argued that the Mon education system is indeed part of an approach that supports 'reconciliation'.

Ethnic education in Karen State: The Karen Education Department and community schools

During the colonial period, Christian missionaries, and later government officials, encouraged a sense of national identity among the previously scattered Karen community, leading to the emergence of Karen social and political movements in the late nineteenth century (Smith, 1999). At the time of independence in 1948, the Karen nationalist movement was well organised, with Western-educated elites coveting independence. This resulted in over 60 years of armed conflict that only ended with a ceasefire in 2012. The KNU subsequently signed the NCA in 2015. Despite the 1962 restrictions on ethnic language education, some churches and monasteries continued teaching informally, particularly in Christian Sgaw and Buddhist Pwo dialects. Only a minority of the Karen population live within the borders of the official Karen State that was established in 1952, with large Karen-speaking populations living in Yangon, Ayeyarwady and Tanintharyi Regions, eastern Bago Region, Mon State, as well as in refugee camps in Thailand.[19]

The education system in Karen-populated areas is highly diverse, reflecting the heterogeneity of this community, numbering approximately 5–7 million people in Myanmar (Lall and South, 2013a).[20] Most schooling is owned and organised by communities with varying degrees of external support, with some other schools having been built by the government, and in some cases having had teachers and rudimentary teaching materials supplied. In such 'mixed schools' resources are sometimes supplemented by materials and teachers supplied by border-based CBOs or EAOs.

The KNU founded schools in areas under its control in the 1950s. In the 1970s, an Education Department was established near the Thai town of Mae Sot. The KNU's Education Department (KED), along with its affiliate organisation the Karen Teacher Working Group (KTWG), operate together as the Karen State Education Assistance Group (KSEAG).[21] They provide teacher stipends, pre-service and in-service teacher training, administrative support and schooling materials. Well suited to local needs, this system diverges significantly from the Myanmar government education system, not least through the use of Karen (mostly Sgaw) as the LoI, with only a limited focus on Burmese. Given the differences between the systems and the lack of recognition of KED schooling, KED school graduates find it difficult to enter the government education system or access opportunities in Myanmar or abroad (Lall and South, 2013a and 2013b).

The KED is part of the KNU administrative governance structure and oversees school administration and policy across 28 KNU designated townships through a network of field education staff, and school management committees/PTAs. These include District Education departments in each of the KNU's seven districts. The KSEAG is in charge of the provision of school and learning materials, while KTWG for pre- and in-service (mobile) teacher professional development. KED and KTWG jointly operate two teacher-training colleges at the Thai–Myanmar border. In 2017–8, they together supported 1,573 schools, from primary to post-secondary education – of which around 330 use the KED curriculum (serving around 23,000 students), 612 use a mixture of KED-MoE curriculum and 631 use the MoE curriculum (both serving around 156,000 students).[22] In 2015, the KED published its Education Policy that amongst other stipulations in its basic principles stated the following:

> Every Karen shall learn his own literature and language.
> Every Karen shall be acquainted with Karen history.
> The Karen culture, customs and traditions shall be promoted.
> Our own Karen culture, customs and traditions shall be made to be respected by the other ethnic nationalities, and the cultures, customs and traditions of the other ethnic nationalities shall mutually be recognized and respected.

The KED system, similar to that of the MNEC, fosters 'redistribution' by supporting equitable outcomes across communities. While the KED schools that do not offer Burmese do not fulfil the aspect of (reverse) 'recognition', the many mixed schools where the KED provides Karen teachers, do support mutual 'recognition' and 'representation' as well as 'reconciliation'. That said, the separatist curriculum used in KED schools which does not allow the children to re-enter the Burmese education system, does not support 'reconciliation' and it is these children that will find it most difficult to engage with Myanmar as their country once the conflict subsides (Lall and South, 2013a and 2013b).

Other Karen EAGs also administer schools in their areas of authority. For example, there are nearly 100 schools in areas under the control of the DKBA. Another ex-KNU faction, the KNU Peace Council, administers

33 schools with around 3,000 students. These include two high schools (up to Grade 10) in Htokoko and We Ler Muh on the Thai–Myanmar Border. These schools receive stationary support from KSEAG, while teacher salaries are paid directly by the Peace Council.

Ethnic education in Shan State

In Shan State, the extremely wide variety of ethnic education stakeholders falls roughly into four main categories that include EAO and non-EAO education providers. The major EAOs mostly offer education services or support in the main Shan language (referred to locally as *'Tai'* or *'Tai Long'*). These organisations have differences on a linguistic basis between those using five tone Tai/old Shan language (this includes education organisations linked to the RCSS) and those using six tone Tai (the reformed version of Shan language as used in northern Shan State), including education organisations linked to the SSPP, Kaw Dai and the Karli paramilitary group/Border Guard Force (BGF) 7th Brigade.[23] There are also CSOs that are involved in Shan education, but are not affiliated to any EAO and do not work directly with any EAO. Others include LCA/LCCs, mostly associated with the smaller non-Shan ethnic minorities across the state, offering education services or support in the ethnic minority languages, the work of which has been discussed in Chapter 6.

There are three non-government Shan-based curricula in operation that include the original Shan language textbooks developed during the country's first parliamentary period by the Shan State Government, based on the books used in the Sabwa era. These were revised by Sai Aung Htun and submitted to the state government and approved in 2012–3 for the teaching of Shan in government schools (KG and Grade 1–3).[24] The curriculum does go further than Grade 3 and is used in certain mixed settings as explained below. These books use five tones. An alternative set of textbooks was developed by the Shan Literature and Cultural Association (SLCA), particularly by Sai Pha and Dr Sao Sang Ai. Although based on the books submitted to the government, they have been revised to use six tones.[25] The content has been updated and photos are used instead of illustrations. These books are printed by the Mandalay-based SLCA as the government refused to accredit a new set of books just two years after printing the first set. Township LCAs decide which books to use (five or six tone) depending on the location and the teachers, with those in the north generally using six tones, while those in the south generally use five tones. Some of the books at the Taunggyi

Figure 7.3 Shan language books developed by the Shan Literature and Culture Association. Source: Author.

LCA are shown in Figure 7.3. Beyond the two sets of books there is also the RCSS curriculum developed by a Shan teacher,[26] which includes Shan language, maths, geography and history up until Grade 6, all in Shan language using five tones (discussed further below).

In Shan State, it is important to understand that the vast majority of rural schools are community owned and administered. The MoE, EAOs, CSOs, monastic networks and others might then help to organise these schools and provide teachers, textbooks, curricula, pathways for examinations and accreditation amongst other things, and then bring these schools under their system. However, such affiliations are not always permanent.[27]

Ethnic Armed Organisation Education

The RCSS[28] provides support to over 200 schools, including over 100 Shan National Schools, which are directly under RCSS administration, most of which are close to or across the Thailand border. The other types of schools are categorised as government, monastic or community schools. The RCSS HQ is at Loi Tai Leng (in the government defined Langkho Township). In 2017, Chairman Yawd Serk established a new

Education Commission to reform and develop the Education Department. The reform efforts focus on improving teacher training, establishing common learning and assessment standards and strengthening MTB-MLE. Responsibilities are divided and devolved: the Education Department deals with funding, teacher training, human resources, finance and curriculum development; the regional education committees that oversee two or three townships each select teachers, monitor schools and coordinate with the HQ to provide assistance.

The first RCSS school was established at the HQ in 2000 to serve the IDPs who had been displaced by conflict. Schools fall into different categories, being on a continuum with decreasing government funding and involvement, with mixed RCSS-government schools that combine the government curriculum and the Shan curriculum (language, history, social norms and culture), and where both government and RCSS provide financial support while communities provide in-kind support for the teachers. The schools are usually government schools, built by the government, but in remote locations where government teachers refuse to serve.[29] The RCSS provides the salaries for the locally recruited teachers. These are local arrangements that involve the local TEO but not the SEO in Taunggyi. A local NGO, the Centre for Rural Education and Development (CRED) and the RCSS Education Department (and occasionally the MoE) provide teacher training and the TEO and village administrator select teachers who have to speak Shan. The mixed RCSS-monastic schools also mix the government curriculum and the Shan curriculum (language, history, social norms and culture), with some teachers in these schools receiving a stipend from the RCSS and the RCSS Education Department, while CRED provides teacher training. There are also RCSS-supported community schools where the RCSS curriculum is taught and communities provide the infrastructure and in-kind support for the teachers, whilst the RCSS provide the teacher salaries and the RCSS Education Department and CRED provide teacher training. Schools that are referred to as 'national schools' are also essentially community schools that teach the RCSS curriculum but do not receive any support from the government at all, and have often been set up under the guidance of the RCSS. There seems to be a subtle difference between National Schools and RCSS-supported community schools as they are categorised separately by the Education Department. Over the last 10 years, the RCSS has been contributing funds more systematically to establish schools, hire teachers and pay teacher salaries. However, schools are sometimes taken over by the government in situations where the Tatmadaw takes control of previously RCSS-dominated areas (or in cases where the RCSS takes back control, reverting back to the community with RCSS support). Overall, there are over 400 RCSS-supported teachers on the Myanmar side of the Thai–Myanmar border.[30]

The RCSS Education Department developed a curriculum in 2002, initially covering Grades 1–6 in seven subjects, that is used in the Shan national schools. The textbooks are copied and distributed by the RCSS. The teacher who designed the curriculum confirmed in an interview in 2018 that she studied the curricula of 10 countries,[31] before designing what she believed was appropriate for Shan children. This curriculum is completely different from the Myanmar government's, making any transfers between the RCSS and the MoE system impossible.[32] The RCSS curriculum does not go to Grade 10, however, the RCSS secondary schools use parts of the Thai curriculum for higher grades as well as some materials translated from Burmese textbooks.[33] The RCSS-supported schools teach in Shan as much as possible, but in some schools of mixed ethnicity respondents reported that in this case Burmese was occasionally used. It is unclear whether Burmese is taught systematically as a subject in Shan National Schools. Some parents were emphatic that it is not taught because the community is against it; others said Burmese is taught where teachers are available. However, RCSS schools in the Loi Tai Leng (HQ) area teach English and Thai, and students who attend these schools are able to continue their studies in Thailand after completing secondary school at Loi Tai Leng.

Other EAO education systems in Shan State include the Karli People's Militia Force, Kunhein Township (previously, the 7th Brigade of the SSA) and the SSPP Education Department. There are 67 schools in the Karli area, 37 of which were previously run by the militia but are now government schools, and 30 of which they still support. Currently, the militia supports 79 teachers in 197 villages (West Salween) and another 20 (East Salween) across a total of 217 villages under their control. The teachers use Shan language and the Sai Pha curriculum (the same as that used in Kaw Dai schools). Burmese is not taught in their schools, and they send their teachers to government schools to teach Shan. The Karli People's Militia Force Education Department, supported by Sai Pha, provides a one-month pre-service teacher training in the summer.

The Shan State Progress Party[34] was established in 1971, as the political party wing of SSA, which had been founded in 1964. Their education programme started in 1971 and mostly supported community schools, including literacy campaigns and out-of-school training. According to Kim Jolliffe, the system has been revamped since 2015 to provide full-time basic education under leaders with experience in NGOs in Thailand and elsewhere, and with funding from the SSPP central treasury. There are currently 3,700 students in 53 'Shan national' primary schools, and teachers are also provided to 20 mixed schools. In total, the system has 88 teachers on full salaries, in addition to 17 teachers that rely on community donations but get training and 'technical management' from the SSPP Education Department. There is also a full high school at Wanhai (SSPP HQ), which uses the full government curriculum. The MoE provides 3 teachers and 15 others are trained and paid for by the SSPP. All the funding and resources for the school come from the SSPP, while the community provides firewood and other assistance. Shan language, history and civic education are all provided during school hours.[35]

Shan national primary schools in that area use the six tone Shan as a LoI, and the curriculum as developed by the Shan LCA.[36] The Shan National School system has only been in operation since 2015, so, at the time of the research, the oldest children were in Grade 3 and there is not yet a functioning pathway for them to continue to middle school. Teachers all do a pre-service three-month 'community leadership strengthening' intensive course which covers politics, constitutional issues, human rights, women rights and basic healthcare. Some of that is supported by CRED, which gets technical support from KTWG.[37]

Non-EAO education organisations

There are many non-EAO education organisations involved in education across Shan State. Two of the most prominent are CRED and Kaw Dai. CRED, previously known as the Rural Development Foundation Shan State (RDFSS),[38] is a CSO that supports education across Shan State including with some of the non-Shan minorities.[39] CRED/RDFSS started in the Namlan area, organising community and monastic schools in rural areas as well as a boarding house in Namlan (built with support from the organisation 'Child's Dream'), so that children from rural villages could move to the town to continue on to middle school. CRED/RDFSS has been attempting to build a network across the Shan education systems, called the Tai Education Network, to move towards common language policy, common curriculum and common training for teachers. In recent years, CRED has increased its collaboration with the RCSS and SSPP[40] along with a number of other community school and monastic networks across the state by providing a range of education services to EBEPs, monastic and MoE schools, including teacher training and support such as teacher stipends and classroom materials.[41]

Kaw Dai was originally established in 1998 as a CSO focused on issues of human rights and community health. According to Guyot et al., *Kaw Dai* means 'Shan association' and has the connotation of a caring community that extends from one's village to the whole Shan people, wherever they may live (Guyot et al., 2016). As of 2005 they started to work in education, opening a school for IDPs. They are based in Karli, Kunhein Township in the territory of the Karli People's Militia Force. They receive financial support from the militia to run both their schools and the Shan Community College. Some of their staff in 2018 are depicted in Figure 7.4.[42] They have a post-primary school from Grades 4–9, with 217 boarding students as well as five other community primary schools (Grades 1–3) across five areas. The 59 teachers for these schools are provided by Kaw Dai, some of whom have been trained under Dr Thein Lwin in Thailand. The post-primary/secondary school in Karli accepts students from beyond their feeder schools as well. The schools use a curriculum developed by the chair of Kaw Dai's, Sai Pha (who reformed the five tone 'old' Shan language to make it six tones), and the organisation benefits from a number of well educated and dedicated staff based in Karli, Lashio and Yangon. The curriculum is all in Shan (using six tones), with their own Shan language, Shan history and geography textbooks, while Burmese, English and Thai are taught as

Figure 7.4   Kaw Dai, Shan State, 2018. Source: Author.

foreign languages. The 11 teachers at the college are mainly graduates from their former Yangon-based programme. Kaw Dai also provides Shan language, history and culture classes to government schools outside of school hours, mainly in northern Shan State. To support Shan language summer programmes, the chair of Kaw Dai (Sai Pha) provides two-week teacher training to high school students around 12 townships across Shan and Kachin States, as well as Mandalay and Bago Regions, for six months every year. They then volunteer to deliver Shan language and literature programmes organised by the SLCA in community centres during the summer. Kaw Dai's mission goes beyond education – they aspire to promote democracy and justice by nurturing young Shan to serve their community with education, political awareness, protection of the environment, community service, and advocacy.[43]

Across Shan State, achievement of the '4 R' framework varies. All education systems help with 'redistribution', as children are able to understand teachers, achieve better outcomes and have an equitable education where they are not discriminated against. However, with regard to 'recognition', 'representation' and 'reconciliation' there are multiple, varying issues. The RCSS curriculum bears no resemblance to the Myanmar government curriculum, and in many of the RCSS schools it seems that Burmese is not taught, so that transfers are impossible. It is also clear that smaller minority languages are not represented and recognised, so that some Shan families are catered for, but not others. This kind of a system does not support 'reconciliation' between groups. There are clearly other mixed schools, some of which receive RCSS support, that do support 'representation' and 'reconciliation', though this appears to be only between the majority Bamar and the Shan, while the inclusion of smaller ethnic groups and their languages is uncertain.

Ethnic education in Kachin State

Kachin dialects include different branches of the Tibeto-Burmese language family. The largest number of speakers use Jingphaw, with 630,000 speakers in Myanmar, 37,000 in China and 5–6,000 in India. The majority of the Kachin in Myanmar are members of different Christian denominations. It is significant that the Kachin almost certainly make up a minority of the population of Kachin State, with tens of thousands Kachin people living in neighbouring northern Shan State (Jaquet, 2015).

The main EAO education system is provided by the Education Department of the Kachin Independence Organisation (KIO). The KIO[44] was established in 1961 and fought for over three decades for freedom and self-determination for the Kachin people. Following a 1994 ceasefire, 17 years of relative peace allowed a strong and dynamic civil society sector to re-emerge. Nevertheless, the 1994 ceasefire is widely regarded as a failure, as it did not result in a political settlement to the decades of armed ethnic conflict, despite the KIO's good faith participation in the then military government's National Constitution Convention. The KIO ceasefire broke down entirely in June 2011, when the Myanmar Army launched new offensives against the organisation. In the nearly nine years since fighting started again in Kachin areas, the KIO has lost territory, much of it of significant strategic importance. The conflict has created over 100,000 IDPs, many of whom live in camps on the Myanmar side of the China border. These people have 'voted with their feet', as some 80 per cent have chosen to flee to KIO-controlled areas, rather than remain under the authority of the Myanmar government (South, 2018).

In the KIO HQ in Laiza on the China border, the organisation acts as a well-functioning government, administering departments of education, health, agriculture, etc., each with their respective and effective bureaucracies and training centres. Larger towns and villages have electricity and internet access, and many of the trappings of a de facto nation-state, including, their own system of car registration, traffic police, fire brigade, etc. Following the 1994 KIO ceasefire, the then military government made a commitment to supporting civilian community rehabilitation jointly with the KIO in two main sectors: immunisation, and allowing KIO high school students to enter government schools and sit matriculation exams. For this reason, the KIO decided to adopt the government curriculum, including using MoE textbooks. The KIO schools' use of government curriculum was modified slightly, removing objectionable elements of the history and some other syllabi (for example, lessons about the Myanmar flag) and the LoI was mostly mother tongue (primarily, but not exclusively) Jingphaw. KIO students at all levels experienced few problems transitioning between the two systems. However, in 2010, following the KIO's refusal to be transformed into a Myanmar Army-controlled Border Guard Force (BGF), the MoE began restricting transfer between the two systems. Transfers were halted entirely by official decree following breakdown of the ceasefire in June 2011 (South and Lall, 2016b and 2016c).[45]

Since the resumption of fighting, the KIO system has started to diverge from that of the government. At present, the curriculum still follows the MoE, but the KIO Education Department has begun printing its own materials, and expects that these will increasingly reflect the Kachin's 'own curriculum' as Kachin education stakeholders start to develop their own curriculum framework.[46] This approach aims to develop an education system based on mother-tongue teaching, with Burmese mostly confined to foreign language status (equal, or secondary, to English and Chinese) and, therefore, likely to diverge significantly from that of the government. This policy raises a number of issues including the likelihood that future KIO school graduates will not speak fluent Burmese.

As of 2018, the KIO Education Department administers 167 schools (including 8 high schools and 17 middle schools) with 1,534 teachers serving over 22,000 students.[47] Before the ceasefire broke down, there were 58 KIO schools in the Eastern Division, now there are only 28; before 2011, there were 24 KIO schools in Shan State, now only 5 remain. Some of these schools have now been replaced by those in the IDP camps. Before 2011, some of the KIO schools were located in government-controlled or 'mixed' areas. With some exceptions in areas of ongoing armed conflict, most are now located in KIO-controlled areas. Several pre-existing KIO schools have seen student numbers more than double with the influx of IDPs. One KIO high school from northern Shan State has moved entirely, to be rebuilt in Mai Ja Yang, together with 540 students and teachers.[48] Because of a lack of qualified teachers, the quality of education in IDP camps is probably declining. IDP children in KIO schools generally do less well in exams than non-displaced children. According to UNICEF, 70 per cent of IDP students drop out after primary school. The KIO has built a new high school at Je Yang (one of the largest IDP camps), and children in camps close to Laiza and Mai Ja Yang can access high schools in these two KIO-controlled towns. For other IDP children, however, access to education is more difficult. Therefore, the KIO Education department, often in partnership with churches, runs a number of boarding houses, allowing IDP children from the camps to stay in the vicinity of KIO high schools.[49] The KIO has had its own teacher training since 1997, with their Institute of Education in Mai Ja Yang providing short and longer courses (between a few weeks and two years), yet at present they cannot train enough teachers for the needs of all schools, particularly so with the recent influx of IDPs.

At the time of the research there were also reportedly over 2,000 KIO high school graduates who had not been able to sit government matriculation exams.[50] For the KIO Education Department, the long-term aim is to develop channels into further education that are not dependent on the government. An impressive range of options already exist, with KIO high school graduates having been placed in tertiary education colleges in India, China, Thailand, Singapore and elsewhere – often with accompanying scholarships. Furthermore, there at least six further education institutes in KIO-controlled areas (a KIA officers academy; KIO agriculture and nursing colleges in Laiza; the Federal Law Academy; the Institute of Liberal Arts and Sciences (ILAS) and the KIO Education Department's Institute of Education in Mai Ja Yang).[51] However, it is unlikely that the KIO would be able to identify sufficient tertiary education places – and scholarships – for *all* KIO school graduates. Therefore, while Kachin education authorities are committed to meritocracy, the risk is that only (or mostly) the children of elites such as the KIO/KIA leaders will benefit from limited opportunities for access to higher education.[52]

In a potentially significant development, in April–May 2018, the Kachin SEO issued an official announcement that children without 'records of achievement' (i.e. KIO schoolchildren, including IDPs) would be able to join MoE schools after taking placement tests, with no further scrutiny. Implementation of this policy seems to vary between townships. For many parents, this was a positive development giving them options. The KIO-ED has remained officially neutral on this issue, allowing children to join government schools on their own volition, but not promoting the practice. Unofficially, there is probably some disquiet at this development as it seems that fairly large numbers of IDP families have been moving from KIO-controlled areas to camps in government-controlled Myanmar in order to access education. The primary motivation seems to be that children could receive official school certificates (especially the Grade 5 and Grade 8 Board Exams; and matriculation so as to enter Myanmar higher education).[53]

Kachin Education Consortium

The main non-state ethnic education providers are grouped under the Kachin Education Consortium (KEC) that also includes the two nationwide 'Kachin' national NGOs, Metta and Shalom foundations, that provide capacity-building/training and other forms of education support, but do not directly administer schools.[54]

The one organisation that has managed to develop an entirely independent Kachin Curriculum in Jingpaw is *SaJaNa*[55] that provides education services for Kachin both in Kachin and Shan States. A Baptist church-based organisation with its HQ in Special Region 5, its curriculum is used in 25 schools in northern Shan State and 24 in Kachin State, mostly located in government-controlled but at times quite remote areas. It was founded with the financial help of a Kachin militia amid profound dissatisfaction with a government system perceived as irreparably damaged and dysfunctional – both in terms of rote-learning teaching practices and a Burman/Burmese-dominated curriculum. With the help of Hope International, SaJaNa has developed a system owned and delivered by local Kachin, primarily Jingphaw stakeholders, delivering student-centred, mother-tongue-based education. According to SIL, SaJaNa is the only organisation that offers a complete MTB-MLE experience, as Burmese is taught throughout the early grades as a second language (Dekker, 2018a: 38 and 57).[56] At the time of writing, the earliest established two schools in northern Shan State are offering up to Grade 7, and they are adding a further one grade-level each year. On previous visits in 2015 and 16, SaJaNa schools were experienced as wonderful learning environments, with committed teachers and engaged children. Potential problems with this system are similar to those discussed above in relation to KIO schools: the lack of accreditation, meaning that SaJaNa school graduates will not easily be able to sit government matriculation and other exams.

The Kachin Education Foundation (KEF) was established in 2014 and has played a leading role in developing education policy among Kachin stakeholders, enjoying a close relationship with the KIO-ED. It currently administers 17 schools in government-controlled areas in and around Myitkyina, Bhamo and Kutkai (northern Shan State). Through its Naushawng Education Centre in Myitkyina, KEF offers a number of short and longer courses to post-high school Kachin students, focusing particularly on English language and computer training. KEF also administers independent schools which follow the SaJaNa curriculum. The LoI is primarily Jingphaw, although KEF is beginning to add some other dialects. Fieldwork by Ashley South in 2018 found that a few parents transferred their children after KEF Grade 1 back to MoE schools due to concerns about relatively limited Burmese language teaching, and lack of accreditation for non-government schools.[57] Beyond KEF, the various Kachin churches also supply volunteer teachers to various government and non-government schools and their contribution has become vital due to the conflict. Some volunteer teachers from the Catholic church are seen at a workshop in Myitkyina in 2015 in Figure 7.5.

In the Kachin context, the resumption of armed conflict since 2011 has led to greater pan-Kachin unity and cohesion around an ethno-linguistic core, identified particularly with the Jingphaw identity. Significant elements among non-Jingphaw communities seem not to object to adopting this dominant dialect as a Kachin *lingua franca*,

Figure 7.5 Kachin State non-government teacher workshop, 2015. Source: Author.

although some sub-groups find the dominance of Jingphaw problematic. Associated with massive and widespread human rights abuses, the renewed fighting has alienated many of those in the diverse Kachin ethno-linguistic community who previously were willing to consider a future as part of Myanmar. Since the resumption of armed conflict, KIO-administered schools have been switching more to Jingphaw and English, and teaching less Burmese. This is part of a general move to disengage from government education, and to develop a more distinctively Kachin school system.[58]

The KIO-ED was similar to the MNEC system in that it met all '4 R's' of Novelli et al.'s peace and education framework. However, the resumption of conflict means that not only KIO schools but also those run by SaJaNa, while supporting 'redistribution' through equitable access to education for equitable outcomes, no longer meet the 'reconciliation' part of the framework. It is also debatable if they meet the 'recognition' and 'representation' elements of the framework. SaJaNa offers Burmese as a second language allowing the children in its care to learn the official Myanmar language, but their system and curriculum does not allow children to transfer. The KIO still mostly uses the government curriculum, which does allow for transfers (when the government is in the mood) but they teach less and less Burmese. Non-Jingpaw speaking groups are neither represented nor catered for in either of the two systems.

Engaging with the government

There are understandable historic reasons for the emergence of separate education systems, and they do offer education in a language the children can understand, making them popular across communities that have developed a historical mistrust of the Bamar-dominated administrative systems. However, these separate systems have some distinct disadvantages: limited options for school graduates if they cannot speak Burmese and have no recognised qualifications, and difficulty for graduates to re-integrate into the Myanmar HE system, or consider themselves citizens of the Union. Furthermore, separate systems marginalise already poor and vulnerable communities, leading to long-term disadvantages. A system of recognition, accreditation and transfer, which includes remedial Burmese language training for those who want to join government schools, has yet to be negotiated.

Although the NESP (MoE 2018, Section 5.2.2) includes a goal to: 'develop a partnership mechanism to support the participation of different education service providers in basic education reforms', the MoE has found it particularly challenging to engage with EAO education departments. It seems that the MoE officials generally believe that the standards offered by EAO schools are lower than what government schools provide.[59] In discussions about possible ways forward, Mon State was singled out as the one place where a possible collaboration between the MoE and an ethnic education system could be developed, as the MNEC broadly uses the government curriculum and the MNEC already has links with the SEO (see Figure 7.6). All other potential collaborations were seen as challenging based on the issues of different content and standards across the systems. The main issue for some MoE officials is a concern that all children in Myanmar should learn the same curriculum content, as well as the requirement that they should reach equivalent standards of learning.[60] For a transfer process to be formalised, at the very least common agreed standards would have to be developed.

The language issue was also seen as a barrier to collaboration in relation to transfer mechanisms, as several MoE respondents felt that the ethnic children who had attended ethnic schools would not speak sufficient Burmese, putting extra strain on already overburdened classroom teachers.[61] This feeling is widespread, despite the fact that the

Figure 7.6 Joint MNEC and Mon SEO workshop 2018, led by Viren Lall with Mi Kun Chan Non translating. Source: Author.

NEL Chapter 7, Establishment of Curriculum and Curriculum Standards, Section 42, states (GoM, 2014b): 'The Ministry, Division or State Governments, and Self-Administered Division or Region Governments shall (i) arrange for the ability to communicate and transfer between government and other schools and (ii) help to open classes to develop the ethnic groups' literature, language, culture, arts and traditions'. Whilst the latter point is covered in the MoE's development of the LC with the various ethnic LCAs (as discussed in Chapter 6), the issue of remedial language support in transfers between systems[62] to promote lifelong learning opportunities for all remains to be addressed.

Developing a relationship with the government MoE is no easier from the EAO side. Demands are similar across systems focusing in the first instance on recognition of their schools and teachers as well as standardising easier mechanisms for student transfers: 'Ethnic schools need recognition by the government, so students can switch to the same grade, with the help of special language upgrading classes. They [the government] need to make rules for this, so that this arrangement is spread throughout the country'.[63]

There are many barriers to collaboration with the government; they include the historical Burmanisation, which has resulted in de facto discrimination and the lack of equal rights for all ethnic nationality communities across the social and economic domains. Some barriers are more structural and include the centralised nature of the government, such as the fact that education decisions cannot be taken at state level, resulting in the government retaining control over the LoI and curricular content (Lall et al., 2020). For the Mon, whose system is possibly closest to that of the MoE, the main concern remains that the Union level MoE does not understand the value of MTB-MLE and that the State Counsellor herself was against MTB-MLE being used as a system in Myanmar schools.[64] It was felt by Mon respondents that since the state level government and the MoE did not have any decision-making power with regard to education in ethnic states, there needed to be advocacy directly to the State Counsellor and the MoE in Nay Pyi Taw by organisations such as UNICEF and Save the Children, who understand that MTB-MLE allows ethnic children to learn better overall when they are able to start education in their own language. The NLD was described as being very 'new' in the matters of politics and governance, and few if any NLD MPs were deemed knowledgeable about different multilingual/mother tongue-based education systems in general and on ethnic education systems in particular.[65]

Despite these barriers, two EAO education departments have taken part in very preliminary discussions.[66] This poses the risk of those willing to engage with the MoE being criticised by 'hardliners' within ethnic communities for engaging with the government. But in the face of the increasing threats to the EAO education systems, such an engagement has become salient. These threats include issues of finance and the related issue of losing teachers.

Financing EAO schools has become a particular problem for all EAO education systems. Before Myanmar's opening to the Western world after 2011, EAOs received cross-border funding, mostly through Thailand from cross-border-based NGOs, that supported schools, teacher training and teacher salaries as well as materials and textbooks for the children. This aid has now largely moved away from the border and the international development partners focus and support is on the reform process within Myanmar (Lall and South, 2018). Communities have always supported their teachers, mainly by contributions in kind, but there is simply not enough money for the system to work smoothly. A particular issue is teacher salaries. In the last two years, a large grant from Norway has helped NMSP to pay its teachers, but nevertheless this salary is a fraction of what government teachers receive. As the conflict has been paused since the 1990s, and MNEC teachers now have direct contact with government teachers, not least in joint government training, this highlights the huge disparity and leads to the risk of losing teachers across all EAO education because of the unstable financial situation.[67] Whilst teachers have a strong commitment they need secure livelihoods so they can remain in the job. During a government school recruitment drive under the Thein Sein Government, some skilled teachers transferred to the government system as daily wage teachers.[68] Those who have integrated into the government system have both job security as well as a pension, an attractive package that the MNEC cannot match. A related issue is the low matriculation rates at the Mon National High Schools, especially in Nyisar, which some parents say is due to a lack of 'skillful' teachers available in such a remote location (interviews 2015).

The quality of teachers and student achievement has become a contentious issue. Previously, the quality of instruction in MNSs was seen as better than in government schools (Lall and South, 2013a and 2013b); this is now the reverse, reinforcing the status government schools have gained in Mon communities, and leading to new parental choices (Lall and South, 2018). During the time of conflict and military dictatorship, parents actively wanted their children to attend Mon National Schools (interviews across Mon State in 2011 and 2012). This was in part for linguistic and nationalist reasons, in part due to the lack of choice in more remote regions. Since the reform process started, more government schools have moved into former conflict areas, changing the education dynamics. In some cases, there has reportedly been coercion by government teachers who visit parents and pressure them to send their children to government schools, in other cases parents chose the government alternative as they know children can continue their education through to university without any of the transfer problems that can occur when the children have to switch systems. According to some respondents (interviews in 2011, 2012 and 2016), those parents who choose to send their children to MNSs for nationalist reasons, to protect their language, literature (script) and culture, are declining in numbers. Since the conflict is seen to have ended some time ago, and the government is no longer seen as a military dictatorship, the 'protest value' of using MNSs has diminished. 'MNSs rely on the community but the community now has more trust to the government school, so this reduces commitment of the community. Under military rule the commitment of the community was stronger, now that the government has changed, they are less anti-government' (Mon Teacher, Mudon, 2018). Teachers and MNEC officials see this as a worrying trend as they believe that without their schools Mon language will not be learnt adequately by Mon children. They are concerned both for the children who come from Mon-speaking households and who in a Burmese language system suffer lower achievement and loss of communication skills, as well as for the wider, more educated urban-based Mon population, where Burmese is sometimes spoken at home, but where there is a risk of losing the essence of Mon culture. 'Education is the essence of the ethnic identity. To have freedom of the ethnic identity is important. Therefore, MNS are important. We can produce good Mon leaders' (Mon Teacher, Mudon, 2018). Many teachers who took part in discussions in 2016 and 2018 thought that parents did not understand the benefits of MTB-MLE, and that the Mon community also needed to be informed about why mother tongue-based learning helps children achieve better in the long run.

Conclusion: Harnessing ethnic armed organisations systems for increased social justice

EAO education officials and ethnic parents who send their children to EAO-run schools generally feel that the government has a responsibility in supporting both the teachers and the infrastructure of ethnic nationality schools on the basis of giving ethnic people equal rights – 'We need government support without their control.' This was justified by the fact that in the remote area where the government was not able or willing to open a school, or where even if there was a government school, government teachers would refuse to stay, the EAO was doing the government's job.

> So there is less responsibility of the government to the remote areas and MNEC is taking the responsibility so children can continue their education. Really good for the MoE. Therefore, MoE should recognise the school. (MNEC official, 2018).

This is a reflection of 'redistribution' – in that there needs to be non-discrimination in access to resources and equitable outcomes in education, 'recognition' – in that the government was seen to have to accept and respect the diversity of its own country as well as 'representation' –

where communities have the same right to participate in setting up education systems. It also links in with the desire by other, smaller ethnic communities discussed in the previous chapter, to have local teachers who speak the local ethnic language in order for the communities to 'own' the system and feel they benefit from it.

It is clear from the above that in order for Myanmar to achieve a sustainable and just peace, educational reform and practices will have to engage with the past injustices and the effects of decades of conflict. Part of the reconciliation process, therefore, is about the recognition of EAO systems, so that ethnic communities feel their language and culture is represented in the Myanmar education system. Only through recognition will equitable redistribution occur. And whilst the NESP text sets out the aim for this to be achieved, the path of negotiation is proving difficult.

Notes

1. Dekker et al. maintain that: 'Of the 11 EBEPs we met, only four (possibly five) are positioned to develop true MTB-MLE programmes in the next 2.5 years. Only KED, MNEC, KEC, KnEDN, and (possibly) CRED have complete control over a sufficient number of "independent [primary] schools." Other organizations support "community schools," but these are transitioning (by intent) into government schools at a fast rate – a process which will accelerate as international funding of the MOE rises. Even long-standing, strong EBEPs like the MNEC and KED are losing schools to the government system through attrition, as community members feel that government funding will alleviate their financial burdens while giving children the opportunity to study the national curriculum (opening the door to higher education and better jobs)' (Dekker et al., 2018b: 11).
2. The NMSP has maintained a ceasefire with the government since 1995.
3. The KIO saw its 17-year ceasefire collapse in 2011.
4. The '4 R' framework is also used in Higgins et al., 2016. However, that report engages only with the government and the Mon education systems.
5. Higgins et al.'s analysis is based on the text of the NEL 2015 and the National Education Sector Plan (i.e. the text developed under the Thein Sein Government by 2015, that was adopted by the NLD almost in its entirety in 2015) rather than the actual reform process that took root after 2015, but that rather confirmed their fears.
6. 'Formal education' is used to indicate regular schooling, whether implemented by government or non-state groups, or a mixture of these; 'non-formal education' refers to extra-curricular (usually part-time) education activities, implemented by a range of (mostly non-state, community-based) agencies.
7. See for example, the Report by the Karen Human Rights Group (2011). https://khrg.org/reports/year/2011.
8. https://reliefweb.int/report/myanmar/ethnic-armed-alliance-extends-ceasefire-rest-year, and https://elevenmyanma.com/news/tatmadaw-extends-unilateral-ceasefire.
9. More details on this in Lall et al., 2020.
10. Plus an estimated 80,000 Mon speakers in Thailand.
11. MNEC Aim: 'To create a society that ever continually makes learning for its capacity improvement so as to build a federal union state that is destined to provide its people at least with basic education and enables all ethnic groups of people to peacefully coexist'. MNEC Objectives: 'For all Mon children to access basic education; To maintain unity in diversity; To develop friendliness among the ethnic nationalities; To maintain and promote ethnic

12 culture and literature; To develop technological knowledge; To produce good sons and daughters of the nation; To help the outstanding students attain scholarship awards for continuing their education up to the international universities.'
12 In February 2012, NMSP leaders re-confirmed a ceasefire with the Thein Sein Government and in 2018 they signed the NCA.
13 In addition to the MNS, many Mon monasteries continued to teach elements of the Mon language and culture through the MSLBC training in a number of monasteries that have expanded over the years. While the extent of MSLBC training activities has expanded as a direct result of the increased space created by the NMSP ceasefire, Mon armed groups were not directly involved in these initiatives. See chapter 3 in this volume.
14 Figures given by MNEC. The SIL MEC Inception report (Dekker et al., 2018c) has different figures: MNEC provides mother tongue-based education to over 25,000 students (11,000 in 133 Mon national school with 610 teachers. 14,000 students with 161 teachers for Mon language in 96 government schools, 12 ECCD Schools, 1 NFE centre, 831 teachers, 20 ECCD teachers, 42 programme staff.
15 Fieldwork was conducted in the course of 2018 across Mon, Shan and Rakhine States.
16 Attended and co-organised by the author.
17 Discussed at length in FGDs in Mon National Schools in 2018.
18 According to interviews with MNEC leaders in 2018, MNEC has representation on the LC development committee for Mon State, but finds itself outnumbered by non-Mon stakeholders, creating new tensions in what the MNEC believes should be a collaborative process led by them working with the SEO.
19 'In the context of the Myanmar Army's brutal counter-insurgency campaigns since the 1970s, hundreds of thousands of Karen and other ethnic nationality citizens have fled the country to refugee camps in neighbouring Thailand. In 2015, some 30,000 children attend 80 schools in the seven Karen and two Karenni refugee camps in Thailand. These camps receive assistance from a range of international NGOs, and are administered by the Karen and Karenni Refugee Committees respectively, with education organised by the Karen Refugee Committee Education Entity (KRCEE), and the Karenni Education Department (under the authority of the KNU and KNPP respectively). Since the peace and reform processes began there have been some voluntary returnees, and there are calls for a more systematic return of these refugees, with declining international aid to the camps.' The Border Consortium. 2015. The Border Consortium Programme Report, January–June 2015 (Bangkok). https://www.ecoi.net/en/document/1431034.html.
20 Karen dialects occupy the Tibeto-Burman branch of Sino-Tibetan languages. There are some 12 Karen language dialects, of which the majority speak Sgaw (particularly in hill areas and among Christian communities) and Pwo (especially in the lowlands and among Buddhist communities). The size of the Karen population is unknown, no reliable census having been undertaken since the colonial period. Many commentators emphasise the Christian identity of the Karen. However, not more than 20 per cent of the Karen population are Christians. There are also some small populations of Karen Muslims.
21 The KSEAG was formed in 2005 by KTWG, KED and various partner organisations. According to KTWG, in 2013–4 KSEAG supported 6,154 teachers, 141,632 students and 1,294 schools. https://ktwg.org/education-assistance/.
22 These figures were provided by a KED official in 2018. Dekker et al. have similar figures: 1,573 schools with 317 schools KED administered, and using MTB; 5,652 teachers; 22,968 students in 1,256 mixed schools; 15,443 teachers; and 152,693 students in mixed schools (Dekker at al., 2018c).
23 Former affiliation of SSA-N Brigade 7.
24 Interviews with Shan Literature and Culture Association in Taunggyi and other Shan stakeholders in Yangon and Shan State in 2018.
25 Sai Pha, who met the author at Kaw Dai in 2018, explained that the six tone system allows to distinguish between similar sounding words, while the five tone creates confusion.
26 Personal interview with the teacher in Taunggyi in summer 2018 who developed the curriculum, but who asked to remain anonymous.
27 Discussion with Kim Jolliffe who has worked on public services in northern Shan State.
28 After decades of conflict, the RCSS signed the NCA in 2015, but has to date refused to consider any formal discussions of collaboration in education with the government.

29 Certain areas are designated by the Myanmar government as 'black areas' where there has recently been, or is continuing, armed conflict. Although government teachers and health workers are sent to these areas (and now also remunerated better because of the risks), many do not stay.
30 During the 2018 fieldwork, no data was collected about the RCSS's support to schools in camps on the Thai side of the Thai–Myanmar border, nor was the RCSS asked about how its system functioned in Thailand.
31 Including India, US, Norway, Thailand, Philippines and Sri Lanka.
32 Respondents told the author there was currently no transfer mechanism and no transfers were taking place.
33 The curriculum developer met the author and explained that she left the RCSS in 2006 and that she had developed materials up to certain Grades: maths only for 2 grades, geography for Grades 2, 3 and 4; science for Grades 1, 2 and 3; and history not all Grades. However, some subjects including Shan were developed up to Grade 8. Other respondents explained that the secondary curriculum is based on the Thai curriculum.
34 The SSPP has not signed the NCA, and is in conflict both with the Tatmadaw and the RCSS.
35 Discussion with Kim Jolliffe who has worked on public services in northern Shan State.
36 Interview with Sai Pha at Kaw Dai in 2018.
37 Interview with CRED officials in Taunggyi in 2018.
38 According to a senior CRED member, RDFSS was advised to register as CRED so that its activities would not be limited to Shan State.
39 CRED facilitated two workshops on Shan National Education Policy and Planning, in March 2017 and December 2016, supported by MEC – but no details in English seem to be available.
40 Although they collaborate with the education departments of the EAOs, respondents were keen to emphasise that while they have good relations with the different EAOs, this does not mean they support them.
41 Much of this support comes under its partnership with the Rural Indigenous Sustainable Education (RISE) network and is supported by the EU via ADRA.
42 The schools received some donor support from the Swedish Burma Committee in the past.
43 Aims as listed on https://www.kawdaiorganization.org/:
    - To build the capacities and skills of Shan youth so that they become community leaders in areas of need in the Shan State.
    - To provide academic education for Shan students so that they can pursue higher education abroad.
    - To provide basic education and home for internally displaced children and poor children across the Shan State.
    - To empower grassroots community through political education to become active citizens.
    - To create sustainable community economy through community learning centre.
44 Other Kachin armed groups include the ex-communist New Democratic Army-Kachin (NDA-K) and ex-KIO Kachin Defense Army (KDA), both of which agreed ceasefires with the government in the 1990s (for more detail see South, 2003: Chapter 5). The KIO has not signed the NCA.
45 At least until 2018 – see developments about this later in this chapter.
46 Author interview in London with Dr Lu Awn, head of the Mai Ja Yang College, April 2019.
47 Actual numbers including IDP schools are likely to be higher. Author interview in London with Dr Lu Awn, head of the Mai Ja Yang College, April 2019.
48 Author interview in London with Dr Lu Awn, head of the Mai Ja Yang College, April 2019.
49 As documented in the unpublished W3 report by Lall et al., 2020. Fieldwork for this by Ashley South. Also confirmed in discussions with Dr Lu Awn in April 2019. See more on the Kachin situation in South, 2018.
50 This was pointed out in a personal interview with KIO Maj Gen Sumlut Gun Maw in Chiang Mai in 2016. He shared the government directive that no longer allowed students from KIO schools to transfer to government schools or take matriculation exams. Interview with Dr Lu Awn in April 2019 (London) shows that this problem is ongoing although there are some changes detailed below.
51 The author visited both Laiza and Mai Ja Yang in 2015 and was shown around most of the tertiary education facilities.

52 Bawk La notes: 'there are not enough places at [KIO FE colleges] ... to accommodate all of the students who wish to pursue higher education ... At least one third of students who have completed standard 10 in KIO schools still need to join Myanmar government-controlled schools ... [However,] despite having attained standard 10 matriculation, students from KIO-controlled schools are forced to re-enter the formal system in government-controlled schools at a level two years lower' (Bawk La, 2017: 17–9).
53 Private conversation with Dr Lu Awn, Rector of Mai Ja Yang College, April 2019.
54 Dekker et al. state that overall the KEC supports 23,000 children in Kachin and northern Shan states with 1,862 teachers; 70 education officers; 217 principals; and 400 school management committees that include the KIO and *SaJaNa* (SJN) – Shan State Kachin Baptist Union schools (Dekker et al., 2018c).
55 Northern Shan State Kachin Baptist Union church-based education.
56 See Lall 2016c for points from the meeting with SaJaNa administration in Lashio.
57 Conversations with Ashley South who conducted fieldwork in Kachin in 2018.
58 Fieldwork in Kachin State in 2015–6.
59 Confidential interviews with MoE officials including a number of director generals from different departments on issues pertaining to ethnic education 2017–9.
60 Confidential interviews with MoE officials including a number of director generals from different departments on issues pertaining to ethnic education 2017–9.
61 Confidential interviews with MoE officials including a number of director generals from different departments on issues pertaining to ethnic education 2017–9.
62 National Education Law (2014, Parliamentary Law No. 41) The objectives of national education are, among others: 'To develop union spirit and to create citizens who respect, value, preserve and develop all the ethnic groups' languages, literatures, culture, arts, traditions, and historical heritage' (Chapter 2 (c) Objectives).
63 Quotes from Mon and Kachin respondents during confidential meetings between 2018 and 2019.
64 This was clearly expressed at a meeting between Daw Aung San Suu Kyi and the NMSP leadership during a meeting that was earmarked to discuss education issues. This came up during one of the interviews with NMSP leadership, the person had been present at the meeting with Daw Aung San Suu Kyi was meeting with Nai Hongsa and other NMSP officials. The fact that Daw Aung San Suu Kyi personally said that she did not support MTB-MLE and even (incorrectly) claimed that Assam in India is dropping the three language formula that is based on MTB-MLE was re-confirmed with the head of MNEC. This was related to the author during a meeting in Mawlamyine in 2018 and re-confirmed in 2019 in Yangon.
65 Conversations with MNEC and other Mon education stakeholders 2018 and 2019.
66 As part of the MEPP that was facilitated by the WB in 2018.
67 The situation is slightly different in Kachin State; first, because the conflict is ongoing, second, because KIO teachers are better paid than those working for MNEC and KED, with higher parental contributions (apart from parents in refugee camps).
68 The same problem was reported in monastic schools in 2013–4 (See Lall, 2016a and c).

Conclusion: Whither social justice in Myanmar?

This book has covered the Myanmar education reform process, how it is affecting Myanmar citizens and what they think about it; it is not a book that looks at Myanmar as a case study with reference to the wider global social justice debates. But since education is a globally accepted pathway to social justice, the country's reforms leading towards a more participatory system (Lall, 2016a) offer an opportunity to make major policy changes across society and the NLD promised such change, it is pertinent to review the massive reform effort undertaken by the government across the different education sectors.

The policy-practice gap

Historically, there has been a large variation in the extent and mix of deprivations experienced across the different states/regions, townships and schools. The presence of widespread poverty and a stagnant economy over decades have been key factors affecting education services and the experience of children and teachers within schools and students and academics in universities. In light of this, the 2015 NLD election manifesto was like a breath of fresh air, promising after decades of oppression to put citizens first, in particular focusing on the most vulnerable, weaker sections of society. Education was presented as a key pillar of the strategy; the NESP[1] addressed all the right headings – aiming for inclusive and equitable quality education accessible to all. One can deduce from the official texts – many of which have been reviewed in this volume – that there is a general understanding across both government and the civil service of the issues the country faces with regard to poverty, ethnic and religious discrimination, and other widening gaps between the most disadvantaged sections of society, both urban and rural, and those who are in power politically and economically.[2] The policy texts indicate that these issues were understood both under President Thein Sein's and

Daw Aung San Suu Kyi's leadership. While Myanmar's citizens might not have expected such changes under the USDP Government, the NLD manifesto promised a social justice agenda, underlining the existing policy texts. What is more – the new policy texts developed under the NLD all re-emphasise the social justice priorities. But in practice, the policies are not being implemented; on the ground one can see much activity but not that much change. There is a clear, yawning policy–practice gap, raising the questions as to why the current reality does not reflect the publically declared intentions.

One reason might be time; while five years is a very short time to judge any government's successes and failures, the reforms started at least five years before the NESP was put into place – and if the decade of JICA and UNICEF work is taken into account, an uneasy picture emerges of education reforms that are repeated and amplified, but that do not change enough on the ground to embed and become sustainable. The CESR and the resulting NESP were supposed to break that cycle, but as the MTR shows, despite some improvements, this has not been the case. This raises the question if the impediments to change are structural, including for example, hierarchies and other barriers that cannot simply be wished away by policy texts using the right discourse. This book has pointed out many barriers for stakeholders, but they have not been engaged with by either the government or the development partners. The issues stakeholders face are well known as reviews of previous programmes pointed to much the same issues – yet it seems that the lessons from programmes before 2010 and between 2010 and 2015 have not been learnt. Another reason might be the dissonance between the neo-liberal development agenda pushed by many (not all) development partners that clashes with the social justice-inspired policy texts, as well as the general uncoordinated approach taken by development partners that have put such a burden on the MoE. Caught between the policy texts written by the government and the priorities of development partners, it feels like ministry-based stakeholders as well as those further below do not own the change process; some claim they do not even understand it. In the end, the responsibility for the success of the reforms (or lack thereof) lie with the current NLD-led government, and not with the development partners. Therefore, another reason could be the NLD's own policy shift from state responsibility to 'self reliance' (McCarthy, 2019). In all likelihood, the reasons for the policy–practice gap is a combination of all the above.

The data in this book shows that important pieces of the puzzle are stakeholder challenges and ownership, which are in turn underpinned by clashing domestic and international policy priorities. Stakeholders (i.e. MoE staff at all levels, teachers, teacher educators, student teachers, students and parents) are experiencing challenges across the changing system and these challenges are not being addressed. Most programmes do *not* ask how their participants perceive and understand the education reforms and in particular what barriers they face. As a result, the reforms are experienced as a top-down enforcement, rather than something that is collectively owned.

In the first instance, the education reforms affect MoE staff across the sector at three levels – at the top ministry level, at the more localised administrative levels such as the State/Region Education Offices and TEOs and at school levels. Currently, there is very little material in the public domain documenting how MoE staff are dealing with the reforms. A My-Equip Organisational Constraints Analysis (OCA) (Fullerton and French, 2019) of certain MoE departments identified barriers pertaining to 'rules, guidelines, policies and systems; work culture; human resources and skills; material and financial resources as well as culture and attitudes'. A key issue seems to be a lack of clarity in comprehending the wider reform agenda. Unless MoE staff understand what is changing and why, they are unlikely to be able to own the process. Discussions held in the summer and autumn of 2018 and the spring of 2019 at the MoE in NPT, showed that staff at all levels require new skills – at the top, director generals and their deputies need to move away from centralised authority to devolved decision making. Further down, staff to whom the work is delegated need new skills, in particular with regard to cross-departmental collaboration and the confidence to contribute to programme design. Since the MoE itself is part of a larger hierarchical government structure and has to fall in line with other ministries and the government, changing hierarchical structures will prove a long-term challenge. It emerges that the new ways of working and behaviour change has in effect to be *authorised* and *directed* in order to be accepted; but much of a devolved decision-making culture actually goes against traditional Myanmar culture where hierarchies rule supreme.

Further down the education structure, many lives are affected. As Chapter 2 on basic education has shown, the principal change for serving teachers is the changing pedagogy linked to the new primary curriculum that is being rolled-out with limited support both with regard to learning aids and classroom-based assessment resources. The JICA CREATE MTR, which reviewed (in a limited way) how teachers felt about the new curriculum, states that teachers complained of a number of barriers. These included insufficient time to prepare the lessons and teaching subjects they had no training in – such as performing arts and visual arts. But the main issue seems to have been the cascade training (Mizuno et al., 2019: 16), where the lower down the cascade, the thinner the transmission of the concepts required for the new curriculum, with teachers struggling to understand and use the new materials.[3]

A preliminary review was conducted by OPM of how the new formative and summative assessment system is affecting teachers (OPM, 2019). It seems that rapid changes have resulted in parallel systems in the same school, which means that some teachers are teaching both the old and the new curricula with both pedagogies depending on which class they were seeing. Teachers are worried as they do not feel they have the pedagogical skills to use the new approach, in particular that they are unable to conduct classroom assessment on individual students due to the lack of experience with the new system and large class sizes.

Teacher–parent relations have also been affected by the new curriculum as parents report they cannot check what children have learnt.[4] This was mentioned both in an interview with JICA (autumn 2019, Yangon) as well as in the JICA CREATE MTR (Mizuno et al., 2019), where teachers explained that parents did not understand the new curriculum and were worried about their child being excluded if they did badly, especially at Grade 5. As the new curriculum, the new teaching methods and the new assessment system are rolled-out, parental support and understanding will be needed if the new curriculum and assessment systems are to become a success.

Looking back, the main difficulties stakeholders face in the current reform process are similar to the ones uncovered in previous research, prior to the roll-out of the NESP, in particular, previous UNICEF programmes, such as QBEP. This shows that previous lessons have not been learnt. The barriers broadly fall into three categories – culture: in particular hierarchies and reporting pathways; structure: particularly lack of sufficient or adequate training and infrastructural: limiting the successful roll-out of the new curriculum and assessment system.

The barriers do not only emerge in basic education, but also in higher and teacher education. The new higher education policies, influenced by global neo-liberal trajectories of higher education around the world are likely to cement inequalities. It has been seen that a three-tier system is being proposed, with Yangon and Mandalay Universities at the helm of an elite system, and regional universities in ethnic states at the bottom of the pile. This will embed the disparities between ethnic students who manage to get into universities close to home, compared to the Bamar students accessing urban higher education provision, in turn exacerbating the already existing social inequalities. Second- and third-tier universities, their staff and students are unlikely to receive the same recognition and respect as their elite counterparts. But in order to compete internationally, Myanmar's HEIs feel they have to play by international norms and rules, despite the domestic costs.

With regard to teacher education (and teaching as a profession), the system is inherently inequitable. Not only do teachers face their own social justice challenges due in part to material constraints and low salaries and in part to the local cultural outlook, but teacher education is also instrumental in reproducing the same social justice issues again and again. The main issues are around gender and ethnicity. Over 80 per cent of teachers are female, but only 60 per cent of female teachers become head teachers and fewer make it to TEO positions. Teaching is seen in Myanmar as a service profession where the teacher serves society and is a role model to the community in which they work. The transfers often mean that female teachers cannot marry, as their husbands might not be able to find a job where they are posted (Condon, 2017). Marginalisation is rife, and remains unaddressed in teacher education and the teaching profession. There are fewer ethnic minority teachers in schools than their Bamar counterparts, in part, because the matriculation exam is offered only in Burmese, which is not the mother tongue of the ethnic students. Recent changes in the 2017–8 academic year in ethnic states suggest access to education colleges appears now to have become more inclusive, but these changes still have to work through the system and it will be years before there are an equivalent number of ethnic teachers to the number of ethnic students.

The book also reviewed how alternative systems provide more social justice to the people they serve than the reformed government provision – possibly without the fanfare of large policy documents and election manifesto promises. Monastic schools, for example, are a key mechanism in Myanmar's education system to combat marginalisation, and aim for the inclusion of the poorest in society. By ensuring that the monastic schools and teachers are supported through donations from society, monastic heads undermine the exploitative relationship of the tuitions system within the government education system to which poor parents are subject.

While monastic schools mostly support poor children and their families, the parallel ethnic systems, many of which are provided by EAOs, offer similar support to remote and conflict-affected children, whose mother tongue is not Burmese. The EAO education officials and ethnic parents who send their children to EAO-run schools generally feel that the government should have a responsibility in supporting both the teachers and the infrastructure of ethnic nationality schools on the basis of giving ethnic people equal rights, that have been denied for many years under military rule. This is cemented by the fact that these schools often offer education in areas where the government is unable or unwilling to go. The government's answer for ethnic students – the roll of the LC – does not reverse the process of marginalisation embedded in the government education system that impacts so adversely on smaller minority groups. In fact, rather than greater inclusion, the manner in which it is being developed and rolled-out seems to be sowing division even within the ethnic groups. So the debate on the teaching of ethnic languages through either a local curriculum, or by developing a full MTB-MLE system continues. The census points to the fact that the lack of MTB-MLE in Myanmar means that the country will retain long-term structural disadvantages for certain groups, and social justice for them and others who are disadvantaged is a long way off.

It is astonishing how well understood all these social justice issues are in policy terms. The NESP MTR underlines the systemic inequities that disadvantage those living in conflict-affected, remote areas:

> In the period since 2014/15 the education budget increased by 63 per cent. The three regions receiving the highest per student budgets are Rakhine State, Chin State, and Kayah State – all conflict affected areas. Rakhine State and Chin State aside from being conflict affected also rank with the lowest matriculation results nationwide. The weak correlation between higher expenditure and lower matriculation results is likely the result of those areas in conflict resulting in disrupted schooling, as well as, inexperienced teachers being posted to remote areas, and using Myanmar language instead of (better understood) local, ethnic languages. (MoE 2020: vii)

The MTR explicitly acknowledges that the 30 per cent of children whose mother tongue is not Burmese have to learn two new languages – Burmese and English – and are therefore at a high risk of dropping out: 'There are no explicit learning strategies to cater for ethnic language speakers across Myanmar' (MoE 2020: ix). And the MTR also recognises that national data masks the disparities in education across regions, states and population sub-groups.

Much of the current data available to the MTR team is not disaggregated by gender or factors of disadvantage such as ethnicity, religion, disability, geographic location and economic status. Data analysed in the MTR indicates that GESI is not integrated across all nine transformational shifts of the NESP, which limits its contribution to improving and strengthening education opportunities for all girls and boys. While inclusion is a focus of one transformational shift in the NESP, the plan does not adequately mainstream GESI across all main sub-sectors (MoE 2020: viii).

The NESP MTR therefore validates the findings of this book, but does not offer much in terms of suggestions of how the policies can be put into practice so as to effect a more socially just system on the ground. The Executive Summary of the MTR states: 'There is a need to manage expectations to what might realistically be expected to be achieved from within and outside government. For the remaining two years of NESP implementation, the MTR team encourages the MoE to remain focused on achieving realistic and planned foundations of reform' (MoE 2020: vi).

It is unclear at the time of writing if development partners have taken on board the results of the MTR in order to tweak their support to the reform process, to adjust to the Myanmar government policy texts (and its social justice discourse), make their programmes more workable, and in the long run more sustainable. Real change for academics, teachers, students and their parents is essential if the reforms are to result in a system that offers hope to the generation currently growing up and who will have little or no recollection of Myanmar's military junta. It is essential that the reforms erase the junta's legacy of injustice and therefore the political parties in charge of the reforms (and one might argue the supporting development partners) have a heavy responsibility that is also time bound.

Educating Myanmar's youth for the future of the country?

When discussing education reforms the outlook also has to be forward – to the future that is held in trust by the adults of today for the youth, the adults of tomorrow. Given the reforms, it is therefore right to ask how the reformed system as it stands at the time of writing is expected to improve the life of the next generation.

It has been seen across this volume that over the last 15 years, the quality of education has been very low. Most urban youth found it impossible to get a job, simply based on the government qualifications.

The rise of parallel private systems focusing on IT and languages (such as English and Mandarin) discussed in Chapter 1 in this volume shows that families looked for alternative and supplementary training, especially in urban areas. An unpublished study by Myanmar Egress conducted in 2007–8 uncovered that young people in Yangon needed to take courses in private institutions in order to get a job in the private sector. But these young people were mostly the fortunate ones whose families could afford to pay the required fees, and those who could afford it would try to get the required qualifications to go and study abroad, guaranteeing them better jobs later in life.[5] These market solutions did not and cannot offer a way out for the wider population. Many more, either rural or poor, were simply stuck with the Myanmar qualifications (either matriculation after finishing school or their university degrees) and then unable to find a job commensurate to their 'training level'. The education reforms were sorely needed and eagerly anticipated.

But have these reforms taken a 'visionary' approach with regard to the needs of the young people that centre on getting employment in a country where the economy is also changing? It is already known that there is a serious skills gap as education is not well aligned with the country's changing labour force needs, even in light of the reforms, and even in light of many development partners professing an adherence to human capital theory where education is essentially a tool to create an educated labour force. The ADB[6] succinctly explains the challenges in terms of: 'Access – while at least 80% of youth complete primary education, less than half (44%) complete even lower secondary education. This leaves a "missing majority" with bleak prospects for entry into modern sector employment.' The summary goes on to explain how and what students learn in schools lacks relevance. Written in 2019, four years into the NESP, and after the same issues were discussed as part of the CESR in 2015,[7] the ADB document shows that Myanmar's economic model, based on unskilled labour and natural resource exploitation, plays its part in limiting the success of the education reforms, especially with regard to more inclusive growth and poverty reduction and underpins the need for a social justice approach. The lack of joined-up thinking is recognised in the NESP MTR: 'Beyond implementation of individual reforms, the MTR team finds that stronger links with industry and stronger connection to future social and economic development policy and plans needs to coherently underpin the next phase of NESP in Myanmar.' (MoE 2020: vi). It emerges that even as budgetary expenditure for education rises[8] and policy documents signal the right intentions, a missing element is the recognition of the needs of the young people – who these reforms are ultimately for – and a vision of their possible future. As has been seen across this volume, if the practice does not follow the policy text, not much will change. Under these circumstances the question remains – what future for Myanmar's youth?

The 2020 elections

The future will not only be determined by the education reforms. Those who will govern Myanmar after 2020 also hold the key to how the reforms and the future will pan out. The planned parliamentary elections at the end of 2020, the third under the 2008 Constitution and the first under the government led by Daw Aung San Suu Kyi, are expected to return the NLD to government. This next step in Myanmar's transition would in itself be a big achievement, given the country's history of military rule. The Union Election Commission (UEC) compiled the list of 37 million eligible voters at the end of 2019.[9] More then 100 parties are expected to contest. As a new generation is allowed to go to the polls, how are the education reforms feeding into the campaign?

More broadly, the reforms are part of the pre-election campaign that started very informally early in 2020. After five years in power, the NLD has engendered a lot of activity, which has not translated into much change on the ground. Certain sections of Myanmar's urban society will be disappointed with the slow pace of change, especially in areas such as jobs, infrastructure and foreign investment. The NLD has not lived up to society's high expectations, and there is disappointment; but given the lack of an alternative and the fact that there is certainly no appetite for a return of the military at the helm of government, the failings of this government are unlikely to make much of a difference at the polls. A survey held by People's Alliance for Credible Elections (PACE) in July 2019 shows that: 'People were more positive about the outlook in their immediate vicinity such as townships than in their states/regions or in Myanmar as a whole. While nearly half (44%) of the citizens stated that their townships were going in the right direction, only one third said the same regarding their states/regions (38%) and the country (37.3%)' (PACE, 2019: 17).

Given the current political context, education and its reform is unlikely to dominate the election headlines; critical issues to influence voters are more likely to be the stalled peace process and the debate around the Rakhine crisis. Callahan states in her 2019 report for United States Institute of Peace (USIP) that the elections will foster division rather than reconciliation. 'Communal, religious, and nationalist claims will certainly be center stage during the campaign, raising the possibility that tensions could boil over' (Callahan and Myo Zaw Oo, 2019: 2).

Not all see the peace process as a key issue. A quote from a Mandalay-based public intellectual in the USIP report notes the lack of interest in the peace process amongst the Bamar majority: 'They watch Amay [mother] Suu give the opening speech at every Panglong (Union Peace) Conference, and they think she has already made peace. It's done for them. So why are the ethnic groups making trouble?' (Callahan and Myo Zaw Oo, 2019: 19). Nevertheless, the peace process is a key issue for around 40 per cent of the population of ethnic nationality, many living in conflict-affected areas. The disappointment in these areas at the lack of progress of the peace process might lead to some electoral gains for ethnic parties, which could recreate an ethnic opposition, as seen during the USDP Government between 2011 and 2015 (Lall, 2016a). This would be easier than in 2015 as the multiple Kachin, Mon, Chin and Karen parties have mostly merged into single ethnicity options that can stand against the NLD and the USDP candidates. Nevertheless, as Callahan reminds us, much will depend on how acceptable the ethnic party candidates are perceived to be by the local voters. It also remains unclear how the EAOs – both signatory and non-signatory – will prepare for the elections.

Not all ethnic issues will damage the NLD. Myanmar being called to defend itself at the International Court of Justice (ICJ) in 2019 will actually help Daw Aung San Suu Kyi as she has been seen standing up for her country against what are perceived as unreasonable international demands. The country's support has been underlined by huge billboards that appeared at Yangon's busy intersections as Daw Aung San Suu Kyi headed to The Hague to defend her country accused of genocide, declaring: 'We stand with Daw Aung San Suu Kyi'.[10] However, in 2018 under immense international pressure, the NLD's Government agreed in principle to the repatriation of the Rohingya from Bangladesh. This was to start with around 2,000 refugees at the end of 2018. To date, none have returned through the formal process. Nevertheless, this agreement will pit the NLD against the Rakhine nationalists. Protests against repatriation have already taken place, led by Rakhine CSOs and monks. The Rohingya issue is likely to be used by political parties fighting the NLD, not only in Rakhine, but in other states and regions as well. In addition, the increased violence between the recently created Arakan Army[11] and the Tatmadaw in Rakhine State has increased the state's fractious politics. The Arakan Army has seen its popularity rise in central and northern Rakhine State, 'having captured the imagination of many Rakhine people through its pursuit of #ArakanDream2020 and the Way of Rakhita, which is a call for a nationwide armed revolution by the Rakhine people in 2020' (Callahan and Myo Zaw Oo, 2019: 21).

Education – the 'litmus test' by which many in the country will judge the reforms in the long run – was originally expected to play a significant role in the pre-election discussion.[12] In fact, the PACE survey mentioned earlier asked those who indicated Myanmar is going in the right direction the reasons why. A large percentage (42 per cent) indicated infrastructure and government services, 30 per cent said administration and governance and 16 per cent pointed to the economy and 36 per cent mentioned better education (PACE, 2019: 56). When PACE's enumerators asked those who responded that things are going in the wrong direction the reasons why, 39 per cent said bad education (PACE, 2019: 57). Education is seen as a key issue. Most families have a link to a school or another education institution through their children, or as young adults through their studies and training. Ordinary families can directly evaluate what has changed and others, more removed from the sector, can also follow changes in public education carefully as it has become an important press item. This is why the MoE saw the MTR report as such an important document and why it needed to show progress against the NESP.

However, the COVID-19 epidemic has dampened the post-MTR education reforms. As of 19 April 2020, Yangon imposed a night-time curfew (10 pm–7 am) and a stay-at-home order on several townships – in the first instance, until mid June 2020.[13] Shan, Karen, and Kachin States and Mandalay, Sagaing, Ayeyarwaddy, and Bago Regions have also adopted restrictions including limiting gatherings to a certain number of people.[14] As schools and universities are closed to reduce the chance of contagion, and citizens have been asked to avoid unnecessary outings, the whole nature of the build-up to the elections is changing. The government has created the country's first-ever joint civil–military 'Emergency Response Committee' led by military-nominated Vice President U Myint Swe to enforce community quarantines and social distancing initiatives. The military has been using social media to show that it is better prepared to deal with a crisis such as COVID-19 than the civilian administration.[15] The government on its side put together a COVID-19 Comprehensive Relief Plan (CCRP) and Daw Aung San Suu Kyi is also using social media to underpin her central and visible role in the crisis.[16] COVID-19 seems to have become a key election issue, eclipsing others that might have played a larger role in the nationwide debate.

In light of this, the MoE has put developing NESP 2 on hold, till it has a clearer picture of when and how schools will reopen in the second half of the year.[17] Development agencies have sent most staff back to their home countries, and many programmes have either slowed down or paused, as they cannot deliver the required changes remotely. COVID-19, despite not having hit Myanmar as hard as was initially feared,[18] also means that the whole election campaign focus moves away from education, to the other basic public service of health.

The date for the polls has been set as 8 November 2020. The UEC has tried to reassure political parties that the pandemic will not result in a rescheduling. However, political parties are concerned that the government should first focus on controlling the spread of the virus and that the virus might also result in fewer voters taking part in the elections, and that it could affect election preparations and management. Political parties, therefore, have asked to be consulted in any possible changes to the polls.[19]

This ends a tumultuous five years in which both much and little has changed. It is a positive development that ministries such as the MoE are aware of the country's challenges, and that these show up in the policy documents. It has to be hoped that the next administration will take up the challenge of translating these policies into a reality for the Myanmar people.

Notes

1. It should be remembered that the NESP is not an NLD document but was conceived under the President Thein Sein USDP Government as a result of the CESR. The NLD took the original NESP and only made minor amendments before it became official Myanmar education policy and the backbone of the reforms.
2. In the Myanmar context, it is unhelpful to think of this in class terms; the military, though part of this structure, is not necessarily middle class.
3. Most of the issues related to in-service training are dealt with in the next section on teacher education.
4. Prior to the new system, when asked, children used to be able to simply recite the lesson back to their parents.
5. Wealthier families opt for private education that can lead to higher education abroad: 'In Yangon, the number of international schools, seen by the elite as a pathway to prestigious foreign universities, rose from 25 in 2012 to 43 by November 2016. Despite soaring tuition fees, enrolment increased by more than 75 per cent in the same period, from 6,700 to 11,800, with locals making up 80 per cent of the intake.' See By Shuyin, 2017.
6. Asian Development Bank (ADB) (2019) 'Support to Myanmar in Strengthening Education and Equipping Youth for Employment' Project Summary Sheet. https://www.adb.org/projects/48431-003/main.

Annex 1 of this document shows that less than 20 per cent of Myanmar's entrants to non-agricultural wage jobs have a Bachelors degree (or higher) and 47 per cent have completed secondary education, some other training or diploma. ADB supporting secondary education and TVET reforms over 15 years including the Equipping Youth for Employment Project (EYE), implemented by the MoE and Ministry of Industry in collaboration with other agencies June 2017–December 2022.

7   CESR presentation on skills gap. Chris A. Spohr (2015) 'Skills for Decent Jobs and a Modern Myanmar: Challenges and Emerging Directions', Discussion with the Confederation of Trade Unions – Myanmar (CTUM) and Solidarity Center, 13 November 2015. Presented by Chris A. Spohr, Principal Social Sector Specialist, ADB Myanmar Resident Mission in Naypyitaw.
8   Budgeted expenditure increased as a share of GDP for MoE from 1.57 per cent of GDP in 2014–5 to 1.88 per cent of GDP. Despite this increase, actual expenditure by MoE as share of GDP has remained stagnant at around 1.7 per cent of GDP. […] The gap between planned and actual expenditure reflects growing challenges of budget execution. Beck et al. 2018.
9   Excluding military personnel and their families as well as those in the five townships of the Wa special region, http://www.xinhuanet.com/english/2019-11/28/c_138589570.htm.
10 https://asiatimes.com/2019/12/suu-kyi-no-shoo-in-at-myanmars-2020-polls/.
11 The AA is an ethnic Rakhine armed group that has its sights set on autonomy from Myanmar by 2020, as laid out in its Arakan Dream 2020 mobilisation campaign.
12 Private discussions with NLD MPs and ministry personnel in 2018 and 2019.
13 Excluding essential workers.
14 https://www.csis.org/programs/southeast-asia-program/southeast-asia-covid-19-tracker-0#Myanmar.
15 The Tatmadaw has also announced a ceasefire until the of end August 2020 to help deal with COVID-19, but not including Rakhine.
16 Kyaw San Wai, Myanmar and COVID-19, 1 May 2020. https://thediplomat.com/2020/05/myanmar-and-covid-19/.
17 Myanmar reopened high schools end of July 2020. However, schools had to close again end August 2020 because of a spike in COVID-19 cases.
18 At the time of writing, end of May 2020.
19 https://www.rfa.org/english/news/myanmar/election-timing-05052020171626.html.

References

Achilles, V. J. (2005) 'Das bildungswesen in Birma/Myanmar: Erfahrungen zum engagement im bildungsbereich'. In U. Bey (ed.), *Armut Im Land der Pagoden*. Focus Asien 26. http://www.asienhaus.de/public/archiv/focus26-031.pdf. Accessed 5 March 2020.

Altbach, P. G. (2009) 'Peripheries and centers: Research universities in developing countries'. *Asia Pacific Education Review* 10 (1), 15–27. https://doi.org/10.1007/s12564-009-9000-9.

Alvaredo, F., Chancel, L., Piketty, T., Saez, E. and Zucman, G. (2018) *World Inequality Report 2018*. World Inequality Lab. https://wir2018.wid.world/files/download/wir2018-full-report-english.pdf. Accessed 23 February 2020.

Anderson, B. (1983) *Imagined Communities: Reflections on the origin and spread of nationalism*. London, UK: Verso.

Apple, M. W. (2004) 'Creating difference: Neo-liberalism, neo-conservatism and the politics of educational reform'. *Educational Policy* 18 (1), 12–44. https://doi.org/10.1177/0895904803260022.

Arnhold, N., Bekker, J., Kersh, N., Mcleish, E. A. and Phillips, D. (1998) *Education for Reconstruction: The regeneration of educational capacity following national upheaval*. Wallingford, Oxfordshire: Symposium Books.

Asian Development Bank (ADB). (2016) *Myanmar: Support for education sector planning*. Project Number: 46369-001. https://www.adb.org/sites/default/files/project-document/185972/46369-001-tcr.pdf. Accessed 16 February 2020.

Asian Development Bank (ADB). (2019) *Asian Development Bank (ADB) Support to Myanmar in Strengthening Education and Equipping Youth for Employment*. Project Summary Sheet. https://www.adb.org/sites/default/files/project-documents/47177/47177-001-46369-001-dpta-en.pdf. Accessed 22 May 2020.

Aung Htung and Lall, M., New Nwe San, Ye Htut Naing, Theint Theint Myat, Lwin Thet Thet Khaing, Swann Lynn Htet and Yin Nyein Aye. (2015) *The Legitimacy of the Current Peace Process in Myanmar*. Yangon and Bangkok: Myanmar Egress and FNS.

Aung-Thwin, M. (1985) *Pagan: The origins of modern Burma*. Honolulu: University of Hawaii Press.

Ball, J. (2011) *Enhancing Learning of Children from Diverse Language Backgrounds: Mother tongue-based bilingual or multilingual education in the early years*. Paris: UNESCO.

Ball, J. (2014) *Children Learn Better in Their Mother Tongue*. Global Partnership for Education. https://www.globalpartnership.org/blog/children-learn-better-their-mother-tongue. Accessed 10 March 2020.

Bawk La. (2017) *Broken Future: A study of ethnic Kachin students in the current Myanmar education system*. Naushawng Development Institute. https://naushawng.org/wp-content/uploads/2019/03/Broken-future-by-Bawk-Lare-edit.pdf. Accessed 11 March 2020.

Beck, H. A., Rahardja, S., Thi Da Myint., Nair, A., Guo, F., Aka Kyaw Min Maw, Reungsri, T. and Kessler, M. (2018) 'Navigating Risks'. *Myanmar Economic Monitor*. Washington, D.C.: World Bank Group. http://documents.worldbank.org/curated/en/986461544542633353/pdf/132847-REVISED-MEM-Final.pdf. Accessed 21 May 2020.

Benson, C. (2004) 'The importance of mother tongue-based schooling for educational quality'. Paper commissioned for *EFA Global Monitoring Report 2005, The Quality Imperative*. https://unesdoc.unesco.org/ark:/48223/pf0000146632.

Borg, S., Clifford, I. and Khaing Phyu Htut. (2018) 'Having an EfECT: Professional development for teacher educators in Myanmar'. *Teaching and Teacher Education* 72, 75–86. https://doi.org/10.1016/j.tate.2018.02.010.

Brady, P. and CESR. (2014) *Myanmar Comprehensive Education Sector Review (CESR) Phase 2: Analysis of the impact of ASEAN integration on labor markets and skill needs in Myanmar.* (Final Version, 25 October 2014). https://www.adb.org/sites/default/files/project-document/202046/46369-001-tacr-06.pdf. Accessed 2 March 2020.

Bray, M., Kobakhidze, M. N. and Kwo, O. (2019) *Shadow Education in Myanmar: Private supplementary tutoring and its policy implications.* CERC Monograph Series in Comparative and International Education and Development No. 13, Hong Kong: UNESCO. https://cerc.edu.hku.hk/announcement/policies-for-shadow-education-in-myanmar/

British Academy and École Française d'Extrême-Orient. (2015) *Language Choice in Higher Education: Challenges and opportunities.* Summary of a workshop discussion organised by the British Academy and École Française d'Extrême-Orient, Yangon, Myanmar. https://www.thebritishacademy.ac.uk/documents/1066/Myanmar_Workshop_Report_English.pdf. Accessed 2 March 2020.

British Council (BC). (2015) *English for Education College Trainers (EfECT) Project: Needs analysis 2015.* Yangon: British Council.

British Council (BC). (2016) *English for Education College Trainers (EfECT) Project: Mid-project report 2015–2016.* Yangon: British Council. https://www.britishcouncil.org.mm/sites/default/files/english_for_education_college_trainers_efect_project_mid-project_report_2015-2016.pdf. Accessed 7 March 2020.

Brown, P. (2001) 'Skill formation in the twenty-first century'. In P. Brown, A. Green and H. Lauder (eds), *High Skills: Globalisation, competitiveness, and skill formation*. Oxford: Oxford University Press, 1–55.

Brown, P. and Lauder, H. (2003) *Globalisation and the Knowledge Economy: Some observations on recent trends in employment, education and the labour market.* Working Paper Series: Paper 43. Cardiff University. http://orca.cf.ac.uk/78087/1/wrkgpaper43.pdf. Accessed 23 February 2020.

Burnet Institute Myanmar (BIM) and Monastic Education Development Group (MEDG). (2014) *Monastic Schools in Myanmar: A baseline study.* Burnet Institute Myanmar and Monastic Education Development Group. https://www.themimu.info/sites/themimu.info/files/documents/Report_Monastic_Schools_Baseline_Survey_BIMM-MEDG_2014.pdf. Accessed 25 February 2020.

Callahan, M. P. (2003) 'Language policy in modern Burma'. In M. Brown and S. Ganguly (eds), *Fighting Words: Language policy and ethnic relations in Asia*. Cambridge, Mass.: MIT Press, 143–75.

Callahan, M. P. (2004) 'Making Myanmars: Languages, territory, and belonging in post-socialist Burma'. In J. S. Migdal (ed.), *Boundaries and Belonging: States and societies in the struggle to shape identities and local practices*, Cambridge, UK: Cambridge University Press, 99–120.

Callahan, M. P. (2017) 'Distorted, Dangerous Data? "Lumyo" in the 2014 Myanmar Population and Housing Census'. *Sojourn: Journal of Social Issues in Southeast Asia,* 32 (2), 452–78.

Callahan, M. P. and Myo Zaw Oo. (2019) 'Myanmar's 2020 elections and conflict dynamics'. *Peaceworks* (No. 146). Washington, D.C.: United States Institute of Peace https://reliefweb.int/sites/reliefweb.int/files/resources/pw_146-myanmars_2020_election_and_conflict_dynamics.pdf. Accessed 22 May 2020.

Castells, M. (1994) 'The university system: Engine of development in the new world economy'. In J. Salmi and A. Verspoor (eds) *Revitalizing Higher Education*. Oxford: Pergamon, 14–40.

Channon, D. (2017) 'Exploring the Dynamics of Higher Education Curriculum Change in Myanmar: A case study of internationalisation in an English department'. Unpublished EdD thesis, UCL Institute of Education.

Charney, M. (2006) *Powerful Learning: Buddhist literati and the throne in Burma's last dynasty, 1752–1885.* Ann Arbor: The University of Michigan, Center for South and Southeast Asian Studies.

Cheesman, N. (2017) 'How in Myanmar "national races" came to surpass citizenship and exclude Rohingya'. *Journal of Contemporary Asia* 47 (2), 1–23. https://doi.org/10.1080/00472336.2017.1297476.

Cheesman, N. (2002) 'Legitimising the Union of Myanmar Through Primary School Textbooks'. Master's thesis, University of Western Australia. https://research-repository.uwa.edu.au/en/publications/legitimising-the-union-of-myanmar-through-primary-school-textbook. Accessed 7 February 2020.

Cheesman, N. (2003) 'School, state and sangha in Burma'. *Comparative Education,* 39 (1), 45–63. https://doi.org/10.1080/03050030302565.

Clifford, I. (2016) 'Agency, Aspirations and Culture in Relation to Pedagogical Change Amongst Myanmar Teacher Educators'. Unpublished MSc thesis.

Comprehensive Education Sector Review (CESR) Team. (2013) *Technical Annex on the Higher Education Subsector*. Myanmar Comprehensive Education Sector Review (CESR) Phase 1: Rapid assessment. http://www.cesrmm.org/assets/home/img/cesr-phase%201_rapid%20 assessment_higher%20ed%20subsector_technical%20annex_26mar13_for%20distrib_cln_newlogo.pdf. Accessed 11 March 2020.

Comprehensive Education Sector Review (CESR) Team. (2014) *Republic of the Union of Myanmar: Support for post-primary education development. Technical Annex on Secondary Education Curriculum, Textbooks, and Learner Assessment*. Myanmar Comprehensive Education Sector Review (CESR) Phase 2: In-Depth Analysis. ADB Project Number: 47177. https://www.adb.org/sites/default/files/project-document/204741/47177-001-tacr-05.pdf. Accessed 4 March 2020.

Condon, M. (2017) 'The Impact of Teacher Trainer Education on Women's Empowerment in Myanmar'. Unpublished MA dissertation, UCL Institute of Education.

Connell, R. (1993) *Schools and Social Justice*. Philadelphia, PA: Temple University Press.

Couch, D. (2019) 'The policy reassembly of Afghanistan's higher education system'. *Globalisation, Societies and Education* 17 (1), 44–60. https://doi.org/10.1080/14767724.2018.1523708.

Cummins, J. (2000) *Language, Power, and Pedagogy: Bilingual children in the crossfire*. Clevedon, England: Multilingual Matters.

Dekker, D., Person, K., Naw Khu Shee and Zin Ei Ei Win. (2018a) 'Field Visits Report: Needs analysis and design of a programme of capacity development support to partners for implementation of effective multilingual education'. Unpublished report. Myanmar Education Consortium (MEC).

Dekker, D., Person K., Naw Khu Shee, and Zin Ei Ei Win. (2018b) 'Future Forward: Programme plan for broad based capacity development support to ethnic partners for implementation of effective mother tongue-based education (Deliverable #4)'. Unpublished report. Myanmar Education Consortium (MEC).

Dekker, D., Kirk P., Naw Khu Shee, and Zin Ei Ei Win. (2018c) 'Needs Analysis and Design of a Programme of Capacity Development Support to Partners for Implementation of Effective Multilingual Education: Inception report'. Unpublished report. Myanmar Education Consortium (MEC).

Department for International Development (DFID). (2019) DFID 8478 Myanmar UK Partnership for Education (MUPE) Lot 1 – Component 1: Towards results in education and English (TREE) contract award. DFID. https://www.contractsfinder.service.gov.uk/Notice/3a7933c0-37e9-487e-9acf-c6ad6210cc53. Accessed 7 March 2020.

Department of Foreign Affairs and Trade (DFAT). (2017) *Strengthening Pre-Service Teacher Education in Myanmar Review Report*. STEM project and management response. DFAT. https://www.dfat.gov.au/sites/default/files/myanmar-strengthening-pre-service-teacher-education-stem-project-review.pdf. Accessed 7 March 2020.

Drinan, H. (2013) *Language in Education in Myanmar, with Specific Reference to English, Comprehensive Education Sector Review*. Unpublished report. British Council.

Drinan, H. and Zin Zin Win. (2017) 'A Situational Analysis of Teacher Education and Continuing Professional Development (TECPD) Approaches and Providers in Myanmar'. Unpublished report. Myanmar Education Consortium (MEC).

Edwards, N. (2018) 'How Important is Mother Tongue Education to the Chin Community in Myanmar?' Unpublished conference paper.

El Thae Thae Naing. (2013) 'Ministry to train ethnic minority language teachers'. *Myanmar Times*, 25 August 2013. https://www.mmtimes.com/national-news/7954-ministry-to-train-ethnic-minority-language-teachers.html. Accessed 1 July 2020.

Esson, J. and Wang, K. (2018) 'Reforming a university during political transformation: A case study of Yangon University in Myanmar'. *Studies in Higher Education* 43 (7): 1184–95. https://doi.org/10.1080/03075079.2016.1239250.

Ethnologue. 'Myanmar'. *Ethnologue Languages of the World*. https://www.ethnologue.com/country/MM. Accessed 12 April 2018.

Fawssett, S. and Gregson, J. (2016) *Investigation of Myanmar's Distance Education Sector and Proposals for Strengthening*. The Open University.

Fishman, J. A. (1973) *Language and Nationalism: Two integrative essays*. Rowley, MA: Newbury House.

Fullan, M. (2001) 'The dynamic forces of change'. In E. Polyzoi, M. Fullan and J. Anchan (eds), *Change Forces in Post-Communist Eastern Europe: Education in transition*. London and New York: Routledge Falmer, 3–10.

Fullerton, V. and French, B. (2019) *Myanmar Education Quality Improvement Program (My-EQIP) – Phase 1 Report: Organisational constraints analysis*. Department of Foreign Affairs and Trade, Australian Government.

Furnivall, J. (1938) 'The fashioning of leviathan', *Journal of the Burma Research Society* 29, 1–137.

Gamarnikow. E. (2009) 'Education in network society: Critical reflection'. In R. Cowen and A. Kazamias (eds), *International Handbook of Comparative Education*, London: Springer, 619–31.

Gellner, E. (1983) *Nations and Nationalism*. Ithaca, NY: Cornell University Press.

Gewirtz, S. (1997) 'Conceptualising social justice in education: Mapping the territory', *Journal of Education Policy* 13 (4): 469–84. https://doi.org/10.1080/0268093980130402.

Giroux, H. (2004) 'Public pedagogy and the politics of neo-liberalism: Making the political more pedagogical', *Policy Futures in Education* 2 (3): 494–503. https://doi.org/10.2304/pfie.2004.2.3.5.

Global Education and Monitoring Report Team. (2011) *The Hidden Crisis: Armed conflict and education*. EFA Global Monitoring Report, 2011. UNESCO. https://unesdoc.unesco.org/ark:/48223/pf0000190743. Accessed 22 February 2020.

Government of Myanmar (GoM). (2004) *Development of Education in Myanmar*. Yangon: Ministry of Education.

Government of Myanmar (GoM). (2008) Myanmar's Constitution https://www.constituteproject.org/constitution/Myanmar_2008.pdf?lang=en. Accessed 16 February 2020.

Government of Myanmar (GoM). (2014a) *National EFA Review Report*. Yangon: Ministry of Education. https://www.themimu.info/sites/themimu.info/files/documents/Report_Myanmar_National_EFA_Review_Report_30June2014.pdf. Accessed 8 February 2020.

Government of Myanmar (GoM). (2014b) *2014 National Education Law: Parliamentary Law No. 41*. https://www.burmalibrary.org/docs20/2014-09-30-National_Education_Law-41-en.pdf. Accessed 11 March 2020.

Government of Myanmar (GoM). (2017) *The 2014 Myanmar Population and Housing Census, Thematic Report on Education*. Department of Population, Ministry of Labour, Immigration and Population. http://www.dop.gov.mm/sites/dop.gov.mm/files/publication_docs/thematic_report_on_education.pdf. Accessed 3 March 2020.

Government of Myanmar (GoM) and DFAT. (2017) *Myanmar Education Quality Improvement Program (My-EQIP) Draft Design*. 28 June 2017. Unpublished.

Guyot, D., Nang Mao Ceng Cett, and Win Myat Thu. (2016) 'Schools popping up like mushrooms: A bilingual school, a cultural organization, and a nunnery'. Paper presented at the 12th International Burma Studies Conference, 6–9 October 2016.

Hanushek, E. (2013) 'Economic growth in developing countries: The role of human capital', *Economics of Education Review* 37: 204–12.

Hardman, F. C., Stoff, C., Hardman J. (Abd-Kadir) and Elliot, L. (2012) *Baseline Study: Child-centred approaches and teaching and learning practices in selected primary schools in child-friendly school-focused townships in Myanmar*. UNICEF. https://pure.york.ac.uk/portal/en/publications/baseline-study-childcentred-approaches-and-teaching-and-learning-practices-in-selected-primary-schools-in-childfriendly-schoolfocused-townships-in-myanmar(fee06629-fabe-4521-bcfd-1d1b1b64a14b).html.

Hatcher, R. (2001) 'Getting down to business: Schooling in the globalised economy', *Education and Social Justice* 3 (2): 45–59.

Herbert, P. M. (Compiler). (1991) *World Bibliographical Series, British Library Cataloguing in Publication Data*. Volume 132. Myanmar: Clio Press.

Heslop, L. (2019) 'Encountering internationalisation: Higher education and social justice in Myanmar'. PhD thesis, University of Sussex.

Higgins, S., Maber, E., Cardozo, M. L. and Shah, R. (2016) *The Role of Education in Peacebuilding Country Report: Myanmar*. Research Consortium on Education and Peacebuilding, University of Amsterdam. https://educationanddevelopment.files.wordpress.com/2014/11/myanmar-country-report-executive-summary-final-jun16.pdf. Accessed 19 February 2020.

Hill, D. and Rosskam, E. (eds) (2009). *The Developing World and State Education: Neoliberal Depredation and Egalitarian Alternatives*. New York: Routledge.

Houtman, G. (1999) *Mental Culture in Burmese Crisis Politics: Aung San Suu Kyi and the National League for Democracy*. Institute for the Study of Languages and Cultures of Asia and Africa, Tokyo University of Foreign Studies. http://www.burmalibrary.org/docs19/Houtman-1999-Mental_Culture_in_Burmese_Crisis_Politics.pdf. Accessed 8 February 2020.

Integrated Household Living Conditions Assessment (IHLCA) Project Technical Unit. (2011) *Integrated Household Living Conditions Survey in Myanmar (2009–2010): Poverty profile*. IHLCA Project Technical Unit, Yangon, Myanmar. https://www.undp.org/content/dam/myanmar/docs/FA1MMRPovertyProfile_Eng.pdf. Accessed 16 February 2020.

International Labour Organisation (ILO). (1989) *C169 – Indigenous and Tribal Peoples Convention, 1989 (No. 169)*. Geneva: ILO. https://www.ilo.org/dyn/normlex/en/f?p=NORMLEXPUB:12100:0::NO::P12100_ILO_CODE:C169. Accessed 10 March 2020.

Japan International Cooperation Agency (JICA). (2013) *Data Collection Survey on Education Sector in Myanmar: Final Report*. JICA. http://open_jicareport.jica.go.jp/pdf/12113635.pdf. Accessed 16 February 2020.

Japan International Cooperation Agency (JICA). (2017a). 'Introduction of New G1 Curriculum and Textbooks'. Press Release, JICA. https://www.jica.go.jp/myanmar/english/office/topics/press170526.html. Accessed 4 March 2020.

Japan International Cooperation Agency (JICA). (2017b) *Data Collection Survey on Civil Service System in Myanmar: Final report*. https://openjicareport.jica.go.jp/pdf/12301099.pdf. JICA. Accessed 7 March 2020.

Jaquet, C. (2015) *The Kachin Conflict: Testing the limits of the political transition in Myanmar*. Bangkok: Research Institute on Contemporary Southeast Asia. https://doi.org/10.4000/books.irasec.241.

Jolliffe, K. and Speers Mears, E. (2016) *Strength in Diversity: Towards universal education in Myanmar's ethnic areas*. The Asia Foundation. https://asiafoundation.org/wp-content/uploads/2016/10/Strength-in-Diversity-Toward-Universal-Education-Myanmar-Ethnic-Area.pdf. Accessed 24 February 2020.

Kamibeppu, T. and Chao, R. Y. (2017) 'Higher education and Myanmar's economic and democratic development'. *International Higher Education*, 88, 19–20. https://doi.org/10.6017/ihe.2017.88.9688.

Kandiko-Howson, C. and Lall, M. (2020). 'Higher education reform in Myanmar: Neoliberalism versus an inclusive developmental agenda'. *Globalisation, Societies and Education*, 18 (2), 109–24. https://doi.org/10.1080/14767724.2019.1689488.

Kapur, D. and Crowley, M. (2008). *Beyond the ABCs: Higher education and developing countries*. Working Paper No. 139. Center for Global Development. Accessed 23 February 2020. https://doi.org/10.2139/ssrn.1099934.

Kaung (1963) 'A survey of the history of education in Burma before the British conquest and after'. *Journal of the Burma Research Society*, 46 (2): 1–124.

Khan, I. (2014) 'Teachers' perceptions of the significance of local culture in foreign language learning'. *Journal of English Language and Literature*, 1 (3): 65–70.

Kheunsai, S. (2017) 'How I became Shan'. In A. South and M. Lall (eds), *Citizenship in Myanmar: Ways of being in and from Burma*. Chiang Mai: ISEAS, Singapore and Chiang Mai University Press, Thailand, 188–92.

Khin Yi. (1988) *The Dobáma Movement in Burma (1930–1938)*. Ithaca, NY: Cornell University, Southeast Asia Program.

Khit Myanmar Weekly. (2006) 'ILBC new class open in Taung Gyi and La Shore'. *Khit Myanmar Weekly* 3 (25). 17 March 2006.

Kosonen, K. (2005) 'Education in local languages: Policy and practice in South-East Asia'. In *First Language First: Community-based literacy programmes for minority language context in Asia*. Bangkok: UNESCO, 96–134.

Kosonen K. (2017) 'Language of instruction in Southeast Asia'. Paper commissioned for the *UNESCO 2017–8 Global Education Monitoring Report: Accountability in education: Meeting our commitments*. UNESCO. http://unesdoc.unesco.org/images/0025/002595/259576e.pdf. Accessed 11 March 2020.

Kosonen, K. (2019) 'Language education policy in Cambodia'. In A. Kirkpatrick and A. J. Liddicoat (eds), *The Routledge Handbook of Language Education Policy in Asia*. Abingdon: Routledge, 216–28.

Lall, M. (2009) 'Education in Myanmar: The interplay of state, civil society and business'. In M. Skidmore and T. Wilson (eds), *Dictatorship, Disorder and Decline in Myanmar*. Canberra: ANU E-Press, 127–50.

Lall, M. (2010) *Child Centred Learning and Teaching Approaches in Myanmar*. Yangon: Pyo Pin. http://marielall.com/wp/wp-content/uploads/CCA_research_report_by_Marie_Lall.pdf. Accessed 16 February 2020.

Lall, M. (2011) 'Pushing the child centred approach in Myanmar: The role of cross national policy networks and the effects in the classroom'. *Critical Studies in Education, 52 (3)*, 219–33. https://doi.org/10.1080/17508487.2011.604072.

Lall, M. (2015) *Becoming a Teacher in Myanmar (Part 1)*. Yangon: British Council.

Lall, M. (2016a) *Understanding Reform in Myanmar: People and society in the wake of military rule*. London: Hurst Publishers.

Lall, M. (2016b) *Becoming a Teacher in Myanmar (Part 2)*. Yangon: British Council.

Lall, M. (2016c) *Diversity in Education in Myanmar*. Yangon: Pyoe Pin.

Lall, M. (2017) 'Education – A renewed political battleground'. In A. Simpson, N. Farrelly and I. Holliday (eds), *Routledge Handbook of Contemporary Myanmar*. Routledge.

Lall, M. and Rao, S. (2011) 'Revisiting the equality debate in India and UK: Caste, race and class intersections in education'. In M. Lall and G. Nambissan (eds), *Education and Social Justice in the Era of Globalisation: India and the UK*. New Delhi: Routledge, 25–55

Lall, M. and South, A. (2013a) *Education, Conflict and Identity: Non-state ethnic education regimes in Burma*.

Lall, M. and South, A. (2013b) 'Comparing models of non-state ethnic education in Myanmar: The Mon and Karen national education regimes'. *Journal of Contemporary Asia, 44 (2)*, 298–321. https://doi.org/10.1080/00472336.2013.823534.

Lall, M. and South, A. (2018) 'Power dynamics of language and education policy in Myanmar's contested transition'. *Comparative Education Review, 62 (4)*, 482–502. https://doi.org/10.1086/699655.

Lall, M., Aung Htun, Nwe Nwe San, Theint Theint Myat and Yin Nyein Aye. (2016) *Myanmar Connecting Classrooms Pilot Baseline Research*. Yangon: British Council.

Lall, M., Nwe Nwe San, Theint Theint Myat, and Yin Nyein Aye. (2015) *Myanmar's Ethnic Parties and the 2015 Elections*. Yangon: EU and IMG.

Lall, M., South, A., Stenning, E. and Schroeder, T. with Aye Aye Tun, Edwards, J., Jolliffe, K., Schroeder, A., Lall, V., Mi Kun Chan Non, Aung Htun, Nangzing Lu Awn and Cin Khan Lian (2020) *From Conflict Towards Partnership Education – The Myanmar Education Partnership Project, Policy Note*. Yangon: World Bank.

Lall, M., Thei Su San, Nwe Nwe San, Thein Thein Myat and Lwin Thet Thet Khaing. (2013) *Teachers' Voice – What Education Reforms Does Myanmar Need?* Bangkok and Yangon: Myanmar Egress and FNS.

Lall, M., Thei Su San, Nwe Nwe San, Yeh Tut Naing, Thein Thein Myat, Lwin Thet Thet Khaing, Swann Lynn Htet, and Yin Nyein Aye. (2014) *Citizenship in Myanmar: Contemporary debates and challenges in light of the reform process*. Report for Myanmar Egress and FNS: Yangon and Bangkok. https://themimu.info/sites/themimu.info/files/documents/Academic_Article_Citizenship_in_Myanmar_Contemporary_Debates_and_Challenges_in_Light_of_the_Reform_Process_Lall_2014.pdf.

Leadership Foundation for Higher Education. (2016) *British Council Myanmar Needs Analysis*. British Council. https://www.britishcouncil.org/sites/default/files/myanmar_higher_education_leadership_needs_analysis_report.pdf. Accessed 12 March 2020.

Lenkova, P. (2015) *Conflict Sensitivity in Education Provision in Karen State*. Thabyay Education Foundation. http://www.burmalibrary.org/docs21/Thabyay-2015-Conflict_Sensitivity_in_education-karen-en-red.pdf. Accessed 11 March 2020.

Lo Bianco, J. (2016) *Myanmar Country Report: Language, education and social cohesion (LESC) initiative*. https://www.researchgate.net/publication/296334128_Myanmar_Country_Report_Language_Education_and_Social_Cohesion_LESC_Initiative/link/56e7450008ae4cbe4d42d590/download. Accessed 9 March 2020.

Lorch, J. (2007) 'Myanmar's civil society: A patch for the national education system? The emergence of civil society in areas of state weakness'. *Südostasien aktuell. Journal of Current Southeast Asian Affairs, 26 (3)*, 54–88. https://nbn-resolving.org/urn:nbn:de:0168-ssoar-336394. Accessed 25 February 2020.

Mackenzie, K. (2013) *Policy Insights for Higher Education: Recommendations for HE reform in Myanmar.* British Council, 16. https://www.britishcouncil.org/sites/default/files/policy_insights_for_higher_education.pdf. Accessed 11 March 2020.

Marginson, S. (2019) 'Limitations of human capital theory'. *Studies in Higher Education* 44 (2): 287–301. https://doi.org/10.1080/03075079.2017.1359823.

Margontier-Haynes, C. (2016) 'Language and Culture: Perceptions of the role mother tongue education can play in the preservation of Pa-O ethnic nationality culture in Myanmar'. Unpublished MA dissertation, UCL Institute of Education.

Marshall, C. (2000) 'Policy discourse analysis: Negotiating gender equity'. *Journal of Education Policy*, 15 (2): 125–56. https://doi.org/10.1080/026809300285863.

Marshall, T. H. (1950) *Citizenship and Social Class and Other Essays.* Cambridge: Cambridge University Press.

May San Yee. (2019) 'Upgrading of Education Colleges to Four-Year Degree Colleges', Presentation. *Higher Education Forum.* http://www.moe.gov.mm/. (In Myanmar language).

McCarthy, G. (2019) 'Democratic deservingness and self-reliance in contemporary Myanmar'. *Sojourn: Journal of Social Issues in Southeast Asia*, 34 (2), 327–65.

Mehta, N., Gray, M., Lall, M., Shah, P. and Sinha, K. (2014) 'An analysis of the delivery of social services in Mon State for children with focus on education: Final Report'. Yangon: UNICEF-Myanmar.

Metro, R. (2011) 'History Curricula and the Reconciliation of Ethnic Conflict: A collaborative project with Burmese migrants and refugees in Thailand'. PhD dissertation, Cornell University. https://core.ac.uk/reader/6103710.

Metro, R. (2017) 'Whose Democracy?: The university student protests in Burma/Myanmar 2014–2016'. In J. Millican (ed.), *Universities and Conflict: The role of higher education in peacebuilding and conflict.* London and New York: Routledge https://www.academia.edu/35138917/Whose_democracy_The_university_student_protests_in_Burma_Myanmar_2014-2016.

Metro, R. (2019) 'Center, Periphery, and Boundary in the New Myanmar Curriculum'. Paper presented at Myanmar Studies from Center, Periphery, and Boundary. International Symposium, 16–7 September 2019, Naypyitaw, Myanmar.

Milton, S. and Barakat, S. (2016) 'Higher education as the catalyst of recovery in conflict-affected societies'. *Globalisation, Societies and Education* 14 (3), 403–21. https://doi.org/10.1080/14767724.2015.1127749.

Ministry of Education (MoE). (1953) *Education in Burma: Before independence and after independence.* MoE. Rangoon: Office of the Superintendent, Government Printing and Stationery.

Ministry of Education (MoE). (2012) Education for All: Access to and quality of education in Myanmar. MoE.

Ministry of Education (MoE). (2014) *National EFA Review Report, March 2014.* https://www.themimu.info/sites/themimu.info/files/documents/Report_Myanmar_National_EFA_Review_Report_30June2014.pdf. MoE. Accessed 19 February 2020.

Ministry of Education (MoE). (2016) *National Education Strategic Plan 2016–21.* https://www.britishcouncil.org/sites/default/files/myanmar_national_education_strategic_plan_2016-21.pdf. MoE. Accessed 24 February 2020.

Ministry of Education (MoE). (2018) *Annual Performance Review Report FY 2017–18.* Yangon: MoE.

Ministry of Education (MoE). (2019a) *Myanmar National Educational Strategic Plan 2016–2021: Data gap analysis report.* April 2019. MoE and UNESCO.

Ministry of Education (MoE). (2019b) *Mid Term Review of the National Education Strategic Plan 2016–2021 Inception Report.* Submitted by the NESP MTR Team in November 2019. Nay Pyi Taw: MoE.

Ministry of Education (MoE). (2019c) *Annual Performance Review Report FY 2017–2018*, NESP, Nay Pyi Taw. MoE.

Ministry of Education (MoE). (2019d) Teacher Competency Standards Framework (TCSF) – Beginning Teachers. Draft Version 3.2. MoE. Ch5

Ministry of Education (MoE). (2020) *Mid Term Review NESP 2016–2021 Final Report.* Nay Pyi Taw: MoE.

Ministry of Education (MoE) and the Quality Basic Education Programme. (2016) *Multi-Level MoE Capacity Gap Assessment and Initial Targeted Capacity Building in Myanmar.* UNICEF.

Ministry of National Planning and Economic Development, Ministry of Health and UNICEF. (2011) *Myanmar Multiple Indicator Cluster Survey 2009–2010*. Nay Pyi Taw, Myanmar.

Min Zaw Soe, Aye Mya Swe, Nan Khin Moe Aye and Nan Htet Mon. (2017) *Reform of the Education System: Case study of Myanmar*. Regional Research Paper: Parliamentary Institute of Cambodia. https://www.pic.org.kh/images/2017Research/20170523%20Education_Reform_Myanmar_Eng.pdf. Accessed 8 February 2020.

Mizuno, K., Tokuda, Y. Ito, H. Win Tun, Ko Lay Win. and Thein Win. (2019) *Japanese Technical Cooperation Project for Curriculum Reform at Primary Level of Basic Education in Myanmar: Joint Mid-Term Review Report*. Japan International Cooperation Agency (JICA).

Mohanty, A. K. (2009) 'Multilingual education: A bridge too far?'. In T. Skutnabb-Kangas, R. Phillipson, A. Mohanty and M. Panda (eds), *Social Justice Through Multilingual Education*. Bristol: Multilingual Matters, 3–15.

Muta, H. (2015) *Evaluation Study on 'Having at Least Five Teachers at One School' Policy in 2014: Has the regional disparity in educational conditions diminished?* Yangon: Ministry of Education.

Myanmar Education Consortium (MEC) (2015) *Myanmar Education Consortium (MEC) Advocacy Strategy 2014–2016*. https://mecmigration.files.wordpress.com/2016/05/mec-advocacy-strategy-updated-march-2015.pdf. Accessed 27 February 2020.

Myanmar Education Consortium (MEC). (2017) *Myanmar Education Thematic Strategy*. MEC.

Myanmar Information Management Unit (MIMU). (2017) *Monastic education in Myanmar: Trends over the 5-year period from 2012–13 to 2016–17*. MIMU. https://www.themimu.info/sites/themimu.info/files/documents/Analysis_Trends_over_5_years_in_Monastic_Education_2012-13_vs_2016-17_30May2017.pdf. Accessed 25 February 2020.

Myanmar Information Management Unit (MIMU). (2018) *Vulnerability in Myanmar: A secondary data review of needs, coverage and gaps*. MIMU. http://themimu.info/sites/themimu.info/files/documents/Report_Vulnerability_in_Myanmar_HARP-MIMU_Jun2018_ENG_Online_version_low-res_0.pdf. Accessed 23 February 2020.

Myanmar Teacher Education Working Group. (2019) *Towards Results in Education and English*. https://docs.google.com/presentation/d/1mTHfHxCGbhsbjSYESV5KjcLASyHR89ME/edit#slide=id.p1. Accessed 7 March 2020.

Myint Aye Aye and Win Myo (2016) 'The Implementation of the Myanmar Teacher Competency Standards Framework'. *AsTEN Journal of Teacher Education*, 1(2), 16–23.

Myint Zaw Soe et al. (2017) *Year 2 Phase 1 and Phase 2 Qualitative Assessment, Myanmar School Grants and Stipends Programs*. Yangon: Save the Children.

Myo Thant 'Upper House passes Private School Bill allowing ethnic language classes', *Mizzima*, 8 September 2011. http://mizzimaenglish.blogspot.com/2011/09/upper-house-passes-private-school-bill.html. Accessed 1 July 2020.

Naidoo, R. (2007) 'Higher education as a global commodity: The perils and promises for developing countries'. *The Observatory on Borderless Higher Education*, 14 (2), 1–19.

National League for Democracy (NLD). (2015) *National League for Democracy 2015 Election Manifesto – Authorised Translation*. NLD. https://www.burmalibrary.org/docs21/NLD_2015_Election_Manifesto-en.pdf. Accessed 23 February 2020.

Naw Say Phaw. (2008) 'New curriculum excludes General Aung San'. *Democratic Voice of Burma*, 26 June 2008. https://sanooaung.wordpress.com/2008/06/27/new-curriculum-excludes-general-aung-san/. Accessed 4 March 2020.

New Light of Myanmar. (2001) 'Introduction of a Single Democracy System to All Countries with Different Backgrounds Impossible: Special refresher course No. 43 for basic education teachers opens'. *New Light of Myanmar*, 18 January 2001.

New Light of Myanmar. (2011) 'Only Education Can Lead to Goal of Reaching Top. Vice-President Dr. Sai Mauk Kham Inspects Mandalay University'. *New Light of Myanmar*, 28 July 2011, 16. https://www.burmalibrary.org/sites/burmalibrary.org/files/obl/docs11/NLM2011-07-28.pdf. Accessed 7 July 2020.

Novelli, M., Cardozo, M. L. and Smith, A. (2015) *A Theoretical Framework for Analysing the Contribution of Education to Sustainable Peacebuilding: 4Rs in conflict-affected contexts*. University of Amsterdam. https://educationanddevelopment.files.wordpress.com/2014/11/theoretical-framework-jan15.pdf. Accessed 10 March 2020.

Ohnmar Tin and Stenning, E. (2015) *Situation Analysis of the Monastic Education System in Myanmar Final Report*. Myanmar Education Consortium (MEC). https://mecmigration.files.

wordpress.com/2016/05/mec-monastic-education-analysis-report-july-20151.pdf. Accessed 25 February 2020.

Olssen, M., Codd, J. and O'Neill, A-M. (2004) *Education Policy: Globalisation, citizenship and democracy*. London: Sage.

Olssen, M. and Peters, M. A. (2005) 'Neoliberalism, higher education and the knowledge economy: From the free market to knowledge capitalism'. *Journal of Education Policy*, 20 (3), 313–45. https://doi.org/10.1080/02680930500108718.

Organisation for Economic Cooperation and Development (OECD). (1991) *Principles for Evaluation of Development Assistance*. Development Assistance Committee. OECD. http://www.oecd.org/development/evaluation/2755284.pdf. Accessed 19 February 2020.

Ouane, A. (2003) *Towards a Mutilingual Culture of Education*. Hamburg: UNESCO Institute of Education. https://uil.unesco.org/literacy/multilingual-research/towards-multilingual-culture-education.

Oxford Policy Management (OPM). (2019) *AERS Report: Inception study on the factors and processes that shape Myanmar assessment and examination realities*. Report compiled by Gregory, K., Saw, Khun Thuza, Hla, Kyaw Zan, Latt, Kyi Zaw and Myoe for OPM.

Peace Interfaith Initiative Myanmar. (2015) *Informal Education and Child Care in Faith based Institutions in Yangon Division 20/02/09*, 23.

People's Alliance for Credible Elections (PACE). (2019) *Citizens' Political Preferences for 2020*. Yangon. https://www.pacemyanmar.org/. Accessed 22 May 2020.

Pyoe Pin (2014) *The Political Economy of Basic Education in Myanmar*. Yangon: Pyoe Pin.

REACH. (2015) *Joint Education Sector Needs Assessment in North Rakhine State, Myanmar*, PLAN International.

Rizvi, F. and Lingard, B. (2010) *Globalising Educational Policy*. London: Routledge, Taylor and Francis Group.

Salem-Gervais, N. (2018) 'Teaching Ethnic Languages, Cultures and Histories in Government Schools Today: Great opportunities, giant pitfalls? (Part I)'. *Tea Circle*, 1 October 2018. https://teacircleoxford.com/2018/10/01/teaching-ethnic-languages-cultures-and-histories-in-government-schools-today-great-opportunities-giant-pitfalls-part-i/ Accessed 9 March 2020.

Salem-Gervais, N. and Metro R. (2012) 'A textbook case of nation-building: The evolution of history curricula in Myanmar'. *Journal of Burma Studies*, 16 (1), 27–78. https://doi.org/10.1353/jbs.2012.0003.

Salem-Gervais, N. and Raynaud, M. (2019a) 'Ethnic Language Teaching's Decentralisation Dividend'. *Frontier Myanmar*, 18 March 2019. https://frontiermyanmar.net/en/ethnic-language-teachings-decentralisation-dividend. Accessed 10 March 2020.

Salem-Gervais, N. and Raynaud, M. (2019b) 'Promising Developments and Daunting Challenges in Using Ethnic Minority Languages in Formal Education (Part II)'. *Tea Circle*, 24 September 2019. https://teacircleoxford.com/2019/09/24/promising-developments-and-daunting-challenges-in-using-ethnic-minority-languages-in-formal-education-part-ii/. Accessed 10 March 2020.

Salem-Gervais, N. and Raynaud, M. (2020) *Teaching Ethnic Minority Languages in Government Schools and Developing the Local Curriculum: Elements of decentralization in language-in-education policy*. Yangon, Myanmar: Konrad-Adenauer Stiftung Ltd. Myanmar Representative Office. https://www.themimu.info/sites/themimu.info/files/documents/Report_Teaching_Ethnic_Minority_Languages_In_Government_Schools1.pdf.

San Wai Kyaw. (2020) 'Myanmar and COVID-19'. *The Diplomat*, 1 May 2020. https://thediplomat.com/2020/05/myanmar-and-covid-19/. Accessed 22 May 2020.

Shalom (Nyein Foundation). (2011) 'Myanmar Language Learning Levels of Ethnic Nationality Children with Different Levels of Burmese Language Exposure'. Unpublished DRAFT report. Shalom (Nyein Foundation).

Shuyin. (2017) 'Breathing New Life into Myanmar's Monastic Schools'. *Buddhistdoor Global*, 19 May 2017. https://www.buddhistdoor.net/features/breathing-new-life-into-myanmars-monastic-schools. Accessed 21 May 2020.

SIL. (2018) 'Needs Analysis and Design of a Programme of Capacity Development Support to Partners for Implementation of Effective Multilingual Education'. Unpublished report. Yangon: Myanmar Education Consortium.

Silverstein, J. (1977) *Burma: Military Rule and the Politics of Stagnation*. Ithaca and London: Cornell University Press.

Smith, D. E. (1965) *Religion and Politics in Burma*. Princeton, NJ: Princeton University Press.

Smith, M. (1999) *Burma: Insurgency and the politics of ethnicity*. London: Zed Books.

South, A. (2003) *Mon Nationalism and Civil War in Burma: The golden sheldrake*. London: Routledge.

South, A. (2018) *Protecting civilians in the Kachin borderlands, Myanmar: Key threats and local responses*. HPG Working Paper. London: Humanitarian Policy Group. http://www.ashleysouth.co.uk/files/AS%20Kachin-ODI%20Dec%202018.pdf. Accessed 11 March 2020.

South, A. and Lall, M. (2016a) 'Language, education and the peace process in Myanmar'. *Contemporary Southeast Asia*, 38 (1), 128–53. https://doi.org/10.1355/csa.2016.0009.

South, A. and Lall, M. (2016b) *Schooling and Conflict: Ethnic education and mother tongue-based teaching in Myanmar*. Policy Dialogue Brief 15. The Asia Foundation. http://asiafoundation.org/wp-content/uploads/2016/12/Policy-Brief_Schooling-and-Conflict-Ethnic-Education-and-Mother-Tongue-Based-Teaching-in-Myanmar_ENG.pdf. Accessed 11 March 2020.

South, A. and Lall, M. (2016c) *Schooling and Conflict: Ethnic education and mother tongue based teaching in Myanmar*. The Asia Foundation. https://asiafoundation.org/resources/pdfs/SchoolingConflictENG.pdf. Accessed 9 March 2020.

Stenning, E. (2018) *Independent Review of QBEP's Child Friendly Schools/Language Enrichment Programme In-Service Teacher Training Programme: Informing the design of a harmonised and scalable in-service teacher training and continuous professional development scheme in Myanmar*. UNICEF.

Stigler, J. and Hiebert, J. (2007) *The Teaching Gap: Best ideas from the world's teachers for improving education in the classroom*. New York: The Free Press.

Stokke, K., Vakulchuk, R. and Øverland, Indra. (2018) *Myanmar: A political economy analysis*. Norwegian Institute of International Affairs. https://reliefweb.int/sites/reliefweb.int/files/resources/Myanmar_-_A_Political_Economy_Analysis_-_Norwegian_Institute_of_International_Affairs_2018.pdf. Accessed 23 February 2020.

Su Myat Mon. (2019) 'Civics education in primary schools is a lesson in discrimination', *Frontier Myanmar*, 5 February 2019. https://frontiermyanmar.net/en/civics-education-in-primary-schools-is-a-lesson-in-discrimination/. Accessed 19 February 2020.

Sweetland, S. (1996) 'Human capital theory: Foundations of a field of inquiry'. *Review of Educational Research*, 66 (3), 341–59. https://doi.org/10.3102/00346543066003341.

Sy, S. (2013) *Republic of the Union of Myanmar: Support for education sector planning – Technical Annex on the Secondary Education Subsector. Myanmar Comprehensive Education Sector Review (CESR) Phase 1: Rapid Assessment*. ADB Project Number: 46369. https://www.adb.org/sites/default/files/project-document/79489/46369-001-tacr-02.pdf. Accessed 16 February 2020.

Taylor, S., Rizvi, F., Lingard, B. and Henry, M. (1997) *Educational Policy and the Politics of Change*. London: Routledge.

Thant Myint-U. (2001) *The Making of Modern Burma*. New York: Cambridge University Press.

Thaung Htut. (1980) *Myanmar raing gnan phongyi kyaung pyinnyayay hamaing (History of Monastic Education in Burma)*. MA thesis, Rangoon University. Rangoon: Ohn Pin Press.

The Border Consortium (TBC). (2015) *The Border Consortium Programme Report, January to June 2015*. The Border Consortium. Accessed 11 March 2020.

The Irrawaddy. (2015) 'Timeline of Student Protests Against Education Law'. *The Irrawaddy*, 10 March 2015. https://www.irrawaddy.com/news/burma/timeline-of-student-protests-against-education-law.html. Accessed 2 March 2020.

Thein Lwin. (2017) 'Comments on the National Education Strategic Plan (2016–2021) of the Ministry of Education, Myanmar'. Unpublished letter dated 10 March 2017.

Thein Lwin. (2000) *'Education in Burma (1945–2000)'*, Second Edition. https://www.burmalibrary.org/en/education-in-burma-1945-2000. Accessed 6 February 2020.

Thornton, B. and Tolmer, Z. (2017) *'Strengthening Pre-Service Teacher Education in Myanmar – Review Report'*. Prepared for DFAT. https://www.dfat.gov.au/sites/default/files/myanmar-strengthening-pre-service-teacher-education-stem-project-review.pdf. Accessed 7 March 2020.

Tonkin, D. (2007) 'The 1990 elections in Myanmar: Broken promises or a failure of communication?'. *Contemporary Southeast Asia*, 29 (1), 33–54. https://www.jstor.org/stable/25798813?seq=1.

UNESCO-IBE. (2006/7) 'Myanmar: Principles and general objectives of education'. *World Data on Education*, 6th edition. UNESCO–IBE. http://www.ibe.unesco.org/fileadmin/user_upload/archive/Countries/WDE/2006/ASIA_and_the_PACIFIC/Myanmar/Myanmar.pdf. Accessed 7 February 2020.

UNESCO. (2016) *Education College Curriculum Review, Strengthening Pre-service Teacher Education in Myanmar (STEM) Programme*. Yangon: UNESCO.

UNESCO. (2019a) *Myanmar participation in education*. Montreal: UNESCO Institute of Statistics. http://uis.unesco.org/en/country/mm. Accessed 2 March 2020.

UNESCO. (2019b) *Strengthening Pre-Service Teacher Education in Myanmar (STEM) Phase II*.; https://opendata.unesco.org/project/XM-DAC-41304-529MYA1001. Accessed 7 March 2020.

UNICEF. (2015) *Meeting the Humanitarian Needs of Children: Fundraising concept notes*. UNICEF.

UNICEF. (2016) *Final Performance Evaluation of QBEP's School-based In-service Teacher Education Pilot Programme: Final Report September 2015–January 2016*. Yangon: UNICEF. https://www.unicef.org/evaldatabase/files/SITE_Revised_Final_Report_FINAL_Edited_Myanmar_2016-012.pdf.

UNICEF. (2017) *QBEP'S Influence in the Classroom: Key findings on teacher behaviour and student learning*. Yangon: UNICEF.

UNICEF. (2018) *Myanmar 2018 Education Budget Brief*. Yangon: UNICEF. https://www.unicef.org/myanmar/media/1901/file/Myanmarpercent202018percent20Educationpercent20Budgetpercent20Brief.pdf. Accessed 16 February 2020.

United Nations. (1992) *Declaration on the Rights of Persons Belonging to National or Ethnic, Religious and Linguistic Minorities*. Office of the High Commissioner for Human Rights (UN Human Rights). (OHCHR). http://www.ohchr.org/EN/ProfessionalInterest/Pages/Minorities.aspx. Accessed 10 March 2020.

United Nations. (2007) *United Nations Declaration on the Rights of Indigenous Peoples*. United Nations. https://www.un.org/development/desa/indigenouspeoples/wp-content/uploads/sites/19/2018/11/UNDRIP_E_web.pdf. Accessed 10 March 2020.

Wolf, A. (2002) *Does Education Matter? Myths About Education and Economic Growth*. London: Penguin Business.

World Bank. (2018a) *Government expenditure on education, total (% of GDP) – Myanmar 2017*. https://data.worldbank.org/indicator/SE.XPD.TOTL.GD.ZS?locations=MM. Accessed 16 February 2020.

World Bank. (2018b) *Proposed Additional Financing and Restructuring From the Myanmar Partnership Multi-donor Trust Fund. Report No: PAD1782*. World Bank. http://documents.worldbank.org/curated/en/767591550129655680/pdf/PAD1782-PJPR-PUBLIC-Project-paper-Myanmar-AF-DFSP-P157231-12-04-2018-for-printing.pdf. Accessed 18 February 2020.

Wright, K. and Stoakes, G. (2017) *HEA Report to the Ministry of Education of the Government of the Republic of the Union of Myanmar*. York, UK: HEA.

Wrigley, T. (2007) 'Rethinking education in an era of globalisation'. *Journal for Critical Education Policy Studies Online*, 5 (2). http://www.jceps.com/wp-content/uploads/PDFs/05-2-01.pdf. Accessed 23 February 2020.

Young, I. M. (1990) *Justice and the Politics of Difference*. Princeton: Princeton University Press.

Young, I. M. (2005) 'Five faces of oppression'. In A. Cudd and R. Andreasen (eds) *Feminist Theory: A Philosophical Anthology*. Oxford, UK and Malden, Massachusetts: Blackwell Publishing 91–104.

Zobrist, B. (2015) *Mapping Teaching-Learning and Operational Experiences in Fifty Monastery Schools Across Myanmar*. A project of Pyoe Pin Programme, Myanmar Youth Forum and Phaung Daw Oo Basic Integrated Monastic High School. https://www.academia.edu/2589750/Mapping_Teaching-Learning_and_Operational_Experiences_in_Fifty_Monastery_Schools_Across_Myanmar. Accessed 25 February 2020.

Zobrist, B. and McCormick, P. (2017) 'Primary and secondary education in Myanmar: Challenges facing current reforms'. In L. H. Guan (ed.), *Education and Globalization in Southeast Asia: Issues and Challenges*, Singapore: ISEAS, 166–94.

Zoellner, H. B. (2007) 'Zeitleiste. Daten zur geschichte Mynamars/Birmas unter besonderer berücksichtigung der entwicklung des bildungswesens'. In H. Geiger (ed.), *Myanmar. Bildung und Entwicklung in einem multiethnischen Staat*. Bonn, Köllen Druck and Verlag, 20–21.

Index

academic freedom 143
access to education 61–5, 101, 105, 105, 131, 145–50, 154–5, 204, 277, 280
agency, lack, of 9
aid programmes 9, 16, 152, 246
alternative education systems 26, 239, 264
Amyotha Huttaw Education Promotion Committee 80
Anawrahta, King 102
Arakan Army 282–3
assessment practices 90–1, 115–16, 276
Association of South-East Asian Nations (ASEAN) 150–1, 164
Aung Htung 202
Aung Min 165–6
Aung San, General 38
Aung San Suu Kyi 1–6, 9–10, 22, 58, 70–1, 141–3, 273–4, 281–3
Aung-Thwin, M. 102, 127
Aung Tun Thet 71
Australia 65, 84, 185–8
autonomy
  academic 11, 134, 137, 140–4, 153–5, 184
  for schools 60
Aye Myint 93, 165

Bachelor of Education degree 160
Bamar ethnicity 36, 39, 91–2, 126, 171, 198
basic education
  aims of 36–7
  reform of 85–92
'block teaching' 162–3
Borg, Simon 185
British colonialism 31, 102–3, 139
Brown, P. 10
Buddhism 9, 23, 35–7, 101, 110–11, 115, 240
budgets for schools 60, 74–5
'Burmanisation' 34–7, 199–200, 204, 240–2, 266
Burma's change of name to Myanmar 37
Burmese language 25, 31–6, 70, 159, 165, 184, 197, 219–26, 229, 240, 244, 255, 258, 264, 268
Burnet Institute Myanmar (BIM) 106

Callahan, M.P. 37–8, 205, 281–2
capacity-building 183
'cascade' model 112–13, 121, 182, 276
Census data 201, 210–16
change agents 18
changes in the last five years 284

Charmey, Michael 35
Cheesman, N. 34–9, 103
child-centred approaches (CCAs) to teaching and learning 22–3 30, 42–7, 87, 101, 111–22, 165, 173–5, 182–4
'child-friendly' schools 40
civics education 92
civil service 9, 167
civil society organisations (CSOs) and groups 17, 71, 94, 97, 241
Clifford, Ian 184
community learning centres (CLCs) 40–1
comparative advantage 13
Comprehensive Education Sector Review (CESR) 17, 19, 22, 65–70, 73, 135–41, 146–51, 202–3, 274
competencies of teachers 122, 165, 182–3, 186, 193
computers, use of 111
Condon, Mairead 171, 190
Connell, R. 15
constitutional provisions 7, 33, 73, 63–4, 149, 281
continuing professional development (CPD) 169, 183
corporal punishment 118
coverage of the present book 22–7
COVID-19 epidemic 283–4
critical thinking 184
cultural imperialism 97, 126, 192, 229
curriculum
  links between schools and colleges 187
  for school pupils 7–8, 37–8, 91, 96–7, 275–6
  for teacher training 159–64, 185
  uniform content of 254
  see also 'local curriculum'
Cyclone Nargis (2010) 112

data collected for the present book 18–27, 274
decentralisation 8, 73–5, 97, 130, 144, 191, 229, 244, 266, 275
decision-making power 140–1, 275
Dekker, D. 238
democracy 8
development partners 66–9, 81–5, 93, 97, 151, 159, 181–3, 193, 267, 274, 279–80
Diploma in Teacher Education (DTEd) 150, 164

disabled students 26, 79, 107, 140, 149
disadvantage from lack of education 201, 229, 264, 278
discriminatory practices 76, 92, 192, 199–200, 224, 266
disruption of education services by armed conflict 241
distance learning 145–6, 149, 183
Drinan, H. 184
drop-out from education 61–3, 75, 117, 200, 224, 278

early childhood centres for education (ECCE) 40
education colleges 160–3, 168, 182–93, 277
 organisational structure of 188
 views from 170–81
Education Directory 49
Education for All (EFA) 40–2, 52, 58, 104
Education Management Information System (EMIS) 40
Education Promotion Implementation Committee (EPIC) 19, 58, 69–71, 141
education reform 3, 6, 18, 22–3
 aim and purpose of 13–16, 200
 beginning of 64–5
 failure of 202, 274–5, 280
 linked to social justice 14–16
 NLD promises about 5–6
 priority for 65, 283
 process of 273
educational attainment 216–18
 related to household wealth 216
Edwards, N. 206
elections 281–4
 in 2010 30
 in 2015 6–10
electricity, access to 5
empowerment 14, 84–5
English for Education College Trainers (EfECT) project 24, 159, 170–85
English language 31–3, 111, 132, 138–9, 184–5
equity in educational provision 148–50, 190, 240, 258, 268, 273, 277
Esson, J. 143, 152–3
ethnic armed organisations (EAOs) 199, 238–40, 245–7, 264–8, 277, 282
 education provided by 241, 253–6
ethnic conflict 239–41
ethnic diversity 36, 58, 107, 126, 131, 147, 150, 155, 171, 197–9, 278, 282
ethnic identity 268
ethnic languages 32, 78–9, 124, 140, 197–210, 219, 227–9, 244, 269, 278
ethnic schools, typology of 242–3
ethnic tensions 7–9, 21, 25, 38
European Union (EU) 65, 151
examination systems 44–6

fairness, lack of 7
financing of education *see* funding
Fishman, J.A. 205
'4 R framework' 229, 239–40, 249, 258, 263
freedom of expression 8

funding of education
 by families 50–1, 110
 by the government 60, 105, 134
 by wealthy donors 102, 122
Furnivall, J. 102
further education 6

Gamarnikow, E. 12
gendered differences 118, 147, 160, 170–2, 192–3, 277
genocide, charges of 282
Giroux, H. 11
Global Partnership for Education (GPE) 84
globalisation 11
Government of Myanmar (GoM) 80, 84, 99, 157, 198, 210–6, 218, 265
Guyot, Dorothy 47, 49, 258

'hardship pay' 167
Hatcher, R. 11
head teachers
 role of 182–3
 training of 182
Heslop, Lynne 150–3
hierarchical structures 275
Higgins, S. 92, 192–3, 240
higher education (HE) 12, 24, 130–1, 154–5, 276–7
 inclusive 146–50
 new institutions 144–5
 number of institutions, students and teachers in Myanmar 134
 reform of 139–41
history of education in Myanmar 31
housing conditions 5
Houtman, G. 37
Htein Kyaw 6
human capital theory 13, 66–7, 280
Human Development Index (HDI) 150–1

identity politics 15
inclusion and inclusivity 97, 140, 147–8, 277–8
independence of Burma (1948) 103
inequality within Myanmar 4, 8, 10–11
information and communication technology (ICT) 169, 185–8
Integrated Household Living Conditions Survey (IHLCS) 60–3
International Court of Justice (ICJ) 282
International Language and Business Centre (ILBC) 48
International Monetary Fund (IMF) 13
international standards 166

JICA 152
Japan 152
Jingphaw language 258
Jolliffe, Kim 246, 255–6

Kachin State 258–64, 283
Kamibeppu, T. 140
Kandiko-Howson, C. 154
Karen State 250–2, 283
Kaung 31
Kaw Dai 256–8

Khan, I. 204
Kheunsai, S. 199
Khin Nyunt 37
Khit Myanmar Weekly 48, 55
King, Kenneth 142
Kosonen, K. 204
Kyaw Yin Haing 133

Lall, M. (author) 17, 43, 116, 154
language issues 25–6, 31–3, 91–2, 126, 131, 138, 147–8, 179, 192, 197, 221–2, 239
Lauder, H. 10
Leadership Foundation (UK) 145
lesson planning 118, 182
Lingard, B. 10–11
linguistic diversity 58
literacy rates 211–12
Lo Bianc, Joseph 203
'local curriculum' (LC) 25, 78, 197, 205–10, 221–3, 228–9, 265, 278
logic of business and logic of education 11
long-term plans for education 65, 81, 144–163

Ma Ba Tha 7
Ma Zar Chi Oo 92
Mandalay Conference (2016) 203
Mandalay University 131–3, 137, 139, 142, 152, 155, 276
Mandalay University Distance Education (MUDE) 145
manifestos 4–9, 273, 277
map of Myanmar 2
marginalisation 97, 190, 192, 229, 240, 277–8
Margontier-Haynes, Celine 225–6
marketisation 11–12
Marshall, C. 16
Marshall, T.H. 12
May San Yee 161
memorisation 185
Mehta, N. 20, 52, 56, 59
Metro, Rose 32, 38–9, 91–2, 140–1
middle classes 11–12, 47, 50, 111, 131, 177
middle schools 105–6, 160
military rule 3, 7, 17, 33, 104, 278–9
Millennium Development Goals (MDGs) 40
Min Aung Hlaing 245
Min Zaw Soe 40, 60, 70
minorities within minorities 197–8, 216, 221–9
missionaries 31
Mizuno, K. 88, 89, 100, 187, 196, 276, 293
Mon State 247–50, 264–7
Mon Summer Literacy and Buddhist Culture (MSLBC) 125
Monastic Education Development Group (MEDG) 121–2
monastic schools 20, 23–4, 31–2, 101–27, 147, 277
  clustering of 120
  fluctuating number of 104–5
  Government recognition of the importance of 126–7
  role in maintaining ethnic languages and culture 123–6

mother-tongue-based multilingual education (MTB-MLE) 25, 197, 200, 203–5, 219, 229–30, 238–9, 244, 247, 254, 266, 268, 278
Muslims, discrimination against 7, 76
Muta, H. 86
Mya Aye 68, 141
Myanmar Education Consortium (MEC) 123
Myanmar Egress (ME) 17–19, 280
Myanmar Information Management Unit (MIMU) 1, 105
Myanmar–UK Partnership for Education (MUPE) 85, 182
Myint Aye Aye 165–6
Myint Zaw Soe 76–7
Myo Thein Gyi 141
Myo Zaw Oo 282

Naidoo, R. 130, 154
National Accreditation and Quality Assurance Committee (NAQAC) 144
National Curriculum Committee 81
National Education Law 140–1, 149, 164
National Education Policy Commission (NEPC) 80–1, 140, 144–5
National Education Sector Strategic Plan (NESP) 22–3, 26, 41, 58, 77–8, 87, 138, 141, 148, 151, 200–4, 228, 240, 244, 264, 269, 273–4
  Mid-Term Review (MTR) of 27, 93–7, 153–4, 164, 188–9, 274, 278–80, 283
  priority areas of 164
national identity 37, 39, 92
National Institute of Higher Education Development (NIHED) 24, 130, 144
National League for Democracy (NLD) 1–10, 16–17, 27, 33, 68–9, 141–4, 266, 273–4, 281–2
  challenges faced by 7–10
  disappointment with 4, 8, 73, 273, 281
  in government (2015–2020) 17, 58, 73–4, 77, 80–1, 197, 203–5, 274
  policies and priorities of 1, 3, 274
National Network for Education Reform (NNER) 22, 58, 68–71
national schools 34
nationalism 31–9
Naw Say Phaw 38
Nay Win Maung 18
Naypyidaw agreement (2015) 245
neo-liberalism 3–4, 10–13, 154–5, 274, 276
  and social justice 10–11
net enrolment ratio (NER) 60
Ne Win 33, 131, 139, 159, 247
Norway 266
Novelli, M. 229, 239, 249, 263

Obama, Barack 143
Ohnmar Tin 105, 107, 121–2, 127
Olssen, M. 15
Open University 146
organisational constraints analysis (OCA) 275
Oxford Policy Management (OPM) 89–90

Pa-O community and culture 125–6, 223–7
parental choices 267

INDEX   299

parental concerns 276
parental involvement in education 90–1, 106, 111, 177
parental views on education 109–11
participation 9
partnerships with foreign universities 152–3
peace-building 150, 240
peace process 8, 147, 193, 201, 229, 239–41, 281–2
  effects on ethnic education 244–7
  setbacks to 245
peer support 182–3
People's Alliance for Credible Elections (PACE) 281, 283
personnel management 167
Pestalozzi Children's Foundation 112
Phaung Daw Oo (school) 23, 101, 108–12, 115, 122, 126
'policy window' for change 1, 6, 16
policy–practice gap 97, 273–81
poverty 224
pre-primary teacher training (PPTT) course 160
prior knowledge 184
private schools 22, 27, 30, 47–50, 107, 172, 280
professional development of teachers 166–7, 182, 188; *see also* continuing professional development
professionalism of teachers 167, 277
protest action 10, 17–18, 22–3, 58, 71–2, 132, 140–1, 145, 267
Pyithu Huttaw Education Promotion Committee 79–80
Pyoe Pin programme 20, 122

qualifications of young people 280
quality assurance frameworks 112, 151, 154
Quality Basic Education Programme (QBEP) 67, 82, 87, 186, 276
quality of education in Myanmar 52–3, 107, 140, 200, 267, 279

Rakhine State 9, 219–21, 238, 281–3
Rangoon University 131–2
Raynaud, M. 191, 204, 209
reconciliation process 269
Rectors' Committee 144
redistributive policies 11
reform programme
  characteristics of 9
  failure of 1, 3–4
  see also educational reform
regulatory functions 11
relational justice 15
religious tensions 7, 9
remedial language support 265
research culture 136–7
rioting 72–3
Rizvi, F. 10–11
Rohingya repatriation 282
rural areas contrasted with urban 1–4, 10, 62, 148–9, 224

Sai Mauk Kham 71, 139
Sai Pha 252, 255–8

SaJaNa organisation 261–3
Salem-Gervais, Nicolas 32, 38, 191, 198, 204–9
Sao Sang Ai 252
Save the Children 266
Saw Maung 33
Saw Tin Tin Shu 68
school attendance 211–15
School-based In-service Teacher Education (SITE) project 182–3
School Grants and Stipends Programme 75–7
Shan State 219–21, 238–9, 252–8
SHARE programme 151
Situational Analysis (SITAN) study 52–3
skills gap 280
Smith, D.E. 103
social democracy 11
social justice 4, 6, 9–16, 26, 30, 64, 66, 78, 80, 97, 110, 140, 153, 155, 160, 190, 193, 200, 205, 229, 247, 273–4, 277–80
  as a basis for educational reform 14–16
  global 273
  in a neo-liberal era 10–11
South, Ashley 21, 37, 210, 235, 262, 271–2
special economic zones (SEZs) 10
Speers Mears, E. 246
stakeholders 274–6
state functions 11–12
  as a regulator rather than a provider 11
state schools 32, 36
Stenning, E. 105
stipends
  for students 76–7
  for teachers 207
Stoakes, G. 137
Strategic Development Goals (SDGs) 78
Strengthening Child Centred Approach (SCCA) 182
Strengthening Teacher Education in Myanmar (STEM) programme 159, 165–6, 182, 185–8
student teachers 160
Su Myat Mon 91–2
summer schools 124–6
sustainability 279
Sustainable Development Goals (SDGs) 1, 14–15

Taungalay Monastic School 123–4
Taylor, Robert 133
Taylor, S. 14
teacher-centric methods 181
Teacher Competency Standards Framework (TCSF) 165–6, 189
teachers
  career pathways of 160–1, 172, 189
  changing behaviour of 87, 183
  as civil servants 167
  education and and training of 20–1, 24, 45, 84–97, 101, 112–13, 118, 121–2, 131, 159–60, 169–73, 182–3, 190, 276–7
  from ethnic minorities 277
  in-service training of 168
  marriage patterns of 190

motivations of 171–2
newly-trained 122
pay and status of 30, 45, 105, 157, 171–2, 180, 207, 267
problems and challenges for 169–70
recruitment of 60, 65, 85–6, 119–20, 168–9, 189, 240
research undertaken by 168
respect for 116–19
shortages of 60, 65
trained by schools themselves 124
transferred between systems 267
untrained 122, 163
worries and fears of 173–80, 275–6
Teachers' Voice study 19
teaching assistants 108, 119–20
teaching methods 101, 111, 116–17, 120
teaching space 106, 119–20
teaching time, lack of 120
testing of skills 13
textbooks, review of 88–9
Thant Myint-U 35
Thaung Htut 231
Thein Lwin 31, 33, 68–9, 72, 77–9, 141, 143
Thein Sein 1, 4, 10, 22, 58, 64–5, 71–4, 77, 81, 140, 167, 172, 183–4, 202, 208, 210, 273
Thura U Shwe Mann 70–1
Towards Results in Education and English (TREE) project 183–5, 191–2
travel to school 61
tuition outside school 50–2, 111, 146

U Myint Swe 283
U Nayaka 23, 101, 111, 121, 126
Union Election Commission 281
Union Solidarity and Development Party (USDP) 4, 6, 274, 282

United Nations
Children's Fund (UNICEF) 51–2, 82, 182, 266
Declaration on the Rights of Indigenous Peoples 78
Educational, Scientific and Cultural Organisation (UNESCO) 107, 166, 182, 185–8, 276
universities
adoption of international practices 155
new role for 12
regional 155, 276
research led by 135–7
selection of students 142
university education 12, 17, 20, 32–3, 47
U Tin Naing Thein 71
U Win Myint 92

vernacular schools 31
vocational education 26, 32–3

Wang, K. 143, 152–3
'WASH' programme 122
Washington consensus 13
Western firms' contracts 3
World Bank (WB) 13, 65, 77, 167
Wright, K. 137

Yangon University 131–3, 137, 139, 142–3, 151–2, 155, 276
Yangon University Distance Education (YUDE) 145
Yaung Zin teacher training programme 122
Yawd Serk 253–4
Young, Iris 15, 23, 97, 126, 229
young people 279–81

Zobrist, B. 104, 120
Zoellner, H. B. 103

www.ingramcontent.com/pod-product-compliance
Lightning Source LLC
Jackson TN
JSHW081257100426
100637JS00007B/42